The Gift Of Choice

THE LIVES AND TIMES OF

LEON Z. RODA and ALFONSO P. RODA

Father and Son

By

Consuelo R. Jackson

TEACH Services, Inc.
Brushton, New York

Copyright © 2003 Consuelo R. Jackson
ISBN 1-57258-246-4
Library of Congress Catalog Card No. 2002114542

Graphic Design for the cover
by
Beryl Dawn Roda

Published by

TEACH Services, Inc.
www.tsibooks.com

DEDICATION

To *Manang* Ely (Elizabeth Roda Roeder)

To *Manang* Es (Esther Roda Sanidad)

***

In the annals of human history, the growth of nations, the rise and fall of empires appear as dependent on the will and prowess of man. The shaping of events seems, to a great degree, to be determined by his power, ambition, or caprice. But in the Word of God, the curtain is drawn aside, and we behold behind, above, and through all the play and counter play of human interests and power and passions, the agencies of the all-merciful One, silently, patiently working out the counsels of His own will.

Ellen G. White, Education, p. 173

***

CONTENTS

Book I, Leon Zumel Roda (LZR)

***

BOOK II: ALFONSO P. RODA (APR)

***

SECTION 2 of BOOK II (APR)
A Compilation:

A Dialogue—Points of View

FOREWORD

When asked to write the Foreword to this book, I readily accepted as an honor in the hope that I might help in the documentation of the Seventh-day Adventist Church work in the Philippines, and the role that the Roda family had in its beginning with Pastor Leon Z. Roda, one of the first three Filipino Adventist ordained ministers, and ending at the demise of his son, Dr. Alfonso P. Roda, the longest-serving president (22 years) of Philippine Union College.

The author, as a second generation PUC alumna, in her own inimitable novel-style of writing, uses second and third person dialogues with local and vernacular colloquialisms which might be strange to the uninitiated of Asian life styles.

I recommend this book as a first hand experience and invaluable resource for those who had worked in the former Far Eastern Division of Seventh-day Adventists, now divided into the North and South Asia Pacific Divisions, and those particularly interested in the history of the Seventh-day Adventist Church in the Philippines. This book portrays the fluctuating currents of human thought and acton unique in those who believe in causes or ideals with tenacity of purpose even in the most inauspicious circumstances.

This immediately brings to the fore the well-known paragraph from Ellen G. White: "In the annals of human history, the growth of nations, the rise and fall of empires, appear as dependent on the will and prowess of man. The shaping of events seems, to a great degree, to be determined by his power, ambition or caprice. But in the Word of God the curtain is drawn aside, and we behold behind, above, and through all the play and inter-play of human interests and power and passions, the agencies of the all-merciful One, silently, patiently working out the counsels of His own will," Education, p. 173.

For indeed, this book touches some sensitive issues about the establishment of the Adventist International Institute for Advanced Studies (AIIAS) and how it would affect the graduate program and the very survival of Philippine Union College (now Adventist University of the Philippines). There appears to be some lack of understanding of how AIIAS would affect an already existing graduate program at PUC by reason of its location (proximity) and the courses it offers.

To the Filipino Seventh-day Adventists and PUC alumni who have ties to the PUC graduate program and to the Seventh-day Adventist Seminary on the campus of PUC, the establishment of AIIAS first as a Division and now as a General Conference institution constitutes a threat to Adventist University of the Philippines for the following reasons:

1. AIIAS, by virtue of a presidential decree, unbeknownst to the now deposed and deceased Philippine president, obtained its charter in a hush-hush manner directly engineered by the FED (Far Eastern Division) officers through the expatriate missionaries then residing in Manila.

2. In a write-up posted in AUP Cyberlink Midweek Forum 010530, Manuel Fauni, professor and former Dean of the PUC School of Liberal Arts wrote, "There was already a movement as early as 1984 led by Seminary and PUC expatriates to get the Graduate School out of PUC with the alibi that the school "seems" to lack an international outlook and is instead very inward focused." Thus there were influential personalities in the Seventh-day Adventist Theological Seminary Far East as well as in the PUC Graduate School who wanted the School of Graduate Studies separated from the administration of PUC. This movement to combine the SDA Theological Seminary and the PUC Graduate School formed the rationale to create an entity with a so-called "international" character. The movement also made it appear that students from other countries (who were upgrading in PUC and who were subsidized by the FED) wanted to be in a graduate program under an international, if not Caucasian, leadership and not under a Philippine identity. In addition, there appeared to be an undercurrent opinion that the graduate school professors, mostly Filipinos, were inferior in qualification and or performance.

3. PUC President Alfonso P. Roda seemed not to have objected to the FED take-over of the Theological
Seminary, but he vehemently opposed the take-over of the Graduate School which PUC had since 1957. When AIIAS came into being in 1987, the annual $50,000 subsidy to PUC Graduate School was cut off, leaving the graduate program of PUC floundering to the point of closure. PUC alumni in the U.S.A., upon hearing that the graduate school program was practically emasculated financially, rallied to raise the annual $50,000 which was cut off by the FED.

4. It is not known whether there ever was the suggestion to convert Philippine Union College into a division or GC (General Conference) institution, including a name change, for the sake of conferring a more prestigious status to the SDA Seminary of the graduate school or the graduate school. After the presidential decree was obtained, by-passing the usual procedure through the Philippine Department of Education, Division and GC funds were quickly available for land and buildings of AIIAS within a 15-kilometer distance from PUC.

5. Perhaps unknown to and not anticipated by the leadership of the Church, at both the Union and Division levels, was the reaction of

the Filipino constituency to the jeopardy into which PUC had fallen. When PUC President Alfonso P. Roda opposed these moves against the acquiescence of the officers of his own North Philippine Union Mission, a call came through the Division channels for A. P. Roda to assume a high Church position in Bangladesh, a call which he promptly turned down. Dr. Alfonso Roda died on March 5, 1987.

6. Thus AIIAS today, with its 200+ enrolment on a well provided campus in contrast to AUP with 3,000+ enrolment on a less developed campus 15 kilometers (9.373 miles) down the road, has even enlarged its curricular offerings to include those that are already offered by Adventist University of the Philippines. Local Union, Mission and or Conference organizations within the South Asia Pacific Division have financial inducements to send their workers for upgrading to AIIAS.

7. Thus it appears that these two Adventist educational institutions, one backed up financially and in every other way by the Division and General Conference, and the other financially handicapped as a local union institution—albeit endowed with university status by the Philippine government to the tolerance of the Seventh-day Adventist Church Educational Department which up to July 2001 has not recognized it as a university—are on a head to head competitive struggle.

My purpose in reciting the above trenchant details, vis-a-vis the two Seventh-day Adventist institutions, is not to re-play the blame game. Perhaps the verdict of history will not be harsh on Church leaders as individuals because all decisions have been sheltered by the mantle of corporate structure in its committee actions.

It is my hope that this book, portraying as it does the beginning of the Seventh-day Adventist work in the Philippines by Pastor Leon Z. Roda, will contribute to a better understanding of the character and leadership of the Filipinos, and help bring a conciliatory closure to the life of Dr. Alfonso P. Roda, the second Filipino president of Philippine Union College.

The Filipinos are a sensitive and sentimental people. And Filipino Seventh-day Adventists will continue to support Philippine Union College, now Adventist University of the Philippines (AUP). They are proud of its alumni who are serving the Adventist Church all over the world. Thought leaders of AUP alumni in the homeland and overseas understand the physics, politics, and psychology of church leadership.

The price has been paid. The future is all that remains. And although humanly uncertain and unpredictable, that future is secure only as we believe that the all-merciful One is "silently, patiently, working out the counsels of His own will."

May this book—<u>The Gift of Choice</u>—be not only of history and its interacting forces but also of peace, above all, the tool for understanding the very roots of variance and resolution—forgiveness.

D. M. Hechanova, Jr., M.D.
September, 2001

***

ACKNOWLEDGEMENTS

This book came to be only with the help of many PUC (now AUP) alumni friends and relatives. For their contributions, my heartfelt and special thanks

To *Manang* Ely (Elizabeth Roda Roeder) who provided the nucleus for Book I, Leon Z. Roda (LZR). In addition to writing all her recollections about her father LZR, and their father-orphaned family life, she sent for my reference a copy of the book Breaking Through, by Dr. Herman L. Reyes.

To Dr. Herman L. Reyes, who gave me permission to use facts from his book, Breaking Through, and also for advising me to visit the Review & Herald Archives, specifying the inclusive dates of issues of The Review and Herald for me to read.

To The Review & Herald Publishing Association library staff for letting me use the Archives. They were ever willing to lend a hand, even to show me how to use their copy machine. My personal thanks to Richard Coffen for writing an authorization for the use of many R&H publications.

To *Manang* Esther Roda Sanidad, for recollecting stories our *Papang* Alvaro Z. Roda and our *Mamang* Maxima C. Roda told about *Tata* (uncle) Leon and *Nana* (aunt) Maria Panis Roda, memories of their occasional three-brother-family get togethers, their individual evangelistic efforts, and for the details of their last family reunion before *Tata* Leon's death.

To Lydia T. Roda, my number one resource person, who had kept the poems her bridegroom read to her on their first nuptial night. She gave these to me in their original forms (some were tattered and there were unreadable parts) but she succeeded in her diligent search for the complete poems. She also read practically every page of the rough drafts. Then during the progress in the writing of the book, we had kept in touch through letters at first and later by email, which sped things up.

To Esther T. Vizcarra, Lydia's older sister, who also read the rough draft when she and Lydia visited at home with me for a few days. Then by long distance phone calls, she continued to give me relevant facts.

To Esperanza R. Idrisalman who, in her regular letters through the years, updated me with MSH (Manila Sanitarium & Hospital) and PUC news. Being MSH chief dietitian during Alfonso P. Roda's admissions to the hospital (many times he called for her) she witnessed his intense suffering.

To Alvaro C. Roda, Jr., for his eye-for-accuracy. He, too, reviewed the rough draft, and jotted down correct dates, names, history, etcetera.

To Elma Lou Roda, M.D., whose interest in getting this book written inspired me to give my best to the task. She read the first draft and jotted down her suggestions. Her fax machine and photo printer came ever so handy—she herself did the errands for me. It was through her prompting that I became a subscriber to the PUC/AUP Cyberlink.

To Mrs. Paz Villanueva Peng, for her recollections of her school days with the older children of Leon and Maria Roda, as well as the close interactions between the Roda and the Villanueva families. Also, the history of the *barong tagalog* came from her Cyberlink posting.

To the late Dr. D. B. Salmin, who, years before her death corresponded with me and voluntarily sent the contents of her file relevant to PUC issues.

To Dr. Demetrio Hechanova, Jr., who was PUC Dean of Men when Alfonso and Lydia were faculty at PUC in Baesa. (For your many long distance calls and for writing the FOREWORD, Sir, thank you from the bottom of my heart.)

To Mrs. Fidela S. Hechanova, the power behind the Hechanova throne, who propelled her busy husband to fulfill his commitments. Acting as Dr. Hechanova's personal secretary, she emailed many letters to me.

To Dr. Reuben G. Manalaysay, for providing accurate information about his father, the late Emilio Manalaysay—one of the Big Three—and for his byline, in Book II, (APR) Section 2.

To Dr. Ottis C. Edwards, former Far Eastern Division president, and earlier, Dean of Faculties and interim PUC president, who took time out of his daily schedule to contribute his byline appearing in Book II, Section 2.

To Dr. Don Van Ornam, former PUC financial adviser, for giving his permission to reprint his letter dated Feb. 24, 1985, and for his bylines—in Book II. (For taking the time out of your busy daily schedule to dialogue with me by email, words are inadequate to express my sincere thanks.)

To Atty. John Tulio, for his permission to reprint his byline published in the IFN, titled, "The Statement of Concern," included in Book II, (APR).

To Dr. Bangele D. Alsaybar, for his permission to reprint his byline also published in the IFN, titled "The Legacy of Alfonso P. Roda," in Book II.

To Cora Arevalo Coo, for sending relevant issues of THE PUC SPOTLIGJHT as well as photos of the Leon and Maria Roda family and their latter generation group photo, and for her reflections on her uncle Alfonso. (For running many errands by email for me, thank you very much, Cora.)

To Ferdinand T. Roda, M.D. (Andy) and wife Loree, for pulling out from their family album pertinent family pictures which they mailed to me, and for Andy's byline, in Book II, (APR). These encouraged me to keep writing.

To F. E. Z. Tauro, editor of IFN (International Filipino Network) for giving his permission to reprint selected articles from the magazine.

To Consolacion R. Mirasol, for sending me pertinent copies of The Link, (the AWESNA Newsletter) and for her encouraging words boosting my efforts in gathering materials to include in this book.

To Dr. Norval O. Jackson (Sonny) for sending me his Macintosh Plus and a Macintosh SE/30 for a spare, when my Macintosh Plus monitor burned, and I despaired over retrieving the manuscripts in Mac memory.

To many others who contributed portions of this book, who wish to remain anonymous, many thanks.

Above all, I thank our all-wise loving Father, high and lifted up, whose leadings He made known, and making His approval in the writing of this book crystal-clear ever since I started gathering materials for it not too long after Dr. Roda's death. Praises to Him for fulfilling His promise to answer even before we call. I believe it was the Lord Who impressed Sonny to box his old Macintosh models instead of discarding them when he upgraded his dental office as well as his personal computer system. Without the Macintosh Plus and the SE/30, the cost of retrieving the manuscripts stored in the McBottom memory would have been sky-high.

May the reading of this book inspire young readers in the conduct of their courtship and as it applies, in raising their families. May it help readers and future leaders to trust in God Who sees from the beginning to the end, and Who holds the future in His almighty hands.

May my dream—for this book to be listed as a required or at least a suggested reading for relevant AUP courses—come true. Above all, may its reading bring healing.... To bring glory to His most holy name!

crj

***

PREFACE

It was after getting over the initial shock on the death of Dr. Alfonso Roda that I conceived of writing his memoir. In sorting out ways to carry this conception, I became aware that I did not know much about him. (Oh, years earlier, he and Lydia came to see me at different times: In Illinois, in Kansas, in Kentucky, in Virginia—the last two places were also to solicit funds for PUC, they called an SOS—Save Our Silang—Crusade. I did not receive a copy of the SOS letter, and therefore I did not then fully understand the implication behind this SOS crusade.)

If I had to carry this conception successfully, I would need help—a lot of help. Who would be willing, who would have the time to lend a hand?

Esperanza (Pancing) a younger sister of mine had been my constant correspondent—she kept me posted of life in the Philippines—so did our own dear mother. In their letters, they brought me up-to-date on the most significant happenings at home, at work at MSH (where Pancing was chief dietitian) and at PUC, where her two girls went to school.

Reading Alumni accounts and opinions about the events that led to the death of Dr. Roda brought a compelling urgency for me to start the task somehow. First, I procured the permission of Lydia, the beautiful wife of Dr. Roda for thirty-three years. That we had been next door neighbors during our PUC days served well. I recall an incident as vividly as it were yesterday, my first time to step in the Jackson-Sevrens Hall to attend PUC vespers. It so happened that Lydia was also entering the door, and she kept in step with me just on time to grab my arm, keeping me from sliding backward on the shiny and slick polished wooden floors. For me, it was the beginning of a casual friendship. We exchanged smiles whenever we met each other. Two years later, we found each other at MSH—she, a student nurse—I, an administrative secretary. Busy days, however, foiled deepening of this friendship. So when I heard and then saw my older cousin Alfonso visiting Lydia, I was ecstatic. I fully approved!

Time flew. Lovebirds Alfonso and Lydia wedded. Busy days did little to progress our friendship. Then came the tragedy of death. From shared grieving came the golden opportunity to work on a common goal—the writing of Alfonso's memoir—a fertile ground for friendship to grow.

With PUC financial problems casting darkening and ever-lengthening shadows, I shared this dream with Lydia, and a goal—proceeds to go to PUC funds. With her permission was a promise to provide factual information. She would share her feelings, her thoughts with me. Thus assured, I prayed for more faith, for self-confidence enough to begin the task. *Lord, how, where do I start?* "**With his family horizon.**" *Thank You, Lord.*

Book I, Leon Zumel Roda (LZR) chronicles the beginnings of the Seventh-day Adventist work in the Philippines. It also tells of LZR's family life—with his parents and siblings as well as his own life as a mature adult.

Book II, Alfonso P. Roda (APR) would be incomplete, lackluster, without Lydia's personal and family life. After all, she had been his better half in their thirty-three plus years of married bliss. Lydia was the silent power behind-the-throne, for she chose a life behind the scenes. Seldom appearing in the lime light with her husband, she saw to it that he dressed appropriately; she reminded him to give due appreciation to individuals when occasions arose, and she supported his mission in life. Caring and devoted to each other, Alfonso, in his travels began writing a love letter to his Dearest the moment he got airborne-settled. I asked Lydia for a few samples of his letters. "Sorry, *kadua* (partner) in my grief and even anger, I burned all of them," she replied in self-reproach. "I regret it now, but then I was too numb with grief, in shock questioning 'why didn't he muster strength enough to live for his sons, for me?' I admit I was too lost to know what I was doing in the immediate months after his death."

In Chicago during the Three-Roda Brothers Family Reunion held in August, 1999, Lydia said, "*Kadua*, I found three letters!" as she handed them to me. She said she found one tucked in her suitcase pocket, and much later, she came upon two more letters between the leaves of a book. These sample letters start the 13th chapter of Book II (APR).

I organized materials as I received them, and jotted down the word-of-mouth. I began writing in earnest. With the ever present conflicts and their consequent partial or temporary resolutions, I thought of going all the way to extend readership. With Lydia's approval, I switched to nonfiction novel style of writing—creative writing, adhering to facts and licensing writers to project their own experiences, thoughts, and imaginations—yet leaving room for the reader's own imagination to play.

Norma R. Youngberg tells this in her book Creative Techniques for Christian Writers: "Creative writing means imaginative writing. Without imagination, the human mind would fail to realize the greatness of God and the infinite variety of His creation.... Imagination is the companion of faith...." I agree. Wholeheartedly.

Dear Readers: As I sat day after day composing page after page, ever trying to find the right words to convey facts, I thought of you. When I shed tears, laughed or thrilled in retracing this father-and-son life *hi*story, I wondered if any of you would know more of their lives, of their steadfast faith in God, their desire to advance God's work, even in their homeland, and their yearning for a conflict-free life. Would you, too, become aware of the ruler-of-planet-earth hard at work blinding eyesights and foresights, as he had done through ages past? Let us rejoice in the Lord's promise of life in the earth made new. There, **we shall understand**. crj

PRINCIPAL CHARACTERS

American Pioneer Missionaries to the Philippines:

Adams, E. M. and wife—1912 assigned to the Visayan Islands; re-assigned in Luzon, North Philippine Union Mission, 1939-WW II.

Caldwell, R. A.—1905–1911, first colporteur to the Philippines.

Daniels, A. G.—1905- President SDA Australasian Union Conference.

Evans, I. H—early 1909–1913, President, Asiatic Division.

Finster, L. V. and wife—1908 to? second missionary couple to the P.I.

Hay, Roy E., with wife and two young children—1913–1921 in the Ilocos provinces, Luzon.

McElhaney, James L. and wife: 1906- first missionary couple to the islands.

Philippine Nationals:

Fernando, Celedonio A.—a neurosurgeon. Lydia's uncle *Tiong Dons*

Manalaysay, Emilio—among the first Filipino converts and one of the first three Filipinos ordained to the Adventist ministry. Father of Reuben G. Manalaysay, the first Filipino PUC president, in whose term the Graduate School was established.

Panis, Bibiano—among the first converts, and one of the first three Filipinos ordained to the Adventist ministry in the Philippines.

Panis, Camilo—influential and wealthy man, among the first converts; father of Teodora (Doray) and uncle of Bibiano and Maria Panis.

Panis, Ciriaca—Mrs. Camilo Panis, mother of Teodora.

Panis, Maria—Bibiano's younger sister and one of the first Filipino converts; married to Leon Z. Roda, she's the mother of Alfonso P. Roda.

Panis, Teodora (Doray)—daughter of Camilo and Ciriaca Panis, married to Dr. Eladio Aldecoa, the dentist who owned a School of Dentistry.

Roda, Alfonso P. (APR)—son of Leon Z. Roda; and the second Filipino appointed PUC president from 1964 to his death in March, 1987.

Roda, *Don* Juan—an influential and wealthy man, a staunch Catholic of Ilocos Norte; and the father of Leon Zumel Roda.

Roda, Leon Zumel (LZR)—son of *Don* Juan Roda; and among the first Filipino converts and one of the first three Filipinos ordained to the Adventist ministry; he's one of the Big Three.

Roda, Lydia T.—the young nurse who became Mrs. Alfonso P. Roda.

Roeder, Elizabeth R.—the oldest daughter of Leon and Maria Roda; one of the first nurse graduates of Manila Sanitarium & Hospital.

Vizcarra, Esther T.—the older sister of Lydia and the wife of Dr. Catalino Chay Vizcarra, Jr. She is the younger Esther in Book II.

Vizcarra, Esther Sr.—the mother of Dr. Catalino Chay Vizcarra, Sr. She is the senior Esther in Book II.

***

THE GIFT OF CHOICE

BOOK I

The Life and Time

of

LEON ZUMEL RODA (LZR)

by
Consuelo R. Jackson

CHAPTER I

THE PROMISE

"Surely the isles shall wait for Me...." **(Isa. 60:9)**

Surely.... Leon bolted upright. Sweat trickled down his forehead, his heart raced. *Where am I?* He blinked his eyes, rubbed them. *Where am I?*

He tried to shake off the... nightmare ? *It seemed so real,* he thought. He drew a long, deep breath. Slowly, like dawn erasing the night, his perception cleared. *I am in the hospital,* Leon mentally affirmed himself. He laid back down and allowed the phantasmagoria to replay on his mind:

I arrived a few seconds on time to an important meeting. I saw a man in white with a kingly and majestic bearing enter. I heard him say, "It's time to take the Seventh-day Adventist faith to the Philippine Islands." His voice was mellifluous, soothing. to my ears. "I know the hearts of the peace-loving islanders and their religious inclination." He brought up His hands—palms nail-scarred, and continued, "They, too, are inscribed in the palms of My hands." Immediately, a voice rasped. "Other faiths are in the coastlands. There is no place for other faiths in my domain."

"Where did you come from?" asked the kingly One. His tone was kind.

"From going to and from the earth—my kingdom—hopping from one island to the other. There are too many churches studding the islands—my lawful territory. I repeat, there's no place for another faith in these isles."

"I have heard the prayers of the islanders, and I have plans for them. Created like you, they, too, have the power of choice and may exercise it."

"Remember you built a fence around Job." The furrows on his face deepened. "Don't do that in my islands, or you'll be sorry," the gruff voice commanded. He stood up, anger flashing in his whole being.

***

How art thou fallen from heaven, O Lucifer, son of the morning! how art thou cut down to the ground.... For thou said in thine heart, I will ascend into heaven, I will exhalt my throne above the stars of God, I will sit also upon the mount of the congregation.... I will ascend above the heights of the clouds; I will be like the most High (Isaiah 14:12–14).

***

MANILA GENERAL HOSPITAL
Manila

Name: *Leon Zumel Roda*   Date of Birth: Feb. 19, 1892
Address: (Home: Sarrat, Ilocos Norte) Current student, Intramuros Manila High School, resides at Men's Hall
Responsible Person: Self (Father, Don Juan Roda, Sarrat, I. N.)
Date of Admission: June 6, 1910 9:10 a.m.
Admitting Diagnosis: *Upper respiratory infection, acute*
Discharge Diagnosis: *U R I, acute, with acute laryngitis, resolved*
Date of Discharge: June 7, 1910 4:22 p.m.
Attending Physician: *P. E. Arnoldo, M.D.*

***

The **Philippines**, poetically dubbed 'The Pearl of the Orient Seas' consists of around seven thousand islands dotting the southeast coast of Asia, between the South China Sea and the Pacific Ocean. The two major islands are Luzon, in the north (40,420 sq. miles) and Mindanao, in the south (36,500 sq. miles). A third group, also in the south called the lesser major islands—collectively called the Visayan Islands—are Bohol, Cebu, Iloilo, Leyte, Negros, Panay, and Samar (38,911 sq. miles). The area of these major islands total about 115,831 miles. In addition, there are countless smaller islands, some inhabited but many are too barren to support life. The islanders are Filipinos, as Americans are to America.

The islands are extremely rugged, many of them largely of volcanic formation. Irregular mountain ranges, clothed with virgin forests and verdant flora, traverse the islands. Between the mountain ranges lie extensive fertile slopes and plains, watered by many lakes and rivers. The climate is temperate with two seasons—dry and rainy. Cyclonic storms, typhoons, occurring mainly in the rainy season, often prove devastating.

Escaping the ravages of these typhoons yet resulting in the strength and beauty that made them famous are hardwoods found in its forests.

The Philippine mahogany, *narra* and *sagat*, are but a few examples of these hardwoods used by manufacturers to make beautiful furniture. Trees that withstand the cyclonic storms produce strong, sturdy lumber. Writers use a coin word—rock-hard—to describe this kind of lumber. Also, these hardwoods provide the materials and inspiration behind the intricate Philippine woodcrafts. Indeed, it would be a sin of omission to bypass the souvenir handicraft stands in the many craft markets in the islands.

(As of this writing, it is regrettable to account that commerce had virtually raped most of these virgin forests. The good report is that a few newly arising ecology-minded groups are pushing hard for reforestation and are coming up with noteworthy results.)

The Filipinos, having been under the Spanish rule for about four centuries, have learned to speak Spanish. During that time, the Spanish language came handy as a communication medium between islanders speaking different dialects. (English has since replaced Spanish.). Of the more or less eight hundred dialects spoken in the islands, Tagalog, Ilokano, Bikol, Visayan, Ibanag, Pampanga, and Pangasinan stand out. These dialects represent the groups of Christian islanders. (The dwarf-size almost black aboriginal race—the Negrito—has become almost extinct.)

Church buildings arising in many inhabited places tell of the religions in the islands. Roman Catholic and the Protestant churches—the Baptists, Christian and Missionary Alliance, Episcopalians, the I.F.I.—*Iglesia Filipino Independente* (Philippine Independent Church, a split from the Catholic Church)— the Methodists, Presbyterians, the United Brethrens, the Muslims, and others.

American Missionaries to the Islands. "Send colporteurs to Manila," said G. A. Irwin, then Australasian Union Conference president, during the Seventh-day Adventist General Conference in 1905. Irwin had made an eight-day stop-over to the Philippines on his way to attend the General Conference session. The Lord impressed him the time had come to evangelize the Philippines. While there, he noted small but important groups of Americans, Chinese, Indians, and Europeans with the Filipinos.

Irwin presented an appeal, a call for pioneer missionaries during the Conference. R. A. Caldwell, then colporteuring in Singapore, responded. He arrived in Manila in August of 1905 and began selling books on health and religion in Spanish, the language understood by the educated class.

The interest of the people in the books spread with astonishing speed. People meeting Caldwell wanted to buy his books. Those who bought books passed word to their friends and relatives of the wealth of information in these books. Caldwell traveled to other cities and towns, and always, the people welcomed him and his books.

In April of 1906 Pastor and Mrs. James L. McElhaney arrived in Manila. They felt it most practical first to reach the American teachers all over the islands. They had faith the teachers in turn would share their new-found faith with their students. The McElhaneys distributed the Signs of the Times (monthly Adventist magazine, name is self-explanatory) to the American teachers there. They wrote personal letters to the teachers, and many of them started to correspond with the McElhaneys. As Pastor McElhaney learned more of the needs of the islanders, he helped prepare truth-filled literature for them to read.

In December, 1908, Pastor and Mrs. L. V. Finster arrived in Manila. Heeding an impression for him to learn the dialect spoken there, Finster hired tutors to teach him. As soon as he learned the basics and could carry conversational Tagalog, he ventured to improve his mastery by practice.

5

So with a prayer in his heart and a smile on his face, he went out to the streets of Manila to test his theory. He stood at busy intersections of the city handing out truth-filled literature and talking with anyone who accepted the tracts. To his delight, the people readily received the reading materials and were also eager to talk to him. They sensed his purpose and sauntered along to hear him and exchange ideas with him. During short lulls when no one was there to talk to, Finster lifted his heart to the Lord. *Bless this effort and the people, Lord. Open the hearts and minds of those who read the tracts. Let Thy Holy Spirit guide Thy chosen vessels to meet me, to bring glory to Thy most holy name, Lord. Thy will be done....*

Before long, he found this strategy working to his advantage much more than what he had hoped for. It came full circle one day when he came face to face with two young men whose body language mirrored discernment on what was going on. He shook hands with them saying, "L. V. Finster," and the young men in turn introduced themselves." Bibiano Panis and Leon Roda, even telling something about themselves: "Bibiano, Bib for short, is a law student. I board with his family," Leon said. "I'm finishing high school, then to Ateneo de Manila..."

"To take priesthood," Bibiano filled in.

They bade farewell, the two went on their way, each with a leaflet.

"A lucky day," Leon said, "its exactly the chance I'd been hoping for."

Bib cleared his throat. "You piqued my curiosity... I don't read minds."

"It all started before you invited me to board with you," Leon began. "After arriving in Manila and settling at the Men's Hall, I came down with a chest cold and a hacking cough that made me hoarse... I had to see a doctor. After giving me a physical check-up, the doctor admitted me to the hospital, 'for diagnostic tests and treatment,' he said. He assured me a few days of complete bed rest should rid most of my problems. As I lay in bed an American with a solemn look arrived at the ward. Amused and curious, I watched as he handed leaflets to the patients. When the man smiled, he looked kind and I really thought he was handsome.

Then he was beside my bed. I accepted the leaflet he offered me, I mouthed a 'thank you' and rubbed my throat. The man said, "May I pray for you?" His eyes and tone were kind, I knew he was a Christian. Never mind if he isn't a Catholic, I thought. I nodded my head, and he bowed. I felt a sense of reverence as he prayed, yet, I tell you, he prayed as though talking to a friend. His prayer sounded sincere—it made me feel he meant everything he said. I mentally compared our Catholic prayers, which to me now came as mere chantings of memorized verses. I thought, "Praying like the American makes more sense..." Leon paused, and drew a deep breath.

"And you decided to try praying like that—as if talking to a friend..." interjected Bibiano. "The truth is, I hardly know how to pray. Go on."

"Then I remembered the leaflet in my hand. I began reading it. **Sunday is not the Sabbath day?** jarred my mind. I determined that as soon as I had a chance, I'd check on those verses in the Bible."

Bibiano glanced at Leon, so lost in thought. "Continue..." he urged.

"The next morning the doctor came in. 'Now, tell me how you feel,' he said. 'I feel fine, Doctor.' I heard my voice, I was surprised to hear there was no trace of hoarseness. It came to me that the Lord answered the prayer of the American. The doctor said, 'The test results came out negative, but let me listen to your chest once more.' You know how it is, Bib, 'Take-a-deep-breath, breathe-out' sort of thing. 'I'm discharging you,' he said. Before leaving he added, 'Young man, take better care of yourself.' Bib, thanks for inviting me to live in your home."

"You are welcome, Leon, but to be truthful, I'd often wished to have someone about my age at home, where girls outnumber boys," he laughed. "It's good to have you with us, Leon, I like you very much. Back to Mr. Finster. I like his kind yet outgoing personality. I couldn't help extending him an invitation to visit with us at home."

The two young men walked on in silence until Leon broke in. "Did you see how the man seemed overjoyed, he accepted your invitation at once? I feel we are in to the experience of our lives! A dream come true. As we teach him Tagalog, we'll be learning to speak English more fluently."

"So, for us to learn more," Bib said, "let's keep the visits to ourselves—you and I with Mr. Finster. No girls or any one else. You agree, Leon?"

After a brief silence, "We'll let time take care of that," he replied. "Let's not deprive our women folk or anyone else of our fortune. Your uncle would love to be in this, too, I'm sure."

"You, perceptive, Leon. Now that you mentioned my uncle, who with his wife took me and my sister under their wing, and their daughter, who welcomed Maria with open arms.... Did you observe how those two are so close to each other? Maria found an *uhtee* (older sister) in Doray and Doray found a sister in Maria. You're right, we can't afford to be selfish...."

"Bib, I'm glad to hear you say that, but let's leave the choice to them."

***

GOD'S POEMS

He placed in the skies
the sun, the moon, the stars
to light the days, the nights
and the seasons to chime
In His endless poem, Time.

He filled the seas
with waters, with corals
with fish to fathom the deeps
and swim the reefs
In His boundless poem, The Seas.

He etched on the hills
the rocks, the grass, the trees
and caused the springs to flow
waterfalls to echo in
His loving poem, The Cross.

He made the man from clay
and breathed in him His life
and placed him in Eden
to tend the garden ...
This poem of poems He called, My Child.

In the passage of time
that saw sin's ruinous reign,
when death did rule supreme
He sent His Son to claim His Child
To offer His poem, Eternal life.

 ***

Chapter II

THE LORD IS MY SHEPHERD

The Lord is good, filled Pastor Finster's mind as he made his way to his home, his heart lifted up with gratefulness. *I feel meeting these young men was of Thee, Lord. I praise Thy holy name. Give me wisdom to equal this seed-sowing opportunity, Lord. Open the hearts of Bibiano and Leon, lead them to Thee. Open their eyes to see the leading of the Holy Spirit. I claim Thy promise, "Whatsoever ye ask in my name, you shall receive...."*

"Honey," Finster greeted his wife who met him at the door, he gave her a kiss. "Today, I met two bright looking young men. It made my day," he said as he sat down and placed his portfolio in the drawer.

"I could tell you were happy by the bounce of your steps," she said. "Dinner will be ready in a few minutes, and while we are at the table, I'd like to hear it all," she added, as she turned to the kitchen.

In his prayer for grace, Finster thanked the Lord for His leadings that day. Before taking any food, he said, "Seeing them walking down the road, an overpowering impression came for me to catch up with them." After taking care of the spoonful of food in his mouth, he continued, "Bibiano is a law student and Leon, the other young man, is a high school senior. I greeted them, "*Magandang tanghali, ho,*" (good afternoon) and handed each a tract they eagerly received. I introduced myself as I shook hands with them, and they gave their names: Leon Roda and Bibiano Panis."

After a while, Mrs. Finster said, "I find it difficult to distinguish people one from the other here, as though I'm seeing multiple sets of twins." She chuckled. "Straight black hair, dark eyes, dark tan complexion." She took a bite of her banana, and having taken care of it, she added, "I miss the handles we take for granted back home: the colors of eyes, hair, and so on."

At that her husband smiled. "I concentrate more on features," he said. "As for Leon, L is slim like him, his face is what we'd call pinched. For Bibiano, B is roundish as his face; and he's also more endowed around than Leon." He half-closed his eyes as if to think. "In fact, I saw in Leon's slightly deep-seated eyes a hint of melancholy, and I got the impression he had recently lost weight. His deep and pleasant baritone gives me the feeling his thoughts run deep." He gave a soft chuckle. "Bibiano, Bib for short, is plucky, extrovert; I'd class his speaking voice a low tenor range."

"I see," she said. "Are you describing potential preachers?"

"We're in sync, Honey. They're not the ordinary run-of-the-mill young men—they surely come from good homes," he said. "And I'd like to meet their parents, too. I can see the Lord leading, answering our prayers. As we talked, I sensed Leon's admiration in my effort to speak in Tagalog, and before long he said, 'I'd like to be able to speak English fluently.' I saw this as an opportunity and boldly told him I wish to give Bible studies in Tagalog and would he coach me in this."

Finster beamed as he continued. "His face lighted up, but it was Bibiano who quipped, 'Come to our home for that.' The two exchanged meaningful glances, then Bibiano added, 'On Saturday evening.' It was also Bibiano who gave me the direction to their home. Soon they began telling about themselves. Leon boards with Bib's family—actually his uncle and his wife who had taken him and his younger sister to live with them when the siblings became orphans at an early age."

"Oh, I'm sorry for Bibiano and his sister," she muttered.

"As we parted and I started for home, my heart opened to the Lord, as I usually do when I have no human to talk to. As I talked to Him, as if the heavens opened and I heard a voice say, 'I give to you the desires of your heart. Nurture these young men for me. I've chosen them to help plant the Word in the islands for My name's sake."

"Praise the Lord!" the couple exclaimed simultaneously, their joy overflowing, and they knelt to pour their gratefulness to their Master.

As they arose, she said, "For dessert we have ripe mangoes," forking a slice on her plate. "The flavor is out of this world," she added after her first bite. "My taste buds say mango is becoming my favorite fruit. I like the different aromatic bananas, too, but mangoes have it all."

"The mangoes we buy back home in the States have been picked before they ripened on the tree," her husband said as he forked a piece into his mouth, "Mmmmm... this is delicious, so smooth and velvety. Not a bit of fiber like the ones I'd eaten back home."

"I imagine if they were peeled, sliced and preserved frozen, we could enjoy them when mangoes are out of season. With a little cream, they'd be a refreshing frozen dessert to indulge in on hot humid days," she said.

He gave his wife a pat on the arm. "The problem here is we do not have the luxury of a freezer, not even a refrigerator. And if we based our eating habits on the inspired writings of Ellen G. White, we benefit the most from eating freshly picked, tree-ripened fruits. Unprocessed." He wiped his fingers and mouth with a napkin. "That was a delicious meal, Dear. I'd like to eat more, but I'd be overeating if I ignored the warning."

She chuckled. "Thanks, they're nutritious, too. You just reminded me our first parents' food in the Garden of Eden were tree ripened fruits, freshly picked from the tree. I can't imagine them cooking their food...."

Chatting along while she cleared the table, she said, "I cut only a mango for each of us to have no left overs," and added, "I hate to see any of this good food go to waste." She glanced at her husband who had taken a sit, and saw him as though lost in his thoughts.

"You're right to think cooking food started only many years after the banishment of Adam and Eve from their Eden home. For generations," he said, "perhaps their children didn't use fire, or refrigeration. I presume it was only after the flood which deformed the earth that humans began processing their food."

"If my thinking is right," she began, "processing food includes drying as a way to preserve food. I believe these tree ripened, non-fibrous, sweet mangoes can be dried. Ellen White counseled people in her time to dry fruits and grains to preserve them for future use. Dried mangoes, like prunes and raisins, could become a profitable business, say as an export product from the Philippines." Chuckling, she said "Oh, dear, a missionary is getting out of focus, out of line, getting into business." She side-glanced her husband when she heard him chuckle.

"In fact, you're right on track," he encouraged. "I deal with Bible doctrines, and people accept Christ as their personal Savior, and you can help the women along healthful and palatable food preparation."

"It may not be practical to conduct cooking classes here in the islands," she said slowly. "Demonstrating how to cook and preserve foods in the islands, for with only the dry and rainy seasons, anyone industrious enough can plant a garden and grow fruits and vegetables throughout the year to supply their tables." She paused briefly. "I'm thinking over the possibilities for marketing these mangoes," she said, her enthusiasm resurfacing.

"Again, I agree with you," he affirmed his wife. "There's no comparison to freshly picked garden produce in flavor and in food value to canned or dried foods. We brought a copy of <u>The Ministry of Healing</u> for resource, didn't we?"

She nodded in reply, then said. "We will learn as we go along... I know I will learn much from even the less educated islanders. Healthful food preparation has always fascinated me. Now we know there are fruits and vegetables new to us here, and it's in this area where I'll have to be open minded. I'd like to try as many varieties of fruits and vegetables as possible."

"I don't mind eating fresh-from-the-garden vegetables and freshly picked tree-ripened fruits," he said. "In eating the food God designed for the human family, we can be healthy and vigorous by eating solely fresh fruits, seeds, and vegetables that grow all year 'round in the islands."

She nodded. "I see it to be less work for me," she laughed softly. "With the variety of fruits, nuts and vegetables we have sampled so far, I see no reason for one to get bored in the eatery section."

**

GOD'S TEMPLE

by Ellen G. White

The Creator of man has arranged the living machinery of our bodies. Every function is wonderfully and wisely made. And God pledged Himself to keep this human machinery in healthful action if the human agent will obey His laws and cooperate with God. Every law governing the human machinery is to be considered just as truly divine in origin, in character, and in importance as the word of God. Every careless, inattentive action, any abuse put upon the Lord's wonderful mechanism, by disregarding His specified laws in the human habitation, is a violation of God's law. ... the human habitation is the most wonderful. Manuscript file #9, 1897

God is as truly the author of physical laws as He is the Author of the moral law. His law is written with His own finger upon every nerve, every muscle, every faculty which has been entrusted to man. Christ's Object Lessons, p. 347–348

It is as truly a sin to violate the laws of our being as it is to break the ten commandments.... (1890) Christian Temperance & Bible Hygiene, 53.

Grains, fruits, nuts, and vegetables constitute the diet chosen for us by our Creator. (Gen. 1:29) ... prepared in as simple and natural ... as possible ... they impart a strength, a power of endurance, and a vigor of intellect....

Ministry of Healing, pp. 295–296

***

Chapter III

THE ISLES

Luzon is the largest of these islands, Finster mused as he followed the direction Bibiano gave him. *Their home must be around here,* he affirmed himself. Then he came to an iron-fenced yard, its gate ajar. Past lofty trees, an impressive building stood. A dog barked as he stepped into the yard. It was a few minutes before seven.

Bibiano and Leon heard the bark, and they met their visitor at the gate. "We'd been looking for you, Sir," Bibiano said as they shook hands. "Please come in." The young men led their guest to the living room, and soon they were making small talk—Finster speaking in Tagalog and the two young men in English. They corrected each other's grammar and pronunciation, sounding like boys bantering with each other.

"The Bible says, 'Ask and ye shall receive,' Finster said. "So now, let's bow our heads and ask the Lord to give us wisdom as we study His word." Three heads bowed. *He's speaking as to a friend,* Leon thought as the missionary prayed. After the 'Amen,' Finster began the study.

He's as proficient in Tagalog as I am, Leon admired inwardly, then quickly brought his mind to the study. He heard Finster say in Tagalog, "If you have questions, please ask in English," as the minister beamed at him.

Bibiano and Leon soaked up everything Finster gave them, and they agreed for their next meeting at the same time the next Saturday evening.

To Bib's satisfaction, no one made mention of the visit the American had with him and his chum. Leon surmised the folk were simply being courteous, and he wished they'd get to be assertive. After supper the next Saturday evening, however, Maria said, "*Kuya* Bib, why just the two of you with the missionary? Why not invite me and the rest of the family?"

With a wry smile, Bibiano mumbled, "Sure, come join us. We were not sure you'd be interested." Hearing a knock on the door, he and Leon got up to meet their visitor. Maria disappeared, returning with five others.

Bibiano introduced them in Tagalog. "Pastor Finster, meet my uncle Camilo Panis and his wife, my aunt Ciriaca; their daughter, my cousin Teodora, and my aunt Enriqueta. Then putting his arm around Maria's shoulder, with a possessive pride, said, "This is Maria, my younger sister."

"I'm pleased to meet you," the missionary said, delight in his voice and countenance as he shook hands with each one. "We welcome you to our Bible study," he added, beaming. The small talk following confirmed his first impression—this was a noble family who reached out to help others. He lifted his heart silently. *I praise Thee, Lord.*

Continuing in Tagalog, he said, "We always ask the Lord to bless the study of His Word." He got down to his knees, bowed his head, and the rest followed, palms together fingers upturned in an attitude of prayer. In Tagalog, the minister claimed God's promise that He would answer every request made in His name, he asked for wisdom in their study. Many voices united in a reverent 'Amen', then everyone quietly settled to a seat.

The missionary turned to Leon and Bibiano. "For the benefit of our new members, would one of you give a brief review of the salient points from our study last Saturday?" Right away Leon said, "We proved the Bible to be the inspired word of God without an iota of doubt. We read in II Timothy 3:16–17, *"All Scripture is given by inspiration of God..."* he quoted. Bibiano, finding the text from his Bible, read the remaining verse: *"and is profitable for doctrine, for reproof, for correction, for instruction in righteousness."* Verse 17, *That the man of God may be perfect, thoroughly furnished unto all good works."*

"Does anyone have any question about the verity of the Bible?" the missionary asked in Tagalog. No one spoke. He saw them slightly nodding their heads, affirming their faith in the Scriptures. "I'm glad to see some of you have Bibles with you," he continued, still speaking in Tagalog. "We'll put them into good use. From its sacred pages, we will learn more of the will of God for us. May the Holy Spirit enlighten our minds."

The study became alive. Time flew as fingers turned the pages of the Book reverently hunting for the Bible verses. Noting the seriousness of his Bible students in their quest for truth, the missionary's heart beat high with thankfulness to the Lord. In his closing prayer, he praised the Lord for His word making wise the simple, and for the home and gracious members opening their hearts doors to God's word. As they bade goodbye, Ciriaca asked, "Pastor, may I invite others to join our study group?" She need not have asked, she knew his reply, but just a matter of courtesy.

"Please do," the delighted minister said. "I'd love for you to do that."

The next day, Camilo and his wife visited their friends and relatives. And their friends and relatives extended the invitation not only to their friends and relatives, but also to their neighbors. The following week, Finster came to a living room filled to capacity. Bibiano immediately began introducing each new attendee to the astonished, awestruck missionary.

In his opening prayer, the preacher let his heart overflow in praises to the Lord for His blessings, for His leadings. As before, he asked those who attended the last session to review the salient points of the previous study. Camilo and Ciriaca Panis participated with enthusiasm. "Before you came, we discussed some points," Camilo confessed. "Blame Bib and Leon," he said. "It was our pleasure and for our own benefit," Bibiano said in English. "They made us do it, we merely acceded so we could proceed to the next lesson," he added with a flare of pride for his share in the review.

Now aware of their familiarity with the Bible, Finster said, "I must admit you have more knowledge of the Bible than I imagined." As though discerning their thoughts, he continued, "I urge you to ask questions as we go along in our study. It's likely you have a different understanding of the Scriptures than I, so please ask whatever is on your mind. Every question is important to me, and we'll let the Bible answer each of your questions." A hum of approval came from the group. Their faces clearly showed relief. They fully subscribed to the idea the missionary had just proposed.

The spirited study and discussion that followed far exceeded the lively session that preceded it. Time sped by. Not a trace of weariness appeared even on the oldest. The preacher believed, however, that too much of any good thing turns counterproductive. "We'll continue our study next week," he said. After the closing prayer, he said, "My wife had been eager to meet with you all, and I promised her I'd ask you first...."

Mrs, Panis interrupted him, "Pastor, we'd been wishing for her to come along with you from your very first visit...."

Before he left, the minister singled out Bibiano and Leon to walk out with him. On their way, he confessed, "I felt confident giving the study in Tagalog to both of you only, but with the group having grown in number, I'm feeling inadequate. You surely took note of it, didn't you," he posed.

"Would you feel better if you gave the studies in English?" Bibiano asked, and without waiting for his reply, "I'll translate for you," he offered.

"God bless you, Brother!" Finster's voice choked with emotion, and firm white hands grabbed Bib's brown ones. "Praise the Lord," he exclaimed. "The Holy Spirit impressed it in your heart, and you obeyed the prompting. I appreciate your readiness to come to the fore... I accept your offer. How will I ever thank you. The Lord bless you," the missionary said earnestly.

"Just give me the Bible verses you'd be using. I'd like to be familiar with them," Bib said. "In case of an emergency and I wouldn't be able to do it," he turned to Leon, "my chum will do it for you." Finster saw Leon nod, he put his hand on his shoulder and said, "Thank you very much."

After bidding their guest goodnight, Bibiano said, "See, I trust you that much, Leon,"and chuckling, added, "I knew you'd want to be my back-up."

"You must have read my thoughts, Bib. How did you know I wished you'd come up with the proposition? Are our brain waves in synchrony?"

Bibiano waved his hand to dismiss the possibility his friend posed.

Leon had been drawn to his sister lately, unlike the brotherly love he originally had for her. He wondered if Bib knew about this, too. *Is this what they say 'falling in love'?* He began probing his heart. To him this was the first kind of stirrings in his heart. *Now I see things differently,* he thought, admitting his feelings centering on Maria: *Slim, wears her clothes modestly, simply. Parts her long, wavy tresses at the middle, gathers it in a bun behind her head, sometimes braids them to crown her head, looks pretty either way. When happy, her eyes sparkle, mirroring the innocence of a young woman's heart. Well formed, unpainted lips curve up in a smile. that reaches to her eyes; she speaks softly yet clearly. Fair unblemished complexion has no need of rouge—never uses any. Standing, she comes to about the level of my ears. Just turned sweet sixteen, yet I think she acts much more mature for her age.*

A verse he'd come across while reading Proverbs, *Who can find a virtuous woman? For her price is far above rubies,* flashed in his mind. *God brought it to me....* he reflected. Since meeting with the American who said his name was 'Coldwell', then getting acquainted with Pastor Finster, the Word of God allured Leon more and more as he was drawn to Maria. He and Bib had often reflected on the **new light** shed in their Bible study with their spiritual mentor and new friend.

Of those attending the Bible study, Leon, however, was most spontaneous in asking questions. Between meetings, those who had not raised questions sought Leon, and always they got satisfactory biblical answers from him. For Leon purposed in his heart to be to his friends and others as the Finsters, the American missionaries, were to him and Bib.

The two were indulging in one of their jovial moods one day when Bib blurted, "I often fear you're wearing out the preacher thin," To this, Leon gave him a quizzical look. "You ask too many questions," Bibiano explained.

"I have to, else I'd burst!" was Leon's immediate reply. And in a more serious tone, he added, "If you grew up believing the Bible should be read only by priests and find this to be untrue, what would you do? Brother, 'Ask and receive,' the Scriptures say.... Don't you feel something good is happening to our lives, Bib? I feel God's love binding us one to another. We are all hungering and thirsting for the truth, aren't we?"

Bib side-glanced at his chum. "I admire your diligence in the Scriptures seeing you perusing the Bible makes me examine my life." *I do have other priorities—my studies—law can be tough,* he rationalized inwardly. Yet how he wished to be like his friend in matters spiritual. "Do you force yourself to do it, Leon? I, too, wish to form the habit of personal study." *Now I'd bared myself,* he berated himself mentally.

"No, no. I don't," Leon replied in undertones. "To me, opening the Bible to study the Lord's will is like getting water to drink and eating when I am hungry."

"Ho-Ho! Leon, you're getting poetical, my friend."

"Thanks, Bib, but ever since Mr. 'Coldwell' offered prayer for my healing, which I believed God answered, though it was the day before I had a nightmare, my desire to serve God grew stronger. It's like my longing to serve God when I was a *sacristan* boy that's now growing in earnest."

"A nightmare?" interjected Bib. "You've fired my curiosity, Leon. I tell you, I had nightmares following the death of my parents. Now, tell me yours," but quickly added, "What do you mean, as a boy you were a *sacristan*? You owe me lots of explanation." Bib waited impatiently while Leon drew a deep breath, his eyes almost closed with a lost expression.

"All right," Leon finally said. "The nightmare first, since you had them, too. It came when I was a patient in the hospital: As if I arrived at a meeting and saw a shining being and heard him say, 'It's time to take the … faith to the islands.' Right away, a grating voice objected and gave a threat, 'Don't be sorry.' Then he turned to me with a menacing look that clearly meant, "You, too!' I woke up sweating." Leon shook his head as if to shake off the memory, "On being a *sacristan*—I helped the priest do his duties. You see, my father grew up in a staunch Catholic family. He wanted one of his sons to become a priest, and he saw a potential in me, and got me into it. I enjoyed working with the priest, and began to believe I was the son to fulfill my father's dream. That's why he sent me to Manila." Pausing briefly, he nudged his chum who had a faraway look. "Your turn," he said.

"Believe it or not, I couldn't remember details of my nightmares. I'm amazed you recall yours. Maria had some… uh… dreams that she recalled."

"Actually, it seems mine started as a dream but turned into something like a nightmare that even now, I could see the threatening look of, I think, Satan. The hideous pictures of him, the look he gave me made my heart race." Again Leon drew a deep breath. "It was only after I realized where I was—on a hospital bed—however, that the full details slowly came back."

"Do you think your nightmare had meaning, like maybe a warning?"

"Bib, let me answer your question this way: You see me reading the Bible. I've finished reading the Book of Job which to me, perhaps is an allegory, like the parables of Jesus—the prodigal son, for example. I had re-read chapter I, the first part in particular, for I found a similarity to my nightmare. The Book of Job made me more aware God wants His people to realize that He, and Satan, are real. Now I am convinced there is a power struggle going on in this earth between God and Satan: The power of good versus the power of evil."

Bibiano opened his mouth in a yawn. "We'd better get some sleep…."

LUCIFER

by Ellen G. White

God created Lucifer... next to Christ, had been most honored of God. Lucifer stood highest in power and glory among the inhabitants of heaven. Before his fall, Lucifer was first of the covering cherubs, holy and undefiled. He glorified in his brightness and exaltation. Angels delighted to execute his commands... he aspired to be equal with God. He diffused the spirit of discontent, working with mysterious secrecy. For a time he concealed his real purpose under an appearance of reverence for God. He endeavored to excite dissatisfaction about the laws that governed heavenly beings. He intimidated that the laws imposed an unnecessary restraint.

Lucifer... became dissatisfied because all the secrets of God's purposes were not confided in him, and he entirely disregarded that which was revealed concerning his own work in the lofty position assigned to him.

Lucifer might have remained in favor with God... exercising his noble powers to bless others and to glorify his Maker... but. little by little he came to indulge a desire for self-exaltation.... Instead of seeking to make God supreme in the affection and allegiance of His creatures, it was Lucifer's endeavor to win their service and homage to himself....

God in His great mercy bore long with Lucifer.... Again and again he was offered pardon on condition of repentance and submission. Such efforts as only infinite love and wisdom could device were made to convince him of his error. The spirit of discontent had never before been known in heaven. Lucifer himself did not at first see whither he was drifting; he did not understand the real nature of his feelings. Lucifer was convinced that he was in the wrong, that the divine claims were just, and that he ought to acknowledge as such before all heaven. Had he done this, he might have saved himself and many angels. He did not at this time fully cast off his allegiance to God. Though he had forsaken his position as covering cherub, yet if he had been willing to return to God.... he would have been reinstated in his office. But pride forbade him to submit. He persistently defended his own course... and fully committed himself, in the great controversy, against his Maker.

All the powers of his master mind now bent to the work of deception. to secure the sympathy of the angels that had been under his command. Even the fact that Christ had warned and counseled him was perverted to serve his traitorous designs. To those whose loving trust bound them most closely to him, Satan had represented that he was wrongly judged.... From misrepresentation of the words of Christ, he passed to prevarication and direct falsehood, accusing the Son of God of a design to humiliate him before the inhabitants of heaven. He sought also to make a false issue between himself and the loyal angels. All whom he could not subvert and bring fully to his side he accused of indifference to the interests of heavenly beings. The very work which he himself was doing he charged upon those who remained true to God. And to sustain his charge of Gods injustice to him, he resorted to misrepresentation of the words and acts of the Creator. It was his policy to perplex the angels with subtle arguments concerning the purposes of God. Everything that was simple, he shrouded in mystery.... and many were induced to unite with him in rebellion....

God in his wisdom permitted Satan to carry forward his work, until the spirit of disaffection ripened into active revolt. It was necessary for his plans to be fully developed, that their true nature and tendency might be seen by all. Lucifer, as the anointed cherub, had been highly exalted, he was greatly loved by the heavenly beings, and his influence over them was strong. God's government included not only the inhabitants of heaven, but all the worlds that He had created; and Satan thought if he could carry the angels of heaven with him in rebellion, he could carry also the other worlds. He had artfully presented his side of the question, employing sophistry and fraud to secure his objects. His power to deceive was very great, and by disguising himself in a cloak of falsehood he had gained an advantage. Even the loyal angels could not fully discern his character or see to what his work was leading....

The discord he...had caused in heaven, Satan charged upon the law and government of God. All evil he declared to be the result of the divine administration. He claimed that it was his own object to improve upon the statues of Jehovah. Therefore ... he should demonstrate ... his claims and show the working out of his proposed changes in the divine law....

To the very close in the controversy in heaven... Satan continued to justify himself. When it was announced that with all his symnpathizers he must be expelled from the abodes of the bliss, then the rebel leader boldly avowed his contempt for the Creator's law....

The Great Controversy, pp. 494–500.

***

Chapter IV

SHALL WE GATHER

Shall *I obey God or honor my father—to obey the fifth commandment and receive the reward—a long life on this land?* raged in Leon's heart. He opened his Bible and asked the Lord to guide in the study of His word. He had just begun reading the Book of Acts, now he came to chapter 5. Verse 29. He read, "We ought to obey God rather than men." Leon got down on his knees, "Lord, I thank Thee for showing me the answer to my plight," his lips moved, and then in a whisper continued, "I do want to make my father happy but Thou art my Father in heaven whom I will obey. I thank Thee for the gift of choice that is mine to use, Lord. Give me tact to tell my parents about this enlightenment—my choice to obey Thee—to be used of Thee as Thou see it best in my life. I thank Thee for leading me, Lord...."

As he got up from his knees, thoughts of Maria filled his mind. *This, too, I commit to Thy will, Lord*, he prayed in his heart, then laid down to sleep. Before long, sleep, restful sleep overtook him.

Up on the second floor, in her own room next to her cousin Doray's, Maria had felt a need to pray—a beckoning urge to unburden her heart to Someone. She knelt down, clasped her hands palms together, fingers pointed upward, and inwardly began to pour out her anxieties to the Lord: *His actions speak louder than his words, Lord, but should these feelings bother me and keep me awake? I just turned sixteen,* She wasn't sure if He would really understand the heart of a sixteen-year-old girl like her, but she continued her silent prayer. *Lord, I lay my... our... future in Thy hands.* How she wished her *Kuya* Bib would let her in his friendship with Leon. She wished she had her mother to talk to. Yet she had but a vague remembrance of her relationship with her. As good as her aunt was to her, she simply did not feel free to go to her on this matter.

As she lay wide awake, Maria asked herself, *Why do I like Leon? Why does this feeling bother me? He's an Ilokano—dark like most of them are—and I heard they're as tight as the bark of a tree, but are industrious. I think he's handsome and brilliant, but his thoughts are deep, his eyes never give away what's on his mind.* The dialogue they had at dinnertime during the first few weeks of Leon's arrival to live with the family played over in her mind. Her uncle was drilling the newcomer of his family, and Leon obliged, answering every question: *Thirteen children, one father, two mothers, Leon's mother was wife No. 2. Two sisters, one from each wife, the youngest was Leon's full sister. I'd like to meet her,* Maria thought, and she imagined this sister of his would be close to her age. She recalled Leon say he had three younger brothers, but she really was eager to get to know his sister. A smile curved up the corner of her lips of the foursome they'd make if or when her brother meets Leon's younger sister. *What a trade-of it would be if Kuya Bib would fall in love with his sister*…. she fantasized.

Now Maria's mind went to more serious matters. She knew Leon and her brother believed in everything they had learned so far of this new faith. They had been vocal about their desire for baptism. Her uncle and his wife had talked in favor of this new faith based on the Bible. And she thought of Doray's remark that she'd go along with her parents' decision. Then it dawned on her she had never told anyone of her stand. *I'd like baptism with them,* she decided in her heart. *I'll tell Pastor Finster* ….With these thoughts, Maria drifted to sleep, and in to *d r e a m l a n d:*

Her heart was light as she stepped into the river and Pastor Finster held her hands with one hand and raised his other hand to baptize her. When she came up from the water, it was Leon's face she saw, and his hands held hers as though he had baptized her. Bib had been baptized ahead, and as she stepped up to stand beside him, she saw him turn and walked away from the group around the river. Where was Kuya going?

Maria awakened, her heart heavy. Questions crowded her mind. *What was that dream for? A warning? Why was Kuya Bib leaving, and who was the little boy clinging to his hand, whom he was leading away? I felt he was my own little boy.* So intense was the feeling she had for the little boy, she had to struggle to wake up to the present, to real life. She knelt down—driven to go to Someone she could talk to—and tears flowed freely as she prayed with only her lips moving: *My wonderful, kind Father in heaven, my baptism made me feel Thy beloved child, but why does the rest of the dream make me sad even though I am relieved it was but a dream. Lord, let it remain a dream. I commit my life, and my future to Thee, Lord. I'll keep trusting in Thee, Lord. Thy will be done in my life.* As Maria got up from her knees, she asked silently, *Where do dreams come from, Lord? If there is a meaning to it, Lord, let me know what I should do to prevent what's making me sad from materializing.*

"Maria," Doray called, her voice was soft. "What's that cloud on your face about…." she demanded as she drew closer to her cousin. "You look dreamy and sad and ready to cry. Tell me…." she said and sat beside her.

Evading her cousin's eyes, Maria only mumbled, "I'm fine, *Uhtee.*"

But Doray would not buy that. "I think I know you well enough that all is not fine with you. Now, tell me," Doray turned to face Maria. "Did you sleep good? Did you have uh…. a bad dream? another nightmare?"

Maria shook her head. "Look at me in the eye, Maria," Doray persisted. "You know, I'm here. Now pour your heart out to your *Uhtee*…. Haven't I been like a real sister to you? Now you're acting like you have no friend. There's no need to feel like a martyr. Trust me. Is it Leon?"

"Far from it, *Uhtee*."

"Is it anything I have said, or done?"

"*Uhtee*, you've been better than a real sister to me. I couldn't ask for a more wonderful cousin than you."

"Have you decided on baptism and now changed your mind? I hope not," and Doray chuckled. "I heard you say once or twice, 'Only fools don't change their minds.'"

Maria broke in a smile. "*Uhtee*, like you I've made up my mind to become a Seventh-day Adventist. I've told *Kuya* Bib about it. You should have seen his face light up as he heard of it, he grabbed me in a big hug. His eyes swelled with tears, he said he'd tell Pastor Finster about my decision to be baptized. Seeing him happy made me happy, too."

"That's better," Doray said. "The glow on your face is returning. All right, I'll let you keep your uh... secret, but I will keep wondering what made you sigh and looked so forlorn as though no one cared for you..."

***

THANK YOU, DEAR COUSIN MINE

More than a sister, you are to me,
A friend always, in joy or catastrophe:
You think nothing to go out of your way
To help me, either night or day,
Always bright'ning our day.

I thought you deserved to know
How very much I appreciate you,
Dear cousin o'mine, million thanks to you.
I will always love and adore you,
I thought you'd like to know.

Your friendship means so much to me,
Heaven-sent angel you are, definitely
Without wings, without harp, you are
Lovely, loving, gentle, a radar
To me, a shining star.

RAJ

***

1911, March 3, dawned bright and clear, the sky a canopy of blue. Friends and relatives gathered by the Pasig River, near Punta, Sta. Ana, near Manila, for baptism, and some to witness baptism by immersion. Heavenly messengers of peace and love hovered around rejoicing and anticipating the baptism of the first group of Filipinos to the Seventh-day Adventist faith. Pastor L. V. Finster, who had given Bible studies to the group, gave the honor of performing the baptism to Pastor I. H. Evans, then president of the Asiatic Division. Surely, the host of heavenly messengers hovered to assist the visiting minister bury these precious souls into their watery graves. Candidates for baptism included the Panis household: Camilo and Ciriaca—husband and wife—and their daughter Teodora; their nephew Bibiano, and his younger sister, Maria; two nieces— Catalina Nery and Pilar Espino—and the Panis' boarder, Leon Roda; Emilio Manalysay, Marcelino Pelejo, Diego Elisterio, and Jose Castro.

Heaven rejoiced as the recording holy angel wrote each name in the Book of Life. (Leon Roda's father, however, promptly disinherited him.)

Pastor Finster organized the first Seventh-day Adventist Church in Nozaleda, and the group met together to worship in his own home. The Charter Members, in addition to the eleven newly baptized members, were Pastor and Mrs. L. V. Finster, Mr. and Mrs. Robert Caldwell; Antero Lazo dela Cruz and Apolonio de Jesus, who joined the Church by profession of faith. (They had been baptized earlier into the Mission Christiana Church.)

Right away, Pastor Finster founded the Bible Institute, which also met at his home. He extended to the newly baptized an invitation to those who felt a call to enter the ministry. He added that as a part of the Bible Institute program, participants would go through a hands-on-training. "That means, you'd be helping me in all of the evangelistic efforts I would be conducting," he explained.

"Let's go for it, Bib," Leon urged his chum, and he himself immediately signed for the program. "I see this an opportunity to fulfill my promise to serve the Lord the rest of my life," he said.

"Let me think about it more thoroughly," replied Bib, referring to his studies. "It isn't wise for anyone to rush and make changes in the middle of the course he had lined up his life for," he added. "Bear with me as I grapple with a hard decision—from law to ministry—I need your prayers."

After much thought and prayers, along with Pastor Finster's gentle encouragement, Bibiano finally enrolled to participate in the training.

***

THE PATHWAY

One day a follower of the Lord knelt before his Father in heaven. With a prayer on his lips, peace in his spirit, and faith in his heart, he gazed into his Father's eyes. He noticed the Lord's eyes were clear, brilliant, and sharply focused. The follower turned to see the Lord looking out at a pathway.

The pathway was only visible for a few hundred yards, and faded from view behind a hill. The follower noted other pathways close by. It was at that time that the Lord spoke.

"The pathway you see is the path that I have chosen and prepared for you. Follow it with confidence, trust and courage. It will perfectly lead you into a place I have for your life. If you ever wonder where the pathway is taking you, simply look down and you will see My footsteps ahead of you and behind you.

As you walk, you will see other pathways close to yours. Some will draw your interest and curiosity. You may be attracted because of flowers that border them, trees that shade them, or the direction in which they are leading. What you don't see is the depth of the valleys, and the steepness of the mountains through which they wind. Those whom I have called to travel these pathways will have My grace for their journey. I do not want you to waste your time imagining what it might be like traveling down someone else's path. If you choose another's path, you will not have My grace upon you, and the valleys and hills will burden you and create a weariness within you.

The time and energy I give you will always be enough for each day's travel, and you will find many resting places along the way. Give yourself completely to the path I have prepared for you. As you do, continue to look upon My face, for My smile will be upon you. Never forget that everything is significant and working together for the good. I know where the path will take you, for I have already traveled it. Believe Me when I say that you can never imagine the incredible things that await you."

—Roy Lessin

***

Chapter V

<u>WAIT</u> ON THE LORD

1912–1913, Navotas, Rizal, was Leon's first evangelistic effort. He was eager to apply the Bible Institute principles he learned. *Now on my own, Lord, I will fully rely on Thee for guidance, for wisdom,* prayed the twenty-year-old bachelor. *Lord, nurture me with the milk of Thy Word.*

Leon purposed to use every available time in his hands in the study of God's Word. His heart spilled over with gratefulness for his recently gained ability to speak Tagalog. Fluency in Tagalog was the assurance he banked on for the Navotas community to understand his preaching, but he faced a problem: No matter how painstakingly he prepared his sermons, he felt flutters in the pit of his stomach as he got up to preach. *I need a loving human touch, but above all I want my heavenly Father's help,* he thought.

It was from my daily give-and-take with Bib that I learned to speak Tagalog. I had encouraged him and with Pastor Finster prayed for him until Bib yielded to enter the ministry, Leon reflected. *It was after completing the Bible Institute training when I found out of his bent for debates. 'All Filipinos like debates,' he chuckled at Bib's generalization. He promised to drop in to check on me.* Now, Leon looked forward to this.

As usual Leon got up before sun-up for his daily personal devotion and study. From experience, he learned his mind was clear and ready for spiritual feast at an early hour. The prayer and study refreshed him. He stretched his torso. "This is the day which the Lord has made; I will rejoice and be glad in it" (Psalms 118:24), he declared. "This is the day Bib comes to see me," and prompted himself, *I'd better eat breakfast and get ready....*

While enjoying his meal of still-hot boiled unpolished red rice and as he shelled boiled peanuts to eat, he pondered on how the sunshine and the rain nourished the rice fields, and with the same elements that made the grains develop and to mature, made the yellow peanut blossoms shed their petals and bury their peg-heads into the ground to form into husked legumes. As he stripped off the yellow banana peel and took a bite of the aromatic, sweet white flesh, wonderment filled him—*of broad-huge banana stalks drawing nutrients from the air and the ground to supply the burgundy banana bud that filled up to mature into a cluster of bananas.* As he sliced the thin yellow green papaya skin, exposing the deep orange flesh studded with round black seeds, he reflected: *The gardener tilled the soil, planted the seeds, God provided air, sunshine, rain, and the nutrients in the soil that nourished the fruit into this melt-in-the-mouth sweet maturity.*

Leon mentally calculated his chum to arrive in four hours. While he arranged the nature bounties he'd be sharing with him on a round woven bamboo basket, his mouth watered thinking about these favorite foods they shared: A hand of *lacatan* (aromatic orange-yellow bananas) a large cluster of *lanzones*, a dozen or so *pilinuts*, two red on-the-cob popcorn and two segments of badilla (sugar cane) to chew on. *To keep our hands busy as we brain-storm while filling our stomachs with healthful food,* he mused. There was nothing new to his version of the pick-up meal the Panis family served on occasion in their home. He placed two *buko* (young coconut in their husk) and a sharp bolo alongside the bounty-laden basket.

Now Leon focused on his appearance. *It won't do* he mentally settled. *I must take a shower and change into clean clothes.* He gave in to a soft chuckle. *Like preparing to see Maria.* An analogy dawned from this getting-ready of his to Christians preparing for the event of events—the coming of the Lord. *Clean up the body, the mind, the spirit; I can hardly wait. I know the time Bib arrives but know not when the King appears.*

"The door is open, come in," Leon called out, as he walked to the door. Bib grabbed Leon's hand for a handshake, soon the two were in a brief hug.

"You look good, Leon. How's your cottage venture coming along?" Bib sniffed and sniffed. "I smell the aroma of *lacatan*. It makes me hungry."

Leon showed him a basin of water, and they washed their hands. He led Bib to the only table in the room. "Take that one," he gestured at a straight back wooden chair. They bowed their heads, and Bib said grace.

"I'm feeling at home and helping myself," Bib stated as he twisted a *lacatan* off its stem, pulled down the peel, and took a bite. "Exactly the ripeness I like," he muttered. He picked up an ear of corn and started rubbing its kernels off into a *bao* (polished coconut dish). Shelling done, he got up, dropped the kernels into the pan, and lidded it. Before long, the popping came on. Soon they were enjoying the crunchy hot popcorn.

"The light crunchiness of this popcorn is really good!" Bib praised. He watched Leon put a skillet on the stove and added brown sugar and poured some oil into it, and soon he was dropping pilinut meats into the syrup, then began stirring in earnest. Then he took the pan off the stove and still continued to stir, "To be sure the pilinut brittle does not scorch," he said.

Bib looked into the pan, stuck his spoon into it, fished a nut out, and popped it into his mouth. His chum gaped. "Whoaooo… hot!" Bib howled. "Of course, it is!" Leon said laughing. He grabbed the bolo, cut off the top of a *buko* and shoved it to his suffering friend saying, "The fizz ought to help." Bib raised the *buko* to his mouth for a cool drink. "That's better," he said. "Thanks, I should have known better." He cast Leon a look of humiliation and again raised the *buko* to his mouth for more cooling drink. "It is helping," he mumbled. He pulled a lanzones off the cluster, peeled off its leathery beige wrap, then popped the white transparent morsel into his mouth. "Hrrrr. bitterr!" he roared. He got up to look for a place on which to unload the horrid contents of his mouth.

"You got one with a seed," said Leon, laughing.

"I know it, I wasn't thinking, I thought the sweet gel would ease the burn off my tongue. A fool I am," he said, with a snicker. "I'm not giving up on the *lanzones*," he assured himself, and took another one to peel. "It helps," he said, and continued pulling *lanzones* off the cluster and peeling one after another, now being careful not to repeat his first bite. "They're sweet and lemony," he said. He picked up one of the *badilla* joints, got the bolo, pared off a piece of the sugar can pith, and chewed on it, swirled the sweet liquid in his mouth, and swallowed. "Ohhh, that really is soothing," he said, sounding much relief. He took another bite off the sugar cane repeatedly to the very last sugar cane pith. "I'm ready for more popcorn," he chortled, "and pilinut brittle." As he finished a biteful, he said, side-glancing Leon, "How are your evangelistic meetings coming along?"

"Fine, Bib. Praise the Lord, He is pouring down His blessings," replied a beaming Leon. "The attendance is steady. As I visit in their homes, I sense their wholehearted hunger for Bible truth. I praise the Lord, and Bib, I thank you for mentoring me in Tagalog."

His chum shook his head slowly. "It's amazing how you learned fast, Leon. I don't feel I had done much in your mastery of my dialect. Come to think of it," again briefly side-glancing his friend, "from zero a few months ago to preaching in Tagalog! I'm so proud of you!"

Also slowly shaking his head, "To God be the glory," Leon said, "for the ability to learn that God gave to His crowning work." Pausing briefly, he continued, "I have a problem I need to confide in an understanding ear."

"Get with it, friend," Bib urged. "I have two good ears. Trust me."

Leon let out a sigh. "It's the flutters," he chuckled. "No matter how carefully I prepare… I get flutterings in the pit of my stomach the moment I step up to preach."

Bib mimicked Leon's chuckle. "Brother, be assured you're not alone in this." Again, he let out a low chuckle. "I overheard others tell about that thing. That's why I like debates. The flutters turn to thrill," he bragged.

"Don't tell me you get those, uh, flutters too!"

Bib waved his hand to dismiss his friends's question, and continued. "Monotony is never an element in a debate. Give it a try, Leon. You might find the experience exhilarating, stimulating even."

"I chose to pass up that exhilarating experience," said Leon. "Debate is not my line. I'll simply put my trust in the Lord. After all, the flutters don't last, I heard some say it's normal to have those start-up flutters."

"Just suggesting, I like debates," replied Bib in an undertone. Then added with enthusiasm, "I find debates challenging." Picking up his voice, he continued, "I believe people who wouldn't think of attending cottage meetings find debates interesting. And, who knows, people who otherwise would not hear of the truth, by listening to debates, would. Remember the parable of the sower, the different types of hearers?" After a brief pause, he continued with more fervor. "In the debates I got involved so far, I always adhered to what the Bible says. A Bible Institute graduate would never deviate from the Scriptures. I believe God's word is sharper than any two-edged sword however or whoever handles it. Who am I to question the Lord's way of planting the Seed? I say, never underestimate the power of debates to reach hearts sincerely seeking for the truth."

"You're right, Bib. The Holy Spirit can touch one's heart in a thousand ways." Leon was well aware of the impressive number of baptisms from the evangelistic efforts his chum had been conducting. "Frankly," he added, "I admire you for taking the challenge other preachers raise to debate on doctrines we differ... notwithstanding the extra time it takes on your part."

"Because Filipinos in general like debates, the pleasure is mine. Now tell me more about your evangelistic efforts," Bibiano prodded.

"I cannot help but keep praising the Lord for working in the hearts of the people using even His fledgling servant. When I visit in their homes, they raise questions—deep, sincere questions. I feel it a humbling experience to see God's hand in it all, using a new child of His. My Tagalog fluency is a definite plus, again thanks to you, Bib. I feel at home with the people that I visit and I think the feeling is mutual. Do you feel as I do?"

Bib almost interrupted Leon, "As I see it, we tend to measure the success of our efforts in the number of people we baptize. In a way that's good," he muttered, but quickly added, "I think real success is in direct proportion to how far we allow God to use us, and striving to live a godly life, by His grace. Only then He can pour out His unprecedented blessings in our individual efforts."

"AMEN," said Leon in a reverent tone. "I find deep satisfaction in leading souls to God. As I answer questions, I, too, find enlightenment."

"Hey," Bib almost shouted. "Was it King Solomon who said, 'He that winneth souls is wise?'"

Leon nodded. "Proverbs 11, the second part of verse 30," he offered.

"I like to think this proverb holds true in our days," Bib said, a wry smile creeping up his eyes. "If all those attending our nightly meetings lined up for baptism—they're souls we helped win—that classifies us wise!"

"There's also an instance when we could win a soul twice."

"Hey, Leon, explain that," Bib demanded, a tease in his tone.

Catching the bait, "I'll not beat around the bush," replied Leon. "I hear whispers that an attractive, rich, and sophisticated looking young woman attending your meetings night after night has stars in her eyes as she sits listening to your preaching. Tell me, Bib," he gave his friend a side-glance, "Is there truth to the rumor that the attraction is mutual?"

"Like you and my sister?" quipped Bib. "Your actions speak loud...."

"Exactly, and I admit. I'm serious... Bib, would I fit in the—your—family?"

"A useless question, Leon. You're my choice for a brother-in-law."

"Thanks," a smile lighted Leon's face. Grabbing his friend's right hand, he gave him a firm, warm handshake. "Bib," he said engaging his chum's eyes, "May I ask another question?" Not waiting for a response, Leon pressed on, "How about the tradition? And do you know each other as much as your charming young sister and I do?"

"That I, the older, should get married before Maria? I'm not sure about... uh... I have no doubts you and my sis do care and love each other, seeing you two relate...tells it all. For my part, I assure you, 'where there's a will there's a way.' I'm also serious." Bibiano drew a long, deep breath.

"In your case and nearing your mid-twenties," Leon muttered, "I don't mean to rush you on. Neither dare I ignore our culture...uhmm...tradition."

Bibiano shook his head. "I'd been praying about this matter of the heart for some time now. Look where our talk is leading me to...." he cleared his throat. 'Two are better than one,' he quoted Ecclesiastes 4:9.

"... woe to him that is alone when he falleth," Leon quoted the next verse, "for he hath not another to help him up." His voice rose a decibel, "It does apply in our case, praise the Lord!" he said. "In all thy ways acknowledge Him, and He shall direct thy paths,' Proverbs 3:6."

"Leon, are you trying to memorize the whole Bible, and showing off?"

"No, the texts appear along with the verses in my mind by God's grace. Bragging, I disdain," he said in an undertone, he had a far-away look."

"Your diligence in God's word is paying off, Leon." I do need to spend more time in the study of God's word, and committing them to memory."

For a few moments Leon was lost in thought, then said, "I find the 3rd chapter of 1st Kings perplexing. After Solomon married Pharaoh's daughter, God asked him in a night dream what he wanted. In that dream, the young king asked for an understanding heart—to discern between good and evil. God granted his request—wisdom for him to judge the people. He also gave him discernment between right and wrong. Sad to say, somewhere along, Solomon started a political roller coaster leave from God's leading. My concern is: Are dreams as meaningful in our days as they were in Bible times?" He paused, deep in thought.

Moments later, he said, "God is the same yesterday, today, and forever. If, in ancient times, God talked to men in dreams, does He, too... in our day? Are we paying close attention to our dreams in the night as people did in Bible times? If we genuinely desire to do His will, would He give us wisdom to understand our night dreams? Intriguing as dreams are interesting are curses. In biblical times, pronounced blessings as well as curses came to pass. For example, Isaac to his son in Genesis 27 and 28. Numbers 22 to 23 show the weight placed on pronounced blessings and curses. God promised Abraham, "I will bless them that bless thee and curse them that curseth thee...." (Gen. 12:3). In Deuteronomy 28–30, Moses laid blessings and curses on the Israelites.

Wrapped in their own thoughts, Bibiano kept nodding in synchrony with his bouncing the rubber-ended pencil on the table but remaining tight-lipped. Leon noted the lost-in-thought look on his chum's face and presumed something weighty was on his friend's mind. In his deliberate manner he said, "Only our waywardness would keep God out of our lives."

Bibiano kept nodding, Leon continued, "The penitent King David received complete forgiveness from his out-and-out sin involving the Hittite and he became a man after God's own heart. I like to interpret the phrase 'after God's ōn heart' to mean, David pursued, he was after God's heart. Ecclesiastes 12 also depicts a repentant Solomon. God forgave him, too. Exodus 20:5 says, 'And showing mercy unto thousands of them that love me and keep my commandments.' However, this intrigues me: God forgave Solomon, who, being considered wise, ought to have known better than to disregard his relationship with God and used politics to win heathens to God and his—should I say womanizing?—was it to keep His promise to King David, who had a lifelong relationship with Him, that He forgave Solomon but not King Saul? Is it to point out the importance God places of a father's role to his children and their offsprings?"

Bibiano raised his eyes. "Saul did not repent," he replied. "But let me ask you this: The Bible says that when God forgives, He casts our sins in the depths of the sea and remembers them no more. Like His forgiving the father-and-son kings, yet these sins are recorded in the Bible! Should we take that 'remember-them-no-more' to mean the forgiven sins would not be written in the Book of Remembrance?" He cast his friend a quick glance, and without giving Leon a chance to answer, he continued, "I love that part—'and showing mercy unto thousands of them that love me and keep my commandments,' he repeated the verse in a poetical metre. "Does this verse refer to the Ten Commandments God finger-wrote on two tables of stones?" Bowing his head, he whispered, "Lord, write Thy commandments in my heart that I may keep them."

THE DEBATE

by Ellen G. White

In some cases, it may be necessary to meet a proud boaster against the truth of God in open debate, but generally these discussions, either oral or written, result in more harm than good.

God is seldom glorified or the truth advanced in these combats....

There are occasions where their glaring misrepresentations will have to be met. When this is the case, it should be done promptly and briefly... In the presentation of unpopular truth, ... preachers should be careful that every word is as God would have it. Their words should never cut. They should present the truth in humility, with the deepest love for souls, and an earnest desire for their salvation, and let the truth cut. They should not defy ministers of other denominations, and seek to provoke a debate.... *The spirit of debate, of controversy, is a device of Satan to stir up combativeness, and thus eclipse the truth as it is in Jesus.... Many have thus been repulsed instead of being won to Christ....*

If the interest steadily increases, and the people move understandingly, not from impulse but from principle, the interest is much more healthy and durable than it is where a great excitement and interest are created suddenly, and the feelings are excited by listening to a debate, a sharp contest on both sides of the question, for and against the truth.... The feelings and sympathies of the people were stirred, but their consciences were not convicted, their hearts were not broken and humbled before God.

... in defending the doctrines which we consider fundamental articles of faith, we should never allow ourselves to employ arguments that are not wholly sound. These may avail to silence an opposer, but they do not honor the truth. We should present sound arguments that will not only silence our opponents, but will bear the closest and most searching scrutiny.

With those who have educated themselves as debaters, there is great danger that they will not handle the Word of God with fairness. In meeting an opponent, it should be our earnest effort to present subjects in such a manner as to awaken conviction in his mind, instead of seeking merely to give confidence to the believer.

Evangelism, pages 162–167

***

Chapter VI

<u>FOR</u> GOD SO LOVED

1914, early November. Leon knocked on the door of his former boarding house. Hearing Maria say "Come in," as the door opened, he stepped in. They exchanged smiles and pleasantries as they walked to the living room. As a habit from the past, they sat down on the rattan chairs facing each other.

Maria listened as Leon recounted the blessings of God to his Navotas evangelistic effort, and that the meetings would end in January. "I'll start a new effort in Norzagary," he said. He became thoughtful for a moment then said he would have a new team mate, one who had recently been married. "I met him and his wife a few days ago," he said, and pausing briefly, added, "And they appeared very happy." Placing his right hand gently over Maria's left hand he said, "seeing them sharing life together made me long for that kind of love and companionship." He looked into Maria's eyes. "*Aking mahal,*" he said, "don't you think it's time we wed?"

Maria's heartbeats quickened, a rush of warmth washed over her. She lowered her eyes at her hands clasping a dampening white handkerchief. "I think you and I are ready," she said in a soft, low tone, a faint smile crept up to her eyes. "If it's the Lord's will," she added in a whisper, as her eyes met his. "But first," she paused but shortly picked up what she wanted to say: "We must let my uncle and aunt know."

During his stay with them, Leon learned to value Maria's relationship with her surrogate parents. Now his regard for her soared. It was about nine o'clock, and they heard footsteps. Maria's aunt walked into the living room. "Auntie," Maria called. Leon stood up to greet Mrs. Panis, who then sat down with them and listened with approval as Leon informed her of their plans. This came as no surprise to Mrs. Panis for Leon had told her husband of his intentions before he left for Navotas. And his visits with Maria proved to the couple that he was serious. They had noted the attraction between the two and had secretly approved of it, for they liked Leon and his gentlemanly manners. Maria's aunts, however, carried out their matriarchal responsibility: Each evening when Leon came to visit, one of them made it a point to be near yet out of sight. And as soon as the clock struck 9, an aunt marched into the living room saying, "It's getting late," loud enough for the two to hear. If her hint went ignored, she would walk in and out of the living room until Leon bade goodbye.

Mrs. Panis called her husband to join them, and both of them gave their approval and blessings to Leon and Maria. "We're happy for you," Mr. Panis said. "Have you set the date?" Mrs. Panis wanted to know. When she received no immediate reply, she suggested they probably should look into Leon's evangelistic schedule and plan their wedding date around it.

After Leon left, Maria bounded upstairs to tell her cousin Doray of the good news. "I knew you were both in love, but I didn't think you'd get married so soon. Oh, I'll be lonesome without you," she wailed. "You've just turned 19," she reminded Maria. "Do you think you are ready…?"

Maria turned pale. "I thought you'd be happy for me," she sighed. She knelt beside her Uhtee and put her arm around her," You are crying," she said. "I'll be around, *Uhtee*. We'll come to see you and hope you will come to see us, too."

Doray wiped her eyes with a handkerchief, "Can't help it," she sobbed.

"Please, *Uhtee*, be happy for me," Maria pleaded. "I don't want to see you cry. Please help make my wedding a happy occasion for everyone."

***

Not long after, Teodora began embroidering a linen table cloth with matching napkins in blue—Maria's favorite color—using silken thread in true-life colors: Green husk and white meat buko, deep orange mango and papaya halves—black round dots for the seeds, purple star apples, yellow bananas. Doray worked in secret at every time she could spare. After near-completion of her handicraft, she spread it over her bed. "*It's very attractive*," she mentally approved of her work. She knew her gift would make Maria happy, and she folded her handiwork in a box to finish later.

Before long, their cousins—Pilar Espino and Catalina Nery—learned of the coming wedding. "The youngest of us and the first to get married," Doray said with nonchalance yet trying to find reason for her sadness. The two cousins empathized with Doray and also asked why they, too, shared this sadness over Maria's forthcoming wedding. They tried to deny an old superstition that sadness before a wedding portends to an ominous future. "We're all young," said Pilar. "It does not apply to Leon and Maria."

At her cousins' insistence, Doray showed them her project.

"Let's give her something practical, something useful… like…" Catalina began. "A gift to make her remember us for a long time," Pilar continued. After some thoughtful moment, Catalina declared, "A set of clay cookware —let's get her a complete set." Pilar agreed yet suggested they needed to go window-shopping. "If we pool our means to get her a gift, it would enable us to give something valuable," she said, and then conceding she added, "Oh, yes! I agree to a complete set of clay cookware—to prepare their food, she would need cookware—and as she uses them, then washes them, she'd think of the ones who gave them the gift."

The three cousins further agreed to the secrecy of the gifts they have planned on giving and to admonish anyone from duplicating their gifts. "It's unlikely for anybody to duplicate your gift," Pilar assured Teodora.

So the following day, Catalina and Pilar set out to town to do their own shopping. Even if shopping meant spending money, shopping was nevertheless fun to them. "Let's enjoy shopping, even the spending part of it," Pilar said in a jovial mood. "Somehow shopping is a lot of fun," she said.

Now alone and turning to her thoughts, Teodora nursed her unhappy feelings, trying to fight them with all her might. As was her habit, she turned to the Lord. *Within me is an aching I don't fully understand. All I know is I wish relief. Lord, let me be happy for Maria and Leon....* Her emotions lifted upon dwelling on Leon's quiet, reserved persona. *Soon he will be my cousin-in-law. Since he became our boarder, he won us over and we had become in many ways attached to him.* She smiled to think of his ways, his quietness. *We admire him for these. His self-confidence would be an asset for his career—ministry.* Her father had pointed that out to her. *He had always been ready to help, to lend a hand. He'd made himself like a member of the family.* Although at times he and Bibiano became quite engrossed in their studies to the seeming exclusion of the rest of the family, her father said, it was expected of them. *Father, ever so understanding of his own gender's ways, he always came to their rescue.* It amazed Teodora how the thinking of the two young men appeared to run parallel in spite of the differences in their personalities:

Imperturbable Leon. Impulsive and rather excitable Bib. Leon, the deep thinker, whose eyes often hinted of sadness, yet the moment he opened his mouth to speak, his face glowed. His deep voice exuded confidence. One got the impression he carefully weighed his thoughts before expressing them in words. And both of them could sing beautifully.

By giving in to this reflection, Teodora's mood turned cheerful.

As for their mother Ciriaca Panis: All day long she kept a running mental monologue as she went about her activities of daily living. *Who else but Camilo and I would give the bride away? I'll wear my new Maria Clara (a Filipina dress). Camilo needs a new Barong Tagalog (Filipino shirt)—I'll see to get that. Doray must decide on the color of her new balintawak (a Filipina costume)—sky blue or green? Either color looks good on her. Of course, Maria will wear an embroidered jusi (pineapple fiber) dress, Ivory white is very becoming on anyone. White stands for purity—it will be strikingly symbolic on her wedding day. Bibiano said Leon had asked him to stand by him—Bib actually offered Leon the favor, and Doray will be the maid of honor. Simple.*

Catalina, Pilar, with Doray will serve at the reception. We'll have the table set up before the ceremony. The girls will help prepare tree-ripened fruits for the refreshment. The ceremony will be in the afternoon yet early enough to allow the visitors to get home before dark. For this, we are serving light food. Leon and Maria plan to leave for Norzagaray after the wedding, that is, after the refreshments. I had better write all of these down, I feel more confident seeing a list of everything we need:

Her list: White puto (steamed rice cake). Drink—*kalamansi* (native citrus) with shredded cantaloupe. *Buko* (young coconut). Bananas, jackfruit, lanzones, mangoes, papaya, pineapple, star apples. *Casoy* (cashew nuts). She re-read her list. *Refreshment is the key word,* she reminded herself. And now she was eager for the girls to join her, she wanted their approval and their opinion on the wedding preparations. When Maria came down, she showed the list to her, "Thank you, Auntie," Maria said, and gave her aunt a big hug. "You have always been so good to me."

They talked about how Leon had confided in Bib of his disinheritance by his father following his baptism. Bib shared the confidence, even Leon's angst over his father's action, to his uncle and aunt, but no one had brought up the matter since. However, as Mrs. Panis started preparations for the wedding, this became foremost on her mind. *Who else would be on Leon's side but his former landlady, and his brothers and sisters in Christ?*

"We are his family," she told Maria. "I'm happy to attend to the details of your wedding. All your cousins will be helping—they're as excited as I am, and, I'm sure as you are." She saw Maria's facial expression, and said, "I see you have something to tell. What is it?"

"Leon said he'd give money to spend, Auntie," Maria said. "He knows that the man's family spends for the wedding. He said he had written to his aunt who had always been very close to him—even after his apostasy from their family religion—and that this aunt of his would come for his wedding, bringing with her someone else from the family. He also gave me the impression this aunt of has shown great interest in his new faith."

"They must find true love flowing freely among us, Maria," Mrs. Panis said. "We'd like to win them over to our faith.... They must see with their own eyes and feel with their hearts the love of God in action in Leon's new faith family. May God send the Holy Spirit to lead...."

Leon and Bibiano kept out of the women-folk's way. After all, as was their custom, the ladies let the men go scott free from all those necessary in wedding preparations. The men had their own plans, they had taken Pastor in their confidence, yet kept some things to themselves.

Their Aunt Enriqueta, however, made them aware of the practice that the groom-elect must never see his bride-to-be any time the day before their wedding. She had given them enough warning, especially Maria, of the misfortune that could mar the happiness of a new couple if they became careless in this matter. "Don't dismiss it as an old superstition," she told Leon and Maria upon discerning their reaction to her warning. So the two agreed to avoid seeing each other all day before their wedding, as a matter of respect to dear aunt Enriqueta.

A few days before the wedding date, Pastor Finster and Leon showed up at the Panis's home for wedding particulars, including the rehearsal. The minister expressed his wish for the wedding ceremony to run perfectly smooth. Leon informed him his aunt (Josefa Edralin Marcos) and his first cousin (Atty. Juliana Roda Edralin Castro) were arriving in the morning of the wedding, and that he would prompt his relatives about their roles.

***

Leon Zumel Roda, one of the Big Three. A great preacher.

MARRYING and GIVING In MARRIAGE

by Ellen G. White

God placed the human race in the world, and it is their privilege to eat, to drink, to trade, to marry, and to be given in marriage; but it is safe to do these things only in the fear of God. We should live in this world with reference to the eternal world. The great crime in the marriages in the days of Noah was that ... those who professed to acknowledge and revere God associated with those who were corrupt of heart ... and married whom they would. Messages to Young People, *p. 456*

True Love. *Love is a precious gift, which we receive from Jesus. Pure and holy affection is not a feeling but a principle. Those who are actuated by true love are neither unreasonable nor blind. Taught by the Holy Spirit they love God supremely and their neighbor as themselves.*

Let those who are contemplating marriage weigh every sentiment and watch every development of character in the one with whom they think to unite their life destiny. Let every step toward a marriage alliance be characterized by modesty, simplicity, sincerity and an earnest purpose to please and honor God. Marriage affect the afterlife in this world and in the world to come. A sincere Christian will make no plans that God cannot approve.

If you are blessed with God-fearing parents, seek counsel of them. Open to them your hopes and plans, learn the lessons which their life experiences have taught, and you will save many a heartache. Above all, make Christ your Counselor. Study His word with prayer.

Under such guidance let a young woman accept as a life companion only one who possesses pure, manly traits of character, one who is diligent, aspiring and honest, one who loves and fears God. Let a young man seek to stand by his side who is fitted to bear her share of life's burdens, one whose influence will ennoble and refine him, and who will make him happy in her love....

However carefully and wisely marriage may have been entered into, few couples are completely united when the marriage ceremony is performed. The real union of the two ... is the work of the after years.

As life with its burden of perplexity and care meets the newly wedded pair, the romance with which imagination so often invests marriage disappears. Husband and wife learn each other's character as it is impossible to learn it in their previous association. This is a most critical period in their experience. The happiness and usefulness of their whole future life depend upon their taking a right course now. Often they discern in each other unsuspected weaknesses and defects, but the hearts that love has united will discern excellencies also heretofore unknown. Let all seek to discover the excellencies rather than the defects. Often it is our own attitude, the atmosphere that surrounds ourselves, which determines what will be revealed to us in another. There are many who regard the expression of affection as a weakness, and they maintain a reserve that repels others .... As the social and generous impulses are repressed, they wither, and the heart becomes desolate and cold .... Love cannot long exist without expression. Let not the heart connected with you starve for want of kindness and sympathy.

Though difficulties, perplexities, and discouragements may arise, let neither husband nor wife harbor the thought that their union is a mistake or a disappointment. Determine to be all that it is possible to be to each other. Continue the early attentions ... encourage each other in fighting the battles of life. Study to advance the happiness of each other....

<u>Ministry of Healing</u>, pages 358–360.

***

Chapter VII

SEEK <u>ME</u>

And ye shall seek **ME** *and find* **ME***, when ye shall search for* **ME** *with all your heart* **(Jeremiah 29:13)**

1915, January 3. *Today*, Leon told himself, *is my big day. I'll be 23 on my birthday next month.* Heart singing, he stepped out of his rented home. Cool, soft breezes blew. *Lord, I feel calm and sure like the morning.*

Not so at the Panis' home in Santa Ana, near Manila. The cousins—Teodora, Pilar, and Catalina—were frenetically perfecting the table for the reception. "We planned ahead, all will be well," Mrs. Panis assured them. "Enjoy yourselves." She put her arm around each of them for a light hug.

Mr. and Mrs. Camilo Panis greeted each guest with a warm handshake, a genuine smile, and some with a hug. Leon escorted his aunt Josefa E. Marcos and his cousin Atty. Juliana R. Edralin Castro, and introduced them to his future 'parents-in-law'. His younger brothers, Alvaro and Antonino, having arrived earlier, exchanged warm hugs with their aunt Josefa Marcos and their cousin Juliana. Visitors quietly sat down, exchanging hushed yet warm greetings with one another. Before long, Pastor Finster stood before them. Leon came to stand beside him, appearing composed and with an air of expectancy in his demeanor. Bibiano went to stand beside him.

Lovely and dainty in her blue *balintawak*, Teodora walked with light steps to stand beside the minister. Eyes and heads soon turned to the radiant bride in white floating on the arm of her uncle, Camilo. A hint of a smile playing in her eyes highlighted her youthful loveliness. With bounce yet with dignity, Leon stepped to meet them, gently taking his bride's hand and placing it on his arm, led her for them to face the minister.

Pastor Finster gave preliminary remarks, then addressing the bride and groom by their names, began: "The advice I will now give you was written by Ellen G. White, whom God called His messenger. Listen closely to this divinely inspired counsel:

'*In your life union, your affections are to be tributary to each other's happiness. This is the will of God. But while you are to blend as one, neither of you is to lose his or her individuality. Of Him you are to ask, 'What is right? What is wrong? How may I fulfill the purpose of my creation?*

'*Your love for one who is human is to be secondary to your love for God. God Himself gave Adam a companion, 'a helpmeet for him ... who could be one with him in love and sympathy.' He took a rib from the side of Adam, signifying that she was not to control him as the head, nor to be trampled under his feet as an inferior, but to stand by his side as an equal to be loved and protected by him. A part of him, bone of his bone, and flesh of his flesh, she was his second self, showing the close union and the affectionate attachment that should exist in this relation.*

'*Neither the husband nor the wife should attempt to exercise over the other an arbitrary control. Do not try to compel each other to yield to your wishes. You cannot do this and retain each other's love. Be kind, patient, and forbearing, considerate, and courteous. By the grace of God you can succeed in making each other happy.*"

After the exchange of marriage vows—to love and to cherish till death do us part—they knelt down, and by his heartfelt prayer, Pastor Finster reached to the throne of grace. He committed and consecrated the new home and the lives of the new couple. The newlyweds stood up following the prayer, faced each other, joined hands and gazed into each others eyes. Soon Leon began singing from the depths of his heart:

Together with Jesus, life's pathway we tread,
As one heart united by His hand are led....
His love e'er surrounds us, His comfort and cheer
Will ever sustain us, Though days may be drear.

Chorus: Together with Him, O love so divine!
Together with Him, O rapture sublime,
Together with Him, Life's pathway we tread.

Together with Jesus, We live for His praise
And pray that His sunshine may gladden our ways,
What God joins together, none other can break
Yes, blessed the union that Jesus doth make.

(Lyric & words by Helen E. Fromn, <u>Rodeheaver's Gospel Solos & Duets</u>)

***

Leon had earlier hinted to his sweetheart of this special number, yet it took her by surprise. His vocal interpretation of the lyrics, a prayer and a promise, swept her heart away attune and in full harmony. With eyes and hands holding each other, Maria purposely focused on the melody and the message, intently ignoring the soft sniffles coming from Doray.

With his arms around the bride and groom, the beaming minister said, "I take great pleasure in introducing to you Mr. and Mrs. Leon Z. Roda."

Hand in hand, the radiant newlyweds greeted their guests, threw their arms to embrace their surrogate parents, Mr. & Mrs. Camilo Panis, and returned hugs and kisses with Doray and their other cousins, with Leon's relatives, and with their many well wishers.

Mr. & Mrs. Camilo Panis led their guests to the reception area. Teary-eyed Teodora and her cousins, wearing pressed-on smiles, stood around ready to serve. The guests were soon admiring the centerpiece: A large *bilao* (round basket woven of fine bamboo strips) lined with huge satiny-emerald banana leaves filled with colorful fruits. Radiating from the center, a clump of star apples (light purple)—in monochromatic order starting from the star apples to resemble petals—slices of cantaloupe, mango, papaya (deep orange) pineapple rings and seeded jackfruit (yellow) the clusters of *lanzones* (light beige) for fringe. On one side of the table sat a tier of white cake *puto* (steamed sugared sweet rice flour) and a punch bowl of citrus drink (*kalamansi*—homegrown mini-lemons) with shredded cantaloupe. Arranged in a row on the other end of the table sat green *buko* (young coconut) halves filled with their own fizzling 'milk' and shredded tender meat. Near it sat a punch bowl of *buko* mix (shredded *makapuno* floating in *buko* fizzling 'milk'. *Bao* (black, shiny half coconut shell) placed around the punch bowl to serve as cups for the refreshment.

The men took *buko* halves, the ladies ladled tender *buko* mix into *bao* dishes for themselves. As the newlyweds cut their wedding cake, the hostesses placed a piece of the cake on a shallow *bao* dish, and as they served, urged guests to help themselves with the finger-fruits, and drinks.

The *bao* (coconut shell bowls) fascinated Mrs. Finster. She ran her fingers over the surface of the black shiny *bao*. "It feels and looks like polished hardwood coated with shellac," she told her husband.

From across the room, Bibiano noted the Finster's focus of interest. He sauntered to stop beside them. "That's a coconut shell," he said. "We make use of every part of the coconut. The fruit, for example. Here, the crafter sawed off about a third of the top of the coconut shell to make a deep bowl. By scraping and sand-papering the surface of the shell—inside and out—it's natural shine comes out. Leon calls the shell *sabot*, it is *bao* in Tagalog. Rubbed thoroughly and buffed, the shell becomes shiny without varnish. Like any fruit, coconuts come in different shapes and sizes. This is a small one," he continued as he picked one up. "The *bao* is sturdy, impervious to water as glass and as breakable. The coconut shell is harder than most hardwoods and is useful in many ways. They can be used as firewood. Coconut shell ember burns slowly, giving out steady heat which makes it suitable for loading a flatiron with which we iron clothes. The husk covering the shell has multiple uses." Turning over his emptied *buko* half, he showed how a husk is used as a floor scrub. "Housekeepers ride them to scrub hardwood floors to a luster. The floors turn slick, too," he chuckled. Riding them to polish hardwood floors is an excellent form of exercise. That's how we stay slim," he said, belly laughing.

"I personally like to drink the water from the young coconut you call *buko,*" Finster said. "Its pure natural fizz beats all other refreshments."

Bibiano turned to Mrs. Finster and asked, "Did you know we extract milk from finely shredded coconut meat?"

"I've heard that," she replied, "but I still have to learn how to milk a coconut," she chuckled. Her husband, too, laughed at the connotation.

"You need a grater to do that," explained Bibiano. "And, of course, a mature coconut gives the best milk." He excused himself and returning shortly, he carried a coconut grater. "This is mounted on wood," he said, and laying the tool on the floor demonstrated how to ride it. Picking up a *buko*, he showed how to hold it to grate the coconut meat. "We hack out the coconut husk first, drain the liquid, then half the big nut before grating. Since this is a *buko,* we need a hand-held grater for it," he said, showing them the hand-held grater he held with his fingers. This is the kind of grater the girls used to scrape the *makapuno* with which they prepared the buko mix. *Makapuno* literally means, filled. The tender meat fills the entire space inside the coconut."

"Thank you," Pastor Finster said. "We appreciate knowing the many possibilities of coconuts." And turning to his wife, "We'll get a coconut grater next time we go shopping," he said.

Mrs. Finster sampled what she called exotic lemonade and asked about the orange particles and other ingredients in it. "Cantaloupe shreds added to ripe *kalamansi* juice, water, and brown cane sugar," replied Bibiano.

"I see," she said, filling her cup. "The shreds of cantaloupe give it a distinctive aroma and taste, and vitamin A fortification to the drink." Her husband, too, filled his *bao* several times.

The Finsters walked to where Maria and Leon stood. "It's part of our wedding cake," Maria said softly, gesturing at a platter of white *puto* mounds sprinkled with creamy freshly grated mature coconut. Sampling one, Mrs. Finster said she liked the delicate taste and the tender texture of the *puto.* She and her husband picked a few more to eat. She leaned to Maria and whispered to her ear, "Would you open your gifts for us to see?"

They ambled to corner at the table piled high with gifts. Leon and his cousin Juliana, and their aunt *Dona* (pronounced donya) Marcos, followed them. Maria opened a brightly wrapped box and lifted Teodora's gift. "Oh, it's beautiful, *Uhtee!*" she exclaimed. "Thank you so very, very much." She passed it on to Juliana, who gasped. "How beautiful!" she ran her fingers to feel the embroidery. Mrs. Finster received it. "May I spread it out?" she asked. "It is life-like," she said. "Life-like fruits," others echoed. "It's a work of art!" they admired.

"This one is heavy," Leon said, helping Maria lift a box. Opening it, Leon addressed the Finsters, "Thank you .... these will build my library."

Maria uncovered a set of dishes and read the handwritten card:

"*An eight-piece place setting for you: Blue is always true. Gold is precious, And so are you.*" (signed) Juliana, your cousin, with love.

"Thank you so much cousin; they're useful and beautiful," Maria whispered to a smiling Juliana, who passed the box to Mrs. Finster.

"Now, I'm all set up for my own housekeeping," Maria declared as she opened the last box. "Pots and pans," she exclaimed, casting a glance at Catalina and Pilar. "I'll always think of you two each time I cook and wash them," she said. "Thank you so much. I'll take good care for them to last a lifetime," she added, with unmistakable joy.

Mrs. Finster clapped her hands, others joined in the clapping.

Again hand in hand, the newlyweds went around shaking hands with their guests and thanking them for celebrating the occasion with them. The guests, too, repeated their best wishes and God's blessings to them in their new life together. The Panis family gave the bride and groom more hugs, repeating, "We're happy for you, and God bless your new home."

A few lingered to talk to each other, taking advantage of the occasion to visit with friends and relatives whom they seldom get to see. Dona Marcos took this an occasion to slip a small envelope in Leon's hand. "Put it in your pocket where my gift to you and Maria won't get lost," she whispered.

Maria excused herself. When she returned, she had on a casual, more comfortable print dress, a sky blue cotton shift. "I'm sparing my wedding dress," she stated. "*Kuya,* may I ask a favor of you? There are a few boxes I'd like to take with me." A faint smile hid her inherent shyness.

The two chums turned to Maria. "You look stunning," Leon said. Without taking his eyes off her, he added, "We must, however, get busy."

Bibiano helped Leon carry their wedding gifts and Maria's belongings into the hired *calesa* (horse-drawn covered cart). They organized Maria's personal possessions in the back of the cart, carefully placing the gifts atop them. "There isn't any more room!" said Bibiano, shaking his head.

"Everything should be there, anyway," quipped Maria.

The men surveyed the *calesa.* "The weight has precariously tilted the cart backward," Bibiano said. "That won't hurt," the driver assured them. "When we get up, our weight should even it up," he explained.

The chums shook hands, then hugged. Bibiano turned to Maria. They fell into each others arms in a long brother-sisterly embrace. As she let go, she noted her *Kuya* let out a sigh upon releasing a deep breath. "Take care Sis, take care, Leon. God be with you … on your way," he said, tears in his voice. He gave them a gentle shove.

Having gotten up first, Leon extended a hand to help his bride step up. They settled inside, in the middle seat. The driver took his place on the front, held the reins, applied a light whip, and the horse pulled to a trot.

The newlyweds sat silently, Leon's arm around Maria. The beating of their hearts and the audible clip-clopping of the horse accompanied their individual thoughts. Breaking the quietness, Maria said in a subdued tone, "I'm embarrassed at how my side of the family behaved…." As if fumbling for the right words, and finding them, she moaned, "a funeral tone." Leon secured his arm around his bride, and with his right hand, took her hands. "*Aking Mahal,*" he whispered, "tears of joy." He kissed her lightly on her temple. "Tears of joy."

"It's beyond me why our wedding turned out, uh… mournful," she said venting her feelings. "*Uhtee* Doray promised me she'd not cry but she kept wiping her eyes with her handkerchief. My aunt and her nieces, too, kept wiping their faces." Inwardly, she wondered, *Did they resent it—me being the youngest yet first to get married—violating the oriental code of marriage? Were they fearful of remaining spinsters?* Then she checked herself. *I must not take their tears personally.* Her faith in God and her love for Leon afforded her the courage to refuse to even listen to the murmured portent of the tears: A foreboding of a life of tears—a touch of fear she determined to keep to herself but share with her heavenly Father.

"I paid close attention to Pastor Finster's words," he said. "Did you hear your uncle reply to the question, 'Who gives this woman…?' I like the answer he mumbled after his, 'We do,' but we're not giving her away. We can only share her with Leon,' his original ad-lib," Leon said with a chuckle.

Maria remained quiet for a while. "I did," she said softly, suppressing a giggle. "My uncle often surprised the family with his humor. You've seen them on occasion becoming quite emotional, haven't you?"

"A few times," he replied. Thereafter Maria sank into a deep silence.

"*Mahal,*" he whispered after a while, "I can't guess what you are thinking of, but I sense you are trying to keep something from me."

"No, but while I was changing into this dress," she began, "*Uhtee* Doray came to my room and gave me a hug. 'Please forgive me for crying,' she said." At that Maria let out a sigh. He tightened his arm around her. "She said it was your song that touched her heart so, and she no longer could hold back her tears. 'You are so lucky to have Leon,' she said. 'I'm so happy for you,' and she began wiping her eyes, and ditto, my dam of tears broke…. We clung to each other and cried and cried."

Fruits native to Philippine Soil: clockwise, form center top: Buko halves (at 9 and 12 o'clock positions), lanzones in clusters, a hand of bananas (a cooking variety); zapote, star-apple, santol (3) and in front of the santol are 2 lanzones; a halved atis (above it and below the cluster of lanzones, is a whole atis); mabolo (found and red, and another atis. (At the corner below it is a bolo—actually an oversized heavy-duty knife useful in husking coconuts as well as cutting buko in half.)

"Who can find a virtuous woman?" Leon quoted softly in her ear. After a dramatic pause, he said, "I have found her." Caressing her hair, he kissed his bride again. "Praise the Lord, I've found her and she's mine."

Lampposts along the road lighted the way as they neared the town of Norzagaray in Bulacan. "We're nearing home," Leon hummed softly. He parted the curtain, stuck his head out, and touched the driver's shoulder. "Turn left at the next crossing," he directed courteously. Then, "Here we are!" he announced. *Mahal,* we're home. Welcome to our home!"

The horse halted in front of a bungalow. Leon emerged out of the curtain, stepped down, and extended a hand to help his bride alight. He unlocked the door, and attempted to pick up his bride to carry her in.

"No, no, you don't," she objected. "I'm too heavy for that, and I'm perfectly capable of walking in on two legs," she giggled softly. Chuckling along, Leon whispered teasing, "*Mahal*, you're conserving my energy…."

The driver helped Leon unload, helped him carry the heavy boxes, and stacked them on the porch. He tipped his hat, bowed low, bade goodby, and started to his cart. "Sir," Leon said grabbing his arm. "Wait, I haven't paid you." Waving a hand, "It's all paid for, Sir," he said. "It's a gift," he mumbled, gently pushing Leon's hand that held some money, "God bless," he said. He pulled himself up to his seat, gave his horse a light whip and tipping his hat, he was gone.

Leon and Maria stared at each other in astonishment. Leon shook his head slowly, "What a gift!" he said, "and a blessing. I didn't think to ask who our benefactor was, nor did it come to mind to thank him. Was he the giver? I should have thanked him. If not, whom should we thank?" He regarded the pesos in his hands and handed them to his surprised wife.

She held both palms out to take it. "Thank you. My first allowance?"

For all you are to me, it isn't enough," he said, gathering her in his arms. "Forget the amount, take it as a token of my love and trust in you."

"I'll have to find a way to spend it. You didn't answer my question," she teased. "Silence means yes," she belly-laughed.

"Did you enjoy our honeymoon trip?" he asked, mimicking her teasing tone. "Just a short bumpy one, wasn't it."

"I did. I enjoyed the ride very much, bumps and all. It's a fair beginning of our journey in this life together. But the ride was a gift—from whom? I'm aching to know."

"*Mahal*, how right you are. The bumps and all are blessings like our *calesa* ride. We must learn to accept every blessing, even learn not to question.... A verse comes to mind, 'Every good gift and every perfect gift is from above, and cometh down from the Father of lights, with whom there is no variableness, neither shadow of turning'" (James 1:17).

"There's still work to do," she reminded him.

"Then let's get busy, *Mahal*. Work, too, is a perfect gift, and I would consider our first home together—humble though it be—as God's gift to us."

***

THE FIRST HOME, A MODEL

by Ellen G. White

The home of our first parents was to be a pattern for other homes....
That home, beautified by the hand of God Himself, was not a gorgeous
palace .... but God placed Adam in a garden. This was his dwelling. The
blue heavens were its dome; the earth, with its delicate flowers and carpet
of living green, was its floor; and the leafy branches of the goodly trees
were its canopy. It's walls were hung with the most magnificent adornings
... the handiwork of the great Master Artist. In the surroundings of the holy
pair was a lesson for all time ... that true happiness is found, not in the
indulgence of pride and luxury, but in communion with God through His
created works. If men would give less attention to the artificial and would
cultivate greater simplicity, they would come far nearer to answering the
purpose of God in their creation. Pride and ambition are never satisfied,
but those who are truly wise will find substantial and elevating pleasure in
the sources of enjoyment that God has placed within the reach of all.

Ministry of Healing, p. 12

***

Chapter VIII

<u>AND</u> A NEW HOME

While Leon lugged in boxes after boxes, Maria began looking over her new home. The front porch led into a living room and dining room in one. A round wooden dining table—covered with a plain royal blue round table cloth, a white lace thrown over it—stood at the center of the dining area. Two wooden straight-back chairs faced each other. At the center of the table, a slender crystal bud vase held a single dark pink rosebud.

As Leon brought in a box, he said, "I think this is for the dining room. He laid the box down on the floor, strode toward the table, picked up the bud vase and offered it to Maria "My best wishes to you, Mrs. Leon Z. Roda," he said, sparkle in his eyes.

"Thank you, Dear" she said, accepting the rose and burying her nose in its opening petals. "So thoughtful of you. It's beautiful and so fragrant."

He lighted another oil lamp, and placing it on the table, he said, "May I, too, have the pleasure of a kiss from my sweet rose? That blossom is no rival to your beauty and sweetness." He took his bride's hands in his. She looked up, their eyes engaging. Drawing her closer, he gathered her in his arms, and planted ardent kisses…. "I never had a chance to do this before," he whispered in her ear. "Someone was always around."

"I wouldn't have let you if you tried… and you know this to be true…."

"All the boxes are in," he said. "I carried them in the rooms where I thought they belong. Let's open only the boxes we have immediate need of for now. It's getting late, we need our rest. It had been a long day filled with wonderful and happy moments, isn't it…. She nodded, a smile on her face. "Almost," she said. "Like the rosebud—beautiful, sweet—with thorns."

"*Aking Mahal,* it's good to be home. Once a bachelor's home, the only love of my life changed it all. It's so good to have you with me from now on, Maria, *aking mahal.*"

Lifting an oil lamp and taking her hand, he led her into the living room. "This will serve for our worship room for now," he said. "You may want to make changes later."

They sat side by side on the sofa. "At break of day, the sun rays find their way into every nook in the room. As the sunshine brightens this room, we, too, will welcome God's sunshine of love into our hearts."

"Our gift from Pastor and Mrs. Finster," Maria said as Leon opened a box. "Inspired messages written by a newly married young woman like you," he said. "Let us lay down our family altar—this our first family worship—in our home. Facing each other with joined hands, they knelt.

"Lord," Leon lifted his head in prayer, "we praise Thee for Thy love, and for leading us. We ask Thee to bless Thy Word now open before us and bless us, too…." Up from their knees, they blended their voices in reading 1st Corinthians 13. Leon pulled out The Desire of Ages, He leafed through the pages, and finding the page, (499) he began to read:

"If you would train a pink, or a rose, or lily, how would you do that? Ask the gardener by what process he makes every branch and leaf to flourish so beautifully, and to develop in symmetry and loveliness. He will tell you that it was by no rude touch, no violent effort; for this would only break the delicate stems. It was by little attentions, often repeated. He moistened the soil, and protected the growing plants from the fierce blasts and from the scorching sun, and God caused them to flourish and to blossom into loveliness….

Encourage the expression of love toward God and toward one another."

Leon closed the book. "These passages," he began, "specifically refer to how parents should regard their responsibility in bringing up their own young children, yet to a wider extent, it encompasses us, God's older children. Being called into the ministry to lead others to Him; even mature individuals new to the Kingdom are like little children to God. We will read this divine instruction again as we raise our own family. Before kneeling to pray, let's read this poem together." He drew a paper out from the inner pocket of his vest and unfolding it, continued, "It is a sonnet composed by James Russell Lowell in 1840, yet it still makes sense. To me. it applies to us."

Maria held the other end of the paper. "I like poems," she said almost in a whisper.

Together, they blended their voices to read:

> "I would not have this perfect love of ours
> Grow from a single root, a single stem,
> Bearing no goodly fruit, but only flowers
> That idly hide life's iron diadem:
> It should grow always like that Eastern tree
> Whose limbs take root and spread forth constantly;
> That love for one, from which there doth not spring
> Wide love for all, is but a worthless thing.
> Not in another world, as poets prate.
> Dwell we apart above the tide of things,
> High floating o'er earth's clouds on fairy wings;
> But our pure love doth ever elevate
> Into a holy bond of brotherhood
> All earthly things, making them pure and good.

***

Leon drew her attention to the lines he underscored, and read it aloud:

But our pure love doth ever elevate
Into a holy bond of—*maritalhood* (he paraphrased)
All holy things, making them pure *as gold* (again paraphrased)

Joining hands and hearts, the newlyweds again knelt before the throne of grace to implore pure love for each other from Him Who is love.

"Our heavenly Father," Leon began in fervent tone, "we kneel to worship Thee. Our hearts overflow with praises and thanksgiving for Thy love—to us. We praise Thee for implanting in human hearts a part of Thee, the power of love. For the sacredness of marriage Thou has gifted our first parents in the Garden of Eden, we thank Thee. For enabling us to have a foretaste of holy union, we glorify Thy most holy name. Lord, we implore Thee to take full control of our human desires, emotions, our passions. Keep us from desecrating this sacred union with Thee, Father, let us know the pleasure in this union as Thou intended for Thy crowning work of creation. As Jesus loves and cares for His Church, Lord, let me likewise love my bride in all purity of purpose. Lord, give us the sensitivity to fully fathom the heavenly joys of married life. Let us bear in mind that Thou art the third person in our marriage, that in Thee, we are one. May we bring only glory to Thy most holy name. These we ask in Jesus' name...."

They stood up together, embraced, and kissed. "In heaven's mathematics," Leon said in a soft tone, "we are one. Our home will be a happy home with God in our hearts," he said in a whisper. "Our Omnipotent God gave Adam, Eve, and He gave me you, *Mahal*.... We first met the day Bib brought me to live with your family. We'll know more of each other in the intimacy of our marriage," he whispered in her ears and caressing her with gentleness. "As Christ loves His pure bride, I, too, will love and care for you, my virgin bride."

The quiet darkness of the night afforded them the privacy and rewards of marital love and a restful sleep.

***

"Good morning, Mrs. Roda," Leon teased his bride, rubbing her shoulders tenderly. "With my one true love, I'll never be alone from now."

Maria opened her eyes. Awareness came to her how fulfilling the beginning of their heaven-approved marriage was.

"*Mahal*, I feel like singing," he said. "May I serenade you? It's still quite dark outside, so make-believe I'm out in the night under your window, and you are looking out paying attention to your suitor. I'll sing this song in Spanish, the language of romance as some say."

"You speak Spanish? I didn't know that."

"My father spoke Spanish at home while we were growing up, and, yes, I learned to speak Spanish, too. He wanted his children to remember his forefather was a conquistador." And with that, Leon drew a deep breath, caught her hands in his, "to my one and only true love, I dedicate this—*El Misterio de la Vida,*" he said.

> *Hoy, al fin halle el misterio de la vida,*
> *El secreto que en el mundo yo busca*
> *Es el ansia, y la dicha que an helaba*
> *Es la ilusion, la fe', que en mi sonar forje'*
> *Pues amor, y amor tan solo el mundo busca*
> *Yo es amor y amor tan solo su cantar;*
> *Es principio, y el final de muestras vidas*
> *Y es el amor que siempre reinara'*
> *Y es amor, amor que solo el mundo busca*
> *Es amor y amor tan solo su cantar;*
> *Es principio, y el final de nuestras vidas*
> *Y es al amor, que siempre reinara*
>
> Spanish by Johnnie Camacho
> Music by Victor Herbert

"*Mahal*, I still feel like singing. May I sing it to you in English?"

Maria nodded, eyes dreamy. She drew a deep breath. "Wish I could sing like you. I wish I knew the song to sing along with you, I do like to hear you sing," she said.

> *Ah, sweet mystery of life, at last I've found thee.*
> *Ah, I know at last the secret of it all;*
> *All the longing, seeking, striving, waiting, yearning;*
> *The turning hopes, the joy and idle tears that fall!*
> *For 'tis love, and love alone, the world is seeking;*
> *And 'tis love, and love alone, that can repay!*
> *'Tis the answer, 'tis the end and all of living,*
> *For it is love alone that rules for aye!*
> *For 'tis love, and love alone, the world is seeking,*
> *For 'tis love, and love alone, that can repay!*
> *Tis the answer, 'tis the end and all of living,*
> *For it is love alone that rules for aye!*
>
> lyric by Riva Johnson Young,
> music by Victor Herbert

"The romance of words," he said. "Which one did you like best?"

"I like the English   which I understand—but I like the depth of feeling you had singing it in Spanish. You sang beautifully each time, *Mahal.*"

"Maria, *Mahal*, come quick!" Leon called excitedly. "What's this?"

"A sewing machine!" Maria danced for joy. "You know it is a sewing machine, don't you. My aunt and my uncle surely got *Kuya* into this! That's what he carried to the *calesa* first. Thank you, auntie and uncle!" she cried, and knelt down to run her fingers all over the sewing machine.

Leon watched, smiling from ear to ear. He fished a handkerchief out of his pocket and began wiping the tears of joy off his wife's face. "I'm happy for you, *Mahal*," he said.

"Auntie taught me and *Uhtee* Doray to sew. Now, I can do my own sewing. *Uhtee* Doray enjoyed embroidery more than sewing. Oh, I feel so lucky. I like to sew," she said, running her fingers over the metal frame.

"I knew you spent hours practicing with needles and scissors," he said.

"Auntie said every girl should know how to sew her own clothes. She taught us how to sew even men's trousers, shirts, and other boy things. We used to go to the dressmaker for our special dresses. Auntie encouraged us also to keep a chest hope, our own hope chest," she corrected herself. *Uhtee* Doray and I dreamed of the time, uh, we looked forward to the time when we would have a home of our own. The Lord is so good to me!"

(And according the treasured Filipino culture, the two cousins pledged each other to guard their purity before God and for their Prince Charming.)

Bubbling over with happiness, Maria recounted the tender moments when she and her cousin Doray shared their intimate secrets with each other—of Doray sharing her dreams and future with Eladio (Aldecoa)—of his ambition to be a dentist, and how she encouraged him to pursue his dream. "It was so romantic when he serenaded *Uhtee* Doray on her birthday," Maria reminisced. "And from then on, her prince charming often escorted her home after school. I told *Uhtee* I liked him for her and that I was very happy that auntie and uncle approved of him. We need Christian dentists as much as the Lord needs evangelists to work for Him."

(Years later, Dr. Aldecoa established the only Adventist dental school in the islands, and through the years graduated many topnotch Adventist as well as non-Adventist dentists.)

"Your dreams for the future with me came down to reality sooner than she expected," Leon interjected, "suddenly, she missed her younger cousin."

"Everyday brings opportunities for me to learn to fulfill my role as an evangelist's wife," she said. "I support your nightly preachings even by my attendance, and I go with you on your visits to the homes of many who wish a preacher's visit. I'm learning how to be a good evangelist's wife."

"You stated that so well, *Mahal*," he affirmed. "I appreciate your full support in my calling. By the grace of God, we will—together—learn to serve Him better everyday. Soul-winning requires total heart, body and mind commitment."

She stretched her arms and gave her husband a hug. "Together," she repeated. "Together with Jesus."

***

CHRISTLIKE LOVE BLENDS HEART WITH HEART

by Ellen G. White

God is love. The love of the Father and the Son is an attribute of every believer. The Word of God is the channel through which divine love is communicated to man. God's truth is the medium by which the intellect is reached. The Holy Spirit is given to the human agent who works to cooperate with divine agencies. It transforms mind and character, enabling man to endure as seeing Him who is invisible. Perfect love can be enjoyed only through the belief of the truth and the reception of the Holy Spirit....

Christlike love blends heart to heart. The truth draws men together. It brings into harmony and unity all who have an earnest, living faith in Savior. Christ designs those who believe in Him to develop and become strong by association with one another. All who work unselfishly in the Master's service bear credentials to the world that God has sent His Son to this earth....

Manuscript 46, March 31, 1902

***

Maria and Leon Roda and children l-r: Eduardo Elizabeth, Mercedes
taken Feb. 12, 1920.

Chapter IX

WE KNOW THAT FAMILY OF GOD

To everything there is a season...a time...to build...
(Eccl. 3:1, 3)

1915, Norzagaray. Like honeybees to flowers, the *Norzagarayans* flocked to attend the evangelistic meetings night after night. Earlier, many had bought from colporteur Caldwell Spanish translations of the books, The Great Controversy, by Ellen G. White, and The Coming King by Edson H. White. And reading the books created a hungering for a deeper knowledge of the Bible. In answer to their longings, they heard the news that a young evangelist was coming to preach in their town, in their own dialect. And that in his previous meetings, he had encouraged people to ask questions. Just what they were wanting—to understand the books they were reading.

Those who attended the meetings invited the preacher to visit them in their homes, and those he visited gave him names of friends and relatives who desired to know about the truth.

Maria accompanied her husband as often as possible. Before they ever stepped out of their home, Leon always prayed and asked the Lord to anoint his lips that he may speak only words to lead hungering souls to Him, and to receive His word. As they called in the homes and became acquainted with them, they noted many of them to be affluent and educated. Proverbs 22:9 popped in Leon's mind: *Seest thou a man diligent in his business? He shall not stand before mean men.* And it was apparent that the people were seeking to satisfy the longings of their hearts. He felt the influence of the Holy Spirit compelling them to draw wisdom from His Word. Leon felt assured the Lord was with him.

At the completion of this evangelistic venture, Pastor L. V. Finster came to baptize the sixty precious souls who had given their hearts to the Lord. From the watery grave, each precious soul arose to be a new son or daughter of the King of Kings. Among the names written in the Book of Life were Mr. and Mrs. Macario Pascual, then respected public school teachers. (In Breaking Through, the author H.L. Reyes stated, "Mr. and Mrs. Macario Pascual became known as Pastor and Mrs. Pascual, and in the hearts of many, among the most beloved teachers.") The Pascuals became pioneers of the Philippine Academy in Pasay, which opened in 1917.

Ilocos Sur, 1913. Pastor Roy Hay and his wife, with their young children, arrived early in 1913 to pioneer the work in the province. Like

Pastor Finster, Hay decided to learn to speak the dialect in that region. He hired Juan Afenir and Sofronio Calderon. Hay put his whole heart in the study, and with the help of his excellent tutors, he was soon speaking in Ilokano. Accordingly, he informed his tutors of his plans to conduct a series of meetings. He extended a special invitation for them to attend. "Bring your families, relatives, and friends," he encouraged them. "I'll preach in Ilokano," he said. "I trust you'd be proud of your student," he added with a twinkle in his eye. And he wrote his sermons in Ilokano.

On July 3 that year, Hay began evangelistic meetings in the barrio of Bukig. Mentally, he had convinced himself that he was now conversant in Ilokano, and thought of perfecting his command of the dialect by practice, in preaching. He fortified this self-confidence by writing his sermons.

Seeing his tutors and their families at the meetings cheered him. As the meetings progressed, however, he began to entertain a feeling that an eloquent Ilokano should do the preaching. The facial expressions before him gave him reason to suspect that perhaps his American enunciation got in the way. He asked the honest opinion of his tutors. "It reflects on us," Juan Afenir replied, "but the people find it hard to follow, uh… they have difficulty understanding most of your words." Mr. Calderon nodded in agreement. Hay appreciated the honesty of his tutors, yet he felt letdown.

Before sailing for the Philippines early in 1913, the burden of his prayers had been for the Lord to show him how to serve Him. He and his wife realized that living in a foreign land would require them to be adaptable, to be flexible. The Review and Herald magazine had carried reports—mostly written by L. V. Finster—of the work in the islands, and then they had opportunity to talk with the Finsters. They thrilled to know that he—Hay and his family and other new recruits—would sail with the Finsters on their return to the Philippines after their furlough.

The long voyage provided ample time for the new missionaries to inquire further about what to expect in their venture. The Finsters obliged and answered all the questions they asked as best as they could. Hay found he'd have to learn a different dialect, not Tagalog the dialect Finster spoke. From hearing the benefits of one's ability to speak the local dialect, Hay made up his mind to learn to speak the dialect of northern Luzon.

In Ilokandia. Hay discovered the territory included other provinces where people spoke the Pangasinan dialect. Fortunately, most of the people there understood Ilokano, and that's what he had learned to speak. When Hay heard about Leon Z. Roda, a young evangelist holding cottage meetings in Norzagaray was from northern Luzon, he requested for him.

Nov. 9, 1915. Red brick cobbled streets, lined at regular intervals with oil-fed lampposts, greeted Leon and Maria as they entered Vigan, Ilocos Sur. "Spanish influence," Leon informed his wife. "The lampposts light the streets and corners at night. The red brick houses built close to the street add a feeling of stability to the community," he concluded.

"It's a big city," Maria said. Her first time in the area, the progressive city filled her with awe.

"It's the Vatican City of the north," said Leon, "and" he added, "I might as well say, of the Philippines. Like my home town, most of the people here are staunch Roman Catholics. *Mahal,* to me, it's like home coming."

A three bed-room brick bungalow, not a great distance from the Hays' home, awaited them. Neat and fairly new, it rented within their means. As the two walked through the rooms hand-in-hand, Leon saw a den next to the living room. "I claim this for my study," he said. After getting a survey of the interior of their new home, Leon began lugging their belongings in. Before long, their next-door neighbors came to welcome them, and offered their help. The couples' friendliness impressed the new arrivals.

As Maria set up housekeeping, she hummed the song, "Love at Home." From room to room she walked, affirming herself mentally, *Our home will be a place where angels love to abide. They'll be our unseen guests every moment of every day.* She stepped out to view the front yard. "Roses ready to bloom!" she cried out upon seeing a rose bush covered with red rosebuds. Then becoming aware she was by herself, continued her musing inwardly. *In a few more days I'll be picking roses to brighten the living room. I will take a bouquet to our next-door neighbor to step up friendship.*

She followed her eyes. "A vegetable garden," she muttered in delight, and walked out to get a closer look: She thrilled to see bell peppers, cucumbers, eggplants, okra, string beans, tomato with ripening fruits. Further on were vines—*ampalaya,* chayote, squash, sweet potato. A clump of banana plants and *kamuting kahoy* (cassava) lined a corner of the lot. In the next corner, a row of papaya cradled blushing fruits. On the opposite corner, *kalamansi* flaunted dozens of pendant green-round fruits. A lone tree, a *sineguelas,* displayed plump purplish elongated fruits on its branches. *Our landlord had in mind a homegrown bounty,* she thought. Humming the tune, she let the lyric of the song fill her heart:

There is beauty all around, when there's love at home,

There is joy in every sound, when there's love at home.

Peace and plenty here abide, Smiling fair on every side,

Time doth softly, sweetly glide When there's love at home.

(Lyric and music by J. H. McNaughton)

***

November 12, Bukig. After the opening song, Pastor Hay stepped up with a newcomer to his right. "I take pleasure in introducing to you our new evangelist, Leon Zumel Roda," he said in Ilokano. Placing his right hand on Leon's shoulder, "My right hand," he added. With a broad smile, he continued, "You should find him easy to understand." He paused to see the reaction from the upturned faces of the audience. He read eager anticipation and acceptance of the Filipino preacher. "Brother Roda speaks your dialect. Tonight, he will preach on the "State of the Dead," he said, and sat down. A brief soft audible murmuring came from the audience.

"Thank you, Pastor Hay," Leon acknowledged the introduction. With a broad smile he made a bow. "It's good to be here with you tonight," he began. "I feel the soft breeze of Bukig welcome, I feel the warm welcome in your smiles." Then in a more serious tone, "I pray the Lord to use His humble servant to serve you in Bukig. May God speak to our hearts tonight. Before we open His word, let's ask His blessings in our study." After a brief but earnest prayer, he posed a question: 'What happens when one dies?' Let us turn our Bibles to Eccl. 12 verse 7 for the answer."

Looking around and seeing upturned faces eagerly listening, Pastor Hay thought, *An eloquent Ilokano makes all the difference."*

***

IN THE HOME OF LEON RODA. Mrs. Hay thought it time to pay Maria a visit. Her husband encouraged her on this and offered he would be home with the children while he did some paper work. The Hays had made a brief visit to welcome them when the couple arrived several days earlier, and it surprised her to see how young Maria was. Eager to get acquainted with the new couple yet thought to give them time, especially Maria, to acclimate to their new environment, Mrs. Hay postponed her visit. She had not forgotten her own experience as a young wife and then as an expectant mother. And how much she had appreciated the help she gained just from talking with those who were veterans in housewifery. Even then, she felt she must be cautious. Unlike her husband, she had not learned to speak their dialect. She found out soon enough. Maria didn't speak Ilokano either, for she was a *Tagala*, but she spoke English quite well. And to her delight, Maria was friendly, though at first shy and reserved, before long her reservation dissolved. In no time, they were visiting like longtime friends. Time flew.

At the dinner table, Maria shared with her husband the grand time she and Mrs. Hay had during her visit. "She said, if I did not mind, she would visit more often," she began. "Of course, I told her I'd love for her to come as often as she found the time. We have no idea of the difficulties missionaries have in adjusting to life in the Islands. 'At first,' she said, 'we had a hard time telling one national from the other.' Maria started to laugh. "She said, Filipinos are all dark tan. All have black straight hair and …" she blurted out between fits of laughter, "all have black eyes!"

"Maria, *Mahal*, did Mrs. Hay give you some … uh… laughing pills?" She wiped her face with the edge of her apron, she kept laughing. *Mahal, aking mahal,*" Leon got up close to his wife. "What's so funny?"

"She said, we are all about the same size…" she convulsed laughing. Catching on and joining in the fun, Leon asked, "Can't they tell a man from a woman?" Then more seriously, "I hope you didn't laugh at her." Maria shook her head. "She said, in the States they have more handles by which they could tell one person from the other. Those handles are nonexistent in the islands. That's why they have difficulty telling…."

"That's interesting," he said. He threw question after question at his giggling wife. "Couldn't they have packed those handles in their luggage? Were those handles contraband? Or did they lose them on their way over?"

"No!" she spat, desperately trying to control herself. "No!" Shaking a finger at her husband, "Wait till I tell you," she said. "The Americans, she told me, have different colors of eyes—blue, brown, green, hazel, or a combination of these colors. Hair could be blond in different shades: golden to light, to dark, to strawberry. There are brunettes—brown in varied shades, light to dark. Darkest brown, off black. Also, red hair! Most have wavy hair, some curly. Some have fine straight hair. Skin of different shades of white. And some are just plain black, both of hair and skin."

"I see," he said. He assumed a far-away look. "Yes," he mumbled. "The hair of the Finsters aren't black like ours. From what you've just told me, they could be brunette. Of course, their skin isn't brown like ours. We belong to the brown race, and they—the white race. To me, their skin is more like pinkish-beige. They're both bigger than most of us, but not much taller than tall Filipinos. Both the Hays and their children have dark wavy hair, but not as dark as ours." A smile played on his lips.

Maria guessed his thoughts were deep, and she kept quiet to give him time to think.

Soon, he resumed his monologue, but now giving awareness that Maria was listening.

"The story of creation in Genesis I tells us how the human race began. God created man—Adam and Eve, parents of the human race—in His own image. The whole human race descended from the man God formed with His own hands from clay. He made our first mother out of a rib from Adam. There's no biblical reference that God made another man." He paused, slowly shaking his head from side to side. "From our first parents came all the races of the world: brown, we are brown. Yellow, the Chinese and the Japanese with straight black hair like ours, also black eyes. The black and the red —I still have to meet—and the white race."

"I'd like to say it is interesting, too, how you manage to turn our talks in to… uh. biblical. I wanted you to laugh a bit," she said. "When you meet people, and even when you preach, I know you smile a lot and I wish you'd try to laugh at home more often." She paused, and sighed. "I'd like to see laughter on your face. I like to hear you laugh at home more often."

Leon chuckled then and admitted he felt better. "I was tired when I came home, but not any more. Maybe I was hungry. It's so good to come home to someone, and to find good food on the table," he said, a boyish grin on his face. Boring his eyes into Maria's, he asked. "Tell me, were you just putting on? That Mrs. Hay didn't actually tell all those funnies after all? Did she influence you to get me to laugh?" His voice turned serious.

"I didn't make up those funnies. I wouldn't have known had she not told them," she replied in a monotone. "They were not funny when she was telling them. Only after she left, and I began thinking about the things she said, and thought she didn't mention pug noses that I started to laugh, but then I thought, a sane person does not normally laugh alone."

It took a few moments for Leon to digest what he heard, and raising his hands as if in surrender, said, "Huh, a merry heart doeth good like medicine (Prov. 17:22)." Stealing a sidelong glance at Maria, he said, "There I go again, *Mahal*. The medicine worked, I feel so much better."

November 14. Pastor handed the full responsibility of the meetings over to Leon. It was a great relief for him to see the young evangelist willingly accept the challenge. The missionary's conveyance of faith in his capabilities flattered Leon, it was also humbling. It spurred him to put his trust more firmly in God whom he loved and served, for he believed He had called him to work for Him. It made him feel the need to connect even more to the Source of all wisdom. And because he asked God to be his constant Guide, He lavishly honored Leon's childlike faith in Him.

November 26. Beaming evangelist LZR stepped up to the pulpit to greet the people. Then he said, "Now I can better understand God's love for His children." After a dramatic pause, he continued, "For now I am a father." The spontaneous applause made his ear-to-ear smile reach his eyes. No one had met his wife but some of the women heard she was in the family way. When the clapping subsided, he announced, "On the 25th my firstborn arrived at Vigan Christian Hospital. We named him Eduardo. Now I have a Viganian son. Mother and son are doing well. With the fathers among you, I share this wonderful privilege of fatherhood. In His wisdom, God shared with us this joy, the privilege and responsibility of being a father."

In response to another round of applause, the new father made a bow, and slowly raising his head, said, "Thank you."

Following the opening prayer, his voice took on an urgent tone: "I will now present to you the doctrine that led me to search the Scriptures. I'd like to share the joy of personal study and enlightenment with you. Those of you who brought Bibles, turn with me to Exodus—the second book of the Bible—Exodus, chapter 20.

The rustling of pages sounded like music to preacher LZR's ear. It gave him joy to watch them turn the leaves of the Bible. He savored each moment and waited for their faces to turn up to him. "Let's look at the Seal of God," he said. "I invite you to read with me verses 8 through 11."

Verse 8: *Remember the Sabbath day, to keep it holy. 9. Six days shalt thou labor and do all thy work; 10. But the seventh day is the Sabbath of the Lord thy God; in it thou shalt not do any work, thou, nor thy son, nor thy daughter, thy manservant, nor thy maidservant, nor thy cattle, nor thy stranger that is within thy gates. 11. For in six days the Lord made heaven and earth, the sea, and all that in them is, and rested the seventh day: wherefore the Lord blessed the seventh day, and hallowed it.*

Through eyes of love, evangelist LZR looked at his flock and prayed in his heart for the Holy Spirit to illumine their minds. A solemn quietness pervaded as the meaning of the verses they had read sank in. It was clear to him the people were eager to give their undivided attention to what he was about to say. *Lord, speak through Thy servant tonight, let the right words flow —to bring glory to Thy name,* he prayed deep in his heart.

"Beloved," he said breaking the quiet, "This is the only commandment that begins with the word, Remember. Our Omnipotent God wish for His children to remember Him, their Creator, Who is love. He created man in His own image, placing him a little lower than the angels. He endowed the human race with the capacity to know Him, for His crowning work of creation to have a corresponding perception of his Creator. He also gave them the gift of choice. Moreover, He placed in man's heart a longing for His companionship as much as He wanted their fellowship. He placed Adam and Eve in the Garden of Eden where they could commune with Him, their Creator. He told them of His love for them as they walked together in the garden. Beloved, when Jesus was on earth, He said, *If ye love me, keep my commandments.* Please turn with me to the New Testament, to the fourth book—John—chapter 14, verse 15."

Seeing they had found the verse, he prompted them to read it together: *If ye love me, keep my commandments.* He paused to allow them to absorb its meaning. "Let's turn to the first book of the New Testament. Matthew 5:18. Let's read the verse together, *For verily, I say unto you, Till heaven and earth pass, one jot or one tittle shall in no wise pass from the law, till all be fulfilled.*"

"Beloved, I love God because He first loved me. Beloved, how about you?" Silently he prayed, *Lord, speak to each heart....*

"Now, let's turn to Matthew, chapter 19, verse 17." He waited until they found the text. "Let's read together," he prompted. After they have read the text, he said, "Please pay close attention to the last part of the verse. Will you read—repeat—the verse together?"

He listened as the voices blended in, *If thou wilt enter into life, keep the commandments.* Again, he allowed time for full absorption of the holy Word. "In keeping His commandments, man finds happiness, for God created in the human heart a desire to please Him. Beloved, it's my sincere desire to enter into a life with Him. A life that leads to everlasting life. My beloved friends, how about you?"

Their united 'Amen' assured him they were comprehending. "Again, let's look at the fourth commandment, The Seal of God."

***

Pastor and Mrs. Hay, Leon and Maria united their earnest prayers for the Lord to bless the hearers of the Word. They asked Him to increase their faith, claiming His promise in Matthew 7:7, *Ask and ye shall receive* and chapter 17, verse 20, *If ye have faith as a grain of mustard seed, ye shall say unto this mountain, Remove… and it shall remove … nothing shall be impossible unto you.* They asked for the Holy Spirit to move the hearts of the people to respond to His pleadings. And the Lord honored their faith. After a season of prayer, the preachers and their families recounted God's answer to their prayers, and they magnified His most holy name.

December 15, 1916 was founding day of the first Sabbath School in Vigan. From the company who regularly attended the meetings, thirty souls joined the Sabbath School.

"The Philippines is now a part of a group studying the world-wide Sabbath School lesson," Pastor Hay announced. With one heart, this group, with other interested ones, sought the will of God, and plunged deeper into the study of His Word.

December 29. The thirty Sabbath School members, with the help of others who faithfully came to listen to God's word, finished building a chapel. Here, they met to study, to worship, and to encourage one another.

***

BEAUTIFUL, DIFFERENT, and SACRED

How amazing that from our first grand-grand
  grand-grandparents—Adam and Eve—
  came all the people of the world:
  the brown, the yellow, the black, the white
  and other colors and tribes between
are equally precious in His sight.

Our All-wise Creator love variety.
  Just look around the shapes and see
  the forms, sizes, textures that be
  on shrubs, on trees, on the vines in the lea
  on birds, insects, animals on land and sea
showing how wonderful the Almighty.

Nature tells of God: lover of beauty
  See it in the hues, in colors
  in twinkling stars, in the bow of promise,
  in flow'rs we revel with a touch, a kiss—
  reminders—all earth, God made in six days.
Let's keep sacred the seventh day.

 ***

Chapter X

<u>ALL THINGS</u> OF PARENTING

Suffer little children to come unto me, and forbid them not for of such is the kingdom of God (Luke 18:16).

1916. The arrival of Baby Eduardo in no way altered LZR's daily work life. He adhered to the schedule he had set for himself when he began his ministerial training: Up, long before sunup to meditate, pray, and to study the Scriptures. After the evening family worship and round of chores, he stayed up late for more diligent study. For his motto, he had adopted the words of Jesus, *I must work the works of Him that sent me...*(John 9:4).

February 3. LZR strode home tired yet happy, the bounce of youth in each step. Upon arriving home and rushing through his usual greetings, he said, "Praise be to God! May He magnify His holy name in this city."

Maria stared at her husband.

"I'm bursting with joy, *Mahal.* Are you eager to hear the reason why? I will not keep you in suspense. *Mahal,* we have organized the first Seventh-day Adventist Church in Vigan, testifying the Holy Spirit is working in the hearts of the people in this great Catholic city.

"Praise the Lord," Maria repeated. She motioned in the direction of the crib. "He's awake," she informed. "Get acquainted with your little boy."

He picked up his wide-awake son, and returning the baby's toothless smile, whispered, "My precious little boy." He kissed his baby's cheek. "Hmmm, you're sweet and soft." Father and son eyes met. "We serve a wonderful loving God! He loves you, He loves your Mama, He loves your Papa, and all the little children of the world. He sent His own Son Jesus to this earth as a baby like you, my little one, many, many years ago."

Baby Arding locked eyes with his father. In his wordless way he was telling, "You can practice your sermon on me, *Papang* I'll listen, I'll retain every word you say. I take note of your smile, the tone of your voice, your facial expression. I feel your manner of holding me. Not one tiny bit of expression of your love for me escapes my watchful eyes. Everything is registering in my fast developing brain. I see a loving heavenly Father in you, my *Papang.*"

Sensing something awry, "Is my little boy wet, or dirty?" he asked and fumbled to feel his baby's bottom.

"There's a pile of clean diapers on the corner of the crib," Maria said. I just folded them. He probably needs a change now."

"All right," came a hesitant reply. Then, talking to Arding more spirit-edly, he said, "We might as well get acquainted with each other all the way, huh, Arding." He side-glanced at his wife and caught her smiling, as he gingerly extracted a soiled diaper. "Wet all right, and dirty, too," he mumbled. He reached for a clean diaper.

Suddenly, in his booming pulpit voice, he cried, "Oops! hey, a geyser!" As a jet of stream shoot up, barely hitting him on the face. He'd ducked his head on time to miss being hit "Your water works saved your Mama a diaper to wash," he said chuckling.

"Thanks, Arding," Maria said, erupting in laughter. The baby kicked his feet, flailed his arms, as if joining in his parents' laughter. Wiping off the wetness, Maria chortled, "That's Arding's way of telling you what you're missing for being away for days and sometimes weeks at a time."

"I'm glad you are aware that God comes first in my life, *Mahal,*" said a penitent voice. "I wish I could be a more present husband and father. I, too, feel deprived of your companionship for keeping busy even when I'm at home. Yet, I feel so privileged for the opportunity of sharing the truth with others." Turning to his son," Arding, I'll try to make you feel more comfortable," he said softly, "but I need your help, baby. If you'd keep still, we'd get this job done right in less time."

Maria watched as her husband pinned the diaper. "Good! Neither of you got stuck with the safety pins," she commended. She sat down beside him. He put his left arm around her. "About your being away a lot," she began, "I was jesting. We should be happy you have more than just a job to earn a livelihood. Never mind that you work day and night, often away from us for days. And, you keep busy even when you are home."

"It's a calling, a noble calling. A duty and a privilege," he agreed. "As I study the Scriptures, I feel nourished. Yet my soul's hungering for God's word never seems satisfied. Like an addiction, pardon the simile," he gushed. "The more I read God's word, the more I crave to know His will. And I feel personally responsible for the souls hungering for the truth."

Maria nodded. Arding started wiggling, and Leon handed her the baby. Cradling her baby, she said, "As I nurse Arding, I often wonder how Mary felt as she held and nursed her baby. She was about five years my junior at that time." She paused, knowing her husband was listening. "Young as she was, did she realize that in her arms, she was holding the Savior of mankind? Of the world?"

"In Luke 1, from verse 26, angel Gabriel appeared to Mary, and began talking to her. Mary was initially fearful, and Gabriel sought to win her confidence. Willingly she yielded and said to the angel, *Behold, the handmaid of the Lord, be it unto me according to Thy word.* In the second chapter, verse 19 it says, *Mary kept all these things, and pondered them in her heart.* Yes, I believe Mary knew she was holding the Saviour of the world in her arms. Mary yielded herself accordingly; she entrusted herself to the Lord."

Quietness held them for some moments, lost in their own thoughts, until Maria broke the silence.

"A childlike faith, for she was but a child," she said. "I was trying to put myself in her place. At fourteen, betrothed but not married. Being betrothed in those days must be tantamount to being engaged in our day."

"I believe you are right. Yes, she was then only about fourteen years old. She grew up in the temple, protected from worldliness," he said. He gazed at his wife lovingly. *Mahal,* were you in her place," he said in a soft tone, "would you have been as willing to take the risk? Yield yourself to God's will as she had, and risk your reputation?"

She shook her head slowly. She continued rocking her son, whose eyes had closed, yet occasionally sucked. Taking a deep breath, she replied. "At fourteen, I probably would have consulted my parents before committing myself. At that age, however, I didn't have my parents." She paused. "Did she really understand the significance of yielding herself?

Leon cleared his throat. "I believe so. Women in those days who acquainted themselves with the Scriptures hoped to be the blessed one to carry the promised Messiah. Now I'd like to ask, Had I been Joseph, that is, before our marriage, would you have come to me?"

She merely shook her head slowly, maintaining her silence. And Leon allowed her in her thoughts. Finally, she asked, "Is there any mention of her being an orphan like me? I wish to have as much faith as she had in the Lord," she added. Again, wrapped in their own thoughts, quietness staged solemnity to the time.

"*Mahal,*" we'll let our imaginations run and let our faith answer your questions," he whispered. "I believe Mary's father served in the temple. The Bible describes her as a virgin, full of grace, obedient to the will of God. On matters where the Bible is silent, we must leave it that way; and take what matters most in our personal relationship with God." He watched his son snug in his mother's arms. They remained quiet, partly to let their baby fall asleep as well as being deep in their own thoughts.

Leon placed his pointer finger over the tips of Arding's fingers. The baby's tiny fingers opened slowly, and like the tendrils of a vine, curled around his father's finger. Overcome with joy to the response to the stimuli, he tightened his arm around his wife. "God sharing His intimate love with us. It warms me to feel his little fingers entwine mine," he said. "That must be how our Father in heaven intends His mature children to relate to Him. ...*I was daily His delight*" he quoted Proverbs 8:30.

"I'll take Arding to sleep in his crib," she said, getting up slowly. Leon helped her up. "Thanks, I'll be right back," she whispered.

Leon followed her anyway and watched her lay Arding down. Both gazed at their sleeping baby in wonderment. "He's growing fast," he said in a hushed tone. "A perfect picture of the helplessness and innocence is a baby asleep. Our son is God's little child as we are His son and daughter." Tiptoeing, the happy parents walked to the living room.

"When God created man in His image, surely He thought of His own Son being born of a woman. This alone should secure our faith in His Word. Fathom this: Could you picture baby Jesus being nurtured by a non-humanoid being? I believe that is the very logic God created us in His own image. I feel truly privileged being a part of the human race, just to think of it. Our bodies are His temple. *Moved by the Holy Spirit, holy man of God wrote the Scriptures.*"

They sat side by side on the sofa, communicating in silence.

"Now what are the thoughts running on your mind," Leon broke the silence. "I perceive you have important matters there. Would you share them…?"

Chuckling, Maria lightly tapped her husband's forehead with her right index finger. "Not a mind reader. My guess is, these questions, too, fill your mind. I suspect you have the same thoughts framed to favor your gender. I'd been wondering where young mother Mary got all the wisdom to raise the growing Jesus. Wasn't she His first teacher?" She paused. "I base my questionings on the few months I'd been in to motherhood. I realize age is a poor gauge on one's maturity. I'm five years older than Mary was when she was caring for her baby. Yet I feel unequal to mother-hood, which is but a part of being a housewife." She let out what sounded like a sigh.

"All these call for a lot of selflessness. Think of her many responsibilities: food, meal preparation and timeliness, house chores—keeping the house clean and orderly at all times, laundry, taking care of children." She gave him a side-glance. "Mary had stepchildren, didn't she? If they were still young and dependent, Mary have had her hands full. Did she have a maid, or a servant?" She drew a deep breath. "Even if her stepchildren were old enough to take care of their day-to-day needs, I'd still feel crushed…."

Now aware where his wife's thoughts were leading to, Leon let out a chuckle and wrapped her in his arm. "You do show sensitivity to the duties of a mother in the tender years of her child, for in the eyes of a child, parents represent God." After a brief pause, he added, "I like to think God gave us Arding to show us how much He loves and cares for us and how much dependent on Him He would have us. To let us experience how our heavenly Father feels toward us. Isaiah 49:15 says, *Can a mother forget her sucking child…? yea, they may forget, yet will I not forget thee.* The metaphor applies to fathers, too. Surely, God had given as much thought in choosing Joseph to father-figure His Son s much as He had for Mary to mother Jesus."

"I'm waiting for a non-biblical answer to my question," quipped Maria.

"There might not be one," he replied, "but let's look at faith. Biblical, yes, we take things for granted. It takes faith to get to most if not all of our day-to-day living. For example, our visiting in people's homes. We walk to their homes following their directions, that's exercising faith that we would find the way, and that they would be waiting for us, and that we would be safe while we visited with them. When we have a bridge to cross to get to their homes, we have faith the bridge would not break down under us. You wash the clothes and hang them out on the line, you are exercising your faith that the sun and the wind would dry them. Wisdom is applied knowledge. You were right when you said, it took a child-like faith for Mary to believe the Angel who talked to her, yes, she was then but a child. Her faith was complete. God-fearing, she let her faith extend beyond motherhood duties. Her full reliance on God for wisdom fitted her to raise the Savior of mankind."

After a moment of silence, he resumed with more earnestness. "Growing up in the temple exposed Mary to the Scriptural foretelling of the Redeemer's birth, and she looked forward to the fulfillment of that prophecy as many young woman in those days hoped and prayed she would be God's choice to give birth to the Messiah."

Leon reached for his Bible, thumbed through to the book of Job. "The biblical answer is in chapter 28, verse 20: *Whence then cometh wisdom?* In verse 28, *the fear of the Lord is wisdom.* James 1:5, *If any of you lack wisdom, let him ask of God....* Having grown in an ecclesiastical setting, away from the evil influences of the world, Mary learned her lessons well."

"Her total reliance on God for wisdom made her ready to accept the charge when it came," she repeated, nodding her head.

"Young Mary obeyed the leading of the Holy Spirit when she paid her older cousin Elizabeth a visit," said Leon, "to affirm her faith and obedi-cnce to the message the Angel had given her. Likewise inspired by the Holy Spirit, Elizabeth called her younger cousin Mary, 'blessed of all women'. Barren in her younger years, Elizabeth was carrying John, the forerunner of Jesus, whom Mary was then carrying. Mary depended on God for wisdom and strength to nurture baby Jesus. Joseph, whom God chose to be His son's earthly father was faithful and obedient to God's command. That's faith in action."

Still nodding, Maria said, "I see. Mary's faith and her unreserved commitment, her obedience and willingness for the Holy Spirit to overshadow her, was a package deal. She believed—she had faith—that

God knew exactly what she needed to raise the Savior, and she received everything according to her faith."

"I'm proud to hear you say that, *Mahal*. The gospels tell that Mary read the Scriptures to Jesus. The inspired writings of Ellen G. White, God's messenger, vividly picture Jesus listening to His mother reading the Bible to Him." Leon enveloped his wife in his arm. "Mary surely enjoyed retelling to her young Son of the Angel who appeared to her, and of the host of angels proclaiming His birth to the shepherds, and of the Star that guided the wise men to where Baby Jesus lay, and of the angel that warned them, and in heeding the warning, led to the slaughter of innocent babies, and of Joseph's obedience to the angel who warned them to flee for the sake of the Baby."

Now Leon was shaking his head. "The incident when Jesus was twelve years of age, when his parents took Him along to the temple, takes me to the time when I was an altar boy, about twelve years old. My father was very proud of me then," he sighed, and continued. "Four days later when Mary and Joseph found Him, they confronted their Pre-teen Son, and told Him of the worry to which He had subjected them. To his distraught earthly parents, the Youth's reply, *How is it that ye sought me? wist ye not that I must be about my Father's business?* (Luke 2:49) clearly tells that Jesus had direction at that young age. He was conscientious of His earthly mission, and this was His way of pursuing His mission. Mary's willingness to do God's bidding compelled her to accept her Son's divinity, giving up her maternal human feelings when Jesus reminded them it was time for Him to be doing His Father's business."

Listening to her husband's every word, Maria said softly, "I pray the Lord to have me be as willing to do His will as did Mary. As Arding grows up, he, too, will hear the Bible stories, especially of Jesus as a growing child. Like Mary, I will make it a priority to direct Arding to know the Lord."

"Mahal, I'm so proud to hear you express about how you feel on our sacred trust. As a husband who is always away, and a father who cares very much about his son, I'm assured—I'm blessed—to have you." He flitted her a side glance. Seeing her bent on listening attentively, he continued.

"There are passages in the Bible that strike me whenever I come across them. Topping these are fathers blessing their children prior to their impending death. Abraham to Isaac, Isaac to his twins—Esaw and Jacob—are a few examples. And still farther on, Jacob blessing his twelve sons. Moses, before going up to Mount Nebo, repeated similar blessings to each tribe. And God honored all these fatherly blessings. If the Scriptures are written for our instructions, my conscience compels me to follow through, to bless our son without having to wait for my death impending."

All these talk from her husband turned Maria into her own thoughts.

After some pensive moments, Leon resumed: "Another matter that had been an enigma to me was the brief life of Jesus on earth—thirty-three years!" He shook his head slowly from side to side mumbling, "Had not His own chosen people crucified Him, would have He lived longer to bless others? I admit, who am I to question heaven's timetable! Yet this finite mind," he placed his fingertips over his temples, "wishes so much to fathom the depths of a good life cut short." He cast his wife a side-long glance. "*Mahal,*" has an early death ever concerned you?"

She nodded her head slowly. "I'd often wondered why my parents died before their children were old enough to be on their own."

More moments of nonverbal communication passed. Leon drew a deep breath, let it out slowly, and muttered. "Jesus died at thirty-three years of age. Too young to die, yet those years were packed full of good works." Again, retiring to his own thoughts, he pondered, *No, I should not question God's ways. I intend to get the answer from Him at the first opportunity in the New Earth. Unless I have the answer before that time."*

Now Maria intruded into the silence. "What I don't understand is—His disciples and other followers believed Jesus to be the Messiah. How could the leaders and many of God's chosen people have missed in recognizing Him as the promised Savior? Instead of giving Him adoraton and being supportive of His ministry to the multitudes, they crucified Him!"

"*Mahal*, they did not study the Scriptures, thus depriving themselves of the truth. They became self-sufficient in their awareness that they were God's chosen, and Satan used their pride to blind them. Even we, who have accepted Him as our personal Savior, and by His grace are obedient to His will, could betray Him in one careless act."

***

LISTENING

I was regretting the past
and fearing the future
Suddenly, my Lord was speaking,
"My name is I Am."
He paused.

I waited. He continued:
"When you live in the past
with its mistakes and regrets
it is hard. I am not there.
My name is not I Was.

When you live in the future,
with its problems and fears,
it is hard. I am not there
My name is not I Will Be.

When you live in this moment,
it is not hard. I am here.
*My name is **I AM**.*
Come, live with Me this moment.

(anonymous)

***

Chapter XI

WORK TOGETHER REWARDING DAYS

...your Father knoweth what things ye have need of,
before ye ask Him **(Matthew 6:8)**

LZR preached every evening. During the day, he called on the homes of interested ones. And again, those he visited gave a list of friends and relatives for him to call on. While walking his way from one home to the next, his thoughts often strayed to his family, and he talked to the Lord about it: *I miss spending more time with my family, Lord. I thank Thee for desiring Thy children to take their burdens to Thee. Thy work takes first priority in my life, and on my time, Lord. I wish I could spend time to be a present husband and a father. I'm aware Arding misses his father, I miss him, too. Lord. I long to hold my baby in my arms.* He breathed a sigh of relief to think that Mrs. Hay had taken interest in Maria and her little one, that she had been showing her how to care for children, and sharing her knowledge on healthful food preparation with Maria. *For this, I thank Thee, Lord. I praise Thee for being with Maria when I'm away.*

Little did he realize that his wife shed tears as she struggled to wash his clothes by hand, as she pressed his thick pants and linen coat with a hot flatiron which she kept filled with coconut shell embers.

While on his way to visit a family blessed with a teenage son, he thought of his own early boyhood, and he let his mind wander to those practically care-free, happy days. *I was then the apple of my father's eye,* he reminisced.

His parents took their children to attend the Sunday mass, and often his father pulled him to his side. He remembered how one day he whispered into his ear, "Watch the altar boy closely. You'll take his place some day." He recalled his eagerness to obey his father, he watched every step and each movement the altar boy made. He recalled telling his father how he wished he could understand whatever the priest was saying. His father told him the priest was speaking in Latin, and that no one need to understand whatever he was saying. "He is the vicar of Christ," he explained. Thinking over this, LZR drew an involuntary deep breath. *I enjoyed being an altar boy, I was trying to please my father, trying to earn his approval. I never wanted to cross him for fear of losing his love. I earned his approval with my good deportment and relationship with him, he sent me to Manila,* he mused. *I thank Thee, Lord, for working all things together for good for me. Thou knowest how much I love Thee.*

Once his thoughts turned to the time since his baptism. when his parents withheld all forms of contact with him. *I love them, and will continue writing them,* he resolved. *I will trust when I cannot see.* He thought of his younger brothers, Alvaro and Antonino (Tony). *With Thy grace, Lord, may they accept the truth.* He knew they had been asking, "What does the Bible say....? *Open the way for them, too, Lord,* he prayed. He envisioned them listening to the small voice showing them the way. Hebrews 11 strengthened his faith. As he meditated on the Bible verses he had committed to memory, he felt close the Lord. *Now the American Bible Society is taking responsibility for its translation into the major Philippine dialects. The Lord is opening the way. I praise Thee, Lord.*

Mid-February, The Lord opened the way for him to start evangelistic meetings in Sarrat, his birthplace. And he was thrilled to know that Alvaro and Tony had helped make this possible. His younger brothers, barely out of their teens, have taken a brave step to prove their convictions.

The tent filled to capacity every meeting night. His brothers missed not a single meeting. Often, they stayed by to clarify points that befuddled their minds. A Bible scholar their brother was to them, they desired be like him. "The Lord gives wisdom to whoever asks...," LZR assured them.

However, *Don* Juan kept at his teenage sons. He reminded them of the fifth commandment, *Honor thy father and thy mother.* "It's the only commandment with a promise," he said. "As a father, I wish for all of my children to live long on this earth. Now, you are making me feel like a failure." He paced, and in becoming desperate, he wailed, "What's happening to my sons, my beloved sons! A disappointment you are to me. You think it an easy matter for me—seeing you three go against the teachings I had carefully brought you up from your early years! Leon, especially!"

When Leon failed him, *Don* Juan had counted on Alvaro to become a priest, but to his dismay, Alvaro and even Antonino stood firm telling their father they felt they were not dishonoring their parents.

"Didn't you also teach us to use our heads, *Papang?*" Leon's tone was humble, solicitous. "Despite the teaching we all heard from the priests, you wanted your children to read the Bible, which you believe is the Word of God. You also taught us to reverence God and to put Him first in our lives. We are honoring you in our choice to go by His Word." Leon reached out to lay his left hand on his father's arm. "If everyone reads the Holy Bible, *Papang,* and do exactly as it says, everyone would become a Seventh-day Adventist. And, *Papang,* I pray the Lord to open your heart, also *Mamang* and all my brothers and sisters, to the wooing of the Holy Spirit."

Don Juan became silent, drawing deep breaths with his eyes closed, he placed his palms on his forehead, slowly shaking his head. The three brothers silently prayed for the Holy Spirit to work on their father's heart. Still shaking his head, *Don Juan* quoted, "Honor thy father and thy mother that thy days may be long upon the land…." What a disappointment you three are to me."

"*Papang,* we're sorry that you feel that way for it is not our intention to disappoint or dishonor you. We love and respect you, but from our personal and prayerful study of the Bible, we find the Catholic Church wanting," Alvaro said. "Yet we're proud of your generosity in donating the lot on which the community's grand Catholic Church now stands. Salvation is a very personal matter, *Papang.* For the three of us, we feel it our responsibility to obey God rather than man."

Alvaro was one of the forty 'Sarratanians' baptized at the close of this evangelistic effort. It, too, prompted his parents to disinherit him, This comeuppance, however, mattered little to Leon and Alvaro, but the severance from family ties was painful. Leon assured his younger brother that they were storing treasures where moth and decay held no power. He made it known to him that his baptism highlighted his effort in Sarrat.

Maria was adjusting well to her husband's frequent absences. As for LZR, the friendship and interest of Mrs. Hay in Maria's well-being re-assured him. Even then, he wondered if his son was growing up thinking his father was but a myth. Yet, he made up his mind to leave this problem to the Lord. In reading the <u>Review and Herald</u> magazine, he found that Elder and Mrs. James White were often away from their young children. *Except,* he thought, "*they went away together working for the Lord. God sent His only Son to this earth that those who believed in Him might live.* With this, a nagging thought returned, *Jesus lived on earth for thirty-three years, He spent three years of this span of life in active ministry—teaching and healing—but not all who heard Him believed.*

As one responsible for leading his younger brothers to leave their family religion, Leon saw to meet their needs. He invited them. "Come live with me until you find more suitable living arrangements."

Concerned over infringing on their privacy, Alvaro wanted to be sure where he stood. He asked, "*Manong,* I'll be on my own shortly, but is your offer all right with *Manang* Maria?"

Leon assured she was agreeable. "She knows you'll be colporteuring in the area and need a place to stay. Your presence at home would assuage my concern over your *Manang's* well-being in my absence."

Later, when another of Leon's younger brothers—Bartolome—leaned towards their newfound faith, LZR, also offered him his home. At that time, Tony was getting more involved in the evangelistic efforts, in addition to his colporteuring, and there were times when he, too, would be away. Maria therefore welcomed Bartolome's happy-go-lucky persona. Yet no sooner than he got settled, wanderlust struck and he left for adventure in a far away land for good.

Maria had treated her husband's brothers like they were her own brothers, even outfitting Tony with her home sewing. "For being so helpful," Maria told him. For Tony carried all the water they needed from the artesian well to their house, and supplied all the wood necessary for cooking their food on the woodstove.

July 8. It had been over a year since Pastor Hay began preaching in Bukig. The prospect of winning many souls to the truth had been bright from the start. Yet as time rolled along, the initial appeal to the message lost its appeal. Pastor Hay had wanted to be very sure the people became thoroughly knowledgeable of the three angels message before their baptism. Those who faithfully attended the meetings night after night became disappointed over the difficulty in qualifying for baptism. Some voiced out a sentiment like, "If it is this hard to become a Seventh-day Adventist, we will try to get to heaven some other way."

Pastor Hay, Roda and their team members continued to pray for the Lord's leading, for souls to accept Christ as their Savior. They re-evaluated their methods and searched their own hearts. They asked searching questions: "Are we taking the Lord's work in our own hands?"

"Is our self-sufficiency displacing our dependence on God, giving no room for the Holy Spirit to work in the hearts of those sincerely seeking for the truth?"

"Had our delivery of the three angels messages, pinpointing the antichrist, disgusting to the hearers?"

"Have we swung to the far extreme to being too careful people understood the message thoroughly and putting too heavy a burden on keeping the ten commandments thus preventing people from taking their stand?"

The evangelistic team also looked at how Jesus regarded the Pharisees in His time: Instead of commending their righteousness, Jesus reproved them, calling them fools and hypocrites. In trying to obey the law, the Pharisees added their own interpretations of the law.

Not one of those who initially attended the meetings with regularity chose to take their stand. There had been no baptism, and to all appearances, the Bukig effort had been a failure. Perhaps there were lessons the Lord wanted the evangelistic team and future preachers to learn from this experience. Only Noah's family—he and his wife, their children and their wives—obeyed to go into the ark to escape the flood that wiped out the inhabitants of the earth.

***

The First Ordination, December 21, 1916. Five Seventh-day Adventist leaders met in Manila for the ordination of the first three Filipinos to the Adventist ministry: Arthur G. Daniells, then president of the General

Conference, John E. Fulton, then president of the Australasian Union Conference, Elvin M. Adams, then serving in the West Visayan islands, L. V. Finster, the superintendent of the work in and around Manila, and on whom the Lord entrusted the preparation of the first group of Filipinos for baptism as well as the first three for this ordination, and Roy E. Hay, then pioneering in the Ilocos provinces. The three on whom they laid their hands for ordination were: Emilio Manalaysay, Bibiano R. Panis, and Leon Z. Roda. The first Filipinos to receive ordination, they were later referred to as **The Big Three.**

The ordination gave the three—Manalaysay, Panis, and Roda—credentials as full fledged Seventh-day Adventist ministers. It qualified them to conduct their own evangelistic efforts with their own team members. Manalaysay and Panis continued evangelistic efforts in the Manila vicinity—the Tagalog speaking regions. Roda remained in the Ilokano speaking provinces.

PROFILES: THE BIG THREE

1. Emilio Manalaysay was a public school teacher before his baptism. As one would expect, he had high hopes for his new found church to open its own school system. He pondered over this, and prayed about how he would share his dream with the Church leaders. A thought came: *Take advantage of your unique Filipino custom—serenade him.* He sounded a few friends, then asked them to join in serenading the conference president Arthur G. Daniells, with this thought: *If Pastor Daniells responds favorably to their serenade, it would mean a GO signal for him to talk about his dream with the Church leader.*

Following his baptism, Manalaysay left his public school teaching post to serve as a translator for Elder E. M. Adams. Having completed the Bible Institute Training course, he was one of the first three Filipinos ordained into the Seventh-day Adventist ministry. With his team, he conducted a series of cottage meetings in Sta. Cruz, winning sixty precious souls.

The Manalaysay team moved on to Tayabas for another evangelistic effort, which was interrupted when malaria struck the young preacher. On July 30, 1921, the indefatigable thirty-one-year-old evangelist was laid to rest from complications of malaria, leaving his grieving wife. On August 21, 1921, a beautiful baby was born to the young widow Elisea, who named her daughter Emilia, in honor of her father. (In years to come, Emilia would become an outstanding PUC professor.)

The following is a brief progress report of Pastor Manalaysay's brain child, plus a fast-forward look on God's leading: On June 12, 1917, Pasay Academy (PA) opened. In 1931, PA moved to Baesa, Caloocan, Rizal, where in 1933, it became Philippine Union College (PUC). During the Japanese regime (World War II) when authorities mandated re-opening of all educational institutions, Reuben G. Manalaysay, the son of Emilio

Manalaysay, became the first Filipino PUC president. Despite the prevailing war-torn conditions during this time, the period of his presidency was one marked with progress. In 1946, after the American forces liberated the Islands from Japanese monarchy, O. A. Blake replaced him as PUC president. Later, Dr. Andrew Nelson filled the presidential office through 1952. Late in 1952, Dr. R. G. Manalaysay was appointed to resume PUC presidency and held the post through 1964. On June 10, 1957, the government authorized the PUC Graduate School.

During the interim presidency of Dr. Ottis Edwards, while Alfonso P. Roda was upgrading in the States, the College Board voted to buy a property in Silang, Cavite. PUC transfer to the new site was completed in 1981, orchestrated by the returned college president, Dr. Alfonso P. Roda. Having achieved a university status, PUC became The Adventist University of the Philippines (AUP) in August, 1996.

2. **Bibiano Panis**, a law student when he accepted the Seventh-day Adventist faith, was among the first group of Filipinos baptized. Following his ordination, he and his team began a series of nightly cottage meetings near Manila. The meetings continued for three months, followed by a month long baptismal class, concluding with the baptism of one hundred eighty-three precious souls. The Panis team moved on to hold a tent effort in San Pablo, where one hundred and four souls were baptized to the Seventh-day Adventist faith. Missionary Finster regarded Panis to be the most eloquent of the early Tagalog evangelists. Panis held vice-presidency of Central Luzon Mission for fours years. For reasons remote, he resigned late in 1919. (Part of his life story is somewhere else in this book.)

3. **Leon Z. Roda**. His life story is elsewhere in this book.

***

YOUR MISSION

If you cannot on the ocean
  Sail among the swiftest fleet
  Rocking on the highest bellows,
  Laughing at the storms you meet,
  You can stand among the sailors,
  Anchored yet within the bay,
  You can lend a hand to help them
As they launch their boats away.

If you are too weak to journey
  Up the mountain steep and high
  You can stand within the valley
  While the multitudes go by;
  You can chant a happy measure
  As they slowly pass along—
  Though they may forget the singer,
They will not forget the song.

If you have not gold or silver
  Ever ready at command;
  If you cannot toward the needy
  Reach an ever-helping hand
  You can succor the afflicted,
  For the erring, you can weep;
  With the Savior's true disciples,
You can tireless watch may keep.

If you cannot in the harvest
  Gather up the richest sheaves,
  Many a grain, both ripe and golden,
  Oft the careless reaper leaves;
  Go and glean among the briers
  Growing rank against the wall,
  For it may be that their shadow
Hides the heaviest wheat of all.

Do not then, stand idly waiting
  For some work to do;
  Fortune is a lazy goddess —
  She will never come to you.
  Go and toil in any vineyard;
  Do not fear to do or dare —
  If you want a field of labor
You can find it anywhere.

Ellen M. H. Gates

***

Chapter XII

FOR GOOD MOVING ON

...My **Father** *worketh hitherto, and I work* **(John 5:17).**

1917, September 25. Baby Elizabeth (Ely) was born to Leon and Maria Roda, who were thrilled to note the baby favored her father's eyes, mouth, the fingers, and the *kayumanggi* (dark tan) complexion. Maria said somehow she knew Ely would identify with her father.

"And she'll take after her Mama's sterling character," he predicted.

"Just like Arding," she said, "who is your shadow when you're home." They were happy to observe Arding welcoming his baby sister with wide open arms.

Like all normal babies, Ely soon began responding to her parents' attention, even returning Arding's own ways with her baby smiles.

I wish I had more time to spend with my children, Leon often told himself as well as to Maria. *My priority is soul winning,* he told his Father in heaven. Daily, he worked late at night and got up early in the morning for he found fulfilment and personal satisfaction in leading others to his Savior. On his Underwood typewriter, he put on paper the thoughts the Lord impressed on his mind during his waking hours. When the Philippine Publishing House opened in 1917, he began writing articles in Ilokano, and also wrote versions in Tagalog. *The good news must reach as many people as could read,* he affirmed himself.

When Pastor Hay heard people in Artacho were wanting to know more about the Seventh-day Adventists faith, he assigned Leon to go and hold a tent effort there. "There had been a split in the United Brethren Church in the area," Hay confided in Leon, "and the disillusioned parties wished to hear more about our faith."

It flattered Leon to learn Tito Atiga, who was colporteuring in Pangasinan, requested for him. It had been Leon's prayer for the Lord to use him anywhere, wherever he could be of service to Him most, and he shared this call with Maria. "You need not move to Artacho with me," he said, "for after this series of meetings, I expect to be back here. I sense that my next assignment would be around Vigan," he said. "We'll live one day at a time," he added, for by then, Leon had become well acquainted with the moving-life of a minister.

"Don't worry," she assured her husband, "Mrs. Hay will be here for a while, so will Tony."

Evangelist LZR found the people in Pangasinan friendly. Although most of them spoke the Pangasinan dialect, in general the people understood Ilokano. They had been buying books from Colporteur Tito Atigo, and reading these books whetted their appetite to know more about the Seventh-day Adventist faith. When the evangelist and the colporteur met, Atiga gave Roda a list of names to visit and invite to the meetings. He also gave LZR a layout of the town and its surroundings. After settling at a place to stay, LZR wasted no time—soon he was out visiting the people. In talking to them, he also got a hold of their dialect and found they could communicate well with each other well. The people he visited also gave the evangelist a list of names of people who would welcome a visit.

"We have no problem understanding Ilokano," they assured LZR. "Just speak clearly as you are now speaking to us."

At the outset of the meetings, LZR found out he had underestimated the community's interest. There were not enough chairs for everyone, but people thought nothing about sitting on the grass, or even standing for the duration of the preaching. After colporteuring all the day, Atiga was there to greet and welcome the people as they arrived for the meetings. He ushered them to available seats, or to a space on the grass to sit or to stand.

1918. As he expected, Leon received another directive from Pastor Hay. He was to go to his own hometown in Sarrat. Juan Afenir would finish the effort in Artacho. Leon took this change in assignment heaven-sent, he would be closer home to his family—to Maria and the children—as well as to his parents and relatives.

Leon was thrilled when he found that his younger brothers, Alvaro and Antonino, had raised two separate groups. As he talked with them and as he prayed about it, he felt impressed to help them simultaneously. Both of his brothers had been studying the Bible, and preparing to preach what they had learned would re-enforce their convictions. He thought they were also in a position to put their feet, so to speak, in the listeners' shoes. And he would be there for them as Pastor Finster had been to the Bible Institute students. This, he thought, could be the opportunity for his parents and his siblings to learn of his new faith, and he prayed that they would yield to the wooings of the Holy Spirit. He left this matter to God.

Young and unmarried, Alvaro and Antonino (Tony) invited many of their age range. The three brothers agreed to pool their all in this, by God's grace. Each group would meet separately on alternate evenings to give Leon time to help each of his brothers. This would also give them a chance to learn from each other. Those interested enough to attend both meetings could, if they wished to. There were surprises that awaited the three.

A young school teacher, wanting to attend the evangelistic meetings Alvaro was conducting but not inclined to go alone, invited a longtime friend of hers to go with her. In trying to convince her, she repeated the description others said of the preacher: he preaches powerfully as he sings beautifully. A lover of good music, her friend agreed to go with her on a trial basis. Upon arriving at the meeting place, the two recognized the preacher to be their former classmate and friend with whom they had hang-out during their school days. Neither of them suspected the preacher to be Alvaro, for all of them have come from staunch Catholic families. Furthermore, they thought Alvaro had gone away to study for priesthood.

At the close of the meetings, the two friends were baptized to the Seventh-day Adventist faith. Before long, they came up with an original aphorism: A good Catholic makes a good Seventh-day Adventist. Two new church groups organized in Sarrat from this evangelistic effort.

Antonino was baptized on November 19, 1919, and at once began his own evangelistic crusade. Leon and Alvaro swelled with pride to hear their younger brother preach with fervor and a deep bass voice that tend to spell-bound even them.

The three brother evangelists rejoiced to see their sister Manuela attend the meetings, and how they wished she had taken the final step.

Don Juan Roda surprised his sons when he relented of his rash act in disinheriting them. The three brothers empathized with their father who couldn't hide his hurt on account of their apostasy from his faith. And they readily forgave him.

Not one to miss this golden opportunity, Alvaro asked a favor. "*Papang*, would it offend you if I donated my inherited lot on which to build a new house of worship?" His curt reply, "Do as you please, it's your property." One of the newly organized churches built a small but respectable church on this lot. (To this writing, according to a reliable source, this church stands as a witness to the mighty working of the Holy Spirit to the Sarrat community. It was in this church where *Dona* Josefa Marcos regularly attended as a chartered member. A grandson of hers, Ferdinand Marcos, would become president of the Philippines. During his time, freedom of worship had never been as free. Peace and order ruled in the country except in the Muslim dominated areas of Mindanao, Sulu and in the National People's Army infested Leyte and Samar.)

When the three were by themselves, Alvaro posed a question. "Did *Papang* sneak in the dark of the night to listen to our preaching?" To them he told of an incidence occurring not long after Leon had gone to Manila. "*Papang* took me with him on his walk. When we came to the edge of our property, he turned very sad. 'This wasn't the end of our property,' he said. 'The river had eaten away many kilometers of our land. The soil erosion into the river kept up even after I'd donated a lot to build on our (Catholic) church.' And he thinks he had lost us, too," Alvaro summed up.

"Since *Papang* truly believed in the Roman Catholic faith, would he be among the saved?" Tony asked, concern for his father apparent. "Don't we believe there are many gates to the heavenly mansions?"

Alvaro addressed his older brother. "You heard *Papang* blame you, *Manong* for the perdition of us three....our names are in their mass novena. They're sure the three of us are walking straight in to purgatory."

"I ruined his dreams, he told me this a few times," admitted Leon. "Time quenches anger. It would take time for one to change his attitude and thinking. Our parents and our siblings are honestly following their convictions. Let us continue to pray for them. Let us continue on loving them and leave the rest to God. He gave human beings the gift of choice."

Sta. Cruz, Ilocos Sur. Leon's next assignment was in Amurao, a Sta. Cruz barrio. He was glad to be close to his family. Arding jumped up and down to meet his father, who picked him up. "I surely missed you, my boy," he said. He hoisted him up on to his shoulder. Arding worked his legs around his father's neck, dangled them on his chest, and little hands found his father's ears to hold on to. Leon caught his son's feet that were drumming merrily on his chest.

"You have a little daughter, too," Maria reminded her husband.

"How can I ever forget my little princess... where's she?"

"She's taking a nap right now," his wife whispered. "Don't you wake her up."

With Arding over his shoulder, he walked, tiptoeing to watch the sleeping baby. Arding knew when to hush up. The happy father whispered to his son's ear, "The beauty and innocence of a sleeping baby. We love your baby sister, don't we?" Just then Ely stirred.

"Sissy," Arding called. "*Papang* home!"

"It's time to wake up, anyway, Ely," mother said, picking her up. "I think you need a change," she said.

"You're growing fast, Arding," father said. "Soon you will turn two. Let me put you down, so I can hold your little sister." Helping Arding untangle his legs from his neck, he tossed him up before easing him down. "That's Papa's good boy," he said, giving his son a few love pats. He reached his arms out to receive Ely from mother's hands.

"My little princess, you feel at home with your Papa, I see," he said as he cuddled Ely in his arms. They walked to the living room—Arding jumping along. Leon sat down on the sofa. "Oh, yes, you know your Papa. Wish I could take you with me when I go around visiting people to tell them of Jesus' love." He stroke Ely's little hand with his index finger. Little fingers uncurled to grip the big finger. "You have a good grip," he said. Then he felt Ely drawing his finger to her mouth. "You're looking for milk, which I don't have," he chuckled. "My finger won't taste good, baby. Your mama can give you what you need." He handed Ely to her mother.

"Come on, Arding," he said. The little boy caught his father's hand, and they tumbled down on the floor. "Want to hear a story, Arding?" he asked. "You and your mama listen." And he began to share with them his passion.

"The people in Amurao are mostly farmers, many of them are wealthy landowners, yet they are unassuming. They are hungering for the truth. The Lord is blessing the meetings with good attendance. Only a few stopped coming, but those who are attending are exceptionally receptive. It is clear the Lord is speaking to their hearts through the Scriptures."

This effort brought forty-three precious souls to the Kingdom. They immediately organized into a church, initially renting a place of worship. As soon as they had the funds, they found a place on which to build their own house of worship. To the visiting preacher they boasted, "We are making provision for membership growth."

Candon, Ilocos Sur. Leon and Maria praised the Lord for this new place of assignment, which was even closer to home. As the evangelist became acquainted with the community, he noted the majority belonged to the Roman Catholic Church, many of them affluent and educated. There was open opposition, yet many came to hear the message. As the effort progressed, the Lord poured out His blessings to the hearers of His Word, and there was a rich harvest of souls for the Kingdom.

✳✳✳

Evangelist's Responsibility to the Interested

by Ellen G. White

They should ... show the utmost courtesy and kindness, and tender regard for their souls.... Testimonies, vol. 6, p. 46 (1900).

...all who design to labor in the cause of God should learn the very best manner of prosecuting their work.... The minister should, by personal effort if possible, become acquainted with all his hearers. If they have interest enough to come out and her what you have to say ... respond to it by a decided interest on your part to make their personal acquaintance.... The discourse given from the desk should not be lengthy, for this not only wearies the people, but so draws upon the time and strength of the minister that he is not able to engage in the personal labor .... He should go from house to house and labor with families, calling their attention the eternal truths in the word of God. If he does this labor in the meekness of Christ, he will surely have the angels of God to work with his efforts.... Manuscript 14, 1887

(Evangelism, pages 156, 157).

***

Chapter XIII

TO THEM BIBIANO AND LEON

*...**work** out your own salvation with fear and trembling* (Phil. 2:12).

A letter from Bibiano bearing a P.S., "I need to talk to you, Leon," came as no surprise. Leon had heard whispers of his chum's predicament. Maria thrilled at the prospect of this visit and began making plans to make his visit a happy one. "How could we please *Kuya,* now," she verbalized.

"Mahal, leave that to Arding and Ely. He will have a ball with them."

"Uhh, let's not tell our third one is on the way," she said. "He'd think we're pushing for nature to hurry up," they laughed at that. Arding caught on, "Hurry up, hurry up!" he repeated, grabbing his sister's little hands to help her clap. Ely giggled.

Leon picked her up and gently tossed her up in the air. "Ely, you're getting heavy," he puffed and laid her down on the sofa. Chanting, *Peckel, peckel, ta dardaras dumakel,"* he massaged the tiny body gently down to the limbs, then tickled her chin.

In his mind, however, he was debating whether or not to ask Bib to preach. An idea came, *We'll sing a special song, a duet.* Mentally, he went through the songs they used to sing, and narrowed the selections to coincide with the topic for the evening. Then he decided to let Bib choose the song. He had thoroughly enjoyed singing with his brother-in-law, harmonizing and memorizing the lyrics that stir his innermost soul. *To preach or not to preach will be his decision to make,* he thought. *An eloquent preacher, it wouldn't be difficult for him to step in and preach the topic for the evening.* Then it occurred to him that Bib spoke Tagalog. Some of the people in Amurao understood conversational Tagalog, but Tagalog in a sermon would perhaps be too difficult for them to follow. *I'll offer to translate for him,* The thought brought him a smile.

The revelation. *Kuya,* you're looking good," Maria said as he grabbed her in a brotherly embrace. "You're looking good yourself, Sis," he said. Leon brought in a few boxes Bib left at the steps.

Bib nuzzled Ely, lifted her up in the air, wiggled her till she giggled.

"Ely is my sister," Arding said, hanging on to his uncle's leg-pant.

"Arding, you're a Panis," he said tousling the boy's straight black hair.

Shaking his head, "No, I'm Arding," the boy countered.

"Well, it's good to see you, Leon," Bib finally said and the two entwined arms over each other's shoulders, patting each other's back. "I came to spend the holiday with you," he said, taking the chair Leon offered him. He checked to see if the boxes were all there. Chitchatting and inadvertently interrupting each other, they tried to catch up on what mattered to them.

Arding sidled against his uncle's knee. "I'm ..." he began, trying to hold down his little finger with his thumb to display three fingers of his right hand to his uncle. "I'm three years old," he said.

"You're growing fast," his uncle said. "Soon you'll be going to school."

"You brought up a favorite subject, *Kuya*." Maria laid a tray of *kalamansi* drink on the table. "*Kuya*," she said. He took a full glass, and gave a glass half-full to Arding. Leon reached for his.

"Take care of Ely, I'll get supper ready," Maria instructed the men. And humming *Love at Home*, she exited to the kitchen.

"*Mamang*, I'll help," Arding said, merrily skipping at his mother's heels.

"What's up, Vice-President?" Leon was eager to find out.

"Vice-President," Bib mimicked, letting out a sigh, and spat out. "The job is like politics—a graveyard." Covering his temples with his palms, he started mumbling. "Often, I wonder, had it been wiser for me to have stayed with Law instead of switching to ministry." He drew a deep breath. "The change is causing problems in my marriage." He drew another deep breath, and continued to unload the burden he carried.

Leon assumed a listening pose, keeping silent for his chum to go on.

"The moment I'd leave for an assignment, Evelyn's parents would take her to their home and keep her from returning to me. They harass her for having an Adventist minister husband, haunt her to hate my religion. It hurts me to see her gradually lose her vibrancy, then her desire to live." He shook his head slowly. "She's so fragile. Aggressively continuing to treat her like their little baby she once was, I fear she's losing her sanity. And I'm to blame for it. I realize she wishes to please her parents." He sighed.

"This day is one of the few times I could be home, wish I'd been able to persuade her to come along. She's quite fond of Maria and you," he said with a hint of a smile, reminiscing their brief togetherness. "It hasn't been too long ago." He drew a deep breath. "I need to talk to you, Leon. I admit that my responsibilities rob Evelyn of the companionship she deserves. Helping others, my own I neglect, but she was well aware of the life I lived before we married. She shared with all of my dreams, my aspirations to serve the Lord, and she was enthusiastic over a selfless life. 'Life would never be dull,' she said." Bib closed his eyes.

Leon agreed that a minister can ill afford to neglect his own family. *They, too, need nurturing,* burned on his mind. *There ought to be a way.* Feeling deeply for his chum, Leon prayed silently for him. *Lord, fill his heart and mind with Thy love. Let me be of help to him, show us Thy way to meet his problems. It is cathartic for him to empty his problems....*

"Evelyn never gave up on me becoming a Seventh-day Adventist lawyer. Her parents hoped this would happen. She takes pride in my Church position, but my being away often, even for brief periods, adds to her feelings of insecurity, especially at night. I did not realize she had a difficult time during her first trimester of pregnancy, but she kept her fears from me. Being an only child, she's still her parents' baby. And when her parents learned of her fears, they misconstrued her feelings and intensified their efforts to take her faith away from her. I only wish her parents knew that, weakened from carrying the baby and then the delivery, she'd become vulnerable. The doctor told me post-delivery depression happens to new mothers. In addition to caring for a baby for the first time, her parents' attitude aggravates her depression. Now she's torn up in spirit and mind. "Lord' where's Thy healing power?" he cried.

Bib clenched his right hand into a fist, pounded on his left palm, he stood up to pace the floor. "God is … a very present help in time of trouble, I will not fear," he quoted Psalms 46:1–2.

"Be still and know that I am God," Leon quoted Psalms 46:10.

"I'm toying with an idea," Bib mumbled, "to move my family to the States, away from this marital intrusion. I'd prefer no one hears of this plan. We will step out in faith, place our lives in the hands of God." After a brief pause, he continued. "Outside the security of seven plus years of church employ, I know I'm taking a risk. I don't know how else to solve this parental harassment. I don't know how she'd adjust to a separation from her parents. I dare not add insult to injury."

Leon could only pray silently for wisdom to help his chum.

"Recently she has become too dependent on her parents. Against her wishes at first, her parents took her to their home. Lately, however, she dared not assert herself," Bib let out a sigh. "Would tearing her away from them hurt her even more? They've convinced their child that her departure from her spiritual upbringing has ruined her for life. She's under their hypnotic spell, wrapped around their little pinkies."

"Have you thought of going to one of our remote islands?"

"For the sake of the precious souls who accepted the faith from my humble efforts, with problems I must surmount, I do not wish to become a stumbling block. Leon, I feel more and more … the priests are using her parents in this battle. The distance I hope would afford a safety valve. I care too deeply for them and for my own." Bib's voice resonated despair.

"I admire you for protecting the flock, Bib."

Bib drew a deep breath. "Yes, to America, the land of opportunity. There we'll try to find a better life. I trust a better future awaits us there. Like Job, I'd say, "He knows the way that I take…" (Job 23:10).

"That makes sense," Leon said. "And when He has tried me, I shall come forth as gold" he finished quoting Job 23:10. "Nothing can separate us from the love of God. It's up to us to keep in personal touch with Him. In our private devotions, a one-to-one with Him." The chums sank in their own deep thoughts.

"We cannot hide from God. And what about your wife? If you'd prefer no one else knew of your plans, what if your in-laws find out?"

Bib only let out a sigh, his eyes cast down. "No," he said, shaking his head slowly. "No, I fear getting her in it would only get everything askew," he added dejectedly. Brightening a bit, he said, I'm trying by His help. I'll continue to keep close to the Lord. May His will be done in our lives." He held his temples between his palms, elbows propped on his knees. "Frankly, I'd be glad when I'm out of the way, out of reach. I'd be careful to let no one know of my whereabouts. I can no longer take being under someone else's control. It's not God's will to have another person control someone else's life. I can no longer take the intrusion into my personal life."

"Bib, God loves you, I love you, too, my dear brother, my dear friend. How soon do you plan to leave, may I ask?"

Bib shook his head. "I don't know, but I know the Lord will lead. I'm waiting for His leading. Let me know soon...." he said. Turning to Leon, he said, "I'd always admired your optimism, nothing ever seems to upset you."

"For me, life is too short for self-seeking. Only Jesus is my life pattern, Bib. I will not allow another human being or circumstances bar me from heaven, for Jesus bought me with his precious blood. I believe problems come to purge us of dross and drive us closer to Him. I consider my life too precious to barter away for immature squabbles."

"Not allow another human being or circumstances bar me from heaven," Bib repeated. "I need that. We all need that reasoning, Leon."

"God created men in His own image and lovingly threw in a gift, the priceless power of choice. This gift to us, He would not violate. Men and women who exercise their power of choice in faith honor God. He enables anyone who yields his will to Him."

Just then they heard a call "Supper is ready." A child's voice echoed the call, "supper is ready." Ely was asleep, the men quietly slipped out.

They settled in their seats, and held hands as Bib offered grace. After saying Amen, Bib looked at his watch. "Good!" he said. "We have plenty of time to savor this scrumptious meal before going to the meeting." He scrutinized the table with the eye of a hungry fellow, a smile spreading over his face. Forking slices of garden ripe tomatoes on his plate, he said, "Very attractive, very colorful! Sis, your culinary prowess progressed!"

Like a little boy, Bib declared his delight over the cross sections of red tomato slices bordered by cucumber cuts over cross-sections of green peppers decked with sculptured radishes resembling red roses. He picked a *dilis* fish with his fingers, popped it in his mouth. "That was light and crunchy," he said. "I better loosen my belt," he grinned. "The papaya slaw complements the mung bean dish and the *camote* tops. Haven't had red rice for a while," he added, heap-spooning fragrant rice on to his plate. "There's Christianity in a meal like this, Sis."

He glanced at Leon, wondering why he was as skinny as he'd ever been. *Brother, it's your own fault you're looking so malnourished,* he said inwardly.

"Thanks *Kuya,*" Maria acknowledged the compliment. "Give credit to Mrs. Hay, my very kind private voluntary mentor. I'm learning to serve a balanced diet, too," she said with pride."She has taught me food preparation for eye appeal and to please the palate, combining foods to enhance nutrition, and to prepare them to conserve nutrients. Now that you're here, I'm showing off!" she bragged, giving her brother a wink.

"Good for you, Sis. I'm happy for you and Leon. I'll have to invite myself to dine with you and help eat your cooking. You know, not only do I like to eat, I also enjoy eating healthful food that please the palate."

"I like boiled sweet potatoes," Arting chimed in. "I like everything good," he boasted, gesturing as his father helped him fill his plate.

"Sorry, Son, I see we have no boiled sweet potatoes tonight, but there are other favorites of yours on the table."

"*Macapuno, puto* for desert, your choice," Maria announced.

"You remember my favorites, Sis." Bib envisioned the tender coconut, and the delicate rice cake. "Arding, our favorites. Let's leave enough room for our favorite foods, heh-heh-heh."

"I've lots of room in here, *Ta* Bib," he said, patting his little belly.

"Know that I appreciate you, *Kuya*. You've been my best friend as far as I recall, not including my uhtee Doray, of course," Maria said.

"A friend loveth at all times, but a brother is born for adversity," Leon quoted. He cleared his throat and tried to hide the mischief on his face.

"A good boy loveth at all times," paraphrased Arding after his father.

The adults exchanged knowing smiles. "You're right, Son," Leon said, running a hand over his son's back. "I'm glad and proud you're my son."

"I'll be like you when I grow up, *Papang,*" the little boy said looking up at his father. Turning to his uncle, he added, "and like my *Ta* Bib."

"Atta boy," his uncle praised, reaching out to pat the boy's head. "I like to hear that. Arding, you make me happy."

Not taking his eyes away from his uncle, Arding asked, "*Ta* Bib, do you have a little boy like me? Or a little girl like Ely?"

His uncle covered his mouth with a napkin coughed softly, and cleared his throat. "Yes, I have a little boy," he replied. "Your cousin and his mother are with his grandparents. They're spending the Christmas with them. When he gets to be as big as you are, maybe he'll tag along to come see you." He tried to sound lackadaisical. "I came alone to see you this time," he smiled and asked. "Aren't you glad I came?"

"I am, *Ta* Bib. Bring my cousin..." he replied with a mouthful of food.

Leon tapped his son on the shoulder. "Arding, did you forget your table manners?" he bent to whisper to his ear.

Arding continued to chew, swallowed hard, and said, "Never talk with your mouth full of food. Sorry, *Papang,* I forgot."

"It's easy to forget when one talks about interesting things," his uncle said, winking at his nephew. "When your cousin grows to be as big as you are, Arding, he will surely want to tag along with me to come to see you."

Arding clapped his hands. "*Ta* Bib, what is the name of my cousin?"

"Ben Samuel. At home we call him Samming, short for Samuel, his second name after Samuel in the Bible. Remember the little boy who went to live in the temple with priest Eli? When God wanted to talk to him, little Samuel said, 'Speak, for thy servant heareth.'"

"Speak for thy servant heareth," repeated Arding. "*Ta* Bib, that is my mem'ry verse in Sabbath School."

Bibiano suddenly cupped his hand over his mouth, and his fork clattered to the floor. Leon and Maria watched as Bib's eyes misted.

"Bit my tongue," he groaned.

"If you're superstitious," said Maria exploding in laughter, "someone is talking about you. Your fork dropped, it's a man!" she managed to say.

"I'm not," Bib retorted. "No, I'm not superstitious, I'm a Christian now."

"With it's precarious location, it's amazing we don't bite our tongue more often," Leon said chuckling yet visibly empathizing with his chum. The happenings when Bib visited him in Norzagaray flashed in his mind.

Bib caught Leon's eye. "Bit it hard this time," he said. Looking down at his nephew, "Do you bite your tongue at all, Arding?" he asked.

The little boy shook his head. "No, *Ta* Bib, my tongue is smart."

"Keep it that way, Son. Don't ever get your grinders do harm," he advised. "Keep your tongue alert and quick at all times, especially at mealtime, heh-heh-heh. Train those grinders to mind their own business."

Bib turned to Maria. "Sis, you ought to know me better than to think I'm superstitious believing in those old wives' tales," he said in one breath.

"You better not, Vice-president," she teased.

"*Ta* Bib, you better not," Arding echoed looking up at his uncle.

"No, I won't," Bib said. He picked a radish, holding the stem with his thumb and index finger, he twirled it slowly. "Like a rosebud with white red-tipped petals," he said. "It's almost too good to eat," he added, popping it to his mouth, and biting off the stem. "Not as pungent as I expected," he said. Having taken care of that bite, he turned to his nephew.

"Arding, you learned your memory verse well. Keep memorizing Bible verses. That's one way to think the thoughts of God, my boy." He saw Arding nod his head, his mouth was full.

They talked about other small things while they enjoyed their meal.

"Sis, thanks for the eye-appealing, palate-tempting nutritious supper," he said, wiping his mouth and hands with a napkin. "It's Doray's work," he said admiring and refolding it loosely, he laid it beside his plate.

"I'm glad you enjoyed the food, *Kuya.* Come over whenever you find the time. Short notice will do. No notice, that's your responsibility."

Pulling a strand of her husband's hair at the nape, Maria whispered, "Take your time, finish eating." To Ardiug, she said, "Stay here with your Papa and get to know each other better. Your uncle and I need to talk."

"Yes, *Mamang.* "

Maria took her brother's hand. Concern written on her face, she pulled him to the living room, faced him and asked, looking into his eyes: *"Kuya,* is it all right with you that her parents must monopolize your wife and your son when it's the only time you could spend together? Is everything all right with you and my sister-in-law?"

Ely stirred, stretched her body, yawned, and opened her eyes wide. Maria picked her up. "My baby, we woke you up," she said rocking her.

Bib glanced toward the dining room as if wishing he'd stayed there. "Hardly, Sis," he muttered. "Hardly. I have handed the case of my wife and our son over to the Lord, I asked Him to take care of them. I have faith in Him. He'll do whatever is best for them—for our family."

"And what are you doing about it? God helps those who help them...."

"Sis," he interrupted, "that's one reason I came here. To talk to Leon. I must decide what to do. Being a prayerful man, he can be more objective over this problem—more than you or I." He drew a deep breath, and after a brief moment, continued. "As for this weekend, your sis-in-law and I talked about it, and since I understood she wanted to make her parents happy, I went along with her wish to please them. After all, she is there only child. I had to put myself in her place. Do you see it?"

Seeing Maria's unchanging facial expression, and reading no recognition of her 'seeing it,' Bib continued. "If I were an only child, I, too, would want to please my parents, to make them happy. And I pray that her parents would soon see the light, that the Holy Spirit would touch their hearts, for them to respond to God's call." He drew another deep breath.

Sensing Maria was listening and did not interrupt his line of thought, he went on. "Did you know that as a family they attended the evangelistic meetings I conducted some time ago? When Evelyn accepted our new found faith, her parents said they'd wait for a while before taking such a big step. They have a wide circle of friends they couldn't abruptly drop. They allowed their daughter baptism because they wanted her to be happy. Evelyn and I had been praying that her parents, too, would soon commit themselves, for them to make their stand to join the Adventist family of God. They love their only child so much they'd give anything for her happiness." He took a deep breath, "and vice-versa," he sighed.

Maria assumed a faraway look. *How similar Leon's experience had been with his parents,* she thought; *and yet so dissimilar. Did belonging to a large family, being one of thirteen children, make the difference?* she wondered.

***

SATANIC FORCES

by Ellen G. White

As we ...work for the multitudes... the enemy will work mightily to bring in confusion, hoping thus to break up the working forces....

Every day, Satan has his plans to carry out... certain lines that will hedge up the way of those who are witnesses for Jesus Christ ... unless the living human agents for Jesus are humble, meek and lowly of heart. Because they have learned of Jesus, they will just as surely fall under temptation as they live, for Satan is watching and artful and subtle, and the workers, if not prayerful, will be taken unawares. He steals upon them as a thief in the night and make them captives ... he works upon the minds of individuals to pervert their individual ideas and frame their plans.

The Lord is displeased with the want of harmony... among workers. He cannot impart His Holy Spirit, for they are bent in having their own way ... discouragement will come in from Satan and his confederacy of evil, but "all ye are brethren," and it is an offense to God when you follow your individual, unsanctified traits of character to be active agencies to discourage one another. Letter 31, 1982

(<u>Evangelism</u>, pages 101–102).

***

Chapter XIV

<u>THAT</u> OLD SERPENT

Hitherto shalt thou come, but no further ;.... Job 38:11

On their walk to the meeting, Bib asked, "Leon, did you tell Maria?"

"No, but if you know your sister as well as I do, you know she'll want to find out everything. Tell me, Bib, are you being assertive on this."

"I've done what I could, Leon," he said under his breath. "Being an Adventist turned minister placed me in a very unfavorable situation from the start. They had counted their daughter on marrying a successful lawyer. Instead, their daughter's husband became an advocate for souls. Logically, wealthy people scorn eternal and spiritual matters more often than not. They firmly believe their only child deserved a better life than I have to offer. Their beautiful, delicate daughter born with a silver spoon."

"Doesn't she stand up for you? You'd been a good husband to her...."

Bib kept silent. He kicked a pebble that went hurtling down the road.

Leon felt his chum grieving, angry. Silently, he prayed. *Lord, grant Bib a sound mind, also his wife and her parents. Send Thy holy angel to enable Bib to withstand Satan's wiles. Rebuke the devil from hounding after him, Lord. Let me say the right words as he empties his burden.*

"As a struggling fellow Christian," he replied at last. "With the touch of parental wand, her parents transforms her into their little baby that she once was. Perhaps they don't realize they're doing this to her. I'd like to think they're doing it unintentionally, but insofar as their daughter has been acting lately, she has been regressing. Initially resenting her parents' attitude, yet being an only child, Satan is capitalizing on her susceptibility."

The chums walked silently, their steps in cadence, thoughts and hearts lifted heavenward, each one pleading for wisdom from the Lord.

"Yes, I know she tried to stand up for me so many, many times, like an advocate," Bib broke in the silence. "She admitted she married me sans a hundred percent of her parents' approval. Their attitude to our marriage had soured even more in suspecting we're having adjustment problems. True, she left the comforts of her parents' home. She worries over having displeased them. She worries over their hostility toward me, and her new religion." He drew a deep breath. "Left alone while I'm away at work, and aggravated by my travels even farther away, these concerns are producing a fatal synergistic effect on her. She's rationalizing over, 'He that loveth father or mother more than me is not worthy of me.'" At this point, Bib fell silent and for some moments, only their steps seemed in motion. Suddenly, Bib cried out aloud in a commanding tone, "Satan, get out of my way!"

Petrolux lamps hanging at strategic places lighted the tent. Leon and Bib cheerfully greeted individuals as they arrived. Soon the tent filled to overflowing. The blithesome chorister bounced to the platform, greeted the people, and asked them to open their song books to the hymn, "Wonderful Love...." He gave the page number, and the organist began pumping the organ. Soon the melody filled the air as everyone joined in the song, some trying to learn it. After the last stanza, "Repeat the chorus," the chorister urged—a chance for them to learn the song from memory.

The ministers stepped to the platform and joined the singing. The chorister stepped aside, Leon gestured saying, "Let's all stand for prayer."

"Our Father in heaven, we thank Thee for this night.... Open our hearts for the Holy Spirit to move us, Lord. Bless the message of the hour, and the speaker, as he breaks the bread of life. Bless each listening heart, Lord... This evening, may we honor and bring glory to Thy most holy name...."

Following the 'amen', and the congregation had sat down, Leon draped his right arm over his chum's shoulder. Beaming, he said, "I take pleasure in introducing to you Pastor Bibiano Panis, from our Conference. Pastor Panis is visiting with me and his younger sister—my wife."

A soft pleasant murmuring rippled through the audience. LZR waited for silence to resume, then continued," Pastor Panis declined to preach tonight, but he has consented to sing a special a duet—with me."

Like two long lost friends who had just found each other, they locked arms around each other's shoulders. Blending their voices in harmony with the swelling pump organ accompaniment, they sang, "In the Sweet By and By," as they used to sing not too long ago. From memory they sang with deep feeling, switching voices from tenor to melody with each stanza.

"There's a land that is fairer than day...." LZR repeated the first line of the first stanza. "Beloved, I look forward to the land where the Sun of Righteousness will be our light, far brighter than these," he gestured at the Petrolux lamps. "I want to be there. How sweet the thought, sweeter yet," making a sweeping gesture with his hands, "with all of you, Beloved."

With fervor, the preacher expounded on The New Earth. "The land where heartaches, pain, sickness, and parting will be no more. Where our bodies and our minds will be in tune with the will of Our Creator. Where we have no desire to let our Lord down. There, sin will be no more...."

To close the meeting, the two men again blended their voices in perfect harmony, singing, "Joy By and By." They invited the gathering to join them in the chorus after each stanza.

"I expect to see all of you, then," LZR said after announcing the topic for the next meeting. "Pastor Panis will offer the benediction," he added. Everyone bowed their heads. After the prayer, they bade goodnight to the congregation, with "We'll be seeing you next evening meeting."

The chums walked silently, retracing their steps to home, absorbed in their owns thoughts, until Leon broke the silence. "I expect Maria will be waiting for us. Why not let her in with what's on your mind, and see what she thinks of it," he said."You know how perceptive your sis is. She's mature enough and deserves to hear of your plans directly from your lips."

Maria greeted them at the door. "The children are asleep now." Then, eagerly asked, "How was the meeting?"

"God continues to bless," her husband replied in an emotion-charged tone. They sat down. "You should have heard us sing our favorite duets."

Maria sat across the men. "The Sweet by and By? And "O, There'll Be Joy…'? I could picture the two of you, hear you singing those lively songs, deep feeling in each word," she said with nostalgia. Turning to her brother, "*Kuya,* tell me…," she demanded.

For what seemed an eternity, Bib kept silent. He looked at his watch. He asked," What do you really want to know, Sis?" Then eyeball to eyeball with his sister, he said, "If you promise to behave, I'll tell you."

Maria raised her right hand. "To the best of my ability, I promise. "

"I told Leon of my plans to go to America."

She stared at her brother. "What for?" she gushed, an I couldn't believe it, clearly written across her face. "What of your responsibilities, Mr. Vice-president? Surely, you can't run away from it all, just like that…."

"You are right, Sis. I have a high sounding job title with corresponding heavy responsibility. To answer your first question, to get away from the mess tied to my faith and to my job. No, I can't run away from myself."

Maria's face registered shock. She turned pale. "Will you explain your last sentence? *Kuya,* don't tell me you're having problems at work with…."

"Sis, I've tried to apply the golden rule—to be kind, to be loving. I don't understand the road blocks looming high. Everything is getting too frustrating." His voice rose a decibel. "The Lord will show me the way."

"*Kuya,* who is mistreating you? Your co-workers? Your superiors?"

"Frankly, none of those…, but a couple is intent on destroying my life. They don't speak kindly to me nor of me, no matter how much love I show them. Like a point of no return, there's no letting go of their hostility."

"So, you are getting away from it all? From our new faith because you see inconsistency in others, behaving like earthly human beings?"

"Sis," Bib lowered his voice. "That's not what I meant. I admit most of my co-workers are Christianity personified. That I collect personal degradings blind me so. Am I getting too sensitive? Where's my faith?" He closed his eyes, his palms pressed against his temples. "A plan only at this time, Sis," he said. He planted his elbows on his knees. He exhaled a sigh.

"*Kuya,* aren't we supposed to look to Christ only and ask Him to fight our battles?" Her voice was soft and pleading, love and worry on her face. "*Kuya*, won't you pray for peace in your heart, so nothing can offend you? And take this as a chance for faith to increase, for you to grow, *Kuya?*"

Not getting the response she expected from her brother, she turned to her husband who just joined them, and attempted to quote, 'Where two or three gather in my name, He will be there.' That is, God will be here with us, the three of us, if we pray. Why not—we pray now—the three of us? She got down on her knees, waited for the men to kneel. "I'll start," she said. "I'll make it brief, after my prayer, *Kuya,* you pray." Placing a hand on her husband's shoulder, she said, "Will you close?"

They formed a tight circle. Maria prayed for the Holy Spirit to calm her brother's mind and that His will be done in his life. They asked for strength, for humility and willingness to do His bidding. For understanding to know His will, for wisdom to act according to His will. They pleaded for a loving heart to love no matter how difficult it may be, as Jesus loves. For God to send His angels to guide and protect them from the evil one.

Getting up from their knees, Bib muttered, "A simple childlike faith, Sis. Right now, I feel I'd be helping God answer my prayers, as well as yours, if I fled from the daily confrontation." His voice was barely audible.

"*Kuya,* you had always met problems head-on, remember? You used to tell me to be a solution to the problem and not be a part of the problem. I truly admired you for that mature position of yours, and your efforts to put it into practice." She drew a deep breath. "And now, you want to run away from the frustrations coming your way. It isn't like you at all, *Kuya.* What happened?" Angst laced her voice. The crease line between her eyes above the bridge of her nose deepened. Concern, sorrow, worry mingled curved the corners of her mouth down, she was in the verge of tears.

Bib stared into space. "Neither do I understand it all," he said. Shaking his head, he mumbled, "Sis, how right you are. I must let go and let God."

A few minutes passed of impenetrable silence. Maria silently prayed.

Leon cleared his throat. "This reminds me of the miracle working prophet," he began. "Chapter 19, the first book of Kings, tells how Elijah ran away to hide after a woman, Jezebel, threatened his life. Even after God—through him—had mightily showed the Baal worshipers that He was God (chapter 18). Despite the miracles the prophet performed, his faith wavered that instant—when a woman threatened him," he said, a mock in his chuckle. "It was a crash after a high. And, the Bible tells God had been with Elijah throughout all this."

"I do not consider myself running away from the problem," Bib explained. "The Bible says, 'Flee from evil.' That's what I plan to do."

"Evil? Pride? Lucifer's downfall." Maria mumbled as if to herself. "As I see it, the missionaries committed themselves to do a job—also a livelihood to them—when they came to our land. I see no evil in that."

Bib blinked his eyes, as if to awaken himself. "You make some sense, Sis. You also made a point. However, nothing I said inferred to our missionaries. They left the comforts of their homes—must be for some adventure in a foreign land on the side—where they learned domestic help costs a pittance, and they can be in control," he monotoned. After a brief pause, he continued, "Don't we place them high on a pedestal? And we practically worship them, hardly question their authority. It pleases them when nationals they'd trained prove capable of carrying a charge." He drew a deep breath, and a smile brightened his face, yet he let out a sigh.

"They trusted me enough to send me as a delegate to the General Conference held in Shanghai, they gave me a responsibility, as they had given Leon. I return their love, their trust." Again, he drew a deep breath. "I would say with all honesty that I think Pastor Finster is a true Christian, a man in pursuit of God's heart. I wish I could love the Lord as he does. I wish I had as much faith as he has. By God's grace, I will," he promised.

Maria stared at her brother, bewilderment on her face.

"There's a quotation," Bib began. "Wealth and authority makes some people grow and others just swell." Shaking his head, he punctuated his quote with, "I'd hate to fall under the latter," he said with a lopsided grin.

Leon cleared his throat. "Pride. Lucifer's downfall," he said softly.

Bib sat up, taking on even a brighter mood. "Are you still my ally, Leon?" he asked. "Friction occurs when two surfaces rub..., right?"

Stifling a yawn, "It's getting late," said Leon. "Time to get some rest."

"You have the living room, *Kuya*. We'll open a cot for you."

"Before you do that," Bib said, "I'd like to open a few boxes." He stood, stepped to the corner where Leon piled the boxes. He opened the box atop, and began drawing out brightly wrapped parcels. "Let the children open their gifts when they get up," he said. "I wrote their names on each. Simple gifts to remember their uncle they seldom see.' He picked up the next box.

Handing it to Maria, "Here's one for you," he said. "Open it now if you wish. I'd like to see smiling eyes on a happy face in my dreams tonight." Pushing the last, a heavy box with both hands toward Leon, he said, "I thought you needed these. Open it now or later, that's your choice."

"Oh, *Kuya!*" Maria cried in delight as she lifted a blue dress in bamboo leaves print. "You remembered my favorite color! I do need a new dress," she said, lifting the dress by its short sleeves to try it for length.

"Your former couturier, the lady you and Doray patronized, sewed it." Giving Leon a wink, he added, "She put a pair of concealed pockets, and made allowance for your having had babies. I hope the dress fits."

"I'll have to work on that fit," Maria mumbled as he put the dress over her. "Carrying babies alter a woman's figure all right. O, it's beautiful, *Kuya!*" she exclaimed. Fingering the dark blue buttons on the front to down below the waistline, she felt a pocket. She thrust a hand in it, fished out an envelope, opened it, saw three crisp ten-peso bills. She sprang up to her feet, grabbed her brother in a hug. "My *Kuya* turned Santa Claus!"

On opening his box, Leon drew out a navy blue linen suit and a pair of matching pants. Then, item by item, he brought out half a-dozen writing pads, three reams of typing paper and a box of carbon papers. More! Out came a box of typewriter ribbons, then a box of No. 2 black pencils.

"Bib, how thoughtful of you," Leon said, his joy spilling over. "You were obedient to the impression. I need these so badly." He moved to Bib and gave his chum a few love pats on the back. "Bib, you've equipped me for a year. Thank you a million times. God bless you, my friend, my ever loving, wonderful, practical brother-in-law!" said Leon, voice choking.

Bibiano's face literally glowed with unmistakable joy.

Leon got busy putting the packs of writing materials back into the box. "I cannot thank you enough, Bib," he said, as he put the box in his study.

"And we haven't thought of getting you anything," moaned Maria.

"Believe me, Sis. I had my reward." Bib tried a curtsy. "Seeing your excitement over my simple gifts....", shaking his head, he couldn't conceal his satisfaction. "That must be how God rejoices when He hears and sees His children appreciating His blessings." Then turning to Maria, he continued, "Sis, the supper you prepared with loving care more than repaid everything you received. I had a feast," he said, rubbing a hand over his abdomen." I had fun with Arding, he's a bright boy," he added, casting Leon a side-glance. "I look forward to repeats of your healthful cooking."

Maria looked at her brother, questions ran on her mind, she kept to herself. "I'm happy to hear that, *Kuya*. I'll be on the lookout for your coming over more often than you had in the past. And I hope your family will come along next time. We need to get to know each other better."

"The clock is ticking away fast," Bib said, covering a wide yawn with a hand. "My eyes are getting too heavy, my bedtime has long arrived."

"You took the words out of my mouth," said Leon in a yawn. Picking up the cot, he opened it. Maria spread out a thick cotton blanket over it and placed a pillow and a folded sheet over. After wishing each other Merry Christmas and goodnight, Leon and Maria left the living room to Bib.

***

CHRISTMAS

by Ellen G. White

The 25th of December is supposed to be the day of the birth of Jesus Christ, and its observance has become customary and popular. But yet there is no certainty that we are keeping the veritable day of our Saviour's birth. History gives us no certain assurance of this. The Bible does not give us the precise time. Had the Lord deemed this knowledge essential to our salvation, He would have spoken through His prophets and apostles, that we might know all about the matter.... the silence of the Scriptures upon this point evidences to us that it is hidden from us for the wisest purposes....

... He has concealed the precise day of Christ's birth that the day should not receive the honor that should be given to Christ as the Redeemer of the world....The soul's adoration should be given to Jesus as the Son of the infinite God.

.... The desire for amusement, instead of being quenched and arbitrarily ruled down, should be controlled and directed by painstaking effort upon the part of the parents. Their desire to make gifts may be turned into pure and holy channels and made to result in good to our fellow men by supplying the treasury in the great, grand work for which Christ came into our world. Self-denial and self-sacrifice marked His course of action. Let it mark ours who profess to love Jesus because in Him is centered our hope of eternal life.

... It is pleasant to receive a gift, however small, from those we love. It is an assurance that we are not forgotten, and seems to bind us to them a little closer. ...

It is right to bestow upon one another tokens of love and remembrance if we do not in this forget God, our best friend. We should make our gifts such as will prove a real benefit to the receiver. I would recommend such books as will be an aid in understanding the work of God or that it will increase our love for its precepts. Provide something to be read during the long winter evenings.

... instead of expending means merely for the gratification of the appetite or the needless ornaments or articles of clothing, one may make the ... holidays an occasion in which to honor and glorify God.

"Shall we have a Christmas tree?" *God would be well pleased if on Christmas each church would have a Christmas tree on which shall be hung offerings, great and small, for these houses of worship. ...*

Christmas and New Year celebrations can and should be held in behalf of those who are helpless. God is glorified when we give to help those who have large families to support.

... Let there be recorded in the heavenly books such as Christmas as has never yet been seen because of the donations which shall be given for the sustaining of the work of God and the upbuilding of His kingdom.

The Adventist Home, excerpts from pages 477–483.

***

Chapter XV

LOVE GOD DAYS OF UNCERTAINTIES

The world, though fallen, is not all sorrow and misery. In nature itself are messages of hope and comfort. There are flowers upon the thistles, and roses cover the thorns. Steps to Christ, *p. 1.*

Leon and Maria prayed for the Holy Spirit to bring peace to Bibiano. For God to impress his coworkers to be more kind, more loving, to be more understanding. It is now, that their brother, who had given of himself in His service, needed true Christian friends.

"I wonder," Maria asked, "had our parents lived longer, would *Kuya* have more strength to bear this—whatever that is discouraging him?"

"Perhaps," Leon replied. He drew a deep breath. "Father tried to train up a child—me—in the way I should go—for priesthood—and when I grew old, I became a Seventh-day Adventist minister, and," shaking his head, he mumbled, "from father's point of view, I proselytized two of my brothers."

For the first time, Maria saw in her husband's demeanor a hint of defeat, a ring of irony in his tone, yet he let out a careless chuckle.

Turning in a pensive mood, he continued. "If only my earthly father realizes how God has blessed his efforts in raising his children. All of us have ambition and self respect. All of us are law abiding, God-fearing. Not one of us became a drunk, a gambler, or a womanizer. Alvaro, Tony and I continue to pray for our parents, leaving the rest to God.... That's what we have to do for Bib. It's the best thing we can do. They are in God's hands."

Maria nodded. "We must keep praying for peace to fill *Kuya* Bib's heart, for his faith to stand fast," she said with a sigh. "Lord God, Almighty to deliver. Omnipotent God, have mercy on my *Kuya.,"* she cried out.

"He promised to look only to Jesus, and to give his plan more thought," said Leon. "And he's biding his time to the end of this year. When the Holy Spirit touches the heart, like Peter, one becomes strong."

The two knelt down to pray. "Our Father in heaven, we come boldly to Thy throne of grace. We thank Thee for the forgiveness of our sins, for the power of prayer, and for Thy word, 'Ask and receive.' We ask Thee to lead Bib, guide him, Lord. Be near him, give him strength to equal the wiles of the devil. Bless his wife and her parents, too. Fill them with Thy Love. Lord, may Thy will be done. We commit Bib in thy loving arms...."

August, 1919. Following the singing, LZR stepped to the pulpit. After his greetings, he began, "The Bible says children are gifts, blessings from the Lord. Tonight, I feel blessed, for on the 23rd of this month, our new daughter arrived. We named her Mercedes, which I'd like to interpret to mean, 'Merciful Lord.' He paused to allow the clapping from the floor to subside. "By God's grace," he said, "Mother and baby are doing well."

After the opening prayer, he said, "Yes, the Lord is merciful, full of grace. He is long suffering." He then went on to expound on The Love of God. "He sent His only Son to live as a human being on our planet, our earth."

Preacher LZR went on to review the miracle of Jesus' birth, and the miracles He performed. To close, he asked them to open their Bibles to John 14. He invited them to join in reading together the first three verses. Then he invited those who wish to accept God's love in their hearts and to accept His invitation to live with Him in the mansions… to join him in front for a prayer of consecration. The audience moved as one to the front.

After the closing prayer, a few lingered to talk to the preacher. A lady pressed something in his hand saying, "Buy for me a gift for the baby."

***

The writing tablet, pencils, typing paper and typewriter ribbons from Bib came handy for Leon. He wrote his sermons and typed truth-filled articles to send to Philippine Publishing House. He translated English articles to Tagalog and Ilokano, and Tagalog articles to Ilokano. *The Lord works mightily His wonders to perform* rang in his mind. *Lord, work mightily for the readers of Thy word, and especially for Bib*…. he prayed.

Then came the shock of their sister-in-laws death. They learned, she was with her parents when it happened. Having been at her parents for months before released Bib of suspicion of her immediate cause of death.

Although her mental and physical health had been progressively deteriorating, her death came as a big blow to Bib. Her temporary separation from him rent him, her death broke his heart. Now, the safety of his son became his consuming priority. Confronting his parents-in-law for his son's custody was as tumultuous as was the care for his wife. He had honored his wife's wish to be with her parents, he relented when she wished her son with her. Now, concerning his young son, he strongly contested for his custody. And he won by God's grace.

It helped that his close kin Segunda willingly offered to take care of his son. He trusted her for she loved the Lord. She was one of his first fruits to the new faith. *Sis Segunda will be super-surrogate mother for my son,* he consoled himself. *Her home will be the ideal home for my son.* It comforted him for his son to be in good hands. Most crucial was for him to grow up a Seventh-day Adventist. Winning custody of his son enabled him to face the reality of his wife's death. It gave him a sense of victory over Satan, whom he believed to be the instigator behind all the affronts.

November. Bib's letter was terse, obviously written in a hurry. It told of his booking for America; the date, port, and time of departure. "No one else knows, no one must," he scrawled and underlined. Leon tucked the letter in his vest pocket and told Maria they were to meet Bib somewhere. Wisely, Maria asked no questions.

Since Bib confided his family problems in him, Leon had made effort to follow-up his brother-in-law's case. He learned that following his wife's death, her parents redoubled their efforts to make his life unbearable. Whenever and wherever Bib set up a series of evangelistic meetings, they were there to disrupt it. When he accepted a challenge to debate, they, or someone else they'd contracted, would be there to shame him. Ignoring the cause of their daughter's death the doctor had explained to them, they used their wealth to make life miserable for Bib. From a reliable source, Leon learned his chum resigned from his conference position, gave up his credentials, for no given reason. He simply bade the leaders goodbye.

"We're going to a very important meeting," Maria told her neighbor, and asked if they could leave their three children with them. Without questioning, their kind friend willingly granted her request. Leon assured their good neighbor they would be back as soon as possible.

On their way out, Maria mumbled, "The Lord didn't answer our prayers after all."

"Maria, *aking Mahal,* Leon wrapped his wife in his arm. "The Lord answers prayers in different ways beyond our human comprehension. I believe the answer to our prayers is, "Wait, I have plans for him better than what you had in mind." In this case, we'll keep trusting God. He understands our brother's circumstances. We'll keep praying for Bib."

Maria determined to relinquish her brother to the Lord and to leave her burdens to Him. *My Lord is in control of man's destinies,* she affirmed herself. Upon arriving at the port, Maria, however, couldn't contain herself.

"Kuya," she cried. flinging her arms on her brother. "Will we ever see you again? Promise to keep close to Jesus," she sobbed.

"We'll have many more years to live on this earth," Bib said, his voice cracking. "I'll return to see you." Trying to appear cheerful, he said, "I'm still alive. I'd like to remember you by your smiling face." Then in a whisper he promised to write, to tell her about his voyage. He gave her a hug, embraced Leon, and walked away. He turned around to wave before entering the ship. Leon and Maria stayed by long enough to see the ship pull out of the harbor and move away, their silent prayers ascending high.

On their way home, Maria's dream years ago flashed back to her mind. "Do you believe in dreams?" she asked her husband.

"I believe in daydreams," he chuckled. "Why do you ask?"

"I had a dream years ago that I recall now as though it came only yester-day," she began, voice faltering. "It bothers me now as it did before, before our baptism. It didn't make sense then...." she drew a deep breath.

"*Mahal,* I'd like to hear the details of your dream," he pressed.

"The candidates for baptism stood in line for baptism," she began, "and were baptized one after another. When it was my turn, the missionary took my hands, raised his other hand and lifted his eyes. I heard him say 'I now baptize you in the name of the Father, the Son, and the Holy Spirit,' and immersed me in the water. When I came out, it was you who held my hands as though you had baptized me. When I stepped out of the river bank, I saw *Kuya* turning to leave. *Where's he going?* I cried." Maria put her hands over her face, drew a deep breath, and a sigh escaped.

The comforting arm of Leon wrapped her. "*Mahal,*" he said. "Go on."

Maria, shaking her head, said, "*Kuya* held a little boy's hand in his and he was taking him away—away from me. And you had disappeared. '*Kuya,*' I cried, 'please don't take my son away.' I awoke. It seemed so real, it really troubled me. How could I have a child without a husband?"

Nodding his head lightly, Leon tried to grasp the import. "So you see now," he said, "as if your dream was a warning. Bib is on his way to a land far away. We had committed him to the Lord, he is in God's hands. If we have faith in God, why worry about it now?"

"Why worry about it now?" she repeated. "That part came true. I'd like to prevent fulfillment of what bothered me most and wished to forget."

Leon was quiet for a long time, Then he said. "I was trying to think of the dreams recorded in the Bible that were fulfilled. There are several of them: Start from Genesis 28. Jacob dreamed of a ladder reaching up to heaven. The Lord actually wrestled with him later. In Genesis 37 Joseph's brothers called him 'the dreamer.' We know the fulfillment of Joseph's dreams. Even the dreams of the imprisoned baker and the butler (chapter 40) that Joseph interpreted for them. In the gospels, an angel reaffirmed Joseph over his betrothed's lot, when he questioned young Mary's appar-ent pregnancy before they became man and wife. And angels warned Joseph in dreams to flee for their Newborn's safety. All these came in dreams."

Maria mentally followed along as her husband recounted the dreams. Once again wrapped in their own thoughts, quiet moments ticked swiftly by. Finally, Maria relinquished. "Let the dream and the meaning belong to God. I'll let Him worry over this dream for me," she said.

"That's a wise decision," he said, giving his wife a pat on the shoulder. "I like to believe that Bib will do something out of the ordinary, like Hosea in the Bible. I pray he'll continue to be God's chosen vessel." After a brief pause, he added, "He promised to write. There are matters one can express in writing more comfortably than verbally. We'll take advantage of this medium. 'For a smoking flax shall He not quench,' Leon quoted Matt. 12:20.

More silence. Maria broke the silence. "You talk as if you know much about what had happened to *Kuya* Bib. He surely confided in you, but I'll not pry. You can tell me whatever you think I ought to know." Then facing him, she said, "Would you do the letter writing for me? Typing is faster than hand writing. Plus, with active little ones to care for in addition to housewife duties, I wouldn't have time to write. I'll try to add a sentence or two to your typewritten letters to him."

***

1920. With hands slightly trembling, Maria carefully opened the envelope bearing a U.S.A. return address. The letter was dated January 1.

Dear Leon and Maria,

Happy New Year! I trust all is well with you when this letter reaches you—probably weeks after the first of the year. As for me, I'm gradually getting acclimated to life in America.

Our ship docked at several ports along the way. In Hong Kong, I went around the shopping malls, but I didn't part with my pocket money. At Tokyo port, I joined a group for a tour to the Imperial Palace, and then we went to the Buddhist Temple. You'd love what they call the temple, Maria. It's actually a garden with quiet-flowing brooks, bright-colored flowers grouped according to their colors. Fleeting birds, occasionally they settle to sing, transform their home to a paradise. A peaceful , yes, a quiet place.—Japanese art in its highest form—they say. The flowers, plants, and trees grow naturally with the slightest manicure touch that bring out their beauty. I felt the influence of the atmosphere , so conducive to meditating on matters heavenly. The temple proves nature is truly God's second book.

When the ship docked in Honolulu, I again stepped out with a group. My impression: Minus the large bodies of water, Honolulu reminded me of Baguio. A bustling city yet the pace of life there, some said, was more country-like than that of a city. Now I wish I could have stayed in Hawaii. A short time it seemed, after our ship left Hawaii, the waters became choppy. We ran into a raging storm—perhaps closer to Hawaii than to California. A really rough sailing. The ship climbed giant waves only to drop from the crest and tossed about by every giant wave. Some became so seasick and thought the sea would be their grave. I prayed as I never had before. and clung for dear life. The storm reminded me of one the disciples went through. They looked for their miracle working friend and found Jesus sound asleep in the hinder part of the ship, his head on a pillow. And I, too, asked, 'Master, carest thou not that we perish?' As though I saw Jesus raise his hands and heard Him say, "Peace be still.' Sharing this similarly harrowing experience with the disciples is one I'll long remember.

It's night time here as I write. Clear across the globe where you are in the Pacific isles, it is daytime. God holds the earth in the hollow of His hand. We know that He owns and rules the universe. He takes care of you, thousands of miles away across the seas, as He takes care of me here.

A temporary job I have, and a place to stay. Use this return address when you write. To you all, I send my love. Hug the children for me.

Always, your brad,
(signed) Bib

Maria re-read the letter. She imagined walking along with her *Kuya.* in distant lands. *Now, I have a glimpse of Tokyo and a little bit of Hawaii,* she told herself. *It's like I'd been there with Kuya,* and prayed silently. *I thank Thee, Lord, for giving my brother a wonderful spiritual experience.*

As she settled more comfortably on the chair, it dawned on her that Bib left them dangling about his job. She wondered if he was preaching, and she hoped so, yet she corrected her thinking. *Unlikely,* she thought. And she remembered that her brother enjoyed doing anything challenging, anything new. She thought, *Surely, he'd behave like an ordained minister.*

She carefully folded the letter. Clutching it to her breast, she prayed, *Lord, continue to be very near and real to my Kuya.* She knew the letter would make Leon happy. *He would write an answer, he's the writer,* she told herself. The melody of the song, 'Praise Him, Praise Him,' filled her heart, and softly, she began humming. She was glad the children were taking their naps. She had clothes to wash, and supper to prepare.

***

September 9, 1921

Dear Bib,

We enjoy reading your letters, they make us feel close to you. Praise the Lord for all His goodness. Know that God continues to bless His work here, and we pray for your return to help spread the gospel message.

Pastor Emilio Manalaysay was conducting a series of evangelistic meetings in Tayabas when he came down with severe chills. On July 30, serious complications of malaria snapped out the life of our strong brother, worker and child of God. It makes us sad to see a courageous man laid down to rest at a very young age, we don't understand why.

Bib, do you perceive the obvious? In my mind, I see Satan returning as in Job's time. Of God asking him 'to touch not his life;' as He requested for Job. Satan snarled at His request—he dared not lose again. Our hearts go out to his grief-stricken young widow and to their young children.

On August 15, a baby girl was born—post-humously. Mrs. Elisea Manalaysay named the baby Emilia, in honor of her father. We pray for baby Emilia to fill the void in her mother's life, and for God to shower His love and care to the father-orphaned children. We pray for the fulfillment of Romans 8: 28 in this, our shared bereavement.

Of the first three Filipinos ordained to the Adventist ministry, do you realize that I am the only one left here? Bib, do you feel what I feel? We're truly lonely for you, for the strength you'd been to God's family. May He bless you and touch your heart. I'm sharing the enclosed clippings with you. They'd been a source of strength to me. The first one is meaningful to me because it was published in the <u>Review and Herald</u> in 1892, four months of my birth. It was written by Mrs. Ellen G. White:

"The opposition we meet may prove a benefit to us in many ways. If it is well borne, it will develop virtues which would never have appeared if the Christian had nothing to endure. And faith, patience, forbearance, heavenly mindedness, trust in Providence, and genuine sympathy with the erring, are the results of trial well borne. These are the graces of the Spirit, which bud, blossom, and bear fruit amid trials and adversity. Meekness, humility, and love always grow on the Christian tree. If the Word is received into good and honest hearts, the obdurate soul will be subdued, and faith, grasping the promises, and relying upon Jesus, will prove triumphant. "This is the victory that overcometh the world, even our faith." (I John 5:4).

Here's the other one, published on July 9, 1908, also in the <u>Review and Herald</u>, again written by Mrs. Ellen G. White, God's Messenger:

"A battle is continually going on between the forces for good and the forces of evil, between the angels of God and the fallen angels. We are beset before and behind, on the right hand an on the left. The conflict that we are passing through is the last we shall have in this world. We are now in the midst of it. Two parties are striving for the supremacy. In this conflict, we cannot be neutral. We must stand either on one side or on the other. If we take our position on the side of Christ, if we acknowledge Him before the world in word and work, we are bearing a living testimony as to whom we have chosen to serve and honor. In this important period of earth's history, we cannot afford to have anyone in uncertainty as to whose side we are on....

"Because thou has kept the word of my patience, I will keep thee from the hour of temptation, which shall come upon all the world, to try them that dwell upon the earth (Rev. 3:10).... If in your life there are defective traits of character that you are not striving to overcome, you may be assured that the enemy will take advantage of them, for he is watching vigilantly, seeking to spoil the faith of everyone.

In order to gain the victory over every besetment of the enemy, we must lay hold on the power that is of and beyond ourselves. We must maintain a constant, living connection with Christ, who has power to give victory to every soul that will maintain an attitude of faith and humility. If we are self-sufficient, and think that we may go out just as we please, and yet hope to come out on the right side finally, we shall find that we have made a terrible mistake. As those who hope to receive the overcomer's reward, we must press forward in the Christian warfare, though at every advance we meet with opposition.

It means all evil agencies must be firmly resisted. Every moment we must be on guard, not for one instant are we to lose sight of Christ, and His power to save in the hour of trial. Our hands must be placed in His, that we may be upheld by the power of His might."

I benefitted much from the above messages. Bib, I believe God placed us on this earth for a purpose. I want to fulfill the purpose He designed for me. Life on our planet earth is brief, a temporary stepping stone to the mansions He has prepared for us. Bib, you and I also believe that "Eye hath not seen, nor ear heard, neither have entered the heart of man, the things which God hath prepared for them that love him." (I Cor. 2:9).

Till next mail,

> *Love as always,*
> (signed) Leon

Chapter XVI

TO THEM A CHRISTMAS GIFT

I am the resurrection and the life … (John 11:25).

December 30, 1921. A beaming preacher stepped on the platform, greeted the people, then said, "Praise the Lord!" Pausing briefly, he added. "Before our song service, I have an announcement to make."

Came a hush and quietness. He smiled and said, "My wife sent me word saying a precious gift arrived at home in Candon, Ilocos Sur, on Christmas day. Our second son was born on the 25th of this month. Earlier, my wife and I had agreed on a name for our fourth child—if a son—to be Alfonso."

A resounding applause congratulated the preacher.

"Thank you," minister LZR acknowledged the applause with a bow. "Mother and baby are doing well." A softer round of applause followed.

The congregation sang with fervor and eagerly listened to the message of **The Coming King of Kings, The Almighty Deliverer.**

LZR arrived home in late January and held his new baby close. "You were born while I was away, Son. I'm so glad to bond with you. You'll be Ponsing to us, but your full name will be Alfonso Panis Roda in the Birth Registry." The proud father registered his son's birth on January 25, 1922.

Looking down at her nursing baby, Maria could not miss the close resemblance between father and son. *A look-alike to perpetuate the family name,* she mused. She could not dismiss a perception that Ponsing would carry out his father's calling. *My baby, you are in God's loving hands.*

"Ponsing is my boy—ours—" Leon said, "but above all, he is the Lord's." He was talking to his baby as well as to his mother. "Each of our children must grow up in the Lord." he continued. After a thoughtful moment, he added, "Before I leave for another series of evangelistic meetings, we'll hold a baby dedication for Ponsing."

So like their older children, they dedicated their newborn son early in his life. Deep in his heart, Leon discerned this child to be a special one. "I agree with you," he told his wife, "Ponsing will carry on the work I started as a young man." Maria smiled and nodded her head in agreement.

Six-year-old Arding begged to hold his baby brother. "My own little baby brother," he bragged. "I'll be careful, *Mamang*," he promised. So his mother made him sit down on the sofa and Arding held his baby brother in his chubby arms." He's warm and soft," he said.

Ely, too, wanted to hold her baby brother. "Your arms need to grow a bit bigger," her mother said, patting her little girl's arms." You can rock him in his crib," she consoled her little girl. "Rock him gently like this," she said, showing Ely and Arding how." Let's sing him a lullaby," she said, and taught them the song, "Rock, rock, rock, little boat...." They watched as their baby brother close his eyes and soon he was sound asleep.

While the baby slept, Arding and Ely played quietly, as their mother instructed them. "You are my big helpers," she told them. And the young mother went about doing her many household chores for the day.

Leon was glad that Tony, his younger brother, lived in their home while colporteuring in the area. By selling truth-filled magazines—Heralds of the Morning and its version in Ilokano, *Ti Damag Ti Pagarian*— he was helping spread the gospel message as well as earn money for his schooling. Tony's burning ambition was to get a Christian education. He carried out the role—deputy man of the house his older brother had committed to him in his absence. The role flattered Tony. He helped his sister-in-law by relieving her of the heavy home chores. He carried water from the artesian well and supplied wood for the woodstove to cook their meals.

While Tony colporteured around the neighborhood, he saw men and women smoking home-rolled tobacco, and little boys and girls aping their parents, grandparents, and uncles. It made Tony long for the time when he'd be at the Academy in Pasay, preparing himself to teach and to preach about healthful living. Healthful living was one compelling tenet that attracted his older brothers to the Seventh-day Adventist faith—keeping the body temple fit for the indwelling of the Holy Spirit. The three brothers saw the link: A Christian keeps his body—God's temple—clean.

It was during the evening worship when Tony had the chance to share his colporteur experiences with the family. The stories entranced Arding, who looked up to his *Tata* (uncle) Tony for a role model. Arding never got tired of listening to the story of Bruno, a boy about his own age.

Bruno's father had been buying every issue of *Ti Damag Ti Pagarian*. Also, he and his wife had been faithfully attending the Bible studies Tony was conducting. Bruno's father told Tony this story, and Tony to Arding.

One day Bruno with his parents went to visit his grandparents. As his practice was, Bruno's grandfather span tall tales for the benefit of his grandson. Stories about the big crocodile that stole a baby girl sleeping under a shady tree at the river bank while her mother washed their clothes closer to the river. Bruno usually sat listening quietly to his grandfather as he spun spellbinding stories. Not at this visit, however. While his grandfather was spinning another tall tale, occasionally puffing a corncob pipe, Bruno kept interrupting him. "But *Lolo*" (grandpa) in an attempt to tell his grandpa something, but his grandpa silenced him with, "Wait, listen to this story," giving Bruno a firm pat.

Suddenly, Bruno stood up, and in as loud as a boy could still show respect, he said, "*Lolo,* you are smoking." He tried to pull out the corncob pipe dangling from his grandpa's mouth.

Amused if not angered, grandpa boomed, "Now, what!"

A childish voice said, "*Lolo*, if you make your body dirty, you will burn up when Jesus comes again." Then in a pleading tone, "I want you to go to heaven with me, *Lolo.* Jesus wants to take you to heaven, too, *Lolo.*"

Grandpa's mouth dropped open. Dumbfounded, he scratched his head, turned to his adult son who was smiling in approbation of his boy. "Did you put those words in my grandson's mouth?" he demanded.

"No," his son said, shaking his head. "No, I didn't."

"*Lolo,* it's in the Bible!" Bruno said. "Please *Lolo,* please stop smoking so Jesus can save you." The little boy's eyes brimmed with tears. "I want you to go to heaven with me, *Lolo,*" he repeated, in almost a sob.

At that point his grandfather's eyes were misting. He swallowed the big lump in his throat. Bruno's parents looked on, but remained silent, their eyes swelling with tears. In the quietness, they heard a songbird singing from a distance.

"Well," grandpa finally said, "I guess you are right." Brushing the tears from his cheeks, he reached out to his grandson, ruffled his hair, and took him in his arms. "I want to go to heaven with you all," he said, hurling his corncob pipe into faraway space. "That's for the birds," he said.

***

Immersed in his evangelistic efforts away from home, Leon rejoiced to see the workings of the Holy Spirit. Every meeting night, the public plaza he rented to hold the meetings overflowed. Each evangelistic campaign lasted for three months. Night after night without the aid of a public address system, he preached. Daytime, most often he walked to the homes of those who asked for visitation.

H. L. Reyes, in his book <u>Breaking Through,</u> described Leon Roda as one 'with fire in his bones working like a blazing meteor.... No evangelist raised more churches in Northern Luzon Mission (NLM) even to the present than he in his ten years of ministry in NLM (1915–1925).' Relying upon the Lord for spiritual as well as physical strength, the Lord blessed the efforts of His humble servant LZR in many precious souls surrendered to Him.

The missionaries had taught the young Filipino evangelists well, and with God's blessings, their efforts were bearing fruit. The missionaries also set role models in soul winning for the young evangelists. They prayed for them and prayed with the young preachers. Philippine soil was fertile ground for seed sowing. Hearts received the gospel message, producing bounteous harvest in earnest precious souls for the Kingdom.

"It's good to be home," Leon sighed. He had been feeling worn out lately. Verved up in proclaiming the gospel, he ignored feelings of malaise. *A few hours of sleep,* he assured himself *would revive my strength as it had in the past.* So he kept his preaching schedule, adhering close to his fixed daily work program: Up long before sunup to prepare his sermons, to write truth-filled articles, translated the articles and the books he had committed to do. In a way, the Press depended on his writings and for his translating The Heralds of the Morning to Ilokano. To LZR, everyday came with a compelling urge to finish as much as he could on that day.

Maria begged her husband to see the doctor for what he called a scratchy throat. "When I have the time," he'd reply, "I will. I must finish writing this article. I must get this translation done on time."

So Maria forced herself to say, "All right, I'll stop nagging, but one day, you'd wish you had listened." She brought her concern over her husband's failing health to the Lord in her silent prayers as she did her home chores.

Then one day LZR's voice gave out. The doctor discharged him after a few days of hospital stay, but gave him an order: "Complete bed rest. Stay in a room alone, by yourself." Diagnosis: Pulmonary tuberculosis.

As though reading Leon's thoughts, the doctor said, "For not heeding your voice box when it clamored for rest, it had gone on strike. Delicate vocal chords stretched beyond its limit, aggravated by infection."

Then the doctor launched a lecture about the nature of pulmonary tuberculosis: "It is highly communicable—contagious and infectious. The bacteria called tubercle bacilli usually come in fine droplets from a person with active lung lesions. Coughing, sneezing, and even talking, could spray the bacteria in the air.

"Sometimes infection results from ingesting milk or other tuberculous cattle byproducts. In this instance, the infection begins in the intestinal mucosa and mesenteric nodes. Skin infection can also occur chiefly on the hands of butchers handling the meat of tuberculous cattle. In your case—pulmonary tuberculosis—the infection is in your lungs, the major organs of the respiratory system.

"To this day the only known medicine for tuberculosis is a strong and healthy body to fight the bacteria. That's why you need to eat nutritious food and take lots of rest to build up your immune system to resist the infection. As a preventive measure to keep from spreading the infection, especially to your young children, you must have your own room. You must have your own eating utensils—dinner plates, forks, spoons, drinking glasses. These must be boiled after each use to kill all bacteria.

"Cover your mouth with a clean cloth when you cough or sneeze. Better yet, wear a mask over your mouth and nose when you talk. If you must spit, do it on a rag or on a container, and burn these articles daily. I repeat, always wear a mask over your mouth and nose when you talk."

Turning to Maria, he asked if she had any questions. She raised quite a few, which the doctor answered to her satisfaction, and added that he expected for her to have more questions later, and that he'd be glad to hear them. "Make him eat food to nourish his body to build up his immune system," he said. And he gave Maria a list of food to prepare and the preferred way to conserve their nutrients to nourish the body.

The doctor repeated to Leon of the importance for him to have complete bed rest to give his body the chance to repair itself.

Leon accepted the diagnosis bravely and submitted to the rules the doctor outlined. He thought he would take advantage of this blessing in disguise to be with his family, to be able to cuddle his children, something he'd wished he could do during the years he'd been away and too busy for them. Then it dawned on him. *The irony of it all,* he thought, *now that I can be home, and have the time, I won't be able to do anything like this. Lord,* he sighed deep in his heart, *Surely Thou has better plans for me.*

Maria prepared a corner bedroom with a wide open window facing east and two smaller ones facing southeast. A *santol* tree, towering above the eastern window filtered the sunshine and the glare. A spreading *lomboy* tree provided shade from the afternoon sun, its leafy branches—nature's air conditioner—also sheltered lively songbirds that infrequently trilled their songs between their feasting on clusters of luscious purple fruits. A *narra* bedside table—with his Bible, a set of E. G. White books including Steps to Christ, a pitcher of water, and an oil lamp—were within his reach.

Feeling imprisoned, Leon continued sharing his thoughts with his Father: *Lord, Who changes not, I feel so helpless. It is Thy will that no one should suffer.* He thought of the first prayer offered for him at the hospital years ago. *I ask for Thy healing hand on my body as Thou answered the prayer of Colporteur Caldwell. I thank Thee for giving me the opportunity to serve Thee.* In recalling the time he and Bibiano first met Pastor Finster on the street, the Bible studies that followed, their baptism, the Bible Institute Pastor Finster conducted, their ordination, and his evangelistic efforts, his burden lifted. *Lord, I feel Thy leading hand in all these.* Now in his mind came the dream that turned into a nightmare when he was in the hospital. *Lord, rebuke Satan from inflicting his threat. That was but a decade ago, Lord. Let Thy will be done in my life.* He thanked the Lord for His promise to answer 'the effectual fervent prayer of a righteous man,' and claimed His imputed righteousness. *I thank Thee Lord for answering my prayer according to Thy holy will...* He drifted off in to a restful sleep.

Leon awakened early as usual, and felt refreshed from his sleep. *This is the day the Lord has made, I will be glad and rejoice in it,* he repeated to himself. He tried his vocal chords. *The doctor was right,* he admitted and recalled his order and thought, *I must do my part to bring my healing.*

He heard distant crowing. *Roosters are early risers,* he affirmed to himself, *like me. In their own way, they are thanking the Lord for the rest and for another day.* As sunshine brightened his room, he took his Bible and opened it to Psalms 91. He asked the Lord to bless in the reading of His Word. An impression to pray for Bib came. *Heal his broken heart, Lord. Guide him today, fill his loneliness with Thy presence in his life.*

He prayed for the flock including his family, his children especially. He prayed for the Lord to spare them from the infection ravaging his body. He reflected on Psalms 23 in his personal life. *David, author, poet, a man in pursuit of God's own heart, like I always wanted, I would today.* He prayed that His will be done. He committed his life and those he always prayed for in God's keeping, *just for today, Lord, In Jesus name, I pray. Amen.*

He turned introspective and reviewed the doctor's discussion about pthisis. *I had come in contact with a person who had active tuberculosis,* jolted his mind. *A healthy body resists the growth of tubercle bacilli, warding off infection.* His mind went to the circumstances that led him to go to Suyok in Lepanto, Bontoc, in 1920. And of S. D. Balutero and his wife who attended the evangelistic meetings he held earlier in Narvacan, Ilocos Sur.

Mrs. Balutero accepted the message but a few matters held her husband from committing his heart to the Lord. Soon after her baptism, she died of tuberculosis. She had pleaded with her husband to meet her in the earth made new, before her death. In his grieving, Balutero became ill. The doctor said he had pthisis and had but a short time to live. Balutero's promise to his wife shook him, and he decided to do something about it. He drafted a petition for a teacher for his village, signed it, and asked others to cosign. *Forty-six families cross-signed the petition,* Leon rejoiced to recall.

He cringed to recount his visit with Balutero for the first time. *He coughed without covering his mouth. He invited me for supper and to stay with him so we could talk about the petition. While we talked, he kept coughing, never covered his mouth. I was extremely vulnerable—tired, lacking rest and sleep, missing nourishment Maria always served at home.*

His thoughts went to the cholera epidemic that swept over the area, the very reason for postponing his move to Suyok. *I escaped the cholera, I caught tuberculosis instead.* Now the connection was clear in his mind: It had been the beginning of his lethargy and feeling spent, yet he kept going —his preaching and studying, with sheer determination to get what needed doing. *I got the death sentence two months before I moved to Suyok!* Now his worry turned to his family, especially for his young children.

Suddenly, he became aware of the direction of his thinking. *A merry heart doeth good like medicine,* flashed in his mind. *I must shake off these morbid thoughts. Lord, by Thy help, I choose to fill my mind with cheerful thoughts,* he prayed. He forced himself to get on a brighter track.

Lord, it's good to think of how a dying woman, new in the faith, let the Holy Spirit guide her to bequeath her large newly built house and a substantial amount of money to the church. I praise Thee Lord for the silent workings of the Holy Spirit in human hearts, he exulted in prayer.

Just then Arding's voice singing, "Lord, in the morning…." floated to his room, blending with the softer voices of his mother and his sisters. Deeply feeling left out, he complained, *Now that I'm home and have the time, I couldn't be present in the family worship.* Again catching himself, he changed the trend of his thinking. *Lord, I join the morning worship in spirit. I praise Thee for the blessings of a virtuous woman in my loving wife. This is from Thee, Lord, I thank Thee. Grant her strength to equal the charge of raising our children in Thy love while she takes care of a sick husband. Lord, I plead, lay Thy healing hand on me as Thou did to the many sick people that came to Thee when Thou dwelt among men. I ask Thee to give me faith even as small as a mustard seed. I thank Thee for not withholding what is good for Thy children, including me, for answering my prayer of faith according to Thy will and loving kindness. I thank Thee for imparting Thy love in my heart to love others. like Jesus… Amen.*

He reached for his Bible and re-read 2 Kings 20:1–11. He was reflecting on the passage when Maria greeted him. "The children are eating and they send their love to you," she said cheerfully. Leon helped her clear his bedside table for her to lay down a tray of food: A small section of a pomelo, a quarter of a ripe papaya, and a *tumoc*. On his plate around a mound of boiled red unpolished rice sat a serving of scrambled eggs and a handful of shelled boiled peanuts.

"Do you think you could clean up your plate?" she asked in a teasing tone, quoting a question he had often asked Arding. He simply smiled. He was hungry. "Enjoy your food," she said. "I'll return soon," He let her read a message he had scribbled on his tablet, and they locked eyes. Before she turned to step out of his room, she flashed him a smile. *"Mahal,"* she said.

She removed her apron, hang it over a peg near the window where sunshine would strike. She washed her hands before returning to her children. "Your Papa sends his love to you," she said as she sat down.

"Will *Papang* get well soon, *Mamang?"* Arding asked.

"Yes, we prayed for him last night and this morning at worship," she replied. "He wrote a note that he let me read, that said, 'To my dear children, Arding, Ely, Ceding, and Ponsing. I love you very much.'"

After Maria had taken care of her first bite of breakfast, she said, "I'm glad to see you have cleaned your plate, Arding," seeing him reach for his *tumoc.* She saw him slit the top end with a small knife, peeled it half-way down the stem, and holding it on the unpeeled portion, he took a bite.

"I like bananas," he said. "This is sweet, and good for me." He swallowed after thoroughly chewing it, and took another bite. Ceding, watching her older brother enjoy his banana, reached for her own, and gave it to Arding. He slit the top end for Ceding and helped her start to peel it. "I like bananas, sweet," Ceding chirped. "They are good for me."

Ponsing stirred in his crib, stretched out his limbs and torso, opened his eyes, and let out a soft cry. His mother picked him up. "Finish your breakfast," she told her children. "I need to take care of your baby brother." On their return, the baby clamored for his breakfast. "All right," she said and began to nurse him. "I'll finish eating my breakfast with you, little one," she said. "I must eat so you would have lots of milk."

"*Mamang,*" Ely stood up. "Can I give Ponsing a bite of my banana?"

"Not now, *Anak,* but maybe soon," she said. "I'm so proud of you for wanting to share what you enjoy eating with your baby brother. It won't be long before Ponsing could eat them—mashed—for him."

"Did I eat mashed bananas when I was little, *Mamang?*" Ely asked.

"Oh, yes," she replied. "All of you liked bananas since you were little."

"I'll eat my papaya, then my suha (native pomelo), Arding said.

"Me, too," Ceding chirped.

"Better eat the *suha* first," their mother advised. "Remember the time you ate the papaya before the *suha* ? You said the *suha* was sour."

The children obeyed. When they bit into the ripe papaya slices, they drummed their feet against the table. "Sweet," they said in their delight.

"Papaya is the best dessert, better than cake or candy," Arding said.

"What are you going to do next?" their mother asked.

"We wash our hands and wipe them dry," Arding volunteered.

Approving with a smile, Maria said, "Children, there's a basin of water and a clean towel hanging near it. Would you help your sisters, Arding?"

"Yes, *Mamang,*" he replied, and holding a hand to each of them, he said, "Come on, Ely. Come on, Ceding." Three pairs of tiny feet pattered to the basin of water, with their mother's smile of approbation.

As the baby's belly filled up, his eyes slowly closed, and his mother laid him back in his crib. "Be quiet now," she whispered to the rest of her children. Putting a forefinger across her lip, she pointed to the sleeping baby. "I'll go and see your *Papang,*" she said. She picked up her apron and slipping it over her head to cover her front body, she was on her way.

Finding her husband's clean plate and a broad smile on his face, she teased, "Good boy." While putting the empty plate on the empty tray, she asked, "Did you enjoy your food?" Nodding, his smile broadened. He saw him holding his Bible, and noted it opened to II Kings. "I see you are in the midst of your study," she said with a twinkle in her eye. "I'll let you continue your study. I must see the children. I'll be back at lunchtime." She paused, then continued. "In the meantime, ring the bell for service." She gave him a smile before leaving, her hands full of the empty dishes.

LZR re-read verse 3 and pondered over it. *Lord, I thank Thee for the story of the healing of King Hezekiah. I, too, by Thy grace have walked in truth with my heart in tune to Thy will, doing all that was right. Would it please Thee to heal me as Thou healed Hezekiah?* the plea ended in a sob. *Thou changes not, Lord. Thou art the same now as in King Hezekiah's days. I have faith in Thy power to clear the infection from my lungs. The sign I ask for my healing is the return of my voice and strength, according to Thy will. I commit myself, and my loved ones in Thy care. In Jesus' name....*"

After his prayer, he felt an overpowering relief. He pondered over Hebrews 11, mentally reviewing the chapter. He repeated the first verse in his mind: *Faith is the substance—the reality—of things hoped for. I hope for healing: The evidence—substantiation—the Lord has laid His hand on me to heal me as he had healed King Hezekiah of his sickness. As He healed Namaan of his leprosy.* He drew a deep breath and imagined his lungs filling with oxygen, disposing of all tubercle bacilli. *The healing properties of fresh air,* he affirmed himself, drawing another deep breath. His eyes wandered out of the window, and watched the sway of the canopy of green leaves by a gentle breeze, permitting occasional glimpses of an azure sky. His thoughts turned to the week of creation, and imagined himself there. The Creator speaking, 'Let there be light,' and it was so. *He created the firmament, the trees, flowers, the grass, every living creature, the sun, the moon, the stars, by His word. Before he formed man in His image, He created the things to meet human needs.* He thought of the perfect pair, untouched by sin walking in Eden. *My Creator, my Friend, I trust in Thee.* Deliberately, he guided his mind to dwell on thoughts uplifting, and he felt Him close even by his bedside.

***

MY BEST FRIEND

I know that I shall never own
   A friend, lovely as the Rose of Sharon.
A Friend whose faithful promises
   Are written in bright, bold letters
In the sky, and on earth's tresses.
   A Friend Who walks with God alway
And walks with me by night and day.
   A Friend Who would my burdens bear,
A Friend Who all my joys I share—
   Upon Whose shoulders I can lean
Who closely listens to my dreams.
   Only in Jesus is this Friend, I find.

(With apologies to Joyce Kilmer, crj)

***

Chapter XVII

<u>WHO ARE</u> FAITHFUL

Blessed is the man who makes the Lord his trust…. **(Psalms 40:4)**

1923, Cuyapo, Nueva Ecija. In answer to LZR's prayer of faith, the Lord restored his voice, his strength, his vigor. A soft distinct voice spoke to him: "Parched souls thirsting for the Word are waiting in Cuyapo." *This is an appointment for me to keep to complete my recovery,* came to his mind. "My God, my strength and healing, I praise Thee," he cried out, his heart overflowing with joy. *Father, use Thy humble servant to lead men and women in Cuyapo seeking for Thee I put my trust in Thee, my God.*

When the people heard of the evangelistic meetings soon to come to their town, they started a 'good-news chain'. They told their friends, their neighbors, and relatives about it. In turn, their friends, neighbors, and relatives told others about it. The news that the preacher would preach in Ilokano spread quickly. The news that the preacher, once a staunch Roman Catholic, would preach straight out of the Bible, tickled their ears.

The community watched as men set up a tent, and as they saw the need for muscle, able bodied men volunteered to help finish the work.

The tent overflowed the first evening. They only had to add more chairs as people came to listen to the preaching night after night. People who attended left satisfied, yet they returned again and again to fill their longing hearts. They opened their hearts and minds to receive the Word.

Soft breezes cooled the noonday heat and gentle rains came down, programmed by Infinite hands. As the rain watered the parched land, thirsty souls drank of the clear water that flowed from the Living Fountain. No longer encumbered by the dogma that priests only had the right to the Bible, they began searching the Scriptures for themselves. And now, they were feasting on the Word of God.

Upon their request, the evangelist visited people in their homes and he became acquainted with them. He found them to be serious Bible students. Generally educated and well-to-do, they were sincere and unpretentious, honestly searching for the truth.

No attendance attrition nor laxity in attentiveness came about. LZR's deep voice speaking of God's love carried through with fervency. God sustained the strength of His servant day by day as he expounded on God's Word. People came to know that the Law—every aspect of the ten commandments—is as immutable as the Author and Creator of all things.

Jesus became real to them, that His grace, His promises, and His power can be theirs to claim. The Holy Spirit illuminated their minds to His Word.

At the conclusion of the evangelistic meetings, sixty-two precious souls were baptized to the Seventh-day Adventist faith. Strains of praises swelled as the Holy Scribe entered each name in the Book of Life.

LZR's heart spilled over with praises to the Lord for surrendered lives, and for his healing. He rededicated his remaining life in His service.

Maria bubbled over with joy as she tore open another letter. The envelope was stamped August 10, 1923. Eagerly, she read the letter:

Dear Leon, Maria, and Children,

It's good to hear that all is well with you, that the children are growing. Your family photo shows Arding to be growing fast, a big brother to his younger siblings. I see the Panis in his eyes, in his mouth, and the determination in his hands. Has it been four years since he declared, "I am Arding," and showing his fingers that he was three years old? Now seven years of age and in Grade I. How the years flew! Don't you laugh:

To Arding, my Boy: To you I bequeath all my books, including the Law texts. In a few years you should be able to read them. The enclosed ten-dollar bill is for your college funds.

Life in this wealthy country is getting routine for me. I get up every morning to go to work. Home after work, eat, read, visit with friends, sleep. My taste buds are surely getting Americanized. The missionary zeal, once glowing in my once young heart is growing old with me. Infrequently, down in my heart, surges a nostalgia for the pulpit and the preaching. Leon, I miss the debates especially. And performing the solemn rite of baptism. Thought you'd be glad to know I found a friendly church. I attend regularly.

Maria, this is especially for you: The newspaper and the radio are hot on the women suffrage issue. Leading and prominent women are pushing for women's rights, for equal opportunity. Believe it or not, the President's wife, the First Lady, is in it. Expect more to hear of the development of women suffrage in the future.

Can you bear a little gossip? A juicy piece that's going around is of the President's illicit affair with another woman. Naturally, the First Lady feels hurt and rejected. It wouldn't surprise me if this gossip propels her into helping lead in this women's rights. It astounds me that Eleanor Roosevelt was a Roosevelt before marrying President Franklin Delano. They're cousins to some degree. That she's level headed and as bright and intellectual as her husband—and perhaps more so—is beyond refute. A real power behind the throne.

I must be honest with you. Don't count on my homecoming. I have obligations to meet that takes time. Unlike the ride at sea I'd been through, my life here is the same—long and arduous, but there's no need for you to worry over this, or about me. I've learned to live one day at a time. I pray that you, too, have come to terms with life on planet earth. I'm embarrassed to admit some feelings akin to hydrophobia within me—for even the thought of sailing appalls me. But don't waste your energy worrying over this, or about me.

I have some brotherly counsel for you both. Take good care of yourselves, Leon, especially. Don't work too hard. To be kind to those you love, be kind to yourself. Need I remind you that time flies fast? Children grow fast, so spend time with them while they're young. In a few years, they'll be gone from you and on their own. I'm very much aware, Leon, that your children are longing for you to spend more time with them. Every bit of time you spend with them during their pliable years, you will value in your memory.

Hey, preach to yourself, Ka Bib, I hear you say. Yes, I'm preaching the same thing to myself. Believe me, I wish I could, but I have confidence in Sis Segunda and her husband taking my place efficiently. I do what I can—I pray for my son as I do for you. I pray for Ben Samuel to grow up to be a good Seventh-day Adventist. Please continue taking him into your family as occasion allows. I feel your prayers for me, and I thank you tons. Hug the children for me. I'll look for a letter from you… till then,

As ever, your loving brad,

(signed) *Bib*

Arding jumped up and down to learn of his uncle's gift to him. He at once started to write a *Dear Uncle Bib* thank you note.

When they were alone, Maria threw question after question at her husband on her brother's use of the word 'bequeath,' "Is he sick and about to die? Did he use that word because he's away? Has he decided not to return? He'd always been careful with his words, is he getting careless?"

"I believe he's using the word with a bit of humor," Leon replied. "That's the poet in him. My guess is, he's trying to introduce Arding to the Law profession."

"Until now he's silent over what he is doing for a living," she said.

"He's reading the newspaper and listening to the news. It's very much like your brother. His interest in politics is reviving. He made mention about being Americanized." Leon grinned at Maria. "I'm no help, am I?"

"By saying he had obligations that took up time, is he hinting that he has a new family? Did he re-marry? Don't you wish he'd tell us more?"

"Why not try asking Segunda?" he suggested. "Surely, she must be asking questions similar to what your mind is puzzling over."

"Having observed how you related to each other, I sensed *Ka* Bib and you became closer than blood brothers. I think he'd be happy to answer any questions you'd ask him. Remember, you have to ask," Maria said.

***

Rosales, Pangasinan,
Philippines October 1, 1923

Dear Bib,

Your most awaited letter came about two weeks ago. We're happy to know you are doing well, as we're all here. A surprise! A new nephew of yours—we named him Arturo, Turing for short, arrived on the 17th. When you see him, you'd likely say, he's a cross between Panis and Roda. I think he resembles Arding. as a baby. We hope Turing will be an additional enticement for you to come home, plus the niece and two nephews you have yet to meet. I'm thankful I'm home to be of some help to Maria for a while.

Arding is a big help in many ways. He jumped with joy for your note and gift to him. He scribbled the enclosed. letter. He'll be eight years old on the 25th of next month. We will celebrate his birthday as you would Thanksgiving Day there. There's so much to be thankful for. Our healthy children, your letters telling you are well, but <u>we long to hear more about yourself</u>.

Your sis says thanks for the women suffrage newsbit. It'll be years before it hits our 'mahinhin-pinay.' (modest women). I get the impression Mrs. Roosevelt is one who feels secure about herself. As you know, our Filipina women prefer to stay home to take care of their families. For this, we are thankful. It's good to come home and find mother keeping everything in order. When I'm away, I have no worries about who's taking care of the children, who is keeping the house clean, cooking good food for them. I always look forward to coming home to Maria's nutritious cooking. Wish I could be home more often, but there's work to do. God comes first in my life.

I'm bursting with joy and I must share my happiness with you. At the conclusion of the cottage meetings in Cuyapo, I baptized 62 precious souls. They'd built a large church expecting their membership to grow fast. What faith! Considering this to be the first time for the message to enter this town, to God be the glory! For the people's receptivity to the truth, I praise the Lord. The Holy Spirit working in the hearts of the people is clear as day. Pray that I'll get rested and well enough to start a new effort not long from now.

We continue to pray for you. We're happy you've found a church you could feel at home. We enjoyed reading your last letter. Maria says she hopes you'll write again soon. With little children to care for in addition to house chores, her hands are full. She wants me to *include a quote from the Ministry of Healing one you doubtless had come across before.*

"Christ will never abandon the soul for whom He has died. The soul may leave Him and be overwhelmed with temptation, but Christ can never turn from one for whom He has paid the ransom of His own life." p. 118.

"Ask him to tell us more about himself—his work, his social life, anything about himself," your sis directed. And she wants to tell you she's still enjoying the blue dress, your gift the last Christmas you spent with us here.

I appreciate the advice you gave me. Yes, I admit I had neglected the care of my body—God's holy temple—by over-driving myself at work. I want to be His living temple for many more years, and by His grace, I'll try to follow your advice. Carried far away in fervor to spread the gospel message to the detriment of my physical health! Lack of rest and sleep, working too many long hours, in addition to inadequate daily nourishment, had taken its toll, I'm fully aware. It does not bring glory nor honor to His name. Thank you for your caring thoughts. God loves you, Bib. To you, we send our love,

> *Your loving brother-in-law and chum,*
> (signed) *Leon Z. Roda*

***

Naturally, the new baby added to Maria's busyness, yet she was grateful for the quiet and secure atmosphere in Rosales so conducive to her husband's recuperation as well as for raising their children. With Arding and Ely in school, Maria welcomed her husband's presence at home, his help with the children's assignments, in particular. Leon delighted in his involvement with the children's school activities, and came home with good news a homebound mother longed to hear: Of Arding's courteous ways, his articulateness, and pleasant outgoing personality.

"Arding is a brilliant and precocious boy," he told Maria. "We won't have a little boy in him before long."

"What about Ely?" she asked. "I'd like her to grow up to be a proper young lady. I wish our first daughter to be an improvement over her mother. She must get the formal education and a profession I didn't get."

"Yes, all our children must get a solid Christian education," Leon assured his wife. "By God's help," he said. *Mahal*, you need not worry about our little princess. She's demur, well mannered, quiet yet alert, she is not shy. She's as sharp as any parent wish her little girl to be."

Both parents had seen how Ely opened her eyes before she opened her mouth. They were proud of their well behaved children. "I'm so happy to be around our children, to watch them grow up in the fear of the Lord," Leon said over and over. And he continued to pray for his total healing.

The surge of energy that sustained him during his evangelistic effort in Cuyapo slowly ebbed away. He knew he had characteristically given of his all in this effort notwithstanding his doctor's advice. He had used the full timbre of his pulpit voice, for he wanted everyone to hear the message. Almost immediately following the baptisms, his voice turned raspy. He left his team the follow-up task. The district pastor came to preach to the new congregation, visited the homes of the new church members, and found them strong in their faith, full of Christian brotherly love for one another.

Maria intensified her efforts in preparing nutritious meals and often urged her husband to eat more and pleaded for him to rest more. Leon, however, was happiest when he was *producing*. He studied as he had always done, he kept up with his translating in the vernacular, and he continued to write articles, so that all who could read would be reached.

Remembering the promise he made to himself while he was away and when he was too ill to spend time with his children, he sat down with them. "Read to your sisters," he told Arding in a whisper he could manage, "I'll be here to help. So Arding became the voice for his father, he was more than glad to be. A good reader, he needed no help, but he and Ely enjoyed being near their father. He was there for them, present in body and spirit for them, and was there approving what they did.

***

We Are Objects of His Infinite Love

by Ellen G. White

The heart surrendered to God's wise discipline will trust every working out of His providence.... Temptation will come to discourage, but what is gained by yielding to any such temptation? Is the soul made any better by murmuring and complaining of its only source of strength? Is the anchor cast within the vail, will it hold in sickness? Will it be the testimony borne in the last closing scenes of life when the lips are becoming palsied with death? The anchor holds....

O *earth, that fallen man is the object of His infinite love and delight. He rejoices over them with celestial songs, and man defiled with sin, "not having spot or wrinkle, or any such thing* (Eph. 5:27). *"Who shall lay any thing in the charge of God's elect? It is God that justifieth."* (Rom. 8:33).

Let every weak, tempest-tossed soul find anchorage in Jesus Christ and not become self-centered that he can think only of his little disappointments and the interruptions of his plans and hopes. Is not the... plan of salvation all-absorbing? If the infinite God justifies me, "who is he that condemneth? It is Christ that died" (verse 34). *He has in His dying for man revealed how much He loves man ... enough to die for him!* ....

Satan will accuse and seek permission to destroy, but it is God that opens the door of refuge. It is God that justifieth him that entereth that door. Then if God is for us, who can be against us?

God lives and reigns. All who are saved must fight manfully as soldiers of Jesus Christ, then they will be registered in heaven's books as true and faithful.... (Letter 2, Dec. 29, 1889 to Mrs. Mary White, who was dying of tuberculosis.)

Affliction and adversity may cause much inconvenience and may bring great depression, but it is prosperity that is dangerous to spiritual life ... will arouse the ... inclination to presumption.

... the Scotch fir tree is one of the best from which Christians may draw inspiring lessons .... it requires less soil for its roots than any other tree. In dry soil and amidst barren rocks, it finds sufficient nourishment.

(Manuscript 145, Sept. 2, 1902, "Diary: from <u>Upward Look</u>.")

Chapter XVIII

THE CALLED

1924. Now, with time in his hands, LZR had no excuse from keeping his doctor's appointment. And he prayed and hoped to get a bill of good health, a license for him to return to the pulpit to preach the Word of God.

After giving him a thorough physical exam, the doctor said, "Resume complete bed rest. Eat more of fresh fruits, fresh vegetables, nuts, seeds and whole grains. These foods are the best sources of nutrients for boosting your immune system and for you to gain weight. Drink lots of pure water between meals. Give your voice some rest if you want it back."

Leon listened quietly, nodding to show he understood, as the doctor repeated the preventive measures to keep from infecting others. He also reminded him that a cheerful heart, "the Bible used the word merry—a positive attitude, I call it trust in divine power," he said, "is good medicine."

The family having moved since his first complete bed rest, Maria took to the task. She prepared for her husband the corner room with a window facing east, and the other facing southwest. Twin *manzanita* trees gave partial shade from the morning sun and glare. Its luscious round red fruits attracted birds to a feast—their flight and antics were free entertainment for the bedfast preacher. A wide spreading mango tree filtered the afternoon sun, its wide satiny verdant leaves, a natural air-conditioning. The wide-open windows allowed free circulation of fresh in the bedroom.

May. "Let's go to Baguio where it's always cool," said Maria to her husband. The dry, cool climate in the mountains is conducive to well-being, it should enhance your recovery." This delighted Leon. He had always liked the cool air in Baguio that kept fruits and vegetables fresh longer. The children helped in the preparation for their trip and vacation.

Before long, the whole family were on their way, riding up the narrow winding, zigzagging roads to the summer capital of the Philippines. They settled in a cabin amidst tall pine trees. Leon got his own room. The rest of the family spread out on the floor in another room to sleep at night, huddling together for warmth. At daytime, they dressed in warm clothes to be comfortable being unaccustomed to temperatures in the low 60's.

Their cheeks turned rosy, their appetites picked up. Slowly gaining in strength, Leon began putting on some weight, but his voice lagged behind his recovery. Now with stamina enough to go outside, he bundled up to keep from chilling. He sat with Maria under the pine trees to watch their children romp around and play, carefree as little lambs, soaking in sunshine and filling their lungs with clean, fresh mountain air.

"Let's enjoy the summer here before we go back home for school," Maria said, 'Let's have a picnic.' She spread out fresh fruits, boiled sweet potatoes, and other nutritious finger foods on the table under the trees.

June. After a prayerful give and take, Leon and Maria decided to move to Pasay, for their children to get a Christian education.

Leon wrote to a couple of friends in Pasay letting them know of his wish to live where sea breezes blow. Mr. Villanueva was quick to reply: "We've spoken for a three bedroom bungalow near the sea, it's now ready for you," brought praises to God and gratefulness for their friends' help.

Late in the month, the Villanueva and the Umali families met their friends and led them to their new home. The welcoming friends had made the house ready for the newcomers to move in. They also filled the kitchen cabinet with food, and placed a few pieces of needed furniture. And they helped carry the few belongings of the family proving they were welcome.

Well rested and having gained strength and some weight—benefits from Baguio's invigorating climate and their carefree days there—Leon was eager to resume his studying, translating, and writing. He chose a corner room away from the children's living space. His room had two large windows, one facing the sea, and the other completed the full panoramic view of the sea and setting of the sun. Near this window, a tamarind tree bloomed profusely, and long slender green pendant fruits hang from its branches. Sturdy limbs reached up high to the sky testifying God is love. Compound minute-pinnate green leaves dressing the branches and doubling as a cooling shade from the afternoon sun, slowly folded when evenings deepened, to stay folded through the night as if in prayer.

The good neighbors allowed time for the newcomers to adjust to their new surroundings. One day Mr. & Mrs. Villanueva dropped in for a friendly visit. Their talk soon centered on the lofty tamarind tree.

"The fruits should start to ripen in a few weeks," Mrs. Villanueva said. "Last year our tree was exceptionally prolific. We expect another good harvest this year," she added. "The ripe fruits are thick-meated, with that sweet and sour flesh we like."

Mr. Villanueva said "She," referring to his wife, "sprinkles brown sugar on the ripe tamarind to make tamarind-*do*. We have the tamarind-*do* to satisfy our *do-tooth* when there are no fruits on the tree, between the flowering and the ripening period," he explained.

"Have you ever used the unripe tamarind to season food?" asked Maria. "We crush the green fruits, put them in a glass container and add a little salt and water," she said. "Leon likes it as a dressing on cooked salad greens, or to season fish dishes," she added.

A trampling of feet materialized in a breathless Arding. *"Mamang,"* he called, after giving a courteous bow to their visitors. "I found this," he said, shoving a bitten-into unripe tamarind for his mother to see. "I took a bite and it's good but sour," he said, mouth contorting. "I need salt, may I have salt, *Mamang?"* His voice pleaded, his eyes riveted on his father.

Heads turned to Leon. He had cupped his hands over his ears and jaws. Having a knowledge of the situation, Maria tried to suppress a laugh. "Still sour," she said. "Salivary glands responding naturally, heh-heh-heh." Her hands flew to press her ears and jaws. The rest of them broke in side-splitting laughter. Everyone felt an achy salivation to the stimulus of the unripe tamarind Arding held in his hand. Leon didn't pass up the fun.

"Look in there ... for the salt, *Anak,"* Maria gestured to Arding. Finding the salt shaker, Arding asked his mother if he could go outside to look for more tamarind. Permission given, Ely asked to tag along. "Yes, but don't eat too much, *Anak.* One should be plenty for you, Ely," her mother said.

After the children tramped outside, Maria asked her friends. "Would anyone tell me what causes the salivary glands to ache at the sight of an unripe tamarind?" The Villanuevas only laughed and shook their heads.

Again, the children came in, each cradling a light green bell-shaped fruit in their palms. *"Mamang"* Arding said, "Look, the seed is hanging, see?" Dangling the fruit by its stem, the light gray kidney bean-shaped seed attached to the bottom of the fruit fascinated the children. Arding asked, *"Mamang,* can I take a bite of this... uhmm... funny-looking fruit?"

"That's a *casoy"* (cashew), Mr. Villanueva volunteered. "When the fruit is ripe, it is sweet and juicy, somewhat spongy in texture. The sticky sap underneath the nutshell, however, is very poisonous. Don't ever try to crack the nut," he cautioned. "If the sap gets on your skin, it will burn your skin. The acid is potent, more poisonous than poison ivy. The nut is tasty, but I advise you not to try to crack the nutshell for the nut."

"Did you understand what Mr. Villanueva warned you about the *casoy* nut, Arding, Ely?"

"Yes, *Mamang,"* the children chorused. "We'll not try to crack the nut."

After a light lunch, Leon noted a bright red glob with the phlegm he coughed up. He kept it to himself thinking the bleeding would stop if he stayed quiet. When he got up, however, he became dizzy. Observant Maria called their houseboy. "Dando, stay with the children," she told him. "I'll take their father to the hospital," and she gave him instructions.

Assured that her husband was comfortable in the hands of the doctor and nurses, Maria whispered to him, "For your lunch tomorrow, I'll bring some of your favorite foods." Flashing him a smile, she headed for home.

Early the next morning, Maria went to the market. She bought vine ripened strawberries, tree ripened zapote, peanuts in their shells, the long eggplants and *ampalaya* (amargoso—also called bitter melon), tomatoes and jalapeno. *These will be in addition to the cafeteria food*, she reminded herself. She cooked the vegetables *pinakbet* —a favorite dish of Leon—and packed the food in the wooden bamboo basket she bought for that purpose.

Before leaving for the hospital, she again gave instructions to Dando, her houseboy. She told Arding what she expected of him with, "Your little brother is your number one responsibility." Nodding his head, "Yes, *Mamang,* I'll be good to Turing," he promised. Handing his mother a small envelope, he said, "Please give this to *Papang.* The angels will take care of us, and you and *Papang, Mamang,"* said Arding. "I asked Jesus."

Maria gave each child a hug, patted her trusted houseboy on the shoulder, and picked up the covered bamboo basket. As she walked away, she breathed a prayer entrusting her family in God's care, and thanking Him for a good next-door neighbor in Mrs. Villanueva. She was happy that their same-age children enjoyed playing together.

Leon was visibly happy to see Maria. "You look so much better," she greeted him. "You came right on time," he whispered. "I'm hungry. What's in your basket?" She lifted the cover to let him peek.

"Arding sent this for you," she said, handing him the small envelope. He opened it, read it, then handed it back for her to read. Written in his own grade school hand writing in cursive letters, Maria read softly, "Dear Papang, We love you and miss you very much. We are praying for you. Your loving son, (signed) Arding." His siblings' signatures appeared below his: Ely, Ceding. Ponsing's was an X, Turing's, a crooked dash. When Maria looked up, her eyes brimmed with tears, so were Leon's.

"I brought enough for your lunch and something for your supper. Eat what you want from the hospital tray, it should be here soon. I must get back to the children. I'll try to be here about this time tomorrow," she smiled. "I'm glad to see you looking better." Before she left, they bowed their heads and Maria offered a prayer for healing, that His will be done.

Ely jumped from the swing to meet her mother and landed with her face down. Maria rushed to her crying daughter, saw her right palm bleeding from a cut, her chin and her knees were bruised. "Arding," she called out. "Help take care of your younger siblings. I must take Ely to the doctor," she said, addressing Dando. "Children, behave. We'll be right back." Mother and child went on their way, Ely clinging to mother's hand.

Dando met them on their return with, "*Nana,* Ponsing fell off his tricycle." Maria found a deep slash on her son's right leg, and a dirty scrape over his right eyebrow. "I'll take Ponsing to the doctor," she told Dando. "Ely, get in the house, *Anak.* Arding, help Dando," she said.

On their return, Ceding and her little friend were crying. "We fell off the swing," Ceding sobbed. Maria saw burns on her chin. Her little friend's eyelid was swollen, there was what appeared to be a deep cut over it, above the eyebrow. The two mothers assessed their girl's injuries.

"I'll take Raquel to the doctor to be sure the bruise on her eye does not get infected," said Mrs. Villanueva.

"Ceding's injuries look superficial," said Maria. "A good washing of her burns with soap and water and a dab of mercurochrome ought to do," she added. "Ceding, did you get scared to see your playmate's eye swollen with a streak of blood over it?" Maria wiped the tears off her daughter's face. "You'll be all right, *Anak,*" she comforted her. Raquel must see the doctor to be sure her injury does not get infected. The eye is a delicate part of the body," she explained. "The doctor will take care of your little friend."

"I might as well give you a bath, Ceding. I see bruises on your knees. I'll be careful so it won't hurt," mother assured. "After you get cleaned up, I'll get supper—fruits and a good, warm vegetable soup. Worship, then to bed early. What a day," Maria sighed, yet glad the day was not any worse.

***

Deep in his heart, Leon longed to visit his hometown. His nostalgia for the town of his boyhood grew the more he thought of it, but he must tread with care. He sent a note to Sergio, the sibling next to him, to sound the way. "We would stay but a few days," he wrote. Sergio would feel the way for Leon. He had not joined his three brothers in apostasy from their religion. Neutral, and he showed no antagonism toward his three 'apostate' brothers. He could safely navigate.

Sergio's "All Clear," reply buoyed Leon's spirits. Sergio had also spoken for a house with nominal rent. "This is where we reap the blessings of having few belongings," said Maria. "We'll take a bus. The travel would be fun and educational for the children," Leon whispered. Maria, too, looked forward to this trip. She had wished to meet the rest of Leon's family all these years, especially Manuela. And the time had come.

They arrived in Sarrat in mid-May. Manuela, the youngest girl in the family, met them with open arms. She embraced Maria and the children. If she felt apprehensive over Leon wearing a mask, she did not let on. They fell in each other's arms in a brotherly-sisterly hug. "You look good, *Manong,*" Manuela said. *Manong Sergio had done a good job*, she thought.

In time, Maria got the family settled in their small rented house in Sarrat. Leon had his own room. Having gained weight and stamina, he took the time visiting the places where he once roamed as a growing boy.

Alvaro and his family arrived next. They had taken a bus from Bacarra, where they had stopped to visit with his wife's folk. Alvaro shed tears as he embraced his older brother. He felt deep sorrow for him but did not let on. His wife Maxima (Memang) also gave Leon a hug. "David is now a year old," she said, gesturing at her son in his father's arms. "We're hoping for a girl," Alvaro said. Leon nodded, seeing the too obvious confirmation of his younger brother's hoping-for-a-girl.

Just then Maria came with Turing in her arms. She and Memang hugged as far as their babies allowed. "You look good, and about to pop," Maria said laughing. "Very soon," Memang admitted, also with a chuckle. "I have five now," said Maria. "Turing is our fifth and probably the last. I think Turing is five months younger than David," Maria added.

The two brothers—Leon and Alvaro—watched their wives with admiration. "They can pass for blood sisters," said Alvaro. "Memang's fair complexion disproves the generalization that all Ilokanos are dark in complexion. She's only five years younger than *Manang* Maria. Memang converted to the Adventist faith on the strength of the Sabbath, like you, *Manong*." Leon nodded, his eyes sparkled. "Having been a Bible woman for the Methodist church before her conversion, she studied the Bible with purpose," Alvaro said. He saw his older brother's eyes fixed on their wives, and Alvaro took the hint. "*Manong,* let's eavesdrop," he verbalized.

"When David was born," Memang was saying, "I quit my job. "With another on the way, I'll be homebound for a while," she laughed. Maria laughed along. "Good" she said. "Join the club, you could win yet."

Manuela and Tony arrived. As Tony hugged his oldest brother, his eyes misted. Patting him on the arm, "*Manong,* you look good," he said. "Your mask cannot hide your happiness. Oh, it's good to see you all," he said as he gave away hugs. Manuela went to greet Maria and they, too, hugged. *"I really like her,"* Maria mused wishing they had met earlier.

Sergio and his family joined them. Tony made the introductions: *"Manang* Maria," he said, draping his arm over his sister-in-law's shoulder, "meet *Manang* Candida (Dedang). *Manong* Sergio's wife. *Manang* Dedang is a Tagala like you, *Manang,* he added. The two women hit it off from that moment. Dedang put her arm around her daughter, "Fortunata, our oldest." she said. "She's four years old, and now memorizing *Ave Maria.*" The four-year-old curtsied with, *"Mano Po,"* taking the hand of Leon first, she touched her forehead on the back of his hand. She went around to each uncle and aunt for a *Mano Po* greeting of respect.

A photographer arrived and set up his camera equipment. He asked the families to arrange themselves, and immediately began clicking. After taking several group pictures, he asked if he should take more.

"No," Sergio replied, and asked when the proofs would be ready.

"Tomorrow morning," the photographer replied, *"Adios,"* he said after packing his equipment. "I'll see you tomorrow," he told Sergio.

Like iron sheddings to a magnet, Arding, Ely, Fortunata, and Ceding drew together. Arding, the oldest of them all, called, "Let's play catch! I brought a soft ball with me." Only Ely had the dexterity to catch the ball. Ceding and Fortunato contented themselves as spectators of their older cousins playing ball. Arding suggested for them to play dodge ball. "I'll throw the ball, you jump or run out of its way," he explained.

While keeping their peripheral visions on their children at play, the parents updated each other. Alvaro and Memang, Maria, Tony and wife Mameng, indulged in Adventist talk. Leon cleared his throat, addressed his Adventist brothers, and whispered. "The lyric of "Is My Name Written There" moves me so," he said in a whisper. After a pause to catch his breath, he added, "Would one of you sing it at my funeral?" His younger brothers exchanged glances. After a few moments, Tony reached out to pat his oldest brother on the arm, "I will, *Manong*, I promise you," he said.

Sergio, Dedang, and Manuela missed the import of the moment.

As they had agreed upon earlier, each family brought a favorite dish for the family reunion. Manuela spread out a red and white cotton-woven table cloth on the table. "This came from our cotton fields, spinned and woven at home," she stated as a matter-of-fact. Alvaro watched his wife finger the cloth, admiring the print work. "It's yours, *Manang* Memang," Manuela said. Alvaro whispered something to his wife who gave a nod.

"*Manang* Maria, I saw you looking at it longingly, take it," Alvaro said.

With a chuckle Maria countered, "I saw Memang's face light up when Manuela said, 'It's yours' to Memang. It's hers. Barong, please no arguing!"

Manuela smiled, she said, "*Manong* Barong, please don't reject my gift to *Manang* Memang. I have another one for *Manang* Maria. Don't think I haven't planned on this," she said. "This is the only time we may meet… and I want my sister-in-laws to take home something to remember me by."

Alvaro beamed with relief. He began arranging the few hands of ripe *lacatan* and lanzones clusters on a large woven bamboo basket. "We stopped by a fruit stand on the way," he said, "even if *Memang*'s folk had packed a basket of food for us." He continued putting food on the table from the basket: *bangus escabeche* (sweet and sour fresh water fish), roasted peanuts, boiled sweet potatoes, ripe zapote. "We harvested from my sister's tree," Memang said. She noted Leon's longing look at the fruits.

"Leon could eat a dozen *zapote* at one sitting," Maria said with a chuckle, "if you let him." They saw Leon nod in agreement.

Sergio's family and Manuela brought food they prepared together: Boiled lobsters, chicken *adobo*, *okoy* with shrimp topping, and a large kettle of boiled aromatic polished rice. Manuela had invited Sergio and Tony and their families in her home. Manuela granted Tony's request for him and his wife Mameng to cook several choice dishes: *dinengdeng* (mung beans with sweet potato greens seasoned with fresh ginger) and *dilis.* (fish); *ampalaya* fruit rings sauteed with garlic and onions scrambled with eggs. Mameng thought of *kalamansiade* for drink, and prepared a large jug of it.

Maria brought out her platter of salad: center mound of yellow cherry tomatoes surrounded by red globe radishes sculptured to resemble rosebuds, decked with green pepper rings, cucumber rounds alternated with carrot coins for edging. "With five children and," she briefly sidelong glanced at her husband, "I'm sorry, this is all I could do," she said.

Manang, how artistic!" exclaimed Memang. "You have nothing to apologize for a healthful dish of fresh vegetables like this," she added.

"A feast," Leon whispered, eyes beaming. With his eyes, he signed Alvaro to say grace.

***

RELATIVITY

Morning and evening.
Sleeping, awak'ning
Talking, listening.

Sun, moon, twinkling stars
Daylight and darkness
Planting, harvesting.

Sunshine and the rain
Joy, sorrow, and pain,
Profit, loss, and gain.

Health and happiness
Gratitude, kindness
Contentment, gladness.

Quietness, loud noise
Shouts, a gentle voice
Hatred, war, peace, choice,

Giving, receiving,
Loving and living
Singing, worshipping.

Whimsy, reality
Faith, hope, charity,
Time   eternity.

Cry ***

Chapter XIX

ACCORDING TO THY LOVING KINDNESS

1925, Pasay. Now, well adjusted to their new home, Leon found it easy to get back to work at a lesser pace. He wrote truth-filled articles, submitting them to Philippine Publishing House for publication. He also continued translating in Ilokano and Tagalog chosen writings of Ellen G. White. The pleasure he derived from his work renewed his mind, body, and spirit. Aware of the spiritual awakening sweeping throughout his homeland, he felt compelled to do all he could with the stamina and time he had on hand. Unwittingly, he resumed to pushing himself unrelentingly.

During the allocated times for his children, he always covered his mouth and nose with a clean cotton cloth. Unable to tell them stories as he once had, they created other ways to make quality time together. He felt strongly that he must make up not only for lost time but also to fill in for the future. So, at worship time, despite his inability to use his vocal chords, he took his usual place in the family circle. Arding and Ely took turns in reading the Morning Watch. On occasion, Ceding read the shorter verses. Led by their mother, they took turns praying during their family worships. The evening worship became a special event for them. In a more relaxed mood, everyone capable took part in discussing the Sabbath School lesson, then they recounted the happenings of the day. Leon thoroughly enjoyed these moments, he looked forward to this family vespers. His heart sang in witnessing the loving relationship of his children one with another.

"Our home is a little heaven on earth," he'd say in whispers. "You, my precious children, are my heritage from the Lord, my priceless gifts and reward. In your pliable years, you have learned to love God, your parents, and each other. Praise the Lord!" he wrote for them to read.

After the children left for school, LZR turned to his writing and translating. Maria, with household chores, in addition to caring for the younger children, had her hands full, yet her ears were ever tuned to her husband's needs. Her silent prayers for him ascended to heaven without ceasing. Fully aware of her husband's sense of fulfillment in keeping busy, she inspired him in his pursuits. In her own quiet way, Maria worked along to advance his goal as a timely instrument in the hands of God.

October. "*Mahal*," he whispered. "would you tell the children to come and kiss me goodnight?" That evening began a bedtime ritual for father and children. He waited with eagerness for his children to come to his room. Maria always placed a clean cloth—often a white handkerchief—to cover his mouth and nose. Tiptoeing quietly to their father's room, the children took their turn—one by one—usually from the oldest to the youngest, and the other way 'round at times. The older ones often lingered to talk and give their father a report on their day at school or at play.

November 22, 1925. Maria held two-year-old Arturo by the hand for his goodnight kiss on his father's cheek. Innocent eyes locked with his father's, as if eager to know his Papa better and to fix him in his memory. "You'll be the medical doctor in the family, Turing," his father said in a whisper, giving him a light pat on his head. The little boy's body language clearly showed his intent to stay longer by his Papa's bedside, but his mother led him on. "Until tomorrow," she said softly, a smile on her lips and in her voice. Reluctantly, Turing waved goodbye to his father.

Alfonso sidled by his father's bed. Suddenly, Leon could not vocalize the thoughts on his mind: *My Christmas baby born about five years ago.* Father and son's eyes met and locked as Ponsing stood transfixed, aware that his father was deep in thought. Ponsing appeared to read his father's unspoken words. "*Papang,* I tried to be a good boy today," he said. I played with Turing nicely…" Standing with his full height, he declared, "When I grow up, I'll be like you, *Papang,* I'll be a minister." He stood tall to kiss his father's cheeks and saw the sparkle in his father's eyes wet with tears. The smile wrinkles around his sunken eyes deepened. "You will be a leader, but a teacher first, my Son," he said in whispers as he placed his right hand lightly on Ponsing's head. "You will lead many of our youth to the Master Teacher." Ponsing listened intently, clinging to his every word. "Goodnight, *Papang,*" he bade. "*Minamahal kita.*" Seeing his father nod, he stepped back, not taking his eyes from his father's sunken ones. "I'll see you tomorrow, *Papang,*" he said, waving a hand tentatively for a goodbye.

"*Papang,* it's me," Mercedes said. She kissed her father on the cheeks. "Ceding, *Anak,* a school teacher you will be, leading little children to the Lord," he whispered, reaching out to pat his daughter on the head. "When I grow up, *Papang,* I will," Ceding said. *Minamahal kita, Papang.*" His eyes smiled to hear her words. He nodded to show his wholehearted approval, and in his thoughts, *The very best teacher, my child, you will be.*

Eight-year-old Elizabeth, who earlier often asked, *Why is Papang away all the time?* bent to hug her father. She kissed him on both cheeks. He held her tightly with all his strength. Responding to her father's hug, Ely said, "*Papang,* don't worry. When I grow up, I'll be a nurse, I will help you get well. *Minamahal kita, Papang,*" she added, tears in her voice. "A good nurse you will be, my princess," he said, "helping your younger siblings." Ely nodded. "I'll see you tomorrow," she said, stepping back from his side.

Eduardo held his father's hand and said, "*Papang,* you are not as strong as you used to be." Arding embraced his father, he kissed his bony cheeks. "You are a bright boy, mature for your not quite ten years of age," his father whispered. "You are the son of my youth, my first pride and joy, your mother's right hand," he said, tears in his voice. "Your mother will lean much on your strength and keen mind," he added in whispers. "I help *Mamang* all I can, I always will," Arding replied. "Goodnight, *Papang, Minamahal kita*. We will come to see you again tomorrow."

This has been the most touching scene ever since we began the ritual, Maria thought. Unwilling for it to end, wanting to immortalize the tender moments, nonetheless, she said. "That's enough for tonight, children." And she guided them out of their father's presence, wishing she had a camera. Glancing back, she said, "Try to rest now. I'll see the younger children to bed. They'll see you again tomorrow." She forced cheer in her voice and a smile on her face. "I'll return to check on you later, *Mahal*," she said.

The tired yet happy man closed his eyes. His thoughts lifted up, heart turned heavenward, he began to pray silently: *Father, I thank Thee for my wonderful wife. My gentle, wonderful companion who stands by me in health and in sickness. A nurturing mother to my children.* He marveled at how much she had matured since they first met some twelve years ago. *I thank Thee, Lord, for Maria—a true virtuous woman—my gift from Thee.*

He allowed his mind to return to the time when, upon returning to school following a day's hospital stay, his new friend Bib invited him to visit his home, then offered a room with him. *Lord, I see Thy hand leading me in all these. I thank Thee for calling us to bring our cares and wants to Thee, for not getting wearied in listening to our many wants. Lord, I do want healing, Please give me faith even as small as a mustard seed to move this mountain of illness out of my life. I thank Thee for Thy love and grace Thou has imparted in my heart that I may be precious in Thy sight. Yet as Jesus submitted to God's will even on the cross, I, too, submit to Thy will.* An involuntary sigh escaped in his effort to draw a deep breath. *To Thy loving hands I commit my life and my family.*

Upon Maria's return to check on her husband, she found him asleep.

She and her children, too, need rest and sleep. In the morning, her heart sang to see her older children carrying out their duties. Ely had helped her younger siblings dress for the day, and then got the breakfast table ready. Arding had boiled the peanuts in their shell, had prepared the scrambled eggs, and placed the food in separate serving bowls. She watched as Ely supervised her younger siblings wash their hands. With everyone seated around the table in their proper places, Arding said, "Ponsing to say grace." They clasped their hands together, bowed their heads and closed their eyes.

"Dear Jesus, I thank Thee for our food. Bless it to make us healthy and bless us, too, especially Papang for him to get well soon. Amen." Ponsing enunciated each word with care.

Arding stood up to help his younger siblings. He helped Ponsing fill his plate with food from the serving bowls. Ely helped Ceding fill her plate as their mother attended to the needs of Turing. And after filling up a plate for her husband, she said, "Children, you eat now. I'll take food to your father. I'll be back as soon as I can."

"*Mamang*," Arding said, "Tell *Papang* good morning, tell him we love him very much."

"We will all be good for *Papang* to get well soon," Ceding chirped.

"Your Papa will be happy to get your loving messages," she said, and picked up her husband's plate of food and fruits with both hands.

When Maria came to her husband, she found him gasping for breath. She took his hands and felt his pulse erratic and weak.

"Our children send their love to you," she said softly.

Between gasps, he whispered, "Maria, *Mahal kita.* Tell our children, I love them all. I leave you all in the hands of our loving Father in heaven." He tried to draw a deep breath. "Be sure each of our children gets a Christian education. Take good care of yourself." Again, he tried to draw a deep breath. "Remind Tony to sing, 'Is My Name Written There?' for me. After pausing to take a deep breath, he added in a gaspy whisper, "He promised me he would. I'll meet you all in the earth made new."

Maria detected a trace of smile in his sunken eyes. She saw peace in them. His eyelids flickered, then slowly closed. Maria prayed as she held his hands, she saw him breathe his last.

Although Maria had prepared her mind for this inevitable to come any time, she suddenly felt alone. Relieved her husband no longer suffered, nevertheless, she felt the pang of emptiness begin to gnaw. Yet a source of strength surged within her. She was calm as she walked out to tell her children. "You must not cry," she said. "Your Papa is now asleep in Jesus. Arding, *Anak,* please run to Mr. and Mrs. Villanueva. Tell them about your Papa. They will know what to do."

"Yes, *Mamang.* "

"Ely, I'll leave Ceding, Ponsing, and Turing with you. Finish your breakfast, then clean up."

Ceding said, "I'll help wash the dishes."

The children did as their mother bade them. Their father had prepared them well for this eventuality, he had often told them he always prayed for them in his private devotions. They remembered how he had prayed during their family worship. He always told them that the Lord would bless them if they chose to obey Him. That He would be their Father no matter what, and their Father in heaven would listen to their every prayer, if they prayed believing and prayed in faith in Jesus' name.

They had felt the nearness of God Who became real to them in their daily relationship with their *Papang*, and the love between their parents. Their *Papang* made them accept death to be as temporary as life. They had repeated the promise in John 14:1–3 from memory. That everyone who believed in God and put Him first in their lives will be with Jesus.

***

LIFE'S CLOCK

The clock of life is wound but once. And no man has the power
To tell where the hands would stop—At late or early hour.

(Author unknown.)

IS MY NAME WRITTEN THERE?

1. *Lord, I care not for riches, neither silver nor gold—*
   I would make sure of heaven, I would enter the fold.
   In the book of Thy Kingdom with its pages so fair,
   Tell me, Jesus, my Savior, Is my name written there?

Chorus: *Is my name written there—on the page white and fair? In the* book of Thy kingdom, is my name written there?   **(for 1, 2)**

2. *Lord, my sins they are many, like the sands of the sea,*
   But Thy blood, O my Savior, is sufficient for me;
   For Thy promise is written in bright letters that glow,
   "Though your sins be as scarlet, I will make them like snow."

3. *O that beautiful city with its mansions of light,*
   With its glorified beings in pure garments of white;
   Where no evil thing cometh to despoil what is fair,
   Where the angels are watching, yes, my name's written there.

Chorus: *Yes, my name's written there, On the page white and fair; In* the book of Thy kingdom, Yes, my name's written there.

Chapter XX

<u>HIS</u> COMMANDMENT IS LIFE EVERLASTING

(John 12:50)

In cleaning her late husband's room (gathering and separating items to put in **Keep** or **Discard** boxes) Maria found an undated letter in his own handwriting. Each stroke evinced his weakened condition, yet it was very legible. She sat down to read, her eyes welling:

My Dearest Beloved Ones:

First, I must thank you, Mahal, for your love through health and sickness, and for the companionship you are to me. I'd been absent from you more than I was bodily present, but my thoughts had often been with you. You understood. Not a murmur of complaint escaped your lips Oh, how much I thank the Lord for you, Aking Mahal. The many blessings, bumps, bruises we'd shared along the way drew us closer to each other. That the Lord made us for each other is beyond refute in my mind. When you read this, I'll probably be gone from this life. Take comfort, Mahal. I can say, we'll meet again on the resurrection day. Our God of love will carry you through many toilsome years. I have faith our children will bring you pride and joy. They are our jewels, gifts from the Lord. Join me in re-dedicating their lives to God, for them to give themselves to serve Him even in their youth. May they always bring you comfort.

And now, My Dear Children: I want you to remember that in the many long days that I'd been away, you've been in my thoughts and in my prayers. When I came home, you knew I was tired and you gave me time to rest. I know you yearned to be near me as much as I longed to be with you. Seeing you growing up in favor with God and men, as did Jesus as a growing child, fills me with awe, that God answers my prayers for you. In our daily morning worship, I always asked the Lord to keep you safe that day. He held you in the hollow of His Omnipotent hands. He always will, if you ask Him.

Arding, it comforts me to see you mature beyond your years— your Mama's ever-willing right hand and strength. As you grow older, you would take more responsibility at home and in the community. I'm proud of you, Son. Let the Lord be your Guide, you can trust Him.

My Darling Daughter Ely: I'm very much aware that you wished your Papa to cuddle you, to tell you the stories you so love to hear. To see you understand why I must be away from you often—you said "because Jesus has work for you to do"—makes me happy, yet sad because I'm too busy for you.

Now blinded by her tears, Maria could not read any further, and sobs rocked her. She took another clean handkerchief to wipe her tears. Drying the tears lifted the weight from her heart. For while taking care of her children and her husband, she had put on a brave front, and shed no tears.

"I'll miss your moral and spiritual support, Leon," she sobbed as though he were there, listening. "You were too young to die, yet I thank the Lord you no longer suffer, safe at last in His keeping until the resurrection day. Yes, *Mahal,* I'll meet you again in the earth made new."

I thought he was writing only for publication, and translating, she mused. She wondered how long it had taken him to write the letter. She gripped the letter harder as she read the next line:

It made me so proud of you, my little princess, to know you wanted to be a nurse so you could help me get well. The Lord said, 'Inasmuch as ye have done it unto one of the least of these... ye have done it unto Me.' I see you as a kind, loving nurse in the Lord's hands, giving healing balm. By your tender caring hands, the suffering will feel the touch of the Healer divine. Looking ahead, I see many stars brightening your crown because of your sympathetic caring, helping allay pain, assisting the sick regain their health.

My Little Sweetheart, Ceding: You filled my heart with joy and happiness when you whispered, "I'll be a teacher...." The best teacher you could ever be, my child. In my mind's eye, I see you a slim young teacher in a classroom full of impressionable children eager to learn. You will, in addition to the 3 R's teach the children about Jesus, who loves all the little children. Bright stars will shine on your crown for leading many to Jesus.

My dear Son, Ponsing: How awesome tt was for me to hear you say you'd like to be a minister like your Papa. Yes, a minister, Son, is first a teacher: teaching others of God's love, how to serve Him, and how to love each other as Jesus loved. Teaching people how to improve their minds, the only avenue through which the Lord could reach fallen man. A heavy load you will carry on your shoulders. Learn to lean on the Lord for strength to carry on. He'll give you the courage to equal the load you bear, go to Him for strength. Stars on your crown will shine for leading many to the Master Teacher.

Ponsing, keep your eyes fixed upon Jesus, Son. Don't give the enemy any space in your life. God is our present help in time of trouble.

My Dear Baby, Turing: Oh, how much I long to carry you in my arms, to hold you, close, my little one. In my dreams, I see you as a doctor, helping heal the sick and the injured, helping them boost their body defenses to ward off illness. Like the great Physician, Son, you'll be kind and loving.

I love you all dearly. Till we meet at Jesus' feet.

Lovingly (signed) *Your Papa*

***

Now Maria came face to face with her status: A thirty-year-old widow with a sixty-peso pension, who must raise her children ranging from two years of age to ten. Alone. Her growing children needed clothes, food, and must go to school. Married in her late teens, she had devoted her life to nurturing her family (she was efficient and happy in that role) but she had no marketable skills. Yes, she realized, Leon was sickness-retired from the pulpit years earlier, but his pen rolled out truth-filled materials that the Philippine Publishing House published. That brought a steady income. And he was **present** for her and the children. Bereft of her husband, his financial and moral support, she must make decisions on pressing issues.

Healing Words and Actions. Maria opened the envelope. She sat down to read the letter dated December 18, 1925:

Dearest Sis, and Children,

My heart aches for you and the children, and for myself. You know how much I thought of Leon—my chum, my brother-in-law, the father of my nephews and nieces. I grieve with you. How can life be so cruel! So my chum breathed his last on November 23, at about 8 a.m. and was buried on the 25th. That's exactly on Arding's tenth birthday!

Glad to know you *received my letter with the check I sent for Arding's birthday. The enclosed personal check is your Christmas gift—one fourth for Arding.*

(For Arding: Add your share of my gift to your bank account toward your college education, or spend it however you wish. Your parents praised you for not being a spendthrift—I appreciate that!).

I do regret my inability to be with you in your, that is, our bereavement. My new responsibilities forbid me from getting away. I promise to answer faithfully all of your letters.

Merry Christmas and a Happy New Year! Much love to you all,

Lovingly always,
(signed) Bib

***

As she refolded the letter, Maria breathed a prayer for her brother. Although his letters had been coming less regularly and he has not as yet given any inkling about his current real life, she and her children never stopped praying for him. *Ever since Arding was a baby, Kuya had been open about his partiality to Arding over his siblings,* she thought. And it hit her. *Arding will have to write his uncle.* The thought settled her mind.

The transfer of Philippine Adventist Academy to Baesa was moving fast. Maria agonized over having to make the decision. Her late husband had always made decisions on matters as this. That was before he died. Should she uproot her family from Pasay to Baesa, where her children could get the Christian education she promised their father? Where would she get the money? How would she go about getting a place for her family to stay in Baesa? Would her house sell? Would there be property she could afford within walking distance of the school?

Lord, I turn to Thee for these demands in my life, her heart cried out. Almost at once, *"In all thy ways acknowledge Him, and He shall direct thy paths* (Prov. 3:16) came to her mind. *I thank Thee, Lord,* she breathed, and promptly claimed the promise, literally. Again, she sensed welling in her the same unbending faith her husband had to God and His faithfulness to His promises. *God will direct our lives,* she affirmed herself.

Late 1930. "Let's go, *Mamang*," Arding urged. "Let's move to Baesa."

True to His promise, someone was ready to take her Pasay property. And she heard there was a newly built two-story three bedroom house with a full basement, within walking distance of the academy, with a **for sale** sign at the front yard. She went to see it: An efficiency kitchen, a pantry, a dining room, three bedrooms, and a den. Only a few major finishing touches remained to get the house completed. And the price was about the same she was selling her property in Pasay. "God fulfilled His promise to us," she told her children. "Praise the Lord!"

Arding proved to be a great help in their move to Baesa, a safe place to be. The community welcomed Maria and her children with open arms.

Settled at last. With the children enrolled in school, the young widow began to find ways to supplement her sixty-peso pension. During the day, she sewed dresses for the missionaries living in campus, for a small wage. Later, she found out—with the children safe at home, Arding in charge—she could go out colporteuring in the evenings. And she did, specializing in The Signs of the Times. With money to spare only for their pressing needs, she sewed the pants, shirts, and underwears for her boys, dresses and other things for her girls and for herself. The whole family wore her home made originals. Her skill spoke well in her becomingly dressed children.

Maria and her children worked hard from morning 'til night, Sunday to Friday, and they eagerly welcomed the Sabbath. A day of rest, Maria and her children appropriated an hour more or less for siesta, which they could ill afford during the week. The siesta proved rejuvenating to them.

Sabbath. A day to contemplate on the many blessings they received sometimes in disguise, that came with unexpected bonuses. *Our move to Baesa, for example*, Maria thought. *The children walk to school and to work in the school grounds. The children are safe, and safer yet from worldly influences. All their classmates come from good Christian homes.* Maria praised the Lord for His leading. Because of the school, her friends with their families, as well as a few relatives, also lived close by. Blessings....?

And some of them often made Maria realize that she was too young to live alone. "What will your life be when your children are all grown and on their own?" they asked her. And some of them went as far as to suggest a well meant match, taking the Biblical duty of a brother to his deceased brother's wife. "What does a few years your junior matter?" A few asked, trying to make her see what she refused to acknowledge.

Maria repeatedly dismissed her friends' insinuation of Tony. "I'm happy and too busy to consider possibilities such as you suggest," she'd say. "Furthermore, the biblical duty of a brother to his widowed sister-in-law refers to a childless situation. My children will always be my children. I live in the love of God and the priceless memories of Leon."

Times came when Maria ran out of cash, regardless of how hard she worked and how much she tried to stretch her budget. Skimping on food for her growing children was unthinkable. Her friend from early youth, Pilar Espino, who became Mrs. Balayo, operated the *sari-sari* (variety store) next door. To these kindhearted store owners, Maria ran when she was short of money and she needed food for her children. The store owners trusted Maria to pay them when her pension money came. Pilar made Maria feel comfortable, she understood Maria's circumstances.

Maria's fast maturing children rallied to their family situation. Of grade school age, they behaved themselves well, helped their mother in many creative ways. Eduardo developed a division of labor schedule and his younger siblings cooperated: Ely, Ceding—clean the house, cook, wash the dishes, wash and iron clothes for the whole family. Ely to care for Turing (until he is capable of caring for himself). Arding, Ponsing—fetch water from the pump well outside, and carry in firewood for cooking. Work outside for pay, and give earnings to mother to add to the family budget.

Infrequently, there were occasions when Maria wished Leon were with them, especially for her growing-up boys. Her reflections came to the time when Arding began asserting himself generally in positive ways. She wondered if Arding had been deprived of his boyhood. Then an incident popped in her mind, of Arding as a boy.

It centered on the tamarind tree at Pasay Academy. Its branches towered up, high to the sky. Climbing the tamarind tree had become a favorite pastime for the boys in school. When the fruits begin to ripen, the boys would climb the tree, teetering far out on its boughs to reach for ripening fruits. Arding liked them when the pulp turned yellow, the mouth-watering ripe-stage, according to him. The school rule: Climb the tree only in the afternoon after school. Arding always cooperated.

One day, while Arding was teetering way up on a tree limb, a boy older than he, who had challenged him too often, began taunting. "Oh, you slow poke, you can't even climb high enough to pick any. Show me if you can. Drop a ripe tamarind if you find any," he challenged. This time Arding thought of giving the upstart a warm surprise. Precise shot! His target sent a piercing howl. And quickly, the whippersnapper started to climb, threatening. "Stinker you, for the shower you gave me, I'll get you."

Arding, not wanting to fight and hoping to outsmart the angry boy, started descending fast, and dropped down with a thud on his knees and hands. He got up and began running at breakneck speed to get home to safety. He passed by his mother, who was hanging clothes on the line. Without saying a word to her, he shot into the house banging the door shut.

A few minutes later, Maria followed Arding, and found him rinsing his bruised knees. At her prodding, Arding confessed what had happened.

"Oh, Arding," she said laughing. "You did it again." She handed him a bottle of iodine. "Apply this on your clean wound," she said. "Ouch!" he

Elizabeth Roda, R.N. "I'll help you get well, *Papang*. I'll be a loving nurse when I grow up," eight-year-old Ely said. Elizabeth's graduation, in cap and white uniform.

Mother Maria and Alfonso stand behind the tomb of husband and father, Leon Z. Roda.

Pre-World War II, l-r: seated: Elizabeth (Ely), mother Maria, and Mercedes (Cheding). Back row: Arturo (Turing), Eduardo (Arding) and Alfonso (Ponsing).

cried out after the first dab, but he knew the sting would not last. He covered the bruises with iodine to prevent infection. That done, he asked, "*Mamang,* what do you mean by 'you did it again'—I never did that before to anyone…"

"Of course, you were too young to remember," his mother replied with a chuckle. "You were barely a year old when your Papa was changing you. I heard him boom, 'Hey, a geyser!' I saw him duck on time to miss getting hit. You shoot out a stream before your Papa could put the diaper on you," she said with a laugh. She reached to ruffle his hair. Arding only smiled.

The deputy-man-of-the-house, Arding carried his responsibility with aplomb. He became his mother's right hand and a strong shoulder for her to lean on. For this blessing, Maria thanked the Lord over and over again.

HAPPINESS

Happiness and misery are in the mind
  Like gold and ore in the rock are mined:
  We can either be happy or sad,
Depressed, dejected, or cheery and glad.

It all depends upon our attitude,
  Thankfulness or full of gratitude.
  Like a trickle of water makes a ripple,
It can be rough or it can be gentle.

Think of happiness and you'll be happy,
  Think of gloom and you'll be gloomy;
  "As a man thinketh in his heart, so is he."
We can be happy or dwell in misery.

Life is what we make it—mournful or cheerful;   Stay on the sunny side and be joyful.
  Life is short, like the sweetness of a rose—
Enjoy it to the full—happiness is close.

Happiness and misery are in the mind,
  Dig in the ore—gold that's yours and mine.   Think of joy, wonderful joy and gladness,
And wear the golden crown of happiness.

                    by Jose Valdez, Jr.
                    from his book Golden Treasures

***

Chapter XXI

PURPOSE

Trust in the Lord …. (Psalms 37:3)

1940. To his contemporaries, Eduardo was walking encyclopedia as his father was Bible concordance to his colleagues. Aware his parents had dedicated him to the Lord in his infancy, Arding sought ways to serve the Lord. Even now as a school teacher, he longed to know more about the intricacies of Law. As early as he could recall, he had been his mother's counselor on legal matters: in business, finances, mortgages, etc. requiring knowledge of the law. As a boy, he recalled seeing his father referring to the books his uncle Bib had left with him, which his parents said were his. And what he read in the books appealed to him. His mind absorbed the theories of law, awakening in him a desire to know more of this profession.

For required continuing education (CE) he took law courses in Manila. To his knowledge, there were no Seventh-day Adventist lawyers. He began to entertain the thought that the Church needed workers knowledge-able in matters of the law. He settled in his mind to seek the Lord's leading and His will on this desire—for him to fill this need.

The future continued to grow bright for Maria and her children. Her 20-peso sustentation pension increase came at the right time to meet the money demands of her family. She counted other overwhelming evidences proving that God honors His promises to those who put their trust in Him:

Her cousin Teodora (Doray) practically financed Ely in her nurse's training, and Elizabeth received her degree with the first graduating class of Manila Sanitarium & Hospital. With her nurse's license and registra-tion, Elizabeth was part of the nucleus that formed the Adventist Church's medical outreach. She was paying Arturo's school bill with commitment to finance his way through medical school.

Mercedes was now a well-loved elementary school teacher. After Alfonso completed an Associate Degree in Commercial Science, Philip-pine Union Mission employed him as a clerk typist.

Maria lifted her heart in gratitude for God's leadings. How she wished she could share these blessings with Leon. She resolved that no matter what the years of uncertainty may bring, she would anchor her faith in the Lord, who proved trustworthy over and over again.

WORLD WAR II. The rumblings of war came just when life was picking up for the family. On December 7, 1941, Japan bombed Pearl Harbor, the U.S. Naval base in Hawaii. The attack came ten hours after

Japan sent its 14-part message to America. President Roosevelt received the decoded message seven hours later. Only moments later, Japanese bombers clouded Philippine skies. The tranquil island of Luzon became a battleground.

Schools closed. Business came to a stop. The Allied Forces sprang to life. The Cavaliers, the Infantry, the Air forces moved with one purpose: to meet the enemies head-on. Able-bodied non-military citizens joined the army of national guards. The deception, nonetheless, gave the deceiver an edge so that after but a few months of resistance, the Philippines fell into Japanese hands. The Philippine flag furled and in its place the flag of the rising sun waved in the Philippine skies.

War, no respecter of persons, brings out the worse in people.

And it trampled down the future of promising Philippine young men and women, including that of Eduardo. The fatherless family were among the community seeking safety from the well-rumored ruthless torturings of the Japanese soldiers in uniform.

Maria and her children evacuated to the town of Binan (pronounced Binyan) in the province of Laguna. Even there, the claws of war reached out to grab the citizen's peace and safety. In their military excursions, uniformed soldiers of the reigning monarch claimed the produce in the gardens the evacuees planted, before they could benefit from their own labors. These were tense moments, having to be on guard for dear life. One must be ever alert for fight or flight any time.

Deprived of nourishing food, rest, and stressed beyond his physical endurance, Arding's immune system gradually weakened. Once subdued by his strong body resistance, the opportunistic tubercle bacilli staged another war in the body of Arding. Tuberculosis infection.

Maria tried her best to nurse her son back to health, but limited by the poor conditions of war, Arding's life ended on January 26, 1945. A grave in Binan accepted the lifeless body of the walking encyclopedia.

Again, Maria stood bereft of a strong shoulder to lean on. A nag bored through her consciousness. *I haven't heard from Kuya Bib. Could it be, with normal business at a standstill, overseas communication was at a halt? Her agony included a question: Is Kuya Bib dead?*

Steeling herself just as she had done in the past, by God's grace, Maria reminded herself that death from this life was but a sleep until the resurrection day. God was still in control. Life must go on. The Filipinos put their trust on General MacArthur's promise to return. His return would lift the oppressions of World War II.

My Jesus, too, promised to return, to put an end to wars. Even the war between powers and principalities on planet earth. Though I walk through the valley of death, I will fear no evil for Thou art with me, Maria prayed.

***

Maria lived to see not only her children reach the pinnacle of success, so to speak, but lived long enough to see her grandchildren. She lived to see her son, Alfonso, elected in successive terms to the presidency of Philippine Union College. She rejoiced to see the fulfillment of her dream, to prove over and over again that she had put her trust in a loving God. She exulted to see the phenomenal growth of the Adventist Church, the faith she and her late husband LZR loved.

Death claimed Maria on June 5, 1975, at Manila Sanitarium & Hospital, three months short of her 80th birthday. She died of heart failure. but her mind remained keen and intact. Her body awaits the Lord's return at the Eternal Gardens in Baesa, Caloocan City, Rizal.

Family photo taken 6–68. Seated, mother Maria. Standing, l-r: Elizabeth, Alfonso, Arturo, Mercedes.

The Walter Roeder family, l-r: Mary Anne, Mom Elizabeth, Dad Walter*, Helen Beth. *Read Walter Roeder's part in the winning of World War II, <u>The Reader's Digest</u>, March, 1992, feature book condensation.

The late Leon Z. Roda and Maria P. Roda family, from 1st to 3rd generations: Front l-r, first row—Helen Beth Roeder, Anne Arevalo, Reginald (Bong) Roda, Carol Pilar Roda, Mary Anne Roeder. 2nd row l-r, Lydia T. Roda, Elizabeth R. Roeder, Maria vda de Roda, Mercedes R Arevalo, Tomasita P. Roda (wife of Arturo), Teresa Arevalo Torres, 3rd row, l-r, standing: Ferdinand (Andy) Alfonso P. Roda, Walter Roeder, Eliseo R. Arevalo, Jr., Eliseo Arevalo, Sr., Arturo P. Roda, Romeo Torres; last row, l-r: Mario P. Roda, Chito P. Roda, Fe Arevalo Poblete, Emmeline A. Corros, Cora Arevalo Coo, Sylvia Arevalo Ramirez.

HE HAS NOT FORGOTTEN

Are you passing through life's rugged roads,
  are your eyes bedimmed with tears?
Do you moan and ask the reason, why it seems God never
  hears?
Why is it that there's no answer to the prayers you offered
  Him,
Why the heavens show no rainbow and the skies with clouds
  are dim?

Do you wonder, ever wonder, if God really understands?
Why it seems that He ignores you and you cannot feel His
  hand?
Do black doubts confuse, assail you, you give in to cruel hate,
Take heart, friend, He still is leading, His great clock is never
  late.

When God tests, He has a purpose, some day the light you'll
  see.
For He wants that you will trust Him, if from dross you would
  be free.
If life's doubts and tears beset you, just remember He is near,
He will ever, ever love you. He will always, always hear.

  When at last these things are over, dear, dear heart you'll
    understand,
  Why for others you did suffer, why you did not feel His hand.
  Why you thought He had forgotten, when it seemed your
    dreams were vain,
  Times when others did the wrong things, and on you, they laid
    the blame.

*Our ways are not always His ways, so till then keep trusting
  Him,*
*Through the sunshine and the shadow, through life's thick and
  through its thin,*
*In due time you'll reap full harvest. These, dear heart, are for
  your sake.*
Bear in mind His clock keeps moving, it is never, never late.
by Jedd A. Pastor-Villanueva
  (first published in the 60's,
  The College Voice

***

GLOSSARY

Listing of Tagalog terms, unless otherwise specified. Tagalog is the Philippine National Language (*Pilipino Wikang Pambansa*).

adobo	a dish, a recipe usually of chicken or other meat, prepared with garlic, onions, soy sauce and vinegar. (For vegetarian dish, use *kalamansi* —calamondin—or lemon juice in place of vinegar.) Care to try the dish as in okra *adobo*? The recipe follows:

20 young okra, 4 TBS kalamansi juice, ½ cup finely chopped *gluten, oil, 3 TBS soy sauce, (try Bragg aminos) garlic, onions and salt to suit your taste. 1 tsp MSG (optional). Wash okra and parboil. Saute *gluten, add garlic, onions, and the parboiled okra. Add kalamansi juice, soy sauce, salt, and MSG. Cover and simmer until okra is tender. *May use tokwa instead.

aking	possessive form for *ako* (me) change o to i and add *ng* as in *aking mahal*, meaning, my love.
alugbati	a succulent green, a vine with a strong flavor, relished cooked vegetable dish by itself or added to other vegetables or legumes.
ampalaya	also called *amargoso*, bitter melon fruits. The tender leaves are used as greens, added to other dishes, as with mung beans.
Anak	Child
balasangko	in Ilokano, literal translation: *balasang*—a young woman. The addition of the possessive suffix *ko* makes an endearing term—daughter mine, not necessarily biological.
bangus	a tasty fresh water fish, commercially raised in fish farms.
bao	halved coconut shell, polished smooth and used as a bowl, dish
barong tagalog	the Filipino dress shirt. Fabric, called *jusi*, is made from pineapple leaves. Fabric is transparent, off-white (but may be dyed in any primary color) with fancy embroidery at the front; pocketless, worn shirttail untucked and without necktie.
bilao	a round shallow, wide bamboo-woven multi-purpose basket.
Binibini	an address for unmarried women, the equivalent of Miss
bogok	(or *sira*) impaired, ruined, spoiled. Often used in context, as in
bogok na	or *sira na* meaning, now hopeless, impaired, useless.

buco, buko	young coconut savored for its soft meat and natural sizzling water content, often referred to as coconut juice/coconut milk.
calesa	a covered horse-drawn open carriage used for transportation.
caretela	a horse-drawn open carriage primarily used for transportation.
casoy	cashew, pear-shaped fruit; the cashew nut, the kernel or seed.
dilis	commercially prepared dried fish consisting of small fry fish.
dinengdeng	an Ilokano dish, cooked mixed vegetable dish.
dippig	Ilokano for the cooking banana, i.e. plantain. *Saba* in Tagalog.
Don	a Spanish-derived term of honor or respect reserved for the learned, rich, wealthy man.
Dona	(pronounced donya) title for a learned, rich, wealthy woman.
garampingat	Ilokano word for a loud, unmannered girl or woman.
Halili	name of a commercial line of public transportation (bus).
Ho	equivalent of Ma'am, or Sir to address a contemporary, or one in authority, or highly educated person or social status. Usually used in place of the person's name. For example, *Magandang tanghali, Ho* (translated, beautiful afternoon, Sir.)
Ilocano, Ilokano	a Filipino tribe originating in northern Luzon; the dialect spoken in northern Luzon.
Inday	an endearing Visayan term for a female friend, relative, or a new acquaintance, used in place of her given name.
Ka	short for *Kuya,* a term of respect for an older brother, a male relative, or any man older than the one speaking. Filipino culture expects a younger person to use a term of respect, by itself or before a person's name (as in *Kuya* Bib) when talking to or referring an older person. See also *Manang, Manong, Tiang, Tiong, Uhtee.*
kababayan	unisex Tagalog word for fellow countrymen, compatriot.
kadua	Ilokano word. Literal translation—companion, partner.
kalachuchi	a flowering tree with fragrant five-petal white flowers ideal for lacing leis.
kalamansi	a citrus tree bearing fruits much smaller than lemon or lime. The fruit itself, or its juice. Calamondin in Florida.
kangkong	an oriental vegetable cooked like most greens, like spinach.

kayumanggi	dark brown complexion. The Filipino complexion.
kundiman	love song. Word derivation *kung hindi man:* were it not so
kuripot	(pronounced coo-REE-put) Ilokano for stingy, tightfisted.
lacatan	*lakatan* an aromatic banana, firm flesh and less slimy than most. Flesh is light orange with a hint of lemon or orange flavor.
liwayay	(pronounced lee-Y-Y, as the alphabet Y is pronounced. In Tagalog, it means dawn. Liwayway is also the name of a popular romance magazine published in Manila.
Lola, Lolo	Grandma, Grandpa.
lomboy	popularly called *dohut* in Tagalog. A tall tree that bears clusters of purple, sweet fruits much like concord grapes, just as juicy, with friable thin skin, it contains one big seed.
lumpia	a Filipino finger food, similar to the Mexican burrito.
macapuno	a tender-meated coconut, its meat filling the entire center.
mahal	love. Add the suffix *ko* (my) —*Mahalko*—it means my love.
mahinhin	unassuming, demur, modest.
malunggay	the tree, its edible leaves that are round in multiple leaflets in twice odd pinnate form, cooked as greens. Prepared (cooked) as in spinach, or used as a mixed vegetable. The nutritious vegetable is distinctly flavorful.
Mamang	Mama, *Papang* Papa. Adding the suffix *ng* shows affection.
Manang	*Manong* in Ilokano, older sister (the letter *a* for female) *Manong*, the letter *o* for male, an older brother. Filipino culture expects that a younger person defer to one older, be they siblings, relatives, or non-relative. When age aspect is clear a younger person uses either term alone, or before the person's name. *Mang* is short for Manang, *Nong* for *Manong*.
Mano Po	literally translated, *mano* (hand)
Po	(ma'am, or sir). In a curtsy, a child greets a respected older relative by taking his hand, and bringing the back of his hand to his (the child's) forehead as in obeisance.
manzanita	literal translation, little apples (manzanas—apple) A tree bearing small sweet syrupy fruits with minute seeds that children and birds love the eat.
minamahal kita	literally means, I love you. The root words are *mahal*. (love) *kita* (I/you). *Mina* is a present progressive tense.

Motorco	a 'topless' double decked commercial public transportation, primarily a joy-ride, cruising the Laguna de Bay highway.
mungo	mung beans
Nana	aunt. It is courteous and respectful to use Nana by itself or before an aunt's name (or for a woman much older than the one speaking), as in *Nana* Maria.
naranja	orange. A citrus fruit larger than the mandarin.
okoy	an oriental dish. Ingredients: grated unripe papaya mixed with flour seasoned with garlic, ginger, pepper and salt, and formed into patties, topped with meat or fish, and fried. Eaten when still hot and dipped in vinegar and soy sauce.
pala	after all, or its equivalent.
pasalubong	a favor, a gift of one who had been away on a trip, given loved ones at home to tell, "I'd been thinking of you."
pekel	Ilokano for massage, a rubdown. It is an Ilokano practice for parents (part of nurturing) to give their pre-to-toddlers massage, smiling chant the cheerful ditty: *Pekel, pekel, ta dardaras dumakel,* while massaging gently. Literal translation: rubdown, rubdown to help you grow fast. The massage ends by tickling the child on the chin or abdomen.
pinakbet	a favorite dish of the Ilokano group. The main ingredients: long, slender tender eggplants, *ampalaya* fruits, mild jalapeno, pepper, garlic, fresh ginger, tomatoes, fish or soy sauce. Placed in a heavy cookware, the longitudinally sliced vegetables are simmered till tender.
Pinay, Pinoy	short for *Pilipina* (*a* for female) and *Pilipino* (*o* for male.).
Po	same as the use of *Ho,* a term showing respect for a much older person than the one speaking, or one with authority or highly educated, wealthy, or high social status.
pomelo	a wide-spreading citrus tree, its large sweet but rather dry thick-rinded fruit.
puto	rice cake, spongy in texture. It is steamed, not baked.
salamat	it means thanks, always with an attached *Ho* or *Po,* as in *Salamat Ho,* or *salamat Po*—Thank you, Sir …Ma'am.
sampaguita	The Philippine National flower. The shrub produces clusters of fragrant small round flowers, the tiny round petals exude perfume akin to the fragrance of gardenia or lily of the valley. The name is a derivation of *sumpa* (promise) and *kita* (I/you): I promise you.
sari sari	a variety store.
sponhada	Spanish origin, meaning sponge-like. Bouncy, wavy hair.

Tia, Tio	aunt (ending in the letter *a* denoting female, *o* for uncle. The addition of the suffix *ng* to the root words forms endearing terms—as in *Tiang* Del, *Tiong* Dons.
tumok	Ilokano for a variety of banana that is soft, sweet, with a melt-in-the-mouth syrupy consistency with a distinctive aroma akin to pawpaw. The *tumok* peel or skin remains green even when the fruit is ripe.
Uhtee	pronounced AH-tee, a form of respect used for an older sister, an older female relative, or any older non-relative female. It may be used alone, or before the given name, as in *Uhtee* Doray. (*Manang.* in Ilokano.) In the vernacular Uhtee is spelled '*Ate*' — which is reason enough for using the phonetic spelling here.
zapote	a robust fruit tree bearing round fruits, when ripening the green fruits turn purplish. The flavor and texture of a tree ripened *zapote* fruit is that of chocolate pudding.
Abbreviations	that may be unfamiliar to many, particularly to the non-Adventist readers:
AIIAS	Adventist International Institute of Advanced Studies.
AUP	Adventist University of the Philippines, formerly PUC.
EGMP	Eternal Gardens Memorial Park
FED	Far Eastern Division (Replaced by two Divisions—Southern Asia Pacific Division and Northern Asia Pacific Division.
GC	General Conference of the Seventh-day Adventist Church.
MVC	Mountain View College
NAPD	Northern Asia Pacific Division, based in Seoul, Korea.
NPUM	North Philippine Union Mission (in Luzon).
PUC	Philippine Union College, now AUP (see above).
SSD	Southern Asia Pacific Division, based in Silang, Cavite, Philippines.
SDA	Seventh-day Adventist. Preferred abbreviation: Adventist.

***

THE GIFT OF CHOICE

Book II

The Life and Times

of

ALFONSO PANIS RODA (APR)

PROLOGUE

"... it is impossible but that offenses will come ... (Luke 17).

Am I hearing right? the question filled the young nurse as she strained to listen to what her patient was saying. She drew closer to her suffering patient. *First, I am a nurse,* she reminded herself, *and last, a recipient of his kindness as a working student.*

The visitors—tearful faculty members—took their turn two at a time, according to ICU rules. Praying silently for their stricken friend and superior, Dr. Alfonso P. Roda, they stepped hesitantly out of the room.

"Why did I sign it... I should never have signed it...." The nurse heard him right the first time. She continued her bedside nursing care vigil: monitoring vital signs, and documenting progress notes on the chart:

"Still complaining of severe headache, nape pain, always thirsty, numbness of left side of the body. Severe pain, lower extremities, particularly the right. Patient is conscious and answering questions.

2:30 p.m. Sudden increase of blood pressure to 170/90; deterioration in level of consciousness; now stuporous, no spontaneous opening of eyes or response to stimuli but responds to pain stimuli with movement of upper and lower extremities.

Glassgow coma scale from 74 to 8. Lapsing in to coma ... Taken to surgery. Pre-op diagnosis: Brain stem medial cerebello-pontene infarct....

The nurse maintained her professional veneer, mentally reviewing his previous admission, when in tears he had confided and shared his angst over the 'unfair manner the leaders had been dealing....' she could not keep her tears from spilling. *Satan is using every possible way to tempt the very elect,* she sighed inwardly. Lifting her heart to God and pleading for mercy, the young nurse prayed earnestly for her patient. *Gracious Lord, deliver ... from the shadow of death ... Thy will be done.*

***

February 26, 1987, Loma Linda, California. Lydia awakened, lifted the ringing telephone wondering, *who could be calling so early in the morning.* She glanced at her clock—about 5:30.

"Auntie, Uncle is in the hospital." Tita Torres was calling from La Sierra to relay the news that her older sister, Cora Coo in Baesa (Philippines) phoned to her.

Within minutes, Lydia was on long distance talking to Bien Capule, president of Manila Sanitariu & Hospital, and friend of her husband. After a brief exchange, Capule handed the phone to Dr. Joselito Coo. Shortly, Dr. Ong, attending neurosurgeon and Dr. Celedonio A. Fernando, also a neurosurgeon, were in phone consultation.

Lydia, a former nursing instructor with a master's degree, grasped the import of the doctors' assessment on her husband's physical condition. Crushed and benumbed, she dialed her son Andy's phone. Following their brief talk, she phoned her uncle, *Tiong Dons* (Dr. Celedonio A. Fernando) in Glendora. Quickly, she called her nurse siblings: older sister Esther Vizcarra, and then her younger sister, Preciosa Pilar. The three agreed to take the next flight to Manila—the same flight—together.

Now, airplane-borne, Lydia began unburdening her fears and her anxieties to her empathizing *Tiong Dons*: "Is he in pain? Is he suffering much? Would he be able to continue his term as president (to Dec. 1989?) Would he be able to talk to me? Will he leave me and our children?"

Dr. Joselito Coo met them at the airport and gave Dr. Fernando a full report of the College President's condition. He led the group to their stricken beloved's room.

Upon entering the Intensive Care Unit, Lydia flung herself at her husband's inert body, pressed her face against his, tears flowed freely. The answers to her questions were clear: Her husband couldn't talk to her nor squeeze her hand. His pupils had dilated. He had no reflexes. A machine kept him breathing and his vital functions going.

Believing the Word to be quick and powerful, Lydia claimed God's promise, "I'll answer when you call." She opened her Bible and in whispers began reading to her husband passages she had underlined during their devotions together. Consoling words from the Psalms. Promises from the books of John. Soaking in the promises, her heartache eased, yet her heart cried out, *Must you go and leave me....?"* Inwardly, she pleaded, *Please Lord, perform a miracle for us.... Give me faith to believe .... Thou art the same loving God who raised Lazarus. Please, do this for us, too, Lord.*

Dr. Fernando, in his own words:

After examining him and assessing his condition, I went out to face a large, eager, anxious group of teachers, students, relatives, and friends. They refused to believe their beloved president, their friend, their teacher, was beyond help. "Aren't you operating? Are you giving up? Isn't there something you can do? Won't you even try?" Prodding questions.

I traveled half-way around the world bringing a bag of neurosurgical instruments.... I would have operated at the slightest indication.... Yes, I would have done everything, anything, if I could ... but the brain waves were flat .... the brain was dead....

Soon Andy and Dr. Roda's sisters—Elizabeth Roeder and Mercedes Arevalo—arrived. They, too, clearly understood the meaning of the flat brain waves. Notwithstanding, Andy, their firstborn, knelt to embrace his father, he cried out, "Daddy, I love you." But there was no response. His once strong and vigorous Dad, whose strength he knew and esteemed all his life, lay unresponsive, lifeless.

After Dr. Fernando committed their loved one to the Lord, Lydia said, voice quivering, *"Sigue, Tiong,* you can turn off the respirator now."

The Student Association. When the students learned about the hospital admission of their beloved president, they became open. They donned shirts, **We Love Dr. Roda** emblazoned at the front, and at the back, a radiant replica of him. Details of the problematic turn of events piling on the man they respected and loved reached their attentive ears. Wanting to show their beloved College President their support, that they were behind him, helping him carry his heavy load, and hoping to hasten his recovery, they rallied to prove they loved him. United, the students paraded around the college and hospital grounds, skipping classes. Also, grieving, the faculty let the students pour out their love and to vent their anger.

As soon as the students heard that their beloved Dr. Roda had lapsed in to coma, their emotions erupted like an angry volcano. They punctured the tires of those they presumed created the stress the president suffered. They carried posters expressing rage to parties they assumed caused the strain that broke down the endurance and broke the heart of their beloved president. Classes suspended for a week from date of Dr. Roda's death.

When the body of Dr Roda arrived at PUC campus, Lydia took her stand. "Please remove the rude posters...." she pleaded. "Please behave in honor of Dr. Roda." Unwillingly, the students complied with her request.

***

MANILA SANITARIUM & HOSPITAL
1975 Donada St, Pasay City

NAME: Roda, Alfonso Panis   **Hospital No**. > > > >

Address: PUC Campus, Silang, Cavite Date of birth: Dec. 25, 1921

Occupation: President, PUC

Responsible Party: Self, wife

Notify: Wife, Lydia T. Roda

Previous Admission(s): February 22–24, 1987 (admitted for check-up)

Date of Admission: Feb. 25, 1987

Attending Physician(s): Dr. Magat, Dr. J. Coo, Dr. Ong

Admitting Diagnosis: Severe headache, severe vomiting

Surgical Procedure: Tube ventriculostomy, Feb. 27, 1987 (Placed on respirator) Autopsy, March 6, 1987

Final Diagnosis: Non-hemorrhagic infarct of pons, vermis & cerebellum with obstructive hydrocephalus

Date of Discharge: March 5, 1987 (6:35 a.m. taken off respirator; 6:55 a.m., death pronounced by Dr. C. A. Fernando

NATURE SIMILES

Speak to me with clarity
Like the yellow rose's
Sweet sincerity.

Whisper to me close
Words like hibiscus
Bow when the wind blows.

Let smile on your lips
Play like gardenia
Scents when the wind dips.

Laugh till your heart fills
Like light cumulus clouds
Cover distant hills.

Pray for faith to crowd
Your sorrows away
Like sunbeams shroud

In bright array
A glorious day.

crj ***

Chapter I

<u>FOR</u> MATTERS OF THE HEART

Evening of March 31, 1951. *She's beautiful,* Alfonso caught himself affirming, as he saw bridesmaid Lydia come in. His heart began beating fast, and the room suddenly became too warm for him. He felt smitten.

It was Remedios' (Mediong) bridal rehearsal at the chapel, at Philippine Union College. Fely Abaya was maid of honor, Esther Dalisay and Lydia Tabucol, the bridesmaids. Bridegroom elect Flaviano V. Dalisay, Jr. (Entong) had asked Catalino Bautista to be best man for him. Jose, his younger brother, and Alfonso Roda (Ponsing) he asked to be groomsmen.

Remedios Quevedo, Ed., MA., felt confident teaching at PUC Elementary School. She enjoyed the classroom full of eager-to-learn children. She was comfortable in her single mobile home on campus, some five-minute walk from her school room. A book lover, she habitually dropped by the library to return a book and to check out another.

One day on her way out of the library, someone suddenly bumped on her, knocking her books to the floor. It was Entong. He stammered about his mind being elsewhere, but he noted the expressive eyes on an amused face, as shapely fingers picked up books from the floor. "I'm sorry," he finally spoke the words he presumed to read in her eyes. He started walking down the steps with her, he offered to carry her books. She handed them to him. *Expressive eyes,* he admitted to himself. Her smile and her eyes sent his heart soaring.

"Were you going to the library?" she asked. "I live only a few steps away" she said, and flashing a smile, "Better go to the library before it closes," she advised. She extended her hands to reclaim her books.

Entong retraced his steps to the library. Her simple manner, smiling eyes, her soft voice filled his mind. *Funny how I knew she was around yet was unaware of her,* he thought. He decided to get to know her better.

Days rolled into weeks, and weeks into months, and that year, their friendship grew. Now, this marching-down-the-aisle rehearsal.

Having gone to school with Ponsing practically from grade school, Entong had kept his friend up-to-date of his love life. From the grapevine he heard of Ponsing's own 'smittenings', but to his knowledge, there had been nothing serious in his life. *Ponsing is a reserved fellow in matters of the heart,* he thought. *Always working hard, maybe he's too careful, too choosy. And Mediong has come up with something to help her distant cousin. I hope this rehearsal will stage a repeat performance for my friend. Maybe,* he mused.

"Ponsing, you've meet Lydia..." said Mediong with a twinkle in her eye. Nodding, Ponsing flashed Lydia a one-sided smile, which she returned accompanied by mini-dimples, one on each side at the corner beneath her lips. The music added to the pounding of his heart against his chest. *Heart behave. I see my dreams fulfilling.* The rehearsal ended too soon for him.

Lydia stepped out of the door with the group, chatting along with them as they walked to the College east gate toward the village. She lived with six siblings in their home a few minutes walk outside PUC gate. An uncle, Celedonio Fernando, *Tiong Dons* to them, became their unofficial guardian when their father remarried two years after their mother died.

Alfonso lived in Baesa *canto* (road) with his mother and Turing. Being single, this was expected of him, notwithstanding his being a PUC faculty. He stepped to walk beside Lydia. For the past year or so, he had his heart made up, but she had been a student. In the meantime, he had made his intentions known in subtle ways but felt the need to take his time. His uncle Tony, with whom he confided, had given him his approval of Lydia.

Having finished pre-nursing at PUC, Lydia had gone for nurses' training joining her older sister Esther, at Manila Sanitarium & Hospital. Felicito (Tito) the oldest sibling, was finishing medicine at MCU (Manila Central University); Preciosa (Precy) younger sister, and three younger brothers, Miguelito (Mike), Orlando (Orlie) and Edgardo (Pepe) were students at PUC.

The Tabucol family are Ilokano, like Alfonso's father. As he walked home alone, Alfonso reflected on his life. *I enjoy teaching, yet I feel unfulfilled, there's something missing in my life.* He had plans to finish his Master's degree as soon as he saved enough money, then on to doctorate. Pride surged within him in pondering over the loving relationships in his family. *Uhtee Ely, still single, is financing Turing in school; we will have a full fledged medical doctor in the family in two years in Turing. Uhtee Ceding married well, yes, she married ahead of Uhtee Ely.* Yet he rejoiced for the happiness of the new couple. His thoughts went to their courtship. Very much in love, Eliseo Arevalo composed a *kundiman* (love song) *Cheding Ang Ngalanmo.* (Cheding is Your Name). *What love can do!* he thought. *A fairy tale courtship and marriage.* He wondered if Turing would follow suit—marry ahead of him. *He's in love with a musician, too.*

"*Mamang*, I'm home," he called as he stepped in the door.

His mother met him. "How was the rehearsal?" she asked.

"Wonderful."

"Is that all, *Anak* ?"

"Mediong paired me with a very beautiful and charming young lady." He deliberately skipped divulging that he had asked Mediong the favor."

"What's her name?"

"Lydia Tabucol, a nursing student." He took the rattan chair across his mother and assumed a relaxed, somewhat dreamy position. "*Mamang,* I believe this is true love."

"It's about time you found one you feel you could live with the rest of your life, Ponsing. I know her—one of the siblings whose mother died not long after they bought a house there." She gestured to the east of their house. "I haven't seen her lately, however," she said.

"She's at Manila Sanitarium taking her nurses' training." *Would she like Lydia?* he wondered. Even at his age, it meant so much to him for his mother to approve of his new choice. *Lydia, motherless as I am fatherless.*

"So thoughtful of Mediong, your second cousin by your *Papang* to play cupid for you." The delight in her voice was assuring to Alfonso.

"*Mamang,* how old were you when your parents died—.my grandparents whom I never met? What caused their death?"

"I was too young to care about the cause of their death. Now, I wish I could remember, even to know at what age I was when they died."

A coincidence ? the thought again struck home. *Lydia and I are both one-parent orphans. She, without her mother; I grew up without a father.*

"Ponsing," she began, she lowered her voice. "At your age, need I remind you of what the Bible says—'beauty is vain, but a woman that feareth the Lord…' you know the rest, *Anak.* The Lord will guide you in choosing a life companion if you ask Him to." She cast him a sidelong glance, and interpreted his pose that he was listening. "I prayed much for your sisters. I gave Ely and Ceding a similar advice. It's Ely that somewhat concerns me, even at her age. Wally Roeder is not of our faith, and he's from a far country. We do not know his personal background, except that he's a chemist and had something to do with winning the war. I'm glad Ely is taking her time. I praise the Lord for Ceding's marriage."

"I believe my parents laid down a good Christian home model for us. It takes two to fight as it takes two to make a marriage work. I recall very little of *Papang,* but in my subconscious mind, I feel my parents planted good marriage seeds. To prove this—*Uhtee* Cheding's marriage. *Tata* (uncle) Alvaro and *Tata* Tony had not always been around, but somehow I'd seen my own father in them. I'm very much aware that *Papang's* influence, by God's grace, won my uncles over to the Adventist faith."

He side glanced at his silent mother, he saw her eyes misting. "*Mamang,* "I want you to know… I'm not rushing in matters of the heart. I am determined not to let my heart dictate whom I choose for a life companion. First, I would learn all I can about the object of my love." He cleared his throat. "*Mamang,* are you listening?" He drew a deep breath.

She looked at her son with a questioning look. "I'm listening, *Anak.* "

"Now," he said, "this time I hope to get all of my kins' full approval." Pausing briefly, he added, "God willing, I plan to live much longer than *Papang,* by God's grace. I plan to live to see my children grow to adulthood, and even live long enough to enjoy my grandchildren."

Maria nodded her head. "May the Lord's will be done," she said.

Clasping his hands behind his neck, Alfonso leaned back. He began reminiscing. "I remember *Kuya* Arding had been in love. World War II deprivations broke down *Kuya's* immune system giving tuberculosis a foothold to thrive. This caused his love and his life. I heard many who knew my *Kuya* personally say, 'What a waste of life! Eduardo was a brilliant man.' The name his contemporaries dubbed him—Walking Encyclopedia—described him well. I, too, miss *Kuya* Arding so much."

Maria assumed a faraway look. "Your *Kuya* was a normal young man, Ponsing," she chuckled lightly as if to console herself, but her voice choked. "Anita Quitolio was a beautiful and intellectual young woman, a winsome Ilokana teacher, gifted with a sweet singing voice." Wiping a tear, she sighed, "Arding grew up fast to be a man, he was my right hand. The war robbed us of your *Kuya* Arding." She flashed her son a faint smile, but you stepped right in his shoes."

After a brief pause, she continued. "*Anak,* tell me why you think you are falling in love… again. I trust nothing amiss comes this time. Just what do you see that you like in Lydia?"

"She gives me the impression of innocence. If simplicity is beauty, it's her pure natural beauty. Shapely limbs, tapered fingers, long dark hair."

"What I call *sponghada,"* his mother interjected. "Considering only external appearances, as beautiful as she is, I pray no one has claimed her love ahead of you."

He shook his head slowly. "I can tell she's not a flirt," he replied in a rather defensive tone. "Choosy would be a term more appropriate for her. Selective." He paused and drew a deep breath. "The Scriptural description of Sarah, Abraham's wife is that she was a beautiful woman, but the Bible is silent about courtship. I'd like to know how *Papang* courted you."

Chuckling, "You're not to copy-cat how your *Papang* courted," she began. "You'll never make it. No girl nowadays would go for that kind of courtship. You've heard your *Papang* was our boarder. He and your uncle Bib met in school and became chums. *Kuya* Bib invited him… to board with us. They understood each other … they thought almost alike!"

Alfonso listened, and noted a day-dreamy look in his mother's eyes. He waited silently for his mother to resume reminiscing.

"At first your Papa treated me like his younger sister, but before we knew it, we began to care for each other, unlike a brother and sister…."

Alfonso's grin reached his eyes. "Chemistry," he muttered.

"We gradually began to understand each other without spoken words. In biblical terms, we had that Christian preferring-one-another feeling, liking and enjoying being with each other. Your *Papang* was a true gentleman." Her voice caught at the words, she drew a deep breath.

"I thought of him as a man who let Christ live in and through him. He was courteous, helpful, noble, hardworking. He said anyone with our hope should be happy." She ran her pinkies lightly over her eyes. "That's why we enjoyed each other. I trusted him."

"You were thirty years old.... Did you fall apart after *Papang*'s death?"

Shaking her head, she replied. "His death came slowly, he prepared me for it. During his last days, he could only whisper, but together we prayed much and earnestly. In each prayer, he entrusted us all in God's care. Because he knew God intimately, he didn't worry about our future. That's the impression I got, it rubbed on me. Complete trust in God. 'When I'll be gone, you will all be safe in God's hands,' he often said. Maria let out a sigh.

Alfonso allowed his mother time for her own thoughts, his eyes closed.

"He wanted to be sure each of you gets a Christian education from our own church schools. I promised him you will all get the formal education deprived me." She forced a smile. "His insight in this life and in the life to come, his presence in my children, especially in you now, Ponsing, comfort me. I'd have missed your *Kuya* Arding more were it not for you." She drew a deep breath. "Money had been a constant problem. Pastor W. B. Amundsen somehow seemed to know when I didn't have money for tuition, he'd come to tell me, 'Send the children to school, anyway.' Only a true Christian school administrator would think of doing that, Ponsing."

"I agree," he said nodding his head. "I remember him—a very kind missionary. I can never forget him," he said. "Speaking of having not enough money, *Mang* Ely spoke of aunt Doray. I know she stayed with aunt Doray while she was finishing her nurse's training. Did she help *Mang* Ely through school? I had been too engrossed with my studies, and ran to work after school, perhaps it didn't matter to me then."

"Yes, your aunt Doray had always been a very caring cousin. When your uncle Bib and I lived with them, she treated us like her own blood brother and sister. Aunt Ciriaca taught us to be helpful—we didn't have any helper—so we did all the chores. Aunt Ciriaca also taught us to sew. Aunt Enriqueta, who never married, stayed with us and it helped, but she was very strict," she chuckled.

"Wealthy but they had no helpers or maids, huh," he mumbled.

"The training helped. When you were all little, your Papa had to be away for his evangelistic efforts, and he came home with all his clothes dirty. I had to wash them by hand—a hard, hard work—often I cried.

Men's clothes at that time were heavy and needed ironing. But as you, my children, grew older, you all helped. I miss your Papa most in wishing he were here to share with me the joys my children are to me."

Alfonso saw her wipe her eyes with her fingers and dry her fingers on her apron. He understood the longing of her soul. He stood up, put his arms around his mother, he held her close and tight, yet with gentleness.

"Tears of joy, *Anak*," she said. "Now, let's get back to … Lydia. Having seen her mostly in church and from a distance, yet as if I saw her blossom into womanhood. I, too, admire beauty. From outside appearance, she has it," she said with a faraway look.

Alfonso saw his mother assume a lost-in-thought frame of mind.

"Now I remember," she finally said. "I was at the Balayo *sari sari* and came upon two students shopping. I overheard one say, 'He fell head-over-heels for her and got crazy when she ignored him. She's young, she knows she need not fall for the first guy.' The other girl mentioned a name, which sounded like Lydia. I'm sure they were talking about someone they called a heartbreaker."

Ho-ho-ho," he roared. "What good ears my mother has!"

"All girls, including older girls enjoy hearing girl gossips," she laughed. "Well, do you want to hear more about it?"

"Sure, *Mamang*. It won't hurt anyone. I'm listening."

"On purpose, I took time in choosing a bunch of bananas. The other girl whispered, 'I heard of another one smitten—a talented doctor—M.D. He sings and plays the violin. He had been composing poems and songs and dedicating them to her, but no way. She wouldn't even consider him. Maybe, because he's much older?' The girls giggled."

"Now, from a boy's point of view, I don't think it's funny. I feel sorry for both boys," he mumbled. "I'm getting old, neither am I good looking." He caught himself mentally praying, *Lord, reserve her for me.* It was a relief to hear his mother repeat what she heard, 'She wouldn't even consider him.' Sidelong glancing at his mother, on impulse he asked a childish question, "Did you think Papa was handsome as a young man?"

"Ponsing, there's more to handsomeness than meets the eye,' she said. "I'd always thought your father was good looking. As the truism goes, 'beauty is in the eye of the beholder.' Change one word: 'Handsomeness is in the eye of the beholder.'

She stood up and pulled down a framed picture hanging on the wall. "Look at this," her index finger pointed to a young man in the photo. "You see this all the time, it no longer attracts your attention. Now, what do you think of it? Your father was about your age when we sat down for this."

"I think *Papang* was good looking. You were young and beautiful…."

"Ponsing, you look very much like your father when he was your age, except there's more flesh on you. That's an improvement. Your Papa never gained weight no matter what. Holding the photo at an angle, she stared at it. "Years have a way of re-making a face," she chuckled. "That was on me," she explained. "I think all of my children are good looking." Stepping closer to her son, she tilted his chin lightly. "You are handsome, Ponsing, she said.

"Naturally, *Mamang*. Now, you need to get some beauty rest to awake refreshed. You worked hard all day. Goodnight." He stood up to leave.

"You, too, *Anak*. Sweet dreams. When I told the truth that you're handsome, intelligent, and talented, I didn't want to blow up your head."

"Thanks, I'm old enough to withstand flattery even from my mother."

"No flattery. Yes, you're right in that you're old enough to be serious about setting up a home of your own. Don't get me wrong. I like you staying at home with me," she chuckled. "To run errands for me."

He was barely five years old when his father died. He must feel as I had —parents-deprived, she thought. *Lord, may the Holy Spirit guide Ponsing,* she prayed in her heart.

As Alfonso prepared for bed, he reprimanded himself, questioning, *What made me feel sore over that 'heartbreaker bit.'*? As his habit was, he knelt down to pray, to pour out his mixed feelings to his Father in heaven. He'd proven prayer to settle his mind, and this moment was no exception.

At the breakfast table, Alfonso told his mother of his plan to go to town. "I'd like to take the 9 o'clock Halili," he said.

"While in town, would you do an errand for me?"

"Give me your list, Ma. I'm happy to spare you the rigors of the trip."

She made her list, handed it to her son with money to pay for her order. "I hear the bus," she said.

"Right on time," he said, hastily stepped out, boarded the Halili, taking a front seat. At the next stop, Lydia came up. *I thank Thee Lord,* he breathed, got up to offer her a hand and dropped her fare in the fare slot.

"Thank you," Lydia said with a smile, taking the seat he offered her. "I need to do some shopping. It's almost impossible to get out of the San," she added, chuckling. "I'm making use of this free time to buy things I need."

"Students and working people must work around their schedules," he said, stealing a sidelong glance at the presence beside him. "I, too, need to do some shopping for myself and for mother. She made a list for me, her errand boy as far as I recall," he said, grinning "How's life at the San?"

"I'm enjoying the challenge, though hectic. It helps that *Mang* Es is there. She said her first year had been the hardest. Perhaps, it's because we'd always lived at home, we never were dormitorians until now."

"My oldest sister, Elizabeth, *Uhtee* Ely, felt the same way. Do you know *Uhtee* Ely is a nurse? She's one of the first graduates at the San. She switched to private nursing some time ago, she likes that work setting."

"Yes, I've heard of her. I've also heard private nursing pays well."

Nodding, he said, "It helps. *Uhtee* Ely had been so kind to help foot her younger siblings' school expenses. That is, *Uhtee* Ceding and me. Now, she's responsible for Turing's schooling. We'd always helped each other. *Uhtee* Ceding taught in grade school but she's now a full time mother."

"So that makes two teachers in your family."

"For me now, it's a stepping stone, like my having been a clerk typist first, then a treasurer at the mission office. I enjoy teaching, and being with young people. My major is Theology. I trust in the Lord ... to continue guiding me. Somehow, I have a feeling that He'll lead me to follow in my father's footsteps. He was an ordained minister who died at a very young age—before I turned five years." He drew a deep breath. "At thirty years of age," he continued, "mother became a widow, but by God's grace, she took very good care of all of us—her five children."

"I'm sorry," Lydia said, yet she warmed up. "My mother died when I was 17. She had myasthenia gravis and died of pneumonia. For a long time I missed her." She paused, looked faraway. She drew a deep breath.

"It took *Mang* Es a lot longer to get over her bitterness," she resumed. "Often she questioned why God let her die and leave seven still dependent children behind. My father took care of us for two years following mother's death. After he re-married, *Tiong* Dons became our guardian."

"Whenever I think of my father's death," Alfonso said, "I also think of Jesus' death. Both died at the age of thirty-three, but father died of tuberculosis of the lungs. As a youngster, I, too, questioned in my mind, *Didn't he ask the Lord to heal him?* But hearing mother and my older siblings talk about how they prayed for his healing, I questioned, *Why didn't God answer?* My maturing mind now accepts that 'there's a time to every purpose... A time to be born, and a time to die....'" (Ecc. 3:1, 2).

"That's life," muttered Lydia. Inside, she shuddered and thought, *It's a wonder he didn't catch the infection.* "Seeing pain and sickness all day at the San, I often think of my mother."

Alfonso became aware they were nearing the shopping area. Side-glancing at Lydia, he said, "I enjoyed the short ride and talk with you. *I pray we'll happen to take the same ride home,* he prayed silently. "Do you have any idea how long it would take you to finish your shopping?"

She shook her head. "I always take my time shopping. It's like a short vacation for me, and I try to enjoy every minute of it."

"Ditto," he said with a grin. "I enjoyed our chat. I hope to continue our small talk. The wedding's in a few hours ... time to snatch some rest."

"Yes, you must be a mind reader," she said, chuckling softly.

"Not exactly." He cast her another sidelong glance, and noting her look of amusement, he said. "I grew up with two sisters and a mother who programmed me and my brothers according to the needs of their gender."

After alighting, they walked together for a short distance, then went on their separate ways. Alfonso kept a prayer in his heart, *I ask a sign, Lord. If it's in Thy plan for me to pursue this friendship, let me know it—let us have a ride home together as we'd taken the same bus out.*

Shortly before noon, Alfonso saw Lydia walking toward the bus stop. With a *Thank You, Lord,* in his heart, he hurried to catch up with her. Lydia, sensing a presence behind her, turned her head to look. Their eyes met and they exchanged smiles. *Had he been on the lookout for me?*

Alfonso stepped up the bus, said "Fare for two," to the driver, dropped the coins in the fare slot, then turned to offer his hand to help Lydia get up.

"Thank you, she said. "You didn't have to pay for my fare again."

"I'm earning and you are not," he chided as Lydia ambled to a seat at the rear, bypassing several empty seats. He sat beside her.

"Your uncle, being a medical intern, does he live at the hospital, too?"

"*Tiong* Dons commutes to the San, but when his schedule includes the night shift, he rests in the medical interns' room."

"It seems your whole family is getting in the medical field," he said.

She shook her head. "Precy, our youngest sister, is taking secretarial, but she might change her mind. The younger boys haven't decided what they would like to do."

"Dr. Arturo Roda is your brother, isn't it?"

"Yes, our youngest."

Lydia puzzled over in her mind why he didn't get in the medical profession. Her uncle *Tiong Dons* had been so convincing in upholding it as the career with a bright future. She liked the dignity that the profession, clad in white caring for the sick and injured, created. The hospital was always clean with a quiet atmosphere despite the stress the sight of pain and the life and death factors behind it all. Even at the dining table, conversation among the medical interns, nurses and student nurses, centered often on their patients, they referred to as 'cases'.

As if in sync with her thoughts, he said, "I enjoy dealing with the mind. Teaching deals with the mind. Physical well-being is a certain reward of an educated mind. Jesus spent much of his time teaching."

"That's another aspect I like at the hospital," she said. "As we help patients gain their health back, an opportunity opens for us to lead them to the Great Physician. Our Christian nursing instructors teach us how to care for our patients and then lead their minds to think of God."

"You said that so beautifully, so inspiring!" he said with genuine sincerity. "To be a patient under Christian doctors and nurses must be a pleasure," he said with a chuckle.

Lydia smiled at that, too. "I'd never thought of it that way, I as a patient," she said. "My point of view is always as a nurse, not one on the sick bed," she said with emphasis on the last phrase. "Perhaps one of the reasons I chose to be a nurse was a wish I'd been able to care for my mother when she was sick. If only she lived a few more years," she sighed.

"Had she been ill in bed very long? I trust she didn't suffer much."

"Mother never complained." *Had I been a nurse then, would mother still be alive?* once again crossed her mind so strongly that she sighed. "Your statement reinforced my belief that father's death did motivate *Uhtee* Ely to take up nursing. She often said she wished she had been a nurse when *Papang* was yet alive. 'I would have tried my best to nurse him back to health,' she'd say."

"Your mother must have been a good nurse. Not one of you contacted what you said your father died of. Could it be that the doctor misdiagnosed his case?"

"*Uhtee* Ely thought about that, too, but father coughed. The infection must have destroyed his vocal chords. Mother had no formal training as a nurse, but she carried out the doctor's instructions carefully. As I grew older, I realized God chose to answer my parents' prayers by safeguarding the family from the infection. With father bedridden and seeing mother working hard, the older children rallied to help her in every way possible. My uncle Tony lived with us for a while—that helped—but that was before father became bedridden. *Kuya* Arding was mother's moral booster."

"In 1945 my parents decided to move from Sta. Ignacia, Tarlac, to Baesa. They bought a house so all their seven children could attend PUC. Then my mother became progressively weak until she no longer could do house work, nor care for the younger ones. A few relatives came to do what they could, but not one of them stayed long. *Manong* Tito, *Mang Es,* Precy and I pulled together to do all the chores."

"I'm sorry," he said softly. His mind clicked back to some poignant memories. In a low tone he said, "As a grown-up, there were nights I heard mother sobbing. I'd go to her room to ask why. "Go back to bed to sleep, *Anak.* I'll be all right," she'd say. I knew she was lonesome for my father."

He cast a sidelong glance at Lydia, and saw her faraway look. In a more cheerful tone, he said, "About healing sickness. When I was in the States, I read of a group of people who practiced back-to-basics. Instead of using drugs—the medicines that come in capsules and tablets—they use herbs to cure or prevent diseases. They claim 75 percent of the medicines come from herbs to begin with, anyway. Garlic, for example for its antiseptic properties, they use fresh garlic to prevent and cure diseases including TB." *If only my parents knew this,* he thought. "They believe our food should be our medicine. It's the food God gave Adam and Eve—'every herb bearing seed and every fruit tree yielding seed'" (Gen. 1:29).

"That's interesting," she replied, quickly adding, "I mean about the Americans practicing back-to-nature. I heard of some folk living in barrios and farms using herbs as medicine." She gave Alfonso a quick glance, then with hesitation, asked, "So, what did you do in the States?"

"I continued my education at Emmanuel Missionary College and lived like most working students. Ever heard of the Finsters? They were among the first American missionaries to bring Adventism to our country. They took me under their wing, gave me a rent-free room—actually, their garage fixed up into a room. Although it became very cold in my room in the winter, I couldn't complain. I felt fortunate I had a place to stay, and with people who cared...." He laughed softly. He gave her a sidelong glance.

"To earn money to keep me in school, I pumped gas. I picked fruits in season—apples, apricots, grapes, peaches, and other fruits." He paused to recall, and again cast a sidelong glance at Lydia. "There's nothing more luscious than tree-ripened fruits freshly plucked from the tree. The orcharders gave to their pickers the blemished fruits, free. I felt like I was in the Garden of Eden." He paused briefly. "I returned home in 1949."

A memory of an academy social in 1947 flashed in Lydia's mind. She cringed to think of her naivete, but mentally relished re-living the event: She saw herself sitting with friends at the gymnasium after a round of marching when he came around. "What's your name?" asked a then younger-looking Alfonso. She winced to recall how she ran away after telling her name, leaving him with her friends. *At seventeen, I should have acted more mature.* Her peripheral vision told her he was perhaps trying to conceal a smile.

He figured out Lydia to be about twenty years old. *I'm twenty-eight,* he admitted to himself. Turning to her, he asked, "How did you like PUC?"

"Very much," she replied. "I liked Friday evening vespers, the faculty organ-piano-violin trio. And I liked the no-classes days," she laughed. "I also enjoyed the social events—the marchings—we called 'the Seventh-day Adventist dance', the skating was fun. At the San, there's not much of social events as we had at PUC. We're too busy for socials, anyway."

"College is serious enough. Beyond that, it is serious business," he said, grinning. He had a faraway look. *All my student life were serious days.*

"Nursing students study hard and work hard, but I find it also fun."

"*Uhtee* Ely believes every woman should take nursing as a career. It prepares them for their God-ordained position in the family. She says it makes them more efficient in their mother-wife nurturing role."

"It's a profession cut out for women, but there are men in our class," she said. She suppressed a smile, sat up a little taller, ran her left hand over her skirt to straighten an imagined wrinkle. And she kept her thoughts to herself.

He wanted to hear more about the men in her class, but she remained silent. He cast a sidelong glance her way, and decided to let her thoughts run, presuming she was framing words to explain things on her mind.

"At first," she resumed, still trying to conceal a smile, "I thought, 'What do they think they are doing in the nursing profession?' Some of the girls thought like me, and in talking about it, we decided to wait-and-see. We surmised they'd come to their senses sooner or later, and may change their minds. One of the girls came up with an idea 'Ask them separately why they had chosen to take up nursing.' We agreed it was a good notion and asked who'd be brave enough to do it. The next day the girls who volunteered to do the job reported that one of them said, "I want to be with you, girls.' We appreciated his frankness—we knew he was trying to cultivate the friendship of a charming student nurse. The other reason rather came as a surprise to most of us. 'I'm being obedient to divine instruction.' he said. 'Ellen G. White stated it was best for women to attend to women in their medical care, and vice versa.'

Smiling now, she added, "Actually, we girls enjoy having the boys around." She gave him a sidelong glance in hopes of catching his reaction.

"I would not think less of them as men. The profession doesn't make them effeminate,' he chuckled, "nor do women medical doctors become masculine. I presume there are male patients who welcome their own gender attending to their medical care. I, for one, would," he said, quickly adding, "Long ago, however, I made up my mind to stay healthy."

"If everyone stayed healthy, everyone would be happier," she said, and in a lower tone, added, "but that would make doctors and nurses jobless, and hospitals bankrupt."

Simultaneously, they laughed softly.

"In that line of thinking, we'll all be jobless in heaven!" he said.

She thought of that awhile, then joined him in a lighthearted laugh.

"Of course, there we wouldn't have to work for a living," he said. And in an effusive tone, he continued, "Oh, but I'll have plenty to keep me busy there. Like King Solomon, I'll study nature, explore other planets, join the heavenly choir, learn to play the harp like David, and perhaps join the orchestra." Drawing a deep breath, he flitted her a side-glance.

Hmmmmm… someone is a dreamer, she thought. In an undertone, she said, "I'll plant a garden. I'll take time to enjoy the flowers, and, I'll eat tree-ripened fruits. No decaying there but endless beauty, endless life!"

A more mature thinking person than I gave her credit for, he mused. "No growing old there," he said. "The tree of life will keep us all young!"

As the bus lurched to a turn, Lydia began gathering her things. "I found a pair of shoes that would match my dress tonight," she said with a smile of satisfaction. "It will be useful for Sabbath shoes, later."

My guess was right, he thought. "I bought a serviceable necktie," he said grinning. "I'd like to know who originated neckties. To dress up, a man must put a tie around his neck, tie his neck," he chuckled.

"Neckties correspond to women's necklaces or even earrings. That's one Adventist standard I'm really glad for," she said. "I need not wear any. They'd just get on the way, dangling, hanging on the neck or ears like that."

Alfonso laughed aloud then. "Fashion. Neckties. Earrings. Vanity."

Lydia cupped her hand over her mouth. Both tried to squelch their laughter when they saw in front of them women passengers with necklaces and dangling earrings. Alfonso just kept grinning, he said nothing more.

The bus came to a stop. Alfonso stepped back to let Lydia out of the row of seats. "Let me help you with your shopping cargo," he offered.

"Thank you," she said, "but they're not heavy, just bulky," yet she handed him one. And they made their way up front to alight.

"I thoroughly enjoyed the ride and talking with you," he said as they started down the dirt road. Lydia became aware he was escorting her home. *What would people think if they see us now?* crossed her mind. *Oh, let them.* On second thought, *It's broad daylight. Tiong Don's won't scold me,* she affirmed herself.

"I appreciate the favors from you," she said softly.

"My pleasure," he said, beaming. "Just a few more hours to the time of the wedding, a few moments to rest to feel good and look blithe," he said.

"Since starting my nurses' training at the San, I learned to take short naps whenever I find it convenient and have the time. I'll do just that soon as I get home. Before long, I'll be back to the rat race," she chuckled.

"Ditto. I truly enjoyed your company. 'I'll be seeing you then," he bade as they neared Lydia's home. Briefly waving a hand, he walked on.

Maria met her son at the door. "I heard the bus, thought you'd be in it. What took you so long? You look happy. Any good news, Ponsing?"

"Huhm," was his reply, handing his mother a small paper sac, and grinning, he said "Yes, *Mamang*, there's good news." And he detailed all of the day's happy happenings to his mother's very attentive ears.

"That makes us both happy, *Anak*. Could you wed before Turing?"

"Hey, not too fast, Ma!" he said, somewhat ruffled. "As of now, Lydia is a student nurse. I haven't even hinted her of my intentions. I'll let the Lord lead, Ma."

***

Dalisay Takes Quevedo. Heads turned to the bridesmaids in yellow ankle-length bouffant frocks in step with the music. No matter how many weddings come and go, watching dainty dressed-alike bridesmaid never loses ones fascination. No matter how many times a lass has been a bridesmaid, it is unthinkable to refuse a request for her to be one. Is it the assumption that being a bridesmaid is a prelude to becoming the bride? This was Lydia's first, she floated with the music, a faint smile on her face.

Alfonso stood awestruck by the glowing presence before him. The music seemed to come with a lyric, *Yours for the asking... but do be careful.* He felt a warmth within him and a reassurance of his worth. Gratefulness filled his heart for living at the present era, and not in the ancient days when parents choose wives for their sons. *My own choice* he affirmed himself yet a thought came strong, *This is in the Lord's hands and in His own good time. I'll not get ahead of Him—there's no reason to hurry.*

Strains of the wedding march now filled the chapel, and the radiant bride in white marching down the aisle took everyone's attention. Now, the bride and the groom stood before the minister. Their exchange of vows melded them into one flesh. After the minister's prayer of dedication, the radiant bride-and-groom turned to face the audience. Dr. Andrew Nelson, the officiating minister, introduced Mr. and Mrs. Flaviano Dalisay, Jr. The beaming newlyweds marched out, her hand on his arm. They ducked from peltering rice guests tossed, figuratively showering them with best wishes.

Close behind them, the bridesmaids took the proferred arms of their escort-ushers. Now the well-wishers started congratulating Alfonso and Lydia. "You make a beautiful pair."

"You are a perfect match." A few went as far as to predict they would be next to march down the aisle.

After the formal picture-taking, the bridal entourage joined the waiting guests at the reception. The celebration was merry as the wedding ceremony was solemn. Following the formal, and sometimes funny speeches, the call came: "All 'bachelorettes' over here!"

It took some persuasion to get the *heli-heli bago quieri* (hesitance before acceptance) maidens to assemble. But there they were—wearing bashful smiles on their faces—waiting for the forecasting game. The bride turned around, her back to the *binibini* (young women). "Ready?" The bride tossed her bridal bouquet to the now alert *binibini* behind her back. Cheers erupted as Lydia caught the bridal bouquet with her own hands.

Back at the San the day following, Lydia plunged herself in to the nursing student life. She had enjoyed her part at the Dalisay-Quevedo wedding, and tucked the memory in the back of her mind. To prepare for capping, nursing students put their all in their schoolwork. Lydia imagined herself wearing a white cap, the symbol of service. Only a few more months to the capping ceremony to receive her white cap.

Lydia was walking down the hall to her room after a full school day when she heard Dean Ruth Reyes call her name. "Here's a letter for you," the dean said, handing her a blue envelope. She thanked the dean and hurried to her room. She noted the Manila postmark and the date—*two days ago*—she thought. Dropping her eyes to the signature, her heart began double beating as she read:

Dear Lydia,

>*Thank you for taking in stride all the jokes at the* Dalisay-Quevedo wedding. *I want to let you know, I have taken the comments seriously, for this has been in my prayers. And I cannot keep silent. Lydia, I think a lot of you.*

>*Would you allow me to come for a visit with you at the San this weekend, on Sabbath? I realize this to be the only free day from classes for you, a student nurse. 'The Sabbath was made for man....'*

She felt her heart awakening to a new feeling. *Brief and to the point,* she mused. She appreciated his foresight in giving her ample time to reply, yet she understood his P.S. *silence means yes'* meant he wasn't taking any chances. Never been a letter writer, Lydia sent no reply; however, she knew better than not to look for him that Sabbath afternoon. She valued his thoughtfulness for giving her time to rest after church and lunch.

"*I'll tell Dean Reyes about this intended visit,* she mentally decided. She could ill afford to jeopardize her life as a student.

"You are both mature," Miss Reyes said with an approving smile. "Meet at the visiting room, or elsewhere you would feel comfortable at. I trust you to conduct yourselves as you are—mature individuals."

"Thank you, Ma'am. We will not fail your expectations of us," Lydia promised.

The change in her feelings amazed her, for in the past, she had little to do with suitors. But Alfonso's gentlemanly manners during the few times they happened to be in each others company had been delightful. He made her feel respected as a young lady, the most important one in his life, and she returned the respect in kind, and possibly more so.

In her bedtime prayer that night, Lydia added, *Lord, this friendship is in Thy all-knowing hands. May it bring glory to Thy most holy name.*

So unusual for sleep not to come, ran in her thoughts as she lay wide awake. She took her Bible, it opened to the Song of Solomon. *Well....* she thought. *I'll read a part of it.* As she read, an incident disrupted her focus: In her mind's eye appeared a slender black-rim-spectacled friendly gentleman who, smiling from ear to ear, and after clearing his throat, said, "I have a nephew in the States finishing his studies." Her ears tingled to hear him say, 'I'd like you to meet him when he returns."

Lydia had heard Pastor Antonino Roda preach—a fiery preacher with a deep bass voice. Now, she was sure Mr. Alfonso Roda was the nephew of whom he spoke. *Except for the family name,* she mused, *I saw little resemblance between them. Pastor Roda with a much lighter complexion....* She liked the name he called her, *Balasangko* (daughter-mine). *They must be taking this as a family affair,* the thought bemused her. An Ilokana herself, how well did she know of the closely-knit family ties, how they safeguarded one another as with an eagle's eye.

Did Mr. Roda confide his feelings to his uncle—of the academy student whose name he wanted to know four years ago? I acted so immaturely, she chided herself. She determined to let the Lord handle this matter and to leave it that way. With these ponderings, Lydia drifted to sleep.

***

NATURE'S REMEDIES
by Ellen G. White

There are many ways of practicing the healing art; but there is only one way that Heaven approves. God's remedies are the simple agencies of nature, that will not tax or debilitate the system through their powerful properties. Pure air and water, cleanliness, a proper diet, purity of life, and a firm trust in God, are remedies for the want of which thousands are dying; yet these remedies are going out of date because their skillful use requires work that people do not appreciate. Fresh air, pure water, and clean, sweet premises, are within the reach of all, with but little expense; but drugs are expensive, both on the outlay of means, and the effect produced upon the system.

Pure air, sunlight, abstemiousness, rest, exercise, proper diet, the use of water, trust in divine power—are the true remedies. Nature's process of healing and upbuilding is gradual, and to the impatient it seems slow. The surrender of hurtful indulgences requires sacrifice. But in the end it will be found that nature, untrammeled, does her work wisely and well. Those who persevere in obedience in her laws will reap the reward in health of body and health of the mind. Counsels on Diet and Foods, p. 301.

These, We Can Do Ourselves: (Letter 35, 1890) *I must become acquainted with myself, I must be a learner always as to how to take care of the body God has given me, that I may preserve it in the very best condition of health. I must eat food which will be for my very best good physically, and I must take special care to have my clothing such as will conduce to a healthful circulation of the blood. I must not deprive myself of exercise and fresh air. I must get all the sunlight that is possible for me to obtain. I must have wisdom to be a faithful guardian of my body.*

I... would be unwise to enter a cool room when in a perspiration. I should not allow myself to sit in a draft, and then expose myself as to take cold. I ... would be unwise to sit with cold feet and limbs, and thus drive back the blood from the extremities to the brain or internal organs. I should always protect my feet in damp weather. I should eat regularly of the most healthful food which will make the best quality of blood, and I should not work intemperately if it is in my power to avoid doing so. And when I violate the laws... I am to repent and reform....

Chapter II

<u>I KNOW</u> LOVE

April 7, 1952. Professor Roda boarded the Halili bus that would take him to Blumentrit, where he would take a jeep to MSH—the San. His heart overflowed with gratitude to God, who controls the destinies of man. He held a wrapped single long-stemmed white rosebud, its opening petals exuding fragrance he reveled in, influencing him in contemplation. *This rose typifies our blossoming regard for each other. As God's power in the sunshine dabbed beauty and fragrance to this rosebud, Lord, let the rays of Thy love touch our lives. By our love—Lydia and I—may we honor Thee.*

Bounding up to the fourth floor, to the nursing students temporary quarters, he stood at the waiting room. Light footsteps took shape in a trim Lydia coming out to greet him. He stepped up to meet her, and looking into her eyes, offered the rose. Lydia's smile brightened the room.

"Thank you, it's beautiful," she said. They took the corner chairs facing each other. Their talk led to the happenings at the wedding, their work, their friends, and about the future. Just being with her made Alfonso feel so much younger than on school days. His somewhat boyish ways, coupled with an unassuming dignity, stirred a responsive chord in Lydia. She felt safe with him. There was an unspoken mutual feeling: *I'll take pride in introducing you to my friends and relatives. I'll be proud to be seen with you, to walk beside you in public places.*

The visit ended too soon for the professor. It was only the beginning of many wonderful shared moments for them in days to come. On Tuesday, he mailed a letter he had written, sharing with her highlights of life in Baesa and at PUC.

On his second visit, Alfonso suggested a walk along Laguna de Bay. *That's the lovers promenade lane,* crossed Lydia's mind, *but why not. It would do us good to get out of the campus.* "It isn't far," she replied. "I like the sea breeze and I enjoy watching the colors play at sunset."

They mingled with other couples walking to the bay. They walked in step with each other as they crossed to the other side, to the seashore.

"Let's sit on the cement walls to watch the waves," he invited. "These guardrails serve well as benches, hard on the rear they may be." They chuckled on that, and they sat down side by side, sideways to face the sea. When an unusually high wave peaked and slapped, they instinctively leaned away, shielding their faces with their palms from the ocean spray. They stayed to soak in the glory of the panoramic sunset, to enjoy the hues in the western horizon turn from light to bright orange to magenta as the red round sun dipped into the sea, silhouetting the distant cordillera ranges.

"There's quiet romance in sunsets," he said. "I never tire watching the clouds, the dust—in refracting the light of the sun—create dazzling prismatic colors. All living things owe life from the sun. Our God of love splashed all this beauty for human eyes to see and to remember Him by."

They listened to the rhythmic ebb and flow of the waves, nature's song no vocal chord or musical instrument could replicate. The cooling sea breeze, soothing the body and the mind dispensed peace, a healing balm. This sharing of the sunset with each other became a favorite weekend pastime for Alfonso and Lydia. The leisurely walk to the seashore and their return to the San at twilight from Manila de Bay proved to be calming and rejuvenating especially to the professor.

"I had a wonderful afternoon with you," Alfonso always said as he saw Lydia safe in the nurses' dorm. "Until next week, adieu, my love."

If I continue in this friendship, Lydia pondered, *to enjoy single blessedness is nil.* The mission stories they heard from Sabbath to Sabbath, like fairy tales were interwoven in the students' dreams that they, too, would someday serve in foreign mission fields. Thinking this over, *He's ready to settle down while I'm not,* somewhat daunted her. Although he has not formally proposed, he had dropped clues making her feel they belonged to each other, and she didn't really know how to deal with this.

The jeep ride back to Baesa allowed Alfonso time for reverie and serious reflection. *I thank Thee for the wonderful time I had with the young woman Thou intended for me, Lord. I thank Thee for Thy leading, for instilling in man a part of Thyself—Thy love. For enabling humans to appreciate beauty. It gives Thee pleasure to see Thy children enjoy the beauty in Thy vast second book all around us. I thank Thee for giving human hearts the capacity to love. This noble emotion, I feel now filling my whole being, is from Thee Lord. To Thee, Author of love, I consecrate these feelings.*

"I'm home," he announced as he stepped in their home. "*Mamang,* you didn't have to stay up for me," he said.

"I wanted to… I wanted to hear about your visit, *Anak.*"

Alfonso let out a low chuckle. He took a seat beside his mother. "If eyes were made for seeing, then beauty is its own excuse for being," he said.

"Quoting whom? Speak from your own heart, Ponsing," she said. "I know Lydia's simplicity is beauty your eyes feasted on today. How was your visit? That's what I stayed up for—to find out."

"We took a walk to Laguna de Bay, sat on the hard guardrails to watch the sunset. Lydia enjoys the sunset as much as I do. She's rather a quiet person, reticent to share her thoughts openly with me at this point. I told her I'll see her again next week. I'll write her a letter before then."

"From what you said, I think Lydia enjoys your company. I'm happy for you, Ponsing. Any sensible young woman appreciates an admirer not rushing up.... I like to see you with a beautiful, calm and unassuming wife." A smile crept up her eyes. "A beautiful, God-fearing wife will always be a complement to her husband's position in our Church work, or elsewhere."

Alfonso yawned. "For God's glory," he said, and stood up. "We've been thinking along the same lines, *Mamang*. I'd like to add, I figured that if Lydia has awareness of her beauty, she does not parade the knowledge. Not a hint of frivolity in her, I like that. I find her very personable."

"*Anak*," she said catching his eye, "doesn't it bother you that you were over eight and a-half years old when she was born?"

He was silent for some moments. He shook his head slowly, but he remained silent, staring into space. "*Mamang*, not at all," he finally said. "Lydia acts so much more mature than her age. Having lost her mother, she and her older sister took over a mother's responsibility for their family." He began pacing the living room. "I do keep myself fit and in shape. I believe chronological age has little to do with one's vitality. If lives of men and women in the Bible were written for future generations, wasn't Abraham ten years older than his wife Sarah?"

"I'm glad you see it that way." She reached out to give his arm a pat.

"Good night, Ma," he said. "Have a good night sleep."

"You, too, *Anak*."

As Alfonso settled in his room, once again he turned reflective. *The Lord communed with Adam and Eve in the Garden of Eden on the Sabbath day. It was His great pleasure. I, too, felt great pleasure in visiting with my love.* In his letter, he wrote of his true feelings left unexpressed during their few hours visiting. But for Alfonso, a letter was a poor substitute for being with Lydia in person.

Lydia, too, had musings of her own. *Did he learn to court properly while he was a student in the States?* She figured out he was in his mid-twenties then. *Did he have a young lady friend there? I'll find this out somehow.* Suddenly, she came to her senses. *What for?* she chided herself. *He makes me feel the most important person in his life. I'll do all I can to meet his perceptions of me.* She re-read the letter in her hand:

Dearest Lydia, My Love,

The beauty of the sunset we shared together last Sabbath gave wings to my thoughts of our heavenly father Who is a God of love. He is also a lover of beauty Who made us in His image so we may enjoy His love for the beautiful.

The poem I memorized as a schoolboy became more meaningful to me as I watched the play of colors with you beside me. You may remember the stanza: 'He gave us eyes to see them, And lips that we might tell, How great is God our Creator, Who high above doth dwell.'

Not only did I thrill to the glory of the sunset, I was also aware of the beauty of my darling beside me. Sweetheart, let me tell you how much you mean to me. Let me tell you how much I love you....

After Lydia finished reading the rest of the letter, she refolded it, and inserted it back in the blue envelope. Reflecting, *blue is my favorite color. Blue means hope.* She wondered if he chose a blue stationery for what the color stood. She tucked the envelope in the drawer of her night stand.

Is this the feeling of one in love? I must never had fallen in love before. He likes all the qualities he says he sees in me. Funny I'm not conscious of any qualities in my person. I take for granted every Christian girl should live up to such standards. Mother's death taught me to live to the fullest. She often repeated, 'Life is too short to fritter away.' He must have learned to appreciate life, with only one parent to look up to. I'd been fortunate to have mother live to my mid-teens. Has the death of his father affect his view of life so that he feels the need to wait for the right person to come along? Am I the right person he'd been waiting for?

These thoughts absorbed Lydia's mind as she prepared to study. Now, awareness came to her feelings of being worn out. She wished she could just plop down in bed for some sleep, but she forced herself to study. And being not a letter writer, with little time to spare, she wrote no reply.

Not Funny. September days lived up to its hot and humid repute to a T. Lydia looked at her watch. 330. *Good, he isn't here yet. I'll snatch a few minutes rest right now.* Peeling off her apron, and still in her inner blue uniform, she flung herself atop her bed. When she heard Dean Reyes call, she got up immediately and walked to the sala. There, her eyes met Alfonso's. She had dozed off, and now aware of her perspiration-soaked underarm sleeve, she felt trapped. And embarrassed.

Alfonso ignored her discomfiture. He put effort to ease her apparent bind and she slowly forgot her predicament as she listened to the adjustments he went through as an adult student in America:

"'I'll see you,' my new friend said as he left, so I waited and waited for him to return. When he did not return, I thought perhaps he'd forgotten. At another time, he said, 'I'll give you a ring,' as he left. I puzzled, 'a class ring?' He called by phone! Lesson No. 3 came a few weeks later. We were talking about job possibilities, when her sister came. 'Meet Ann, my baby sister. She's in sixth grade,' he said. 'Dad wants you home,' she said. 'You're pulling me leg,' he said. She stuck her tongue out at him, then she left. 'Aren't you going home?' I asked. 'Say that again,' he said. I did. 'Say that again,' he repeated. I complied. He burst out laughing. 'What's so funny?' I asked. 'Don't worry, some day you'll learn,' he said."

Lydia joined in the laughter.

"I saw my unfamiliarity with American idiomatic expressions posing a threat to my social life. I made up my mind to pay close attention to their verbiage. I began questioning the hidden meaning of any unfamiliar phrase. Though a few made fun of me, most of them were kind enough to enlighten me with the American idiomatic expressions." He shook his head slowly, cast Lydia a sidelong glance, half a grin on his face stayed put.

"Now, thinking about our missionaries in campus," he continued, "I suspect they go through a similar experience, except that we are more eager to help them. We go out of our way to make them feel comfortable. I like to think that they can trust us. The difference is that I was a student there while our missionaries here are leaders." After a brief pause, he mumbled, "We virtually worship them. We put them on a high pedestal."

He's trying to give me a picture of life in the States, she thought.

"Maybe some day, your dreams of becoming a foreign missionary will come true," he said with a twinkle. "A foreign missionary to America."

You'd better not make fun of me, flipped in Lydia's mind. "Other than the colloquial-idiom problems, how's life in the States?" she asked.

"Anyone willing to work hard for an education can make it there."

"Like many students in PUC," Lydia mumbled. "For my tuition, I had worked at different places:—at the laundry, at the business office, and even at PPH (Philippine Publishing House).

"Our closely knit and extended family ties are bonuses for us here. The modern conveniences in the States make it easy for any ambitious student to earn his education. Some of my classmates said they were earning their way piecemeal. Some take advantage of student loans—they pay the loan after graduating. There are those who, getting a job as a grocery store checker, or busboy at a fast-food restaurant, skip the rigors of getting an education. With their earnings, they make a down payment on a car, and finance their own car instead of investing in an education."

As Alfonso started to leave, Esther came around and accompanied him down the flight of stairs. "It's a surprise birthday party for Lyd," she said in a hushed tone. "Just a simple one for lack of time. Could you come?"

Drawing out a little notebook from his shirt pocket, Alfonso jotted down the time and the place to meet.

"After sunset, we will ride the Motorco along Laguna de Bay, so dress for it," Esther advised.

So thoughtful of Esther to surprise her sister with a birthday party, Alfonso reflected as he walked away. Instead of meeting them at the place she designated, however, he would show up at the nurses' dorm as usual, but earlier. *Lydia would worry something happened to me or would suspect something was up. Plus,"* he thought, *roses wilt if exposed to the wind.* He knew the winds along Laguna de Bay to be gusty, and the Motorco had no protection from the wind. He thought about the time. *Did Esther feel riding the Motorco tantamount to 'doing your own pleasure on the Sabbath day'? She cared enough not to cause a stumbling block.*

Alfonso looked forward to the Sabbath day for reasons more than to keep it holy. To be with Lydia. *Jesus said, The Sabbath was made for man and not the other way around,* Alfonso reminded himself. He couldn't empathize with the Jews who took the revolutionary ways of Jesus' Sabbath keeping, as in healing the sick, for desecrating the Sabbath.

Lydia received his weekly letter. In it he implied he had matters he wanted to talk about in person. *His life in America,* she thought.

September 27. The unusually heavy traffic caused an unexpected delay for Alfonso. A smiling Lydia met him. "Thanks, I got some rest," she replied to his apology for being late. "Almost 5 o'clock," he sighed, then beaming he sang, "Happy birthday to you…." and handed her the three long-stemmed dark pink roses he had chosen with care early in the week.

"My birthday is past, but I thank you so much for these fragrant beauties," she said, burying her face in the petals. "They will brighten my room." Then eyeing at his clothes, she muttered, "You must not have come from your missionary work in Muntinglupa."

"Someone pitched in for me today, I'll make up for it next Sabbath," he said. "Some of the men are seriously studying the Bible with us," he added.

"I'd never been there," she said, and thought, *I'd loathe going there.*

"It's common knowledge that prisoners are lifelong evil men who'd committed crimes, but like the Japanese prisoners of WW II, many of them had been victims of circumstances. Some of them take a serious look at their lives for the first time while in prison. PUC is reaching out to those desiring to better their lives. The Holy Spirit is ever seeking to work in the hearts of men longing to improve their lives. We are all prisoners of sin."

Preciosa burst in on them. Her eyes met Alfonso's. He stood up. "Let's go," they said. "for a walk to Laguna de Bay."

"I need to get something," Lydia said, she went to her room, and returning with a bandanna, she said, "Okay, let's go."

As they reached Laguna de Bay highway, the Motorco stopped in front of them. Gesturing at the steps, Esther called, "Come on up." In her hand were two large red balloons. Flanking her, Alfonso and Preciosa each took a hand of Lydia. And breaking out in laughter, the three new passengers stepped up after Esther.

"You both sit back there," Esther gestured, giving the balloons to Alfonso. "Sorry, there's not enough room here for all of us," she added. Preciosa followed her older sister to the front.

"Hello there, both of you!" Catalino Vizcarra said. "I'll have to sit up front so as not to be a crowd back there," he said, his eyes disappearing.

"Did you mastermind this?" Lydia asked Alfonso.

"Not guilty, Dear."

"Yes, I'm getting old," she moaned.

"Who isn't?" he said, grinning.

"Uh, your question last Sabbath," he began. "I didn't give the complete answer. Didn't have the chance," he said. "No, I had no girlfriend in America." he whispered. "But," he said, clearing his throat again and again.

"I hope you are not catching a cold," she said with a hint of concern.

"No, I don't think so," he chuckled. "I'm confessing that when I was in the States, you were often in my mind. What beauty I saw in the 'gals' reminded me of you." After a brief pause, he continued. "Before I left for the States, I shared my heart throbs with my uncle Tony. Then by the grapevine I heard many young men were at your doorstep."

My supposition was right, she thought, remembering Pastor Antonino Roda telling her of a nephew in the States he'd like her to meet when he returned. "Do you want to know the truth?" she asked. She gave him a sidelong glance and saw him nod. She hesitated, keeping him in suspense.

"I'm waiting to hear the truth, Dear," he said.

"Before I left PUC," she began, "friends told me that one student went crazy over me. This was a surprise to me. No one, in person or in writing, let me know of... only later... I heard he was afraid of rejection and never came out openly ... to me. I'm sorry, but I can also say, 'not guilty.'

"Oh," he muttered, then asked. "What about the bright and gifted doctor, a talented violinist, who composed poems, dedicating them to you?"

For some moments, Lydia was silent, eyes faraway. Then in almost a whisper said, "Frankly, I honestly felt we were not right for each other."

***

MAKE HASTE SLOWLY

by Ellen G. White

... I would like to warn the young who are of marriageable age to make haste slowly in the choice of a companion ....

Those who are contemplating marriage should consider what will be the character and influence of the home they are founding. As they become parents, a sacred trust is committed to them. Upon them depends in a great measure the well-being of their children in this world and their happiness in the world to come. To a great extent they determine both the physical and the moral stamp that the little ones receive. And upon the character of the home depends the condition of society; ....

Weigh every sentiment and watch every development of character in the one with whom you think to link your life destiny. The step you are about to take is one of the most important in your life, and should not be taken hastily. While you may love, do not love blindly ....

The Adventist Home, pages 44–45.

***

Chapter III

THE THOUGHTS OF TRUE LOVE

As the graduating Class of 1952, in their crisp, spotless white uniforms and caps marched in cadence, Lydia felt pride for her older sister, mixed with longing for her own graduation.

Following the commencement exercises, Lydia wended her way with others congratulating each graduate. She gave Esther a hug and handed her a neatly wrapped gift. "Your turn will come next," Esther said. "A big hurdle is behind me," she said, relief in her voice. "Graduation makes all the hard work worth it." Then remembering what lies ahead, she mumbled, "It would take less time to review for the board exam."

The graduates were grateful that the San had a place ready for every graduate who wanted to stay and join the nursing service. A few of them, however, inspired by the thrilling in-the-service-of-the-King mission stories they heard from Sabbath to Sabbath, answered mission calls.

"Hello, everyone!" Catalino Vizcarra, Jr. (Jun) said as he joined the crowd. "I got off duty on time to congratulate the graduates," he added with a smile. "Let me help you carry those," he said extending his hands to Esther. "You have only two hands, many hands lighten load," he added.

Lydia belly-laughed. "Funny, isn't it, I had to gift-wrap and bring this gift over when we room together," she said.

"It looks good to give gifts when people are looking," Jun quipped. "And we wrap them so we could watch their reaction as they unwrap...."

Addressing Jun, Precy asked, "Will your graduation be as grand as this?" Then doubting her statement, she added, "Do doctors have commencement like... uh....the nurses... or other professions?"

"Of course!" Jun assured her.

"You'll have to send me an invitation," Preciosa gibbered.

Pasay Adventist Church, the graduation venue, but a few minutes walk to the hospital, closed its doors as soon as the last graduate or guest left. Upon arriving at the San, the group saw a waiting line at the elevator.

"Come on," Jun called. "Let's take the stairs," he suggested and began walking up.

Lydia groaned. "Please," she said. "The elevator will be here soon." Heads turned to Lydia, and seeing her body language opposing the very idea, assented. Jun retraced his steps to join them.

While waiting for the elevator, Jun began, "I remember a story I heard my mother tell. Anyone wants to hear it?" He heard some say, "Go on," and saw interest in some faces. "It's a favorite tale my mother, a school teacher, had at her fingertips. Remember that in each re-telling of a story, little changes are common, but I'll do my best." At that, he proceeded:

"Long ago, a Chinese farmer had an only horse that helped him with his work. It pulled the plow to till the soil, helped in the harvesting chores, and pulled the cart for transportation. It was the farmer's most faithful friend, taking him places he needed to go."

Just then the elevator came down, and opened for them. The group boarded, and upon reaching the fourth floor, they bee-lined to the nurses' temporary dorm. "Come on in," Esther called out, and after everyone got settled, she said, "Okay, Jun, continue your Chinese tale."

"One day a hornet stung the horse. Frightened, it galloped away, leaving the farmer bereft of his friend and workhorse. Neighbors came to express their sympathy. With a lackadaisical shrug, the farmer said to his neighbors, "Good luck, bad luck, who is to tell?""

One lucky day, the workhorse returned, and following him were twelve wild horses. His neighbors came to congratulate him for his good fortune. Again the farmer replied, "Good luck, bad luck, who is to tell?"

Said one, "Tame a wild horse and you'll have a hard working horse."

The farmer's son at once saddled the workhorse and lassoed a wild horse. Delighted with his success in taming the first, a second one, and a third, he attempted to tame a fourth. Oh, but this was one wild horse. It jumped, it buckled down, and threw the rider off its back. The farmer's son fell down hard and his right leg broke in different places.

Once again, the neighbors came to sympathize. The farmer again replied, "Good luck, bad luck. Who is to tell?"

Then the war broke. All able-bodied men were drafted into the military. Because of his broken leg, the farmer's son was rejected from the service. The war raged long and hard. Then the news quickly spread all over town. All of the drafted men whom they knew were wiped out. Not one of them came home.

"Good luck, bad luck," said the farmer. "Who is to tell?"

Student Nurses Annual Physical Check-up. To date not one of the new pre-clinical students had reason for worry. The physical check-up assured students of their fitness to continue with their training. And if perchance an irregularity showed up, its early detection insured snipping the problem in-the-bud. The School Director called only students whose physical check-up were in question. In the past, a few students had had special tests run as a safeguard. Being in close contact with the sick, their immune system must be strong to withstand exposure to infectious diseases. For the protection of their patients, it was important they were not the source of infection. Special tests done in the past for a few of the students proved dispensable.

December, 1952. Lydia heard the Nursing Director call her name. "Please come to my office," she said. Miss Enola Davis informed her that an irregularity appeared in one of her physical exams. "I'd like you to go with me to see the Medical Director," she said.

I wonder what it is about, Lydia asked herself. She hoped to find solution to her worn-out feelings of late, at least anyway.

Dr. Willis G. Dick was intent at viewing a chest film when they reached his office. Acknowledging their presence, he pointed to a spot in the left apex. "It could represent minimal pulmonary tuberculosis," he said.

Lydia admitted to her recent all-was-not-well feelings but attributed this to her heavy class load as well as the stress in adjusting to life away from the familiarities of home. After a thoughtful moment, she said, "I'd been careful when giving Bible studies to my townsmate who is in the TB ward. Despite her negative sputum results, I always wore a mask. I had put effort to make her feel loved—as we were taught to do: I answered all her questions, we prayed together, and knelt close to each other."

Then it struck her. "My tuberculin tests had always been negative," she muttered. "I had no antibodies to fight TB bacilli!"

Dr. Dick and Miss Davis reached a decision. For her own sake, as well as for others, Lydia would stay in a room alone at the temporary nursing students' dorm. Not in absolute isolation, but she would rest in bed, and sputum tests will be done at regular intervals. Except for her clinical practicum, which would wait, she would remain a student.

This arrangement gave Lydia hope. Inwardly, *I'm thankful that now TB is curable, unlike a quarter of a century ago,* she affirmed herself. *I'll accept the curtailment of my training and take the treatment,* she decided.

"I don't look forward to staying in bed all day, nor do I relish the delay of my graduation," she said softly.

On their way out of the doctor's office, Lydia said, "May I request... no one outside the School of Nursing learns of my diagnosis or whereabouts...."

With innate womanly empathy, Miss Davis assured her. "I'll ask Dean Reyes to inform the students of your wish and to honor it," she said.

Lydia perceived beyond her words and thanked Miss Davis for being kind and understanding. The assurance fostered in her a resolve to bring something positive out of this adversity. She would waste no time delving on the how or why she came down with the infection. And introspecting, *The experience would be of value in teaching me, a nurse-in-the-making, to be more compassionate to the sick. I'll take this as a challenge for my faith. I'll be brave,"* she determined in her heart, *by God's grace.*

Yet that night as she lay wide awake, she sobbed, *Why me, Lord? I'd recently learned to accept my mother's death. You answered my prayers by helping me meet the required grade points for acceptance to the clinical division. I appreciate it, Lord, but here, only to dump this on me. What have I done to deserve it...?* Tears rolled down her cheeks. *For the first time, I'm beginning to consider love.... Didn't You give it to me? And now, I must give it up. Lord, it hurts even as I think of giving it up.*

She didn't feel like worshipping. Sleep evaded her. She forced herself to say, *Lord, give me a text,* half-demanding. She turned the lamp on and opened her Bible. Sobbing, she read and re-read the text before her: "For I know the thoughts that I think toward you, saith the Lord, thoughts of peace, and not of evil, to give you an expected end." (Jer. 29:11).

She knelt down to pour out her gratefulness for the assuring passage. *The real issue is doing something about it, find the strength to meet the ordeal that lay ahead.* In all fairness to Alfonso, she clung to a decision: *I'll find a way to get out of the relationship. This situation could be an opening for the fulfillment of my dreams to be a nurse in a foreign land.*

On Saturday afternoon when Professor Roda arrived and Lydia did not meet him, he inquired. Aware of their blossoming friendship, and he, being a mature and principled person, Dean Reyes told him the truth.

"May I see her?" he asked. Permission granted, he bounded up to the fourth floor, and knocked on her door. Although Lydia preferred no visitors, she didn't refuse to see him. *I must be courteous, decent and be realistic to the gentleman,* she told herself. Having pleaded with God for help in her decision, she had carefully weighed the words to say.

"Please understand," she began, "but I want to end our relationship **now.** I would like for you to look for another girl—a healthy one…"

"Look, Sweetheart," he interjected. "This illness that pronounced a death sentence on my father twenty-five years ago is conquered. My firm and final decision is, I'll marry you even if you die tomorrow."

Not until their exchange of serious thoughts did Lydia accede.

"You will become a full-fledged nurse, apply all your knowledge to fight this infection head-on, by God's grace. The Lord loves us, and both of us love Him. We know that in all things God works for the good of those who love Him" (Rom. 8:28 paraphrased).

He picked up the Bible from her bedside table. Leafing through its familiar pages, he stopped at 1 Corinthians 13 and began to read:

"Though I speak with the tongues of men and of angels, and have no charity, ('that is, love,' he said) I am become as sounding brass, or a tinkling cymbal. 2) And though I have the gift of prophecy, and understand all mysteries, and all knowledge, and though I have all faith, so that I could remove mountains, and have not charity (love), I am nothing 3) And though I bestow all my goods to feed the poor, and though I give my body to be burned, and have not charity (love), it profiteth me nothing. 4) Charity (love) suffereth long and is kind; charity (love) envieth not; charity (love) vaunteth not itself, is not puffed up. 5) Doth not behave itself unseemly, seeketh not her own, is not easily provoked, thinketh no evil; 6) Rejoiceth not in iniquity, but rejoiceth in truth; 7) Beareth all things, believeth all things, hopeth all things, endureth all things. 8) Charity (love) never faileth."

Pausing briefly, he looked deep into the eyes of Lydia. "Sweetheart," he said, "this is the love I have for only you."

He resumed reading, often glancing at Lydia who was reclining in bed, and read through to 13: And now abideth faith, hope, charity (love), these three; but the greatest of these is charity (love.) 'Amen,' he said.

Visits Unlimited. The next Sabbath afternoon, Alfonso arrived holding a neatly wrapped three long-stemmed red roses. "Direct from Mr. Parago's rose garden," he said beaming, and offered the gift to Lydia.

"They're so beautiful," she said. "You're spoiling me," she teased. On a small heart shaped card attached to a rosebud stem, printed in his own firm handwriting, Lydia read, *A Get-well wish from the garden of my heart to my Dearest.* She gave the petals a lingering kiss before placing them in the crystal bud vase on her bedside stand. "They're fragrant as they're lovely," she said. "Thank you very much."

He began to tell the story he knew so well:

"The College rose garden is a paradise to many students, notably the male gender. When a student selects a rosebud early in the week, Mr. Parago, or one of his assistants, tags the rosebud. On Friday, before the nursery closing hour, the young men return to pick up their orders. On rosebud tags read names like 'Amador-Eleanor, Conrado-Esther, Rudy-Purita, Leslie-Gloria, Minyong-Lagrimas....' You probably know more name combinations," he said. "In church every Sabbath, the roses float on young ladies' crisp blouses, creating a magical change. The commingling of two beautiful faces, the rose and the young lady's, enhances each other's beauty. Truly, God's crowning work of creation—we—the human race."

Mini-dimples, one beneath the corner of her lips, flashed when she smiled. Turning to look long at the roses, she said, "I'll enjoy them longer left on their stems and in water in the bud vase."

"I miss you coming down to meet me at our trysting place," he said, referring to the alcove behind the pharmacy. "Sylvia gave me a warm greeting as I passed by their department. Mrs. Mercado (chief pharmacist) was leaving, but she flashed her sweet smile and waved a hand."

"Both of our hospital pharmacists think very highly of you. They always let me know they approve…. Sylvia likes you very much."

Looking deep into her dark brown eyes, he said in a deliberate low tone, "I trust you like me as much." And without waiting for a reply, he continued, "This is a book I wanted to read through but so far I had only skimmed…. Would you care if you and I spend time reading it?"

He held a brand new copy of <u>Happiness for Husbands and Wives</u> by Harold Shryock, M.D. The word HAPPINESS in bold gold capital letters, against the white hardback cover, stated the purpose of the book, and 'For Husbands and Wives' also in gold but in small case immediately below the word HAPPINESS defined its target. Cursorily leafing the book, he said, "A good Christian doctor, happily married and with children, the author wrote this book from firsthand knowledge. I'll enjoy perusing its pages with you."

My intuition was right, she mused. *He's ready to settle down while I'm not.* Quickly, she resolved to live one day at a time, but first, she must deal with the infection and tackle her training following her recovery.

"After you graduate," he hesitated momentarily and looking deep into her eyes, he said, "we'll get married."

Lydia dropped her eyes and fixed them on the rosebuds. Profound silence. There was not a trace of a smile on her face. Did he read from her eyes—hope? Assurance? Or dismay? Did it come too suddenly for her, she wasn't sure what was in her heart, nor in her mind?

That's three years from now, she thought. *My dream of traveling to foreign lands as a missionary nurse must not be a part of my future. Someone is definitely re-arranging my life for me.* Nonetheless, she was surprised that, rather than sounding repulsive, the idea of falling in love and the dream of every woman—marriage and home—touched in her heart a responsive chord. Being a typical young woman, the thought of wearing a white wedding gown marching down the aisle, then settling down with the man she loved suffused her with a warm feeling. She kept to herself the surge of emotion, a longing to finish her training, her wish to hasten her graduation, and her wedding. In her mind, she saw herself beside him, a pure bride. *Lord, Thy will be done,* she prayed silently.

"Silence means yes, I presume," he said, a question in his tone. "A typical Filipina, an Ilokana you are," he mumbled, a faint smile on his face. "I assume my presume is correct," he added teasingly. The smile spread on his face so expectant of affirmation. He took note of a slight blush on her cheeks. Still getting no reply, he said. "You look well rested. Your imposed bed rest is working to your advantage."

"Doing nothing, I'm gaining so much weight, and I don't like it. I sleep good and I feel good, and wish I could get on a diet and…."

"Now, now, don't worry, Darling," he interjected, still smiling. "You're pleasantly plump in the right places," he added. "Dr. Dick is a good doctor."

"Yes. He's very happy to see the negative results of the sputum tests, but as to reading of your book," she gestured at the book in his hand, "you'll have to do the reading. I promise to be your attentive listener."

"I solemnly accept the task," he said in all seriousness. "And you be my quiet listener and absorber. I will permit interruption of my reading anytime you need to ask a question or to make a comment. I, too, will stop reading to elaborate on a passage as necessary. So, this reading is an invitation to an open give-and-take between the two of us."

"I'd like that," she replied, "but don't expect much from me."

Thus began the Sabbath afternoon worthwhile hours they both looked forward to. Prelude to reading, Alfonso always knelt down to pray for God to grant them wisdom and understanding in their reading. Before leaving, he also prayed, committing themselves to their Father's care.

During their Sabbath afternoon reading, gems opened to lively discussions. He underlined these passages and jotted notes at the margins. On the chapter, 'Disappointed in Marriage?' Lydia said, "My only wish is for you to remain a decent man, for you to uphold your good name at all times. I will not tolerate any kind or hint of 'playboy' or 'woman-chaser' bit," she said. "It must never mar our relationship, must never come between us. I also own accountability as a Christian woman," she added.

And both of them pledged to safeguard their reputation, to uphold each other, to mind their actions and relationship to each other, and above all be true to God, by His grace.

While reading the chapter, 'Maturity of Personality,' Alfonso said, "I believe the Lord will not take any wish lightly albeit trite. My wish is for our firstborn son to favor your good looks and your calm disposition."

"A son to look like me? I wouldn't want to disappoint you but your wish is one beyond my control!" Lydia blurted out. As soon as it came out, she felt silly about it, and said so, which gave them something laugh about.

"Good looks isn't all," Lydia mumbled, and quickly added, "He'd better grow taller than us. Above all, I'd like for them to conduct themselves wisely, to make use of their brains. There's no excuse for them to be 'unbrainy', what with the Panis-Roda blood coursing through their veins."

"No excuse," he said. "I agree with you, that, coupled with the genes from their mother's side." And with a grin, he continued, "I'm glad to hear you use the plural form for our future offsprings. Come to think of it, we both come from large families!"

Almost interrupting him, "Not to get out of the subject matter," she said, "but didn't Paul boldly ask God to restore his eyesight? Didn't he have faith even as a mustard seed to get a positive answer to his prayer? Why didn't the apostle worry God enough until He gave him back his eyesight?"

"Paul did ask, and God assured Him His grace was sufficient for him, and the apostle was compliant to the will of the Omnipotent, Who knew Paul would be more effective in His service with his weakened vision." Pausing and locking eyes with Lydia, he continued. "Back to 'braininess.' Let's not overlook preconceptual and early childhood environment, which includes good nutrition. Our Creator instructed our first parents on the food to nourish their bodies. That original diet holds true to this day, to us—but paramount is our personal connection to the Source of brain power—'The fear of the Lord is the beginning of wisdom.'"

"My mother already likes you very much," Alfonso said when they were reading the chapter, 'Parents-In-Law.'

"Thank you," she said. "I will love her as my very own mother," she added softly, and even in a softer tone, "I'm not sure if I can be as close to my father as I had been to him before he re-married. You might need to deal with Tiong *Dons*. He's even more puritanical than my own father."

If it struck Alfonso that Lydia's uncle was his contemporary, he let none of this feeling show. "I admire and respect your uncle," he said.

While reading the 'Maturity and Personality' chapter, he underlined the passage: A husband or wife should not play the role of parent to the other. for a relationship to develop which is comparable to the parent-child relationship would be perpetuating the … emotional immaturity which now serves as a handicap. They should work out a plan of joint responsibility for the affairs of the home by which the husband and the wife each assumes their share of the burdens incident to maintaining the home…. Unselfishness in action takes the form of service for others.

By the end of March, they had completed reading, Happiness for Husbands and Wives. They had taken time to absorb the instructions Dr. Shryock presented in his book that included many passages from Ellen G. White's writings. Both felt they had gained an honest practical view of Christian home relationships.

At his next visit, Lydia told Alfonso that Esther had arranged to rent an apartment in the village, and that she had invited her to room with her.

"Will you show me the place?" he teased.

"Of course not!" softly laughing, she quickly added, "We will walk around the place on our way to Laguna de Bay. We're transferring the first of the month. The place is about five minutes walk from the hospital grounds. It is a safe and quiet neighborhood, as peaceful as Baesa."

Alfonso kept nodding his head, and Lydia continued:

"It is a three-bedroom apartment. *Mang* Es and I will room together, Mrs Crescencia (Cresing) Saldivar and her husband will have one, and her aunt will have the other room. Actually, we are converting the place into an apartment." After a brief pause, "My brothers will help us carry the heavy things," she said. "We don't have a lot of things to lug."

***

CHARACTER OF TRUE LOVE

by Ellen G, White

Love is a plant of heavenly origin. It is not unreasonable, it is not blind. It is pure and holy. But the passion of the natural heart is another thing altogether. While pure love will take God into all its plans, and will be in perfect harmony with the Spirit of God, passion will be headstrong, rash, unreasonable, deficient of restraint, and will make the object of its choice an idol.

In all the deportment of one who possesses true love, the grace of God will be shown. Modesty, candor, simplicity, sincerity, morality, and religion will characterize every step toward an alliance in marriage. Those who are thus controlled will not be absorbed in each other's society, at a loss of interest in the prayer meeting and other religious services.

If men and women are in the habit of praying twice a day before they contemplate marriage, they should pray four times a day when such a step is anticipated....

<u>Messages to Young People</u>, pages 459–460.

***

Chapter IV

<u>THAT</u> PRELUDE TO HOMEMAKING

Esther and Lydia packed and packed. "Can't find much to discard to lessen our junk, only to regret having thrown them away," said Esther.

"We'd been living temporarily in a temporary place, that's why," Lydia said. "What I'm looking forward to is my graduation from the fourth floor," she added laughing. "And this is one sure way to make some of my dreams come true. I will be able to eat so as to lose most of this junk weight." She let out a chuckle, lifted her right leg and spanked her thigh.

Esther said, "You are not alone in wanting to lessen the extra baggage you are lugging everywhere you go." She belly laughed.

"I don't like what bed rest and institutional cooking are doing to me! I don't like the feel and the looks of it," Lydia continued self-depreciating. "My tastebuds finally got used to the San food and basking in the freedom from planning what to prepare for the next meal...." Sideglancing her older sister, she added. "Sorry, *Mang* Es, a lot of work may have fall on you. But I promise to do what I can to help you. At least we can put less calories in what we eat when we prepare our own food." She gave a sigh. "Perhaps we should try a fruitarian diet—no cooking—that's less work!"

"That's a good idea," Esther replied. "I hope you are serious."

"I am, and glad you think of it as a good idea. Let's begin thinking of the fruits available all year round: bananas—with its many varieties—we need not get tired of any kind." Then, she said in an undertone, "if we have time to go marketing."

"If you are serious about eliminating cooking, or at least much cooking, we can eat fruits at one meal, and vegetables at another, in accordance to the health rules outline in <u>Counsels on Diet and Foods</u>. I'm thinking of sweet potatoes, loaded with nutrients, but I prefer it boiled or roasted, not raw, like others I know eat them. Even then, boiling isn't all that much work. We need not add any more calories to them—just peel and eat them while they're still hot, adding nothing since they are naturally sweet."

"My mind is still on fruits," Lydia said. "Let's start from letter A. *Atis*, avocado, bananas, *buko*. "Is *buko* a fruit or a nut? I'll classify *buko* as palm fruit, never mind the 'nut' at the end of its name. Cantaloupe, *Chisa,* the texture of baked sweet potatoes, and we eat *chisa* raw. Jackfruit, giant of fruits. *Lanzones, lomboy, mabolo,* mango, papaya; pineapple, pomelo, star apple, strawberries, tomato, watermelon, zapote. I'll jot more down as I think of tree ripened fruits that we can eat fresh, that is, raw—uncooked—without cooking."

"I will make a list of vegetables that need no cooking," Esther said. "Cucumber, bell peppers, lettuce, for start. And I like *sinkamas* (Jicama), just peel the heart shape root, they're crispy and sweet. You mentioned tomato. It's fruit all right, but I think it's classified as a vegetable. We'll add nuts and seeds— legumes and grains—for a balanced diet. After some thought, she added, "*Mang* Cresing and her aunt might even suggest for us to prepare our meals together and eat as a family. Knowing her, a nurse and an Ilokana at that, I think we'll have fun. I like her cheerful disposition. Anyway, her husband is away in the service most of the time."

"I hope they won't mind our entertaining our visitors," said Lydia.

"*Mang* Cresing has been through that herself not too long ago," Esther said. "She would understand, I'm sure of it."

In the next few days as Esther, Lydia, and their apartment-mate friends began adjusting to their new living arrangement, they shared the same feeling of belonging. Like one big busy family, every one pitched in to the day by day home chores, including that of food preparation.

First Friday. Esther and Lydia, engrossed in their effort to make the living room a statement of their femininity, were unaware their apartment mates were observing them. Satisfied with their work in the living room, Lydia said she would 'do' their room, since Esther had to go, to be on duty.

Eager to see how they arranged their room, Cresing poked her head in and saw Lydia trying to hang a picture on the wall. Exchanging smiles, Cresing drew closer to look at the picture.

"Our last family picture taken not long before my mother became too weak to be up and about," Lydia explained. With her pointer finger, she identified her mother.

"Lovely," said Cresing. "I see Precy's face on your mother's." Then, making sniffing sounds, she said, "My aunt put on the stove a big pot of black beans with garlic, onions and tomatoes for that nothing-like-it flavor. I'll add the *bangus* and the *malunggay* tomorrow just before lunch. We'll have red rice, *camote tops* (sweet potato) with ripe tomatoes for salad."

"*Mang* Es plans to saute ampalaya with eggs and onions. We'll have *lacatan* and *pilipit* for dessert. I'll squeeze *kalamansi* to make a drink," Lydia said. "I'll lay the dishes out on the table before we go to church."

Soon after arriving from church, the 'new family' sat down around the dinner table to enjoy lunch together. Esther and Lydia declared the black beans scrumptious. They also agreed that every dish complemented each other. Cresing's aunt volunteered to clean the table and do the dishes.

"Thanks for a delicious meal," said Lydia. "I have to get the bed rest the doctor ordered. And it is Sabbath, a time to rest from labor," she chuckled as she stood up to leave for her room.

Shortly, Alfonso arrived. "I'm taking extra bed rest to regain the energy I spent during our moving-in and fixing our place," explained Lydia.

"The quietness around is conducive to a restful rest," he said. "Esther made a wise decision in taking this place. Surely, she had your welfare in mind. So very kind of her."

Lydia nodded her head. "That's *Mang* Es, she'd always been like that."

"How is she and Chay, Jr., the jolly fellow, coming along?"

"Fine. *Mang* Es likes him very much. We both like his easy-going personality," she replied. "You know his father, don't you? Dr. Vizcarra, the surgeon famous for thyroidectomies? Jun's mother was a school teacher." After a brief pause, she said, "I think they're talking of getting married after Jun completes his medical internship."

Alfonso reached to take Lydia's hand. "Holding hands is not yet a Filipino practice," he said. "I see nothing malicious in it. In the States, college students who like each other hold hands while strolling along. Is it all right with you?" From her facial expression, her reply was clear. "Soft, beautiful hands," he said. "Loving and caring nurse's hands. Don't you think we've had enough reading for a while? Diversion refreshes. Working people profit from taking regular vacations," he said.

By the smile that brought out the dimples beneath the corners of her lips, he understood that she agreed with him. "No reading today," he said.

He followed Lydia's eyes, he stood up for a closer look at the framed picture hanging on the wall. "Your family picture, isn't it?"

"Yes, the last family picture we had, taken before mother became too weak to get around." Her voice was soft, her eyes and manner spoke of nostalgia for her mother, and perhaps for the happy days with her.

Your mother was very attractive," he admired, "healthy-looking in the photo. "I see," he added, "Precy shows resemblance, and, I think, you favor your father's… facial features."

She nodded. "In many ways," she chuckled. "Very puritanical. In my growing-up years, whenever he heard me laughing boisterously, he'd say, 'Better practice to be more ladylike. No man respects a woman who laughs the way you do.' She paused to see his reaction. "He said rowdy and wild laughters may be all right for some men like Tiong *Dons* and *manong* Tito, 'but **never** for you,' father maintained." Alfonso noted her bemused look.

"I hope you don't mind me on bed rest. I think I over-exerted myself in our transferring and settling, otherwise we would have taken a walk to Laguna de Bay. Now, I must follow the doctor's order," she sighed.

He gave Lydia's hand a light squeeze. "I would remind you to follow the doctor's order if you did not."

"The closer I follow the doctor's order, the sooner I'd be able to get over his total bed rest order." Both chuckled over that.

"A good nurse is a good patient," he said. "I was too young to recall the details when my father was on total bed rest." He sat up taller, and drew a deep breath. "Now, I understand why father succumbed, perhaps he didn't know any better. In his eagerness and zeal to preach the gospel, shall I say, he cheated himself." He drew a deep breath. "Of course, we cannot dismiss this universal fact: Satan and his legion are hard at work. Yet, God gave to each of us the gift of choice. I believe father loved the Lord above all else, he chose to work hard to lead others to his God of love."

He turned contemplative, Lydia let him be. He cleared his throat.

"By God's grace, I resolve to do better, even as a husband and a father," he said. His face brightened and his tone came alive. "There's a newly published book, a compilation of Ellen G. White's writings titled, The Adventist Home. The author herself, a mother and a wife, backed up this book from personal experience. Of more significance is, the Lord directed her to write down and deliver the messages God revealed to her." He paused briefly as if to gather his thoughts, then continued:

"Whenever I think of the tragic accident she had when she was in third grade, Romans 8:28 comes to mind. Are you familiar with her life?" Presuming he read a question mark on her facial expression, he continued.

"Little Ellen and her twin sister were walking home after school when they became aware of someone angry behind them. Ellen turned to look. At that exact moment the angry classmate hurled a stone that struck the nose of Ellen. Little Ellen fell unconscious to the ground. The accident cut off her chances to continue her formal education. She became so fragile that when she returned to school and tried to write, her hand trembled and she broke in a sweat. Any effort she made in trying to write spent her, but look at the volume of articles and books she had written by hand. Over twenty-five million words! During her lifetime, she penned, literally hand wrote, thirty-seven books. She allowed God to lead in her life. After her death, the trustees of her estate compiled at least thirty-two books out of her written counsels and articles. Many of these books are now in over a hundred language-translations. A woman lacking a formal education but loved God, and desired to serve Him, accomplished much in her lifetime."

"In serving God, did she enjoy a problem-free life?" Lydia asked.

Shaking his head. "No," he replied. "Throughout her life, she discerned Satan making it hard for her and her family. Yet, her connection and faith in God gained strength with each problem overcome, by His grace. Then God's chosen protector of her youth, the companion of her life, the sharer of her labors and afflictions, died. She became a widow at age 54."

He reached into his shirt pocket and drew out a newspaper clipping. Unfolded it to show, "Smiling Armi Kuusela, the new Miss Universe," he said. He read to her the article written of the Finnish beauty-and-talent. After reading, he looked into Lydia's eyes. "I have my own Miss Universe in beautiful you," he said. His face showed he spoke from his heart.

As the afternoon progressed, Lydia became uncomfortable. *Gas filling my abdomen? Please, no,* she willed in her mind. Embarrassed to get up, she wished he'd leave, but it was not to be. He arrived at about one-thirty, and because she felt she needed her bed rest, they couldn't walk to Laguna de Bay, and now she wished they had gone for their regular Sabbath stroll. The exercise and fresh air would have helped. She enjoyed his company and presence, her increasing discomfort made her wish he'd leave. Five o'clock. No sign of him taking leave. To invite him for supper was out of the question. Still she wondered what plans her sister had. Not having the faintest clue of her predicament, Alfonso seemed to enjoy even her silences. He glanced at his watch. "I didn't realize it's past 6 o'clock," he said and stood up. "Till next week...." Squeezing her hand lightly, he said, "I love you, my Miss Universe." He bowed and prayed. "Mizpah," he said.

Soon after he stepped out, Lydia had to get relief. Esther heard it, and ran to their room laughing. To Lydia's query, she replied, "He had stepped off the stairways when I heard something." It assured Lydia, and they burst out laughing the loud laughter their father said was the laugher of a *garampingat.* "It must be the black beans," said. Lydia.

"And the combination of all the food we ate," Esther said.

They reviewed the different dishes they ate of heartily, including the fresh fruits and vegetables. No fresh vegetables, but they drank *kalamansiaide* during the meal and ate the *lacatan* after the full meal.

"My poor weakened gastrointestinal system," moaned Lydia. "Did I overeat? I was hungry, it was past our regular lunch time, and the food was so good. We should have gone for a walk instead of bed resting."

June 6, 1953. Lydia joined the 1953 Nursing Class commencement exercises. All her classmates received their diplomas, she didn't. Passing all the required courses alone did not qualify a nursing student a diploma. The doctor's order for complete bed rest, which interrupted the completion of her clinical practicum, left Lydia three more months to complete the required hours. Only then would she receive her diploma.

The Tabucol clan, her friends, Alfonso's siblings and their mother, attended the Nursing Class of 1953 graduation.

"Your complete uniform in white is very becoming on you," Alfonso whispered in to Lydia's ears, as he handed her a neatly wrapped gift.

"Complete bed rest, nourishing food, my determination to heal, by God's grace, coupled with love," she cast him a sidelong glance, "all worked together to strengthen my immune system," she said. "I praise the Lord. I feel strong physically, and I'm eager to complete my clinical practicum."

Alfonso's statement in December, "After you graduate, we'll get married," filled Lydia's mind. The adage, "Love conquers all," now held more meaning for her. She would be entering sacred matrimony with the one she loved and respected. Every normal young woman's dream. And she felt ready to go anywhere, even to the remote barrios with her would-be-minister husband, wherever the Lord would have them be.

As a nurse, I'd represent the right hand of the Message, working along with him, supporting his preaching, a missionary to my 'kababayan'. These thoughts burned in her heart. She visualized herself teaching young mothers how to care for their babies, their little children, their families, and giving them a hand in time of need. *With Christ on our team, we'll be working with Him, Who holds the future in His hands.* She envisioned what an extraordinary team they would make, with the Lord's blessings.

With each passing day, these dreams became more real to Lydia. Her clinical practicum hours were ticking away, she was enjoying every minute of it. She felt she was learning more each day. Now she understood. The months she spent on bed rest taught her lessons of empathy to the sick and injured, flowing freely out as she performed bedside nursing care.

*** *

THE GREAT ENCOURAGER

We all need some encouragement
  Along this life of days,
And there are always those who help
  In their own kindly ways:
A spoken word, a flashing smile,
  A visit, letter, call.

Within our hearts we realize
  That each of them stands tall
But there's a great encourager,
  Above and over all,
And He will always lift us up
  If we on Him will call.

He is the Christ, the living Lord,
  He is our strength and stay,
He is the great Encourager
  Along this life of days.
In Him we can completely trust,
  Our great Encourager.

by Loise Pinkerton Fritz
(last 2 lines added by crj)

***

Chapter V

<u>I THINK</u> OF THE WEDDING

The wedding invitation:

RODA - TABUCOL

WEDDING

Mr. Felix A. Tabucol	**Mrs. Maria Panis Vda. de Roda**
requests the honor of your presence	*requests the honor of your presence*
at the marriage of his daughter	*at the marriage of her son*
LYDIA	**ALFONSO**
to	*to*
Professor Alfonso P. Roda	**Miss Lydia M. Tabucol**

Tuesday, the twentieth of October, nineteen hundred and fifty-three at four o'clock,
Pasay English Church near Manila Sanitarium & Hospital

***

BACKDROP: Two large intertwining hearts in a sampaguita-bloom wrap, a symbol of two hearts that soon will be one. It was the original of Dr. Arturo Roda.

Redolent of sampaguita fragrance, the church was spilling over with well wishers. A few seconds before 4:00, Nestor Zamora walked to the organ, his nimble fingers touched ivory keys, and soft music filled the chapel. Nestor looked at his watch: 4:20. *Where s the bridegroom?* he wondered. Arturo and a younger cousin, Samuel Roda, and a friend, Enrique Z. Tauro continued ushering guests. Officiating minister Pastor Edwin Gibb stood at his place. Lydia's heartbeats accelerated. Maid of honor sister Preciosa, bridesmaids Concejo Caspe and Felicitacion Garcia cast anxious glances at each other.

Nestor Zamora checked his watch: It was 4:25. Now, the ushers stood beside the minister. Nestor turned to look and saw the cue; the bridesmaids in shimmering pink. He pushed the pedal, and strains of the wedding march swelled, filling the chapel. The maid of honor in blue followed the bridesmaids, all keeping step with the music.

The bride stood alone at the foyer, waiting. Questions jabbed at her heart. *Did he forget his own wedding? Did he change his mind? Did he meet an accident? Lord, take care of him,* her lips moved. She turned to the open door. There, she saw him exit a cab, saw him run up the steps.

"Sweetheart, I'm sorry, will explain later," he said on his way to the front. He took his rightful place beside the minister.

At the last minute, Bible bearer-elect Eliseo Roda Arevalo, Jr., refused to march.

Alfonso on his graduation

Precocious Arden Brion stepped in time. Dainty flower girl Boots Dalisay Valdez followed, scattering sampaguita petals on her way.

The liquid voice of Mrs. Ruth Mitchell Fisher flowed, interpreting "O Perfect Love...." The organ swelled to "Here Comes the Bride."

Heads turned to watch the beautiful bride in white floating with the music. In her hands she carried a bouquet of white butterfly orchids, pure as she. Surely, Alfonso's heart filled almost to bursting with happiness as he watched his lovely bride in white marching down the aisle.

Now, the minister's words: "Beloved, we are here to witness .... It is no ordinary attainment for two people to become one. Nothing on earth is so delicate and so easily moved as the human heart.... If two stringed instruments are to produce a melodious harmony, they must be in tune with each other...."

Following the exchange of vows—to love and honor till death do us part—Mrs. Fisher

Lydia and Alfonso on their wedding day, Oct. 20, 1953

sang "The Lord's Prayer"—a fitting benediction. Pastor Gibb introduced the happy, radiant Mr. and Mrs. Alfonso P. Roda.

During their group picture taking, Alfonso announced of his mother's invitation for a *salo-salo* (potluck) party at her home. "At the home I'm leaving," he said. "This is a special get-together for the new in-laws and our relatives with you," he added. The smiling newlyweds hand in hand led the wedding retinue to the church campus lawn for the refreshments.

The many guests, seated in chairs that filled the church lawn, stood up to welcome the bridal entourage by a hearty clapping of hands.

While enjoying the cookies, punch, and ice-cream, the bride's uncle Dr. Celedonio Fernando emceed in the program that featured Lorenzo Lacson and his group, singing love songs dedicated to the newlyweds. Then the emcee called out: "Attention! All single ladies please come forward." It was for the throwing of the bridal bouquet.

One by one—but only after quite a bit of gentle urging by the emcee—the bridesmaids, the maid of honor, and other single ladies went up to compete in catching the bridal bouquet. Cheers erupted for Concejo Caspe (now Mrs. Chun, class- mate and close friend of the bride) who caught the bridal bouquet.

The wedding entourage with Pastor Edwin A. Gibb behind the bride and groom. From l-r, nee Concejo Caspe, nee Fely Garcia, nee Preciosa Tabucol, Miss Enola Davis, groom's aunt Teodora Panis Aldccoa, the groom's mother, Maria Roda, the bride and bridegroom, the bride's father Felix Tabucol, Dr. W. C. Richli, Dr. Reuben Manalaysay, Dr. Arturo Roda, Enrique Z. Tauro, Samuel Roda. Front: Flower girl Boots Valdez, Bible bearer Arden Brion.

The newlyweds then went around to thank each guest for "sharing with the never-to-be forgotten wonderful occasion in our lives."

***

Their honeymoon trip by car—a favor from Mrs. Teodora (Doray) Aldecoa—was the thirty kilometer-drive from Pasay English Church to Alfonso's mother's home, (for the *salo-salo*) and then to their new home.

The bridegroom attempted to carry his bride up to their apartment, but she said, "No, let's walk up together." So, hand in hand they walked up the flight of stairs to the second floor of the newly built home of Mr. and Mrs. Basilio Bautista, friends of Alfonso from school days.

Recently married themselves, the Bautista couple were happy to share their home with their newlywed friends. "We're using only the first floor," they said. (Basilio worked at the Philippine Publishing House (PPH) about five minutes walk to Philppine Union College campus.)

With the help of Alfonso's aunt Doray's chauffeur, the last gift package was finally deposited on the corner of the long sala. Now, by themselves, the newlyweds began opening their wedding gifts. They were anxious to see the gifts from their many friends from MSH, NPUM, PUC, and PPH. They piled the opened gifts still in their wraps in the corner of the sala.

Earlier, Alfonso had taken Lydia to the apartment—for her approval—at which time she had made a mental note on what she would need to dress up the apartment: First in her note was, curtains for the long window.

"We could use these gifts right now," Lydia said, handing her new husband two large pails. She laid a large wash basin aside. With a pail in each hand, he descended the steps to the first floor, and came up with the pails filled with water. With the water, they washed their bodies clean. It had been an exciting and long yet a day of ecstasy for them.

"Mrs. Roda, may I escort you to our bedroom?" he offered, pulling her hand. "We need to talk, Sweetheart. Still sore at me for being late to our wedding?" he began. "Honest, I started counting down one hundred days to our big day. I knew our wedding day to the second. I hang up my white coat in my clothes closet and seeing it there always reminded me…. I hired a cab in plenty of time but on the way, I chanced to brush my chin…"

"Absent-minded professor," interrupted Lydia with a chuckle. "All right, Sir, unburden your heart."

"I was lucky to have hired a cab driver who was kind enough to drop me off at a barbershop. After the barber gave me a quick shave, I paid him, said 'keep the change,' and ran back to the waiting cab."

"Haste makes waste," Lydia muttered. "I never doubted when you kept counting down to our wedding day each time you came to see me." Despite her assurance, he kept repeating that their wedding day never left his mind. "I was too full of happiness, I simply forgot myself. I didn't want to appear unshaven on our big day." Briefly pausing to study his bride's reaction, he continued in a lower tone.

"At my urging, *Mamang* recounted their wedding day. I thought it worth emulating, and I'd like to make it a family tradition. That is, if you agree with me, Sweetheart," he added, gathering her in his arms. "Oh, how I wanted to do this before, but was never brave enough to do it," he said, planting kisses on his bride. "It feels good holding you close to me."

"I thought you know me well enough. I wouldn't have let you if you tried," she said, "but I'm anxious to know whatever you said 'if I agree."

Opening the drawer of their night stand, he drew out a small notebook. "We both like poems," he said. "I'd like to perpetuate a—ritual—if you please. *Mamang* recalled father taking a poem out of his inner vest pocket, 'close to his heart'," she said, a poem that he read to her before they knelt down for their first bedtime prayer together. That had been many years ago, but she remembered that the poem was about love. After reading the poem to her, together they read chapter 13 of 1st Corinthians.

He picked up the Bible. "We will read now, Sweetheart," he said and kissed his wife tenderly. Before beginning to read he said, "Sweetheart, I never forgot the day and time of our wedding, I'll always remember it."

Lydia had the urge to laugh the uproarious laughter her father said was unbecoming to a lady, but she gave in to a soft belly laughter, and managed to say, "Darling, I believe you the first time you said it, and I'd forgiven you for it." The gleam she saw in his eyes spurred her to confess. "For a while, I worried over the possibility of your having met an accident. I prayed for your safety. When I finished praying, I saw you alight a cab. I thanked the Lord with all my heart. So, please, forgive yourself, too."

"Thank you, Sweetheart. I'll forever be grateful to have married a beautiful and forgiving wife." He wrapped her in his arms, kissing her again and again. "So soft, so cuddly. The title of this poem is, 'To My Wife,' written by Robert L. Stevenson. I'd like to dedicate it to you, my own wife:

> *Trusty, dusky, vivid true,*
> *With eyes of gold and bramble dew.*

Side glancing her, he said, "Let me change the word 'gold' to brown. Now I'll re-read the first two lines to personalize it, make it more realistic:

> *Trusty, dusky, vivid, true,*
> *With eyes of brown and bramble-dew*
> *teel true and blade straight*
> *The great Artificer made my mate.*

Honor, anger, valor, fire,
A love that life could never tire,
Death quench nor evil stir,
The mighty Master gave to her.

Teacher, tender comrade, wife,
A fellow-farer true through life,
Heart-whole and soul-free,
The august Father gave to me.

"That and more expresses my own feelings, Sweetheart," he said wrapping her in his arms. I have more true-to-life modifications, however. I'd add dark to the brown eyes, instead of gold," he said with a grin, "and a nurse, in place of 'teacher.' Poets have a way with words, choosing them carefully and arranging them in the beauty of lilt and rhyme that reaches deep yet tenderly tugs at the heartstrings.

"Here's a poem titled 'A Prayer, by Mary Dixon Thayer that tells how I handled the days between my weekend visits with you. Would you like to read it with me?"

She reached to hold the other end, and together, read:

I pray for you, and yet I do not frame
In words the thousand wishes of my heart.
It is a prayer only to speak your name,
To think of you when we are apart.
God has not need of words. He hears our love.
And though my lips are mute, I bow my head,
And know He leans to listen from above,
And understand the things that are not said.
For love is prayer—and so prayers for you
Mount upward unto Him eternally—
They are not many, and they are not few,
All are as one that ever seems to be.
Thus do I pray for you, and cannot say;
When I begin, or when I cease to pray.

"It's a beautiful prayer poem," she said.

"Here's another poem, 'Prayer Of Any Husband,' by Mazie V. Caruthers. Let me read it to you. As I read, please believe that I, too, wish for you the sentiments in this prayer poem:"

Lord, may there be no moment in her life
When she regrets that she became my wife,
And keep her dear eyes just a triple blind
To my defects, and to my failings kind!

Help me to do the utmost that I can
To prove myself her measure of any man,
But, if I often fail as mortals may,
Grant that she never sees my feet of clay!

And let her make allowance—now and then—
That we are only grown-up boys—we—men.
So, loving all our children, she will see,
Sometimes, a remnant of all the child in me!

Since years must bring to all their load of care,
Let us together every burden bear.
And when death beckons one its path along,
May not the two of us be parted long!

"I really like that. And, yes, I'll do my best," she said. "I'd also like to change from 'husband' to 'wife,' and make other corresponding changes."

"Here's an ode by Edgar A. Guest, 'A Father Wants To Know.' I'll make believe your father sent it to me:"

You would take my girl away? What is there that I can say
Save the things that all fathers think, seldom put in printer's ink?
Little care I for your fame, or the glory you may attain,
Or the fortune you may earn. These are not my deep concern,
This I really want to know: "Will you love her so?"

It is fine enough to tell that today you're doing well;
I appreciate your skills, and I think some day you will know.
Climb the ladder of success to your lasting happiness.
But if all these should be had, and my little girl be sad,
I'd regret my whole life through having given her to you.

Will you always love her so? That is what I want to know.
Will you comfort her and stay at her side from day to day?
Knowing she must bear your name, will you shield her from all shame?
All that matters is to know whether you'll always love her so.

"Sir, I promise, by God's grace," he said solemnly to an imagined presence of his father-in-law. "I will always love your beautiful daughter so." He reached for his Bible. "Let's now read about true love, let's find the depth of true love from the words of our Father in heaven Who is love."

After reading I Corinthians 13 together, he closed the Book reverently, laid it on the bedside table, and reached for Lydia's hands. Together, they knelt down, facing each other, hands clasped.

Alfonso praised God for the sanctity of marriage, for loving the Church as His bride. He thanked Him for his own beautiful bride and for the beauty of purity. From the depths of his heart, he asked Him to bless their new home with His holy presence.

"Lord, let us experience Thy love as Thou had intended to share part of Thy divinity when Thou created man in Thine own image," he implored. "Let us not mar Thy image. Lord, in all that we do, let us honor and glorify Thy most holy name. Let my wife and I be one in Thee in intimacy."

Touched by his sincere prayer, Lydia prayed. "Lord, I thank Thee for leading in my life, for giving me a loving Christian husband, and for his godly parents. For health, for life, for love, I thank Thee, Lord. We consecrate our new lives—our love and our home—to Thee. We invite Thee to live with us and in us, and make our home truly a home where angels would abide, to bring glory to Thy holy name. In Jesus' name, I pray."

Their voices blended in 'AMEN.'

They got up from their knees, held each other tenderly, caressing and kissing ardently. He reached to switch the light off.

Wednesday Morning. Sunrise painted the eastern sky a muted reddish orange. Well rested from a blissful sleep together for the first time, they stood at the window to soak in the glory of a beginning day.

"I'm glad," she thought, *that I had set the table and laid out the cookware to prepare for our first breakfast together. Now, I have this leisure time to soak in the glory of the rising sun with my love.*

They sat down holding hands, and after Alfonso offered grace, he said, "You're a good cook."

"Thank you. I'm glad you like this simple fare," she said with a smile.

"Healthful fare," he said. "As a good wife, you are planning to stay home today…."

She shot him a questioning glance. "I'll put the gifts away and start writing 'Thank You' notes, then I must go shopping for curtains," she said turning her head to the lone and naked window of the sala.

"You know, the ride to town is best in the early afternoon," he said.

"I should leave after lunch," she replied between bites of *lacatan*. "I have in mind what I want and I think I know where I can find them."

"How much money do you need?" He said, reaching for his billfold.

Lydia chuckled. "Not much, and I have enough in my purse."

"Wish I could go with you for a honeymoon-shopping spree," he said. "As soon as we find the time, we'll go sight seeing. We might have to go by airplane to do that." Both chuckled at that.

"With my schoolwork and our wedding over, I'll go for a diversion."

He gave her a quizzical look.

"After I get the window dressing up, I'll focus on my review for the board exam," she explained with a laugh.

He gave his wife a lingering kiss, hugging her tight yet tenderly. "I can never get enough of this," he said. Before she stepped out, he added, "Thank you for forgiving me for being late for our wedding." He locked eyes with her, "And for letting me steal my first kiss on the eve of our wedding day. By then I knew you wouldn't ask me to look for another girl. And I was sure it would have been too late to call the wedding off."

"I didn't let you steal that kiss, and I'll never forgive you for that," she said, face and voice serious, pushing his hands off. "I never will. I so wanted to be able to say, 'Never been kissed until after my wedding', but you spoiled it all." She gave him a gentle push. "Darling, I must catch the early afternoon bus and get a ride home before the traffic gets heavy."

"You see, I wanted to find out how it felt to steal a kiss from a pure young maiden. I enjoyed it—the only wild oat I'd sown." And grinning, he waved her a "Bye, Sweetheart, take care." He saw her board the Halili bus. *I thank Thee, Lord, for giving my sweetheart a safe ride out, a good shopping trip, and a safe return home,* he prayed in his heart as he watched the bus speed down the dirt road.

When the air had cleared enough of the dust, he started walking to PUC, covering his nose to keep from breathing in dust. In his heart, he looked for the day when the Baesa road would get a good solid asphalt. Each passing bus or jeepney stirred up dust causing air pollution not at all conducive to good health. *This air pollution has steadily worsened through the years. During the rainy season, when the dust turned to mud, the muddy road was no improvement over the dust-problem,* he thought. *Surely, the Lord has better plans for the College,* his thoughts ran.

With his own eyes, he had seen Baesa grow and become the home of many Seventh-day Adventist families who had moved in from faraway barrios and provinces that their children may obtain a Christian education. *This is in the hands of my Almighty Father,* he settled inwardly. *Without these problems, the early morning walk to the college and afternoon walk home double for a good exercise for everyone who walked the road.*

Then his thoughts turned to Lydia and their future. His steps became more bouncy and elastic. *While she reviews for the board exam, she will also be adjusting to married life.* He was thankful they lived close to his mother and his sisters, as well as Lydia's own family. *A good support system. Lord, I thank Thee for leading in our lives,* he prayed in his heart.

Now settled in the bus, Lydia's heart lifted in adoration for the Lord's goodness. She savored the euphoria of her new life—the release from school work, the joys of new challenges ahead. *Lord, I thank Thee for the advancement in medical science, for conquering bacterial infections.* Her reverie was interrupted when she heard her seatmate say something.

"I'm sorry," she said, smiling as she turned to her seatmate "My mind was elsewhere, I'll give you my undivided attention now," she said.

"You probably don't know me, but I live farther up the road from you," her seatmate repeated. "You were a new student at the college when I left school to get married. I heard you married a teacher whose classes I attended," she said. "You are now Mrs. Alfonso Roda, isn't it?"

Lydia nodded, "Yes, you're right," she said.

"I'd like to say you married a very good man. So soft-spoken at our history class that put most of us working students to sleep," she took a deep breath to control a giggle, "but I passed his class. My parents were not at all happy when I quit school. They said people thought I only went to school to meet... to get a husband!" She giggled. "A typical Filipina, I'm not but they were right," she said, then asked, "Are you working now?"

"No, not for pay, anyway," Lydia replied with a smile. "I'm getting my house organized and soon I'll be reviewing for the nurses' board exam."

"Studying did not appeal to me. I enjoyed reading *LIWAYWAY* (dawn) and other romance magazines," her seatmate confessed. "But I know better now, and I'll teach my children a better way of life. I plan to send them to PUC from grade one through college. I think I learned enough from attending PUC to know and wish a better life for my children."

Lydia noted her seatmate wore jewelry and concluded she must not be an Adventist. "I'm glad to hear you say that," she commended her seatmate. "I'll be praying for you," she added. "May I know your name?"

"Luzviminda, Luz for short. My parents gave me a name—short for Luzon Visaya and Mindanao," she explained. "Once in a while my husband and I attend the Baesa Church. I like PUC church and vespers better," she said. "I'm glad to have sat with you and talked with you, Mrs. Roda," Luz said, as she got up. "I shop there," she said gesturing before she alighted.

As Lydia walked to get the materials for her curtains, her heart once more lifted in prayer. *Lord, I ask a retentive memory to review for the nurses' board exam.* The reputation of MSH-PUC nursing graduates topnotching in the recent board exams boosted her confidence. *All I ask for is to pass the board exam. I'll not give a thought of failing it.*

It took but a few minutes for Lydia to finish her shopping, and as she stepped out to the street, she heard a jeep driver calling, "Baesa, PUC," he was waving his hand as if to get her attention. *He must know me,* she thought and hailed for the jeep to stop. She took the only seat available.

"I thought I knew you'd be going to PUC," the young driver said. "I went to PUC a few years ago and I remembered seeing you there. I'm trying to earn some money so I could get back to school," he added.

"Thank you for stopping for me," said Lydia. "I'll alight at PUC gate."

I have time to drop the material to Precy, she told herself. She got up the stairs without bothering to knock. Preciosa met her at the door.

Precy admired the material, "A pretty red printed organdy," she said unfolding it. "I'll finish sewing it now if you have time to wait, *Manang,* It's only 3:25. Give me an hour or so," she added, and began to work.

"You've added to my lucky day," Lydia said, admiring her sister's deftness with the material and the sewing machine. "Thank you so much."

At suppertime, Lydia shared her day's experience with her husband. "I think the curtains give the sala a festive aura," she said.

At their evening worship, while singing the closing song along with her husband, he held her close. "Sweetheart, you have a beautiful singing voice. I like it," he said.

"Thanks for the flattery," she responded, "but I think 'how to sing' is another matter. My parents sang in congregational singing, and we, the children sang, too, but no one motivated us to sing beyond that. We enjoy singing and even more so, listening to gifted singers. I enjoy music."

"I'll teach you how to sing yet, Sweetheart," he promised.

"I'd like for our children to be musical like you," she said. "I'll help motivate them to appreciate good music. They'll learn how to play the piano and maybe, violin. They'll love to sing like you." She saw him nod, saw him grinning. "I see all of you are musical. Is musicality inherited?"

"Inherited and learned. Children naturally learn to like what their parents enjoy doing. As you know, God created man in His own image. Music is a part of Him which He imparted to man. The Bible speaks of heavenly music, angels singing praises to His name I like the phrase, "Music is a universal language, like a smile."

Alfonso helped Lydia write the thank you notes to their well wishers. And Lydia's life forthwith began to fall into a comfortable rhythm. There were changes she welcomed—having student help, who for doing certain household chores, earn their board and lodging. And now she's getting adept at handling her husband's school teacher's salary. Dreams of being able to add to his monthly salary and start saving came to her mind often.

While her husband went to teach and *Inday* and other students attended their classes, she reviewed for the board exam. The quietness added to the blessings she counted day by day. She felt in tune with heaven, she felt safe in a beautiful world. Taking her afternoon siesta as a safety precaution, as well as from a habit formed from Day One of the doctor-ordered bed rest, helped her relax, enhancing a retentive memory.

On Sabbath, they walked hand in hand to church, and in the afternoon they took a leisurely stroll around the campus to enjoy nature. Infrequently, Lydia accompanied her husband to Muntinglupa for the missionary work to the prisoners. Even their long courtship left room for them to know each other even better.

Six long months of waiting for the results of the board exam at long last came to pass. True to her expectation, she passed the board exam. "Now, I may add an R.N. to my signature," she said, short of dancing for joy. Her dreams of adding to the family income came to life.

"That milestone won," said her husband, "it's time to revive my dream, my wish to have our firstborn son to be as handsome as you are beautiful."

There goes my dream, and quickly, *I'll put it on hold,* flashed in her mind. "All I wish is for our baby for him to be healthy and normal in every way." After a brief pause, she added, "Considering our genetic backgrounds—yours and mine—there's nothing to worry about. And to herself, *I must continue preventive health measures, work on my attitudes to secure the health of my unborn child.*

Their talk drifted to the reading of <u>Happiness for Husbands and Wives,</u> When delving deep into their family lives, they found no notable mental or psychological problems, nor gross anatomical or physiological anomalies on either side. That is, except for his father's death at 33 from acquired pulmonary tuberculosis, and her mother's myasthenia gravis that led to pneumonia, her immediate cause of death, before she turned 41.

They had agreed on her to be a stay-home mother for their growing family. *It's for me to let go and let God, He knows what's best for me,* Lydia admitted inwardly. She would bend her wishes according to His leading. And they toyed over offering their home to her younger brothers. For after graduating from secretarial, Precy decided to switch to nursing.

At dinner, Alfonso suggested for them to celebrate her passing the board exam. They agreed to hold it on a Saturday night with a simple get together for their immediate families. He said he would call his mother to pass word on to his siblings. Lydia liked that informal invitation way. She would call her older sister Esther to relay the invitation to the family.

They made plans accordingly, taking into consideration the musicality of Alfonso's family. There would be background soft music with room for spontaneous singing. "The key to enjoyment," he said," is flexibility. Make everyone feel at home and enjoy each other."

Esther and Jun arrived first. At once Esther began scrutinizing the food on the table, kept saying, "Good, good." Grasping what her sister was up to, Lydia said, "I learned the lesson, *Mang* Es. Obeying physical laws is as important as obeying the Decalogue. I dare not throw away the lessons I learned while I was on bed rest," she chuckled. "It was when I realized that my body is God's temple, and my duty to keep my body in good health had its impact. He gave us the means to keep our bodies healthy and strong. I learned that sickness and unhappiness are hard to separate."

When everyone arrived and seated, Alfonso said, "Before we ask the blessing, I'd like to thank God for His goodness to me and Lydia. And I'd ask each of you to share with us things you are thankful for. You all know that Lydia graduated from bed rest," he said grinning, "she completed her clinical practicum, got her diploma, got a husband," he said with a wink, "and successfully passed the nurses' board exam. Above all, I thank the Lord for giving me a beautiful and forgiving and a very loving wife."

Immediately, Lydia said. "I thank the Lord for what you have just heard. I thank God for a very loving, thoughtful and unselfish husband. I want to thank *Mamang* for raising a son to be my husband." She stepped to embrace her mother-in-law, and then to give her husband a hug.

"I'm so happy Ponsing waited patiently for Lydia—I'm very sure they are heaven-matched," Maria said. "Think of Ponsing's *Papang*. Now, I don't want to emphasize the sickness that took him away from us," she said, her voiced choked, she wiped a tear, and a sob escaped. Alfonso and Lydia right away enveloped her in their arms. When she got control of her emotion, she said, "Tears of joy. I'd like to share with your two Bible verses that I think are relevant to my life. First, 'All things work together for good to them that love God,' you know the rest of the verse, Romans 8:28. The other is, 'He knoweth the way that I take, and when He has tried me, I shall come forth as gold,' Job 23:10."

An awesome solemn quietness ensued.

Everyone had their say but Esther. Finally, "My turn," she said. "I'd like to remind you of a good medicine—laughter. I'm thankful for this free and enjoyable medicine. I'm also thankful for the bounties of nature on the table, prepared by an enlightened mind. I thank the Lord for divine inspiration instructing us on what to eat—the bounties of nature—and how to eat for good health. One I'd like to point out is, eating at regular meal time. That is, not eating between meals, especially just before bedtime, and not overeating. These rules promote good health. Taking a brief walk outdoors after a meal to enjoy the beauty of nature promotes digestion."

Shooting Lydia a furtive glance, she resumed, "To begin with, I said I was thankful for laughter. I'd like to give you a dose of it now." Stealing another glance at Lydia, she took a deep breath that ended in a giggle. "Well," she said, "I thank *Papang* for calling attention to the girls in the family—Lydia, Precy, and I—to refine our *garampingat* manner of laughing." She turned to Lydia and caught her message.

"And Dr. Catalino Chay, Jr., is one who laughs easily," Lydia interjected.

The boys whistled, and a few clapped their hands. Jun signed a victory with his fingers, he smiled from ear to ear, eyes receding.

"*Papang* never stopped the boys from laughing out so uproariously, though," Esther resumed. "They can have the good medicine any time, aren't they lucky. Anyway, we never outgrew our ever-looking for the funny side of things." She saw Lydia gesturing, and understood too clearly.

"*Salamat* (thank you) *Mang* Es," Lydia said. "If no one else has any thing more to say, the table has been ready, waiting for us. I'm hungry, let's eat before it gets too late." She led the rest to the dinner table.

***

SOURCE OF TRUE HUMAN AFFECTION

by Ellen G. White

Our affection for one another springs from our common relation to God. We are one family, we love one another as He loved us. When compared with this true sanctified, disciplined affection, the shallow courtesy of the world, the meaningless effusive expression of friendship are as chaff to the wheat. Lt. 63, 1896 (SD 101)

To love as Christ loved means to manifest unselfishness at all times and in all places, by kind words and pleasant looks.... Genuine love is a precious attribute of heavenly origin, which increases its fragrance in proportion as it is dispensed to others. (MS 17, 1899. SD 101).

Let there be mutual love, mutual forbearance. Then marriage, instead of being the end of love, will be as it were the very beginning of love. The warmth of true friendship, the love that binds heart to heart, is a foretaste of the joys of heaven....

Let each give love rather than exact it. (MH 360–361, 1905).

Mind Character, and Personality, Vol. 1, p. 211

***

L-r: mother Adelaida Tabucol, Mike, and Lydia

Alfonso in his younger days

An athletic, he played baseball and tennis in his younger days. Later, for exercise, he jogged and walked around the college campus. Andy said he never beat his father in any of the matches they played.

A late afternoon stroll

Chapter VI

TOWARD NEW BEGINNNINGS

"It is part of God's plan to grant us, in answer to the prayer of faith, that which He would not bestow did we not thus ask..." **Ellen G. White The Great Controversy, p. 525.**

Beside her lay her husband sound asleep. *Hmmm the adrenaline must still be coursing through my blood stream,* Lydia mused, *what with all the excitement. I might as well make use of these sleepless moments.*

She replayed in her mind passages from the chapter, "Parents' Legacy to Children," in Dr. Shryock's book, Happiness for Husbands and Wives. While reading the chapter, they discussed on the 'Law of Heredity', particularly on "offsprings perpetuate the physical and mental condition the parents.... Whenever the habits of the parents are contrary to physical law, the injury done to themselves will be repeated in their future generations. By physical, mental, and moral culture, all may become co-workers with Christ. Very much depends upon the parents, whether they shall bring into the world children who will prove a blessing or a curse. The nobler the aims, the higher the mental and spiritual endowments, and the better developed the physical powers of the parents, the better will be the life they give to their children. In cultivating ... the best in themselves, parents are exerting an influence to mold society and to uplift future generations."

Now every blessing God had showered on her life came to her mind floating like cirrus clouds: The stages on her healing and the circumstances contributing to it—the role her sister Esther played, and then the true love her then ardent suitor, now her loving husband, and Dr. W. G. Dick, who sought divine consultation for her treatment. These hastened her healing.

Expecting. The waiting months heaped happiness to the new prospective parents. "Sweetheart, you look radiant. You're getting lovelier everyday," Alfonso would say and wrap her in his arms.

"Darling, I feel good and I'm happy."

Both of them had an intuition that their first baby would be a boy.

Before long, Esther and Lydia were comparing their individual status. Esther was not too far behind her younger sister. There were things they agreed on: their knowledge gained as student nurses prepared them for this event, they knew what to expect at each stage, and on how to care for themselves and for the life growing in their womb. They found their knowledge in anatomy and physiology practical.

Lydia and Alfonso had given Esther and Jun for their wedding gift the book, <u>Happiness for Husbands and Wives</u>, by Dr. Shryock. Being both in the medical profession, Esther and Jun found their perusal of the book to have deepened their awareness of their responsibility for the mental, physical, and spiritual health of their unborn child. The reading of this book added points the expecting sisters shared with each other.

May 10, l955. Lydia, under ether, barely heard the cry of her firstborn. As her nervous system overcame the effects of the anesthesia, she felt a weight on her abdomen and forced herself into awareness of the baby in her arm. Feeling the baby close to her made her forget the delivery pains. Settling in her room, Lydia's arms ached to hold her baby close. *This must be how the Lord longs for His children*, came to her mind.

When the doctor dropped in the check on her patient, she came upon the new parents sharing their pride over their baby. She could relate with their joy. For it had not been too long ago when she luxuriated in the wonderment of first-time parenthood. "A baby Roda with the face of mama Lydia," she said. "I see pride on the new father's face," she added. After making sure all was well with the new mother and her baby, she turned to Alfonso, mischief in her tone. "It's about time you had an heir," she said. After exchanging small talk, Dr. LaMadrid left the new parents to bond with their baby.

Earlier, Alfonso had told Lydia that he and Dr. Ruth attended PUC from the grades through college. He described her to be an outstandingly bright student. "All of them," referring to her siblings, "use their gray matters wisely," he said. "Instead of burying their talents, they improve on them. Direct consequences of God fearing parental influences."

The new father watched his little one suckle. "The wonder of it all!" he said his voice deep in awe. "Parenthood, miracle of miracles." He laid his hand lightly over his tiny baby. "You're hungry, Son, and your mama has lots of nourishing milk for you. Eat and grow fast...."

"Right now," she interjected, "what he's sucking is colostrum. It is nature's provision for babies to build their immune system to resist infection. For two to three days, a breast-fed newborn baby gets nothing but colostrum. The clear liquid contains mainly serum and white blood corpuscles loaded with natural antibodies that the mother passes on to her nursing baby. It's one of God's wise ways to safeguard the baby's health."

"Oh," the puzzled father muttered. "Then he gets milk after that, I suppose. He's sucking well, he must really like colostrum."

"Exactly. At this time a baby's tastebuds are not perverted," Lydia said with a laugh. "No formula can take the place of the baby's own mother's milk for her baby's health. That is, if she eats sensibly, for whatever food the mother eats, naturally is what gets in her breast milk."

"God created man fearfully and wonderfully in His own image, and in His wisdom, provided the minute details for a baby to grow," Alfonso said awe in his voice, and at that solemn moment, he whispered," My little boy, my son Ferdinand Jonathan. The wonders of parenthood!" He bowed his head, and Lydia joined him in a parental prayer of baby dedication.

"We thank Thee, Father in heaven, for the joys of parenthood. We realize our son is Thine for us to nurture for Thy glory. By Thy grace, we take this responsibility. Give us wisdom to train him, Lord. We dedicate our firstborn son to Thee. In Jesus' precious name, we pray, Amen."

***

How to Raise a Child

1. *Remember that a child is a gift from God, the richest of all blessings. Do not attempt to mold him in the image of your neighbor. Each child is an individual and should be permitted to be himself.*

2. *Don't crush a child's spirit when he fails. And never compare him with others who have outshone him.*

3. *Remember that anger and hostility are natural emotions. Help your child to find socially acceptable outlets for these normal feelings or they may be turned inward and erupt.*

4. *Discipline your child with firmness and reason. Don't let your anger throw you off balance. If he knows you are fair, you will not lose his respect or his love. And make sure the punishment fits the crime.*

5. *Remember that each child needs two parents. Present a united front. Never join your child against your mate. This can create emotional conflicts in your child as well as in yourself.*

6. *Do not hand your child everything his little heart desires. Permit him to know the thrill of earning and the joy of deserving. Grant him the greatest of all satisfactions—the pleasure that comes with personal achievement.*

7. *Do not set yourself up as the epitome of perfection. This is a difficult role to play 24 hours a day. You will find it easier to communicate with your child if you let him know that Mom and Dad makes mistakes, too.*

8. *Do not make threats in anger or impossible promises when you are in a generous mood. Threaten or promise only what you can live up to.*

9. *Do not smother your child with superficial manifestations of love. The purest and healthiest love expresses itself in day-in, day-out training which breeds self-confidence and independence.*

10. *Teach your child that there is dignity in work whether it is performed with calloused hands that shovel coal or skilled fingers that manipulate surgical instruments. Let him know that a useful life is a blessed one.*

11. *Do not try to protect your child against every small blow and disappointment. Adversity strengthens character and makes us compassionate. Trouble is the great equalizer. Let him learn it.*

12. *Teach your child to love God and to love his fellow man. Don't send your child to a place of worship—take him there. Children*

learn from example. Telling him something is not teaching him. If you give your child a deep abiding faith in God, it can be the strength and his light when all else fails.

from Ann Landers column, published in <u>GRITS</u>.

***

Chapter VII

<u>YOU</u> GROWING UP

"The best legacy you can give to your son is to love his mother."

"How's my little boy today?" Alfonso asked, locking eyes with his son. "Ferdinand Jonathan is a big boy's name. What about Andy for short?

Lydia agreed. "Andy," she repeated. "God's precious gift to us."

Caressing the arm that cradled their baby, he said, "This little one gave you a new name, Sweetheart. You are now Mommy; and I am Daddy. Baby Andy is mighty capable of dispensing titles."

Alert little eyes followed his father's voice.

"He's listening," she whispered. "He learned to identify your voice long before his birth. Babies have good ears. When he grows up, I hope Andy will be singing with you."

"You need a rocking chair to lullaby him. Now that he's wide awake, may I take him? You relax now," he ordered, offering his arms. "Jesus loves you, dear Andy," he sang softly. "Your mommy is right, you'll be singing not long from now, but I won't rush you." He looked down at his baby, deep satisfaction welling in him. "Our pride and joy," he said, and to Lydia he said, "Hard to believe, some 24 years ago you were a baby like Andy."

As the impact of his statement sank in, she laughed softly and like a boomerang, it came back to him. "Thirty-two some years ago, you were a helpless baby in diapers like little Andy."

"Listen to your mommy, baby. You've really set her flight of fancy afire. Look at your mommy, isn't she beautiful?" And with that, he smacked her forehead with a kiss.

Andy rewarded his dad with a hint of a smile, a flail of arms and legs.

"I interpret that expression on his face as amusement," he said. "Are your brain cells recording our chatter, Andy? He tickled his chin, and the baby responded with more smiles, kicks and flailing of arms and legs.

"There," she said chuckling. "Babies respond to mirror the look on faces they see, then add their own charm with a disarming smile," she said tickling his chin. "Queer isn't it, a baby's toothless smile is captivating while that of an old person's is horrendous... uh... repulsive even."

"Shhh, Sweetheart, please," he said. "Babies respond to what they see and hear," draping his arm around her.

235

"At this age, babies respond to the care parents give on their demand. His eyes tell it's time for a nap," she sing-sang softly. "I'd better take him to his crib."

Alfonso slid the baby into her waiting arms. Little eyelids flickered momentarily as she laid him down. They watched their sleeping son. "So trusting," he said in awe. "I see it now. This is how our heavenly Father wants His children to trust Him. How much easier for me to understand how the Lord would have us relate to Him now that we have Andy. A lesson in faith, a new angle on how 'A little child shall lead them.'"

Arm around her shoulder and her's around his waist, they walked out of the baby's room. "Man made life so complicated for himself." Alfonso continued articulating his thoughts. "All God wanted from His children was total confidence in Him. We have lessons to learn from watching our son relate to us. He's so dependent on us just as we in actuality are on God."

"Now I remember when I was a little girl, before I started school," she said. "*Nong* Tito, *Mang* Es, and I often tagged along with my father when he went fishing. There were large rocks to skip on as we crossed a rivulet. At times the rocks were too far apart for my legs to manage, so my father picked me up. I enjoyed those moments, trusting him to skip the rocks with his wide strides, I on his shoulder. When he let me down, I'd grab his hand and walked holding on." She paused. "Did you ever go fishing?"

He shook his head. "No, I grew up without a father." He watched her fold diapers, admired her shapely tapered fingers move with grace as she stacked the neatly folded diapers in a box. "Thank you for trusting me, too, Sweetheart," he said.

She reminisced how her uncle (*Tiong Dons*) provided the permit The Nursing School required before any student nurse could go out with special friends. "*Mang* Es typed the permit *Tiong Dons* dictated," she said with a giggle. A mature person for me though only two years plus my senior."

"A permit from a father figure who was younger than I," he said. "I felt it rather absurd, but rules are rules. We needed to get to know each other better on less formal grounds."

She explained that it was to save time that she and her classmate and friend acceded to meet them at Taft Avenue, across PWU (Philippine Women's University). You already had a long jeep ride from Baesa."

"In a group, that is," he said. "We always got there ahead of you."

"We walked from the San, crossed San Juan to Donada St., then to the main street to catch a jeep—a time well spent. We got the exercise and some sun. *Hoy*, we'd tease each other. "A college professor and a budding journalist taking student nurses out to the Icecapade show and snacking on the sweets they brought.' An escape from the demands of nursing school schedule was like a vacation for us. We enjoyed every moment of it."

"Eking and I also welcomed the diversion from our jobs. Indeed, didn't Jesus and His disciples escape to the lake for carefree moments?"

She nodded. "It is good to get away from routines," she said.

"Even if I'd been unable to afford a videotape of our wedding, which you so much wished to have, we now have Andy. Our baby is by far a more precious reminder of our wedding vows than any videotape. Yet I'm sorry I didn't have the means for it. You see, I never believed on spending beyond my means. 'No borrowing' is a motto I uphold."

"I should have worked for even a few months after my graduation to earn enough for a few luxuries," she said. "But because you'd waited long enough for me, I had no nerve to suggest a later date than the day you picked. I thought, over five years for you was long enough waiting time."

"Because you were aware time was ticking off on me," he quipped as he gathered her in his arms. "Also, I'm aware of your canceled dreams."

"If only I had not come down with that infection!" She sighed. "Yet, I'll forever be thankful for the strength I gained from it. Some day, He'll make it plain to me. In His love and wisdom, he allowed the ordeal to come that I may learn even if only to entrust my life completely to Him."

"Sweetheart, I'm glad you chose to be a stay-home mom for Andy. Our God will also teach you how to stretch a teacher's salary."

"I'm learning lessons fast," she laughed. "Learning that the Lord is still multiplying barley loaves and small fish. He'll provide for a family of four that we had planned—two children."

"Congratulations, Mrs. Roda," he said, patting her back. "I see how a hands-on experience is helping. This is your third year balance-budgeting and I haven't heard you complain about my spare teacher's salary."

"Most of our wedding gifts gave us a good start," she explained. "The rattan furniture set *Mamang* gave us, for example, will last us a lifetime. So would the two burner gas stoves a group of faculty and staff pooled in as their group gift. The set of baking dishes our American ladies in campus gave us are so useful, also the two sets of five-set dinner plates, complete with cups and saucers, and the complete set of silver ware and carrying trays. So practical for a four member family we had planned."

"Was it Dr. & Mrs. William C. Richli, who, with other couples, pooled to give us books, including a set of the <u>Impending Conflict</u>?" he asked.

Lydia nodded. "I like the practicality of some friends who gave us a high-sitted unisex urinal. I need not get out of the comfort of our bedroom, I only have to squat to relieve myself. Heh-heh-heh-heh."

Alfonso laughed along. "Did you say you haven't had chance to use some gifts?" he asked." What unused presents are crowding *Inday* out?"

"Most of her room crowders are empty boxes," she explained. "I'm saving them for packing their original contents when the time comes for us to move elsewhere. Our place is perfect for now, but our kind friends will surely need their upstairs when their family starts growing in number. For our next place, we need to look for at least a four bedroom house."

Alfonso grinned. "You must have in mind for our next child to be a girl. I'd like to have a baby girl who would also favor your looks. If our next child turned out to be another boy, couldn't the boys room together? I really think it would be ideal to have a little girl…. Think of it…."

"Darling," she practically interrupted him. "I want to be flexible, but as Happiness for Husbands and Wives advices, we must be practical. How many could your salary provide for, comfortably? I could go to work for us to be a two-income family, but no one could take the place of a mother in her child's life. I'd like to raise our own children myself. I wish to enjoy every minute of their formative years."

"Amen, Sweetheart, and the more I think it would be wonderful to have a beautiful daughter in addition to two boys. Half of her genes from you, the other half from me, but now, we'll live one day at a time. Let the Lord handle our future. Remember, we both come from large families."

"As we'd talked about during our courtship days, two children would be plenty. Neither of us are all that young anymore," she mumbled. "I believe in the wisdom of planned parenthood, its application as we learned from our readings. I appreciate your bringing those books for us to read."

The high spirited parents eagerly watched their sons's growth and development. In his baby book, Lydia described every progress Andy made from day to day. Being breast-fed, he was healthy with the robust appetite of a normal growing boy. There had been no setbacks in his physical and mental development. He got his immunization shots on schedule. At about nine months, he needed more than his mother's milk.

"I'm so glad Andy likes bananas. He never tires of eating them," she said to her husband. "Ripe bananas are nutritious and very digestible."

"You're right. I see Andy likes the different flavors, too. *Mamang* used to tell us exactly the same. She said she was always thankful bananas grew locally and were not expensive, she'd buy a whole bunch at a time, getting different varieties. On occasion, she'd buy *saba* (cooking variety). Boiled, they're chewy and sweet. Sometimes she'd cut up the boiled *saba* in small chunks and sprinkle them with freshly grated coconut. It was a treat for us. We liked all the different varieties, not one banana spoiled."

"Did she ever say what your favorite kind was? *Tumoc? Tundal?*"

"No, but I'm partial to *lacatan*. It never gets mushy. I like the hint of orange flavor, the distinct aroma of the firm light orange and firm flesh."

Shaking his head slowly from side to side, he began reminiscing. *Mamang* worked so hard. Daytime, sewing clothes for others; nights, colporteuring. In many ways I felt how much she missed *Papang."* He let out a sigh. "About spending money wisely, *Mamang* never preached to us. She set the example. Once she said in a jest that they—the Tagalog—branded the Ilokano as *kuripot* (tightfisted)."

He grinned and cast his *Ilokana* wife a sidelong glance. "You do understand why your husband isn't a spendthrift," he chuckled. "Half Ilokano, yes. *Kuripot*, no. I view God holds us responsible for the way we manage our money. In my readings especially of Ellen G. White's divinely inspired writings, I find this viewpoint to stand out."

"We're responsible for using all our blessings wisely," Lydia affirmed.

"Exactly. Talents, time, opportunities. It's His design that we improve on these gifts for the glory of His name." He reached out to the bookshelf, pulled out <u>Messages to Young People</u>, found the page and read:

"If we make the most of our talents, the Spirit of God will continually lead us to greater efficiency. To the man who had faithfully traded with his talents, the Lord said, "Well done, good and faithful servant, thou hast been faithful over a few things, I will make thee ruler over many things...." He drew her close to him. "Somehow, that passage always touches me. I want to hear the Lord say to me, "Well done, good and faithful servant...."

Hearing light footfalls, they turned to see Andy carrying a book.

"Sto-we, momma."

Lydia reached down to receive the book, relieving her son's swayback for holding the Bible Story book. He scrambled up to his mother's lap to listen to the story of baby Moses.

Alfonso's eyes brimmed, joy sweeping over him as he watched the magical sight: His beautiful wife, on her lap her mini-look alike son.

"Story 2. Baby Moses to the Rescue," she read. Andy turned the page with eagerness, they were coming to his favorite part of the story. "One day a baby boy turned up in the home of Amram and Jochebed. These godly Hebrews had a little girl ... Miriam, and a little boy ... Aaron, and they wanted another little boy so much. But now? ...."

After reading the chapter, an idea leaped on Lydia's mind. *I'll find out how my just turned-three son would relate to another baby.* "Andy," she said, wrapping him in her arm. "Would you like to have a baby brother, like baby Moses?"

The little boy looked up to see his mother's face as if trying to understand the question. Then his face lighted up with a smile. "For me, momma?" Then clapping, he declared. "I want a baby brother!"

Lydia turned her son to face her, took his little hands and placed them, palms down, over her rotund abdomen. "Your baby brother is growing in here," she said softly. "When he gets big enough, he will come out. You were in here over three years ago. Your daddy and I loved you very much even then. When you were ready, you were born, and we loved you even more. You were a beautiful baby and a very good baby."

Andy looked up at his daddy, who gave him a wink, an approving nod and a smile. "Yes, Son, your mommy is right. You have a little baby brother growing in there. When he's big enough and ready to come out, he will be more safe with us than baby Moses had been. There will be no wicked ruler to order babies to be killed. We will not have to hide your baby brother in a little basket to float in any river."

The little boy's eyes flitted to the book his mother had laid on the sofa beside her. Eyes wide with wonder, he looked up at his mother, then at his father. He wriggled over to pick up the book, stared at a page, then slowly turning page after page, he studied the pictures.

"Do you want me to read some more?"

Andy shook his head slowly. Timidly putting his palms over his mother's abdomen, he turned his face up to his father. Little brown eyes wide, delight and wonderment in them. He hugged his mother's girth. "My baby brother, come out!" he said.

Maneuvering Andy's head, Lydia gently pressed his right ear against her rotund abdomen. His eyes grew wider with excitement and he giggled saying he heard noises. Again he looked up at his father, then at his mother. He turned to press his left ear against her belly. "Come out my little brother. Come out and play with me," he cried out.

"Your baby brother will come out when he is ready, Son. And like you, he will arrive at the hospital, but for a while he'll be too little to play."

For a few seconds, Andy wore a perplexed face. Again, he switched his glance to his father, then to his mother. "How will he know when he is ready?" he asked.

The parents exchanged quick glances. "Son, time will tell," he replied. That seemed to satisfy the little boy. Then taking hold of his daddy's hand, he asked. "When are you going to the hospital to get him?"

"Soon, Son. Your mommy and I will."

"Can I come with you, Daddy? Mommy?" came the quick request.

At that instant, the baby moved, giving something like a slight kick. Andy's eyes grew wider yet. "My baby brother wants to come out now," he squealed.

Lydia took Andy's right hand, spread out his little fingers. "Follow me count," she instructed. "We'll count how much longer you'll have to wait to meet your baby brother." Pointing at his little pointer, "One," she said. "One," a child's voice echoed. Moving her finger to his middle finger, "Two," she said. "Two," he said. Lightly tweaking his ring finger, "Three," she said. "Twee," mimicked a voice with glee. The little boy waited patiently as his mother bent his thumb down and his little pinkie to his palm, and covered them with hers. "In three months. That is how much longer for you to wait for your baby brother."

"How long is three months?" the little boy wanted to know.

His daddy got up and took the calendar hanging on the wall. "Look here,"he began, and explained how days became a week, and weeks turned into a month, and so on. That, too, satisfied the little boy.

"Now let's get back to our reading," Lydia said, passing the book on to her husband. Andy went to sit beside his father. Toward the end of the second page, the little boy's attention began to lag. Alfonso looked at his watch. "I think it's bedtime," he said. They walked to Andy's room. He found Lydia's hand, and they knelt down. Andy knelt down without prompting. Lydia clasped his hands in hers. Alfonso prayed, then said, "Andy, repeat after me." Two voices blended, a man's leading and a child's voice following. "Amen." They tucked their son to bed with a hug and kiss.

On their way to the living room, she said, "I wish the Bible authors included hints on how biblical mothers raised their children. Surely, they had human feelings like mine. For although raising a child is not an easy task, I find fulfillment in watching our son grow. So trusting, so spontaneous, so responsive to nurturing love."

"I'm happy to hear you say that, Sweetheart," he said, squeezing her hand. She returned his with a steady grip. Side by side they sat down.

"We know the Holy Spirit inspired in the writing of the Books," she continued, "but I wish they'd given a little thought to women readers!" She chuckled. "I'd very much like to have an idea on how biblical mothers raised their children in addition to 'in the fear of the Lord.' I wish to read even just an inkling on how women prepared themselves for motherhood."

"Like labor pains? forgotten when a mother holds her baby for the first time?" he asked, sounding his way. "Yes, biblical authors were not garrulous. Had they been, what of the volume the Bible would be! I think there's romance in leaving room for the imagination to play. Furthermore, the culture in biblical times was so remote from our own upbringing, and think of the future's.... Take the Asian countries—China, Indonesia, Japan the

Philippines. Our straight black hair is the closest we have in common," he chuckled. "Comparing Asian to western culture, America for example, only intensifies the differences. The first time I heard younger individuals addressing much older folk by their first names, *how disrespectful,* I thought. Getting closer to home, in Luzon: comparing the Tagalog to the Bicolandian, to the Ilokano and the different upbringing from family to family—differences galore! Yet, we read the same Bible. Perhaps future versions would be more accommodating."

"The King James Version meets my needs," she said. "Never mind that it leaves room for my imagination, for example, to details on how the teenage Mary nurtured Jesus from birth to maturity. The family ate fish, it's clear. They also ate part of their sacrificial animals, clean kosher meat. The chosen of God did not eat unclean flesh as specified in Leviticus 11. Did Mary do the marketing? Did she worry over how much money to spend? Did she prepare all their meals? If so, what food? How did she serve them—fried? sauteed? The sacrificial animals were roasted, that's clear. Did they serve vegetables raw? They ate figs, fresh or dried, we know. Did they eat three times a day, at regular mealtime hours? Did they eat snacks? Who did the dishes? Who washed their clothes? My imagination is very poor. Are these matters unimportant to salvation?"

"Uhuh, I think you missed something, Dear," he said, he was grinning.

"That Mary was only fourteen years old when she was married to an older widower who had several children?" she sounded irked, perplexed.

"Guess again. Think of modern culture, anywhere in the world."

"They wore jewelry. I read in the Old Testament that even men wore them. That tells those men were pagans."

"Maybe, but my mind happens not to be on matters of jewelry."

"Oh." she said. "They danced. Seventh-day Adventists don't dance. Vertical embrace even in public is tantamount to the horizontal kind. They painted themselves, too. Glad our Church doesn't sanction either."

"So, are you saying that Adventist regulations on dancing, jewelry, wearing make-up are man-made and SDA-imposed? And therefore it isn't sinful to go dancing, or to wear jewelry, or to use lipsticks or rouge?"

Lydia shook her head lightly. "I see no reason why some of our young people paint themselves. Nothing like natural beauty—simplicity is beauty."

"Since you haven't guessed what I have in mind, I'll tell you. Ready? In Bible times, husbands and wives lived in separate tents."

She gave a chuckle at that. "Perhaps, but didn't Adam and Eve live together in the Garden of Eden? When did the married people start living separately? Is it to support their paganese polygamous practices? And would you like to live in separate tents as they had in biblical times?"

"Before I answer your question, Dear. I'd like to hear your answer to your last question first," he said.

Chuckling, she said, "It's not cost-effective to keep two houses. That arrangement would be anathema to good family relationships."

"Is that all?" he was now grinning from ear to ear.

"You are pulling my leg," she said, laughing.

"Oh, you remembered that. Say that again." He laughed.

Lydia laughed along.

"I conclude your answer to your original question is…," he resumed, "you're glad that husbands and wives live in the same house and sleep in the same bed and that you don't call me, 'Lord.' I like to hear you call me 'darling,' once in a while. Honestly, I enjoy cuddling. Cuddling my own beautiful Miss Universe."

"In that sense, the Bible is not giving instructions or examples."

"Hardly. As children of God, we must use our own discernment. When our hearts are in tune to our Omnipotent Father, we can only bring glory to His name. He sees our hearts, He knows our thoughts, and He desires His crowning work of creation to be happy, to enjoy his companionship."

***

Chapter VIII

SAYS THE LORD, RALPH REGINALD

Mercy unto you, and peace, and love, be multiplied (Jude 2).

August 28, 1958. A 7-pound 21-inch bouncing baby boy announced his arrival with a lusty cry. His parents had a name for him—Ralph Reginald.

"Congratulations on your new healthy baby boy!" Dr. Roy Jutzy, the attending physician, applaud the new parents. "His face is a miniature of his father's," he said, giving Alfonso a wink. Turning to Lydia, he added, "This being your second made the delivery easy. I'll check on you and your baby before you go home," he said.

Andy looked into the blue bundle his parents brought home. His eyes widened to see baby eyes peering back at him. "I hold," he said. His mother asked him to sit on the sofa, to hold out his arms, palms up. "You can hold him until he gets too heavy," she said.

Beaming with pride, Alfonso watched his two sons, watched as his older son stretched out his diminutive arms to receive his baby brother. Looking into the little one, Andy said, "I love my baby brother. Can he sleep with me in my bed, Mommy?" eyes begged for a positive answer.

"Son, he'll sleep in the crib like you did when you were like him."

"Andy," his father said, "your baby brother's name is Ralph."

Wide-eyed Andy watched his mother peel off the baby's wet diaper and folded it, saw her drop it in the diaper pail. His eyes followed her hands wiping tiny bottom clean and placing on him a clean diaper.

"Mommy," he leaned close to his mother, tugging at her skirt. Lydia smiled at her son's upturned face and bent to kiss his forehead. "Yes, Andy," she acknowledged her son claiming some attention. "Mommy, did you put a diaper on me, too?" His mother touseled Andy's hair. "Of course, I did. When we brought you home from the hospital, you were littler than Ralph is now, but you grew fast. Ralph will grow fast like you, too."

"Andy," his father said, "look how tiny those toes are. And look at those little feet. Yours were maybe as tiny, did you know that?"

The little boy looked at his baby brother's feet and toes, then looked down at his own. "Those tiny toes of my brother will grow fast, too. His feet, too. When will he walk, Daddy?"

"Son, not so soon. He'll crawl first, but watch out! Before long he'll be running around with you. You might not even be able to catch him!"

"I'll teach him how to walk and to run, Daddy." Andy reached to touch the tiny feet. Then he planted a kiss on each teeny foot. "They're soft, they smell good. I love you, my little baby brother Ralph," he said.

"We must be doing something right, Lydia told her husband. "Ralph is growing so fast, he practically skipped the usual newborn adjustments. He'd been sleeping through the night—almost—since he was born."

"Be thankful he has not given you a sleepless night," he said beaming. "It's probably... he had an overdose of your improved colostrum."

Lydia laughed along with him. "Since Ralph looks very much like you, I suspect *Hoy gaya mong kabait* !(He's as sweet-tempered as you are!)"

"Ahem, Sweetheart, thank you. I appreciate hearing that." Wrapping her in his arms drawing her to him, he said, "Do you know what I think?"

"No, Sir. Even up to this time, I haven't learned to read your mind."

"I believe you are more calm now than your first 'round of mommyhood. Caring for Andy gave you a hands-on training, like clinical pacticum. *Mang* Cheding says it gets easier each time. You'll see."

"Also, with Andy's chatter and patter, not just old people's, Ralph feels secure in his new world." Lydia said, ignoring his last remark.

"Hey, hey, I don't like to her you say 'old' of yourself. I don't feel old myself." He slipped his arm down to give her a gentle loving back rub. "Oldness is a state of mind. Some are old at 30, others are young at 60. I for one had felt so much younger since Andy and Ralph came to our lives."

Soon toddling, Ralph's cheerful presence brightened their home even more. He followed Andy around, mimicking all of his older brother's ways.

"Our boys are getting along so well," the proud father verbalized. "We're seeing the power of example with our own eyes, Sweetheart," he said and cleared his throat. "As we'd read in Happiness for Husbands and Wives, as well as Mrs. White's writings, prenatal influences do set a child's temperament. It pays to study and learn from writers who fear the Lord."

Lydia couldn't agree more. "It looks as if Andy is Ralph's favorite teacher," she said. "Look at how his eyes follow Andy, who is acting so much more mature than his age. I haven't noticed any sibling rivalry, have you? Practically inseparable, they're like twins in many ways," Getting no response from him, Lydia cast him a glance his way. His eyes had a faraway look, his facial expression of deep contemplation.

"I'm trying to think how I related with Turing when we were our boys' age," he said finally. "Believe me, I could relate to the feelings Andy has for Ralph. Belonging, comradeship, loving, protective relationship—all of it—and more. I felt that Turing hero-worshipped me. How proud I was of my little brother. I recall growing up with this feeling. Our sisters were older, and they were girls," he chuckled. "Turing and I were boys."

It was Lydia's turn to reflect and verbalized, *"Mang* Es and I related to each other similarly," she said. She quickly brushed aside an old saying, *good children die young,* and wondered why it flitted on her mind. She forced her mind to a plan she had talked about with her husband earlier. *I'll take a few courses toward my B.S.N.E.* Her intense ambition to go back to school kicked back to life.

Addressing her husband, she said, "Since Ralph is growing fast and is behaving so well, I ought to start taking a few classes toward nursing ed."

"I see why not," was his quick reply that buoyed her up. "Arrange for someone to be with the children when you're in school."

"It's such a blessing to live right on campus," she said. "I'd just walk to my classes and back to check on the children. *Inday* is trustworthy."

On her first class, however, Lydia felt an uneasiness, adjustments perhaps? She shared her feelings with her husband and together they prayed about it. Also, they'd pray about it in their own private prayers. In their morning family worship, they committed their lives, especially their active boys to the Lord. For holy angels to hover around them at play. *I'll need to exercise my faith here,* Lydia often reassured herself. *It's the Lord's bidding for His children to improve on every opportunity that opens—gifts, talents, time, open doors for personal and professional growth.* Now the portion of the Lord's prayer, 'Thy will be done' presented a new dimension. Whereas in the past, it had not carried much weight.

A family stroll
L-r: Andy, Mom, Dad, Ralph.

Ralph's first steps. L-r: Mom, Ralph, Andy, Dad.

Four in the family: L-r: Andy, Mom, Dad, Ralph.

***

Of this photo Andy says: "My brother Ralph and I climbed up and down this Kalachuchi tree, in front of our house, for hours. When it came time for annual family picture, it was natural that we chose our favorite playground." L-r: Mom, Andy, Dad, Ralph.

Andy says of the photo: "Here I am about
age six. Dad was my hero. To me he was the
strongest, the fastest and best in everything.

October 19, 1960, a.m. Five-and-a-half-year-old Andy burst into the
library to his mother, who was deep in study. "Mommy, Ralph got hurt," he
cried softly, his frame shaking. Lydia wrapped him in her arms. "My
brother got hurt," he sobbed. Just then a faculty came.

"Mrs. Roda, Mr. Hechanova rushed your little boy to the hospital."

Quickly gathering her things, Lydia got up without asking questions.
She took Andy's hand and hurried out the door and down the road in a run
to their home. The girls met them. "Andy stay with *Inday*—I'll go to the
hospital, and gave instructions to the girls. "Yes, Ma'am," they said.

Miss Veninda Tamayo offered to go with Lydia. They flagged down a
jeep. "Manila Sanitarium & Hospital," Lydia said and they boarded. The
driver sensing the urgency took them on. After what to Lydia was infinity,
they arrived at the San, only to find Ralph not there. The front desk informed
Ralph was taken directly to MCU (Manila Central University). MSH
accountant Gershon Brion offered to take her in the hospital van to MCU.
Mike, Lydia's younger brother, a medical intern at MSH, jumped in the van.
He knew his sister would need all the support possible.

Deep in her heart, Lydia continued her vigil in prayer as they drove in silence. *Lord, Thou art the great Physician, please save my son. We have dedicated him to Thee at his birth. Lord, give me faith to move this mountain of fear. Fear for my son's life, Lord, rescue him, nothing is too hard for Thee.* Painful though it be, she relinquished, *Thy will be done.*

Alfonso was anxious to get home. He had taken Mrs. Esther Vizcarra, Sr., to the pier to sail for the States to join her son Jun. Feeling satisfaction for having done a good deed that day, he was humming a tune. As he came by MCU E. R. parking lot, he recognized the car of D. M. Hechanova, Jr., PUC Dean of Men. He knew Hechanova was a student there, but his heart double beat, fearing he could have taken his mother there. It had not been too long ago when she had a heart attack. He swung in to the E R. parking lot to park his Old Reliable.

He inquired at the ER desk. "My Son, my son," he cried upon hearing the news. "Is my wife here?"

Alighting from the MSH van, Mike took his sister's hand, leading her to the E.R. entrance. Alfonso rushed to meet her and folded her in his arms. No words were necessary. They simply clung to each other silently sharing the bitter cup, hot tears mingling. Lydia's sobs rocked her whole being. Awashed of strength, she turned limp. Tears could not flow fast enough to assuage the pain searing her heart. *Why? Why should my innocent well behaved little boy die so young? Lord, let me awaken to see my little darling smile. Ralphie, my darling baby. Wake up to your Mommy. Lord, let me awaken to see this to be but a dream, a nightmare. Ralph, I cannot bear to leave you here, not in the morgue. Please, Lord....*

Alfonso led his limp Lydia outside to the sunshine for fresh air. He felt her pain, his own pain. He lifted his thoughts to the One Who understands. Silently, he prayed in his heart. *Lord, let us be brave. Let us take the ending of life at its face value, as Thy children. Just as we cherished our dear Ralphie's life, let us fling ourselves into Thy comforting arms. Make us realize that this parting and its resulting pain, too, will pass.*

The convoy of jeeps rambled on through the dusty road of Baesa and in to the College campus. *Coming home has lost its appeal.* Lydia dreaded to open the door. No cheerful chatter of their toddler met them. They found Andy sitting, sullen. As soon as he saw his parents, he began to sob. "It's my fault," he cried. "Daddy, Mommy, where's my little brother?" Lydia knelt beside him. She couldn't force herself to smile. Alfonso held him close. "Son, tell us what happened," he said.

Between sobs, the anguishing parents got the pieces together:

Andy's friend about his age, were playing outdoors with Ralph. Wanting to amuse himself, Ralph ran toward the water tank, somewhat behind their house. To reach the chain hanging on the front end of the tank, he jumped, and getting a hold of it, he tiptoed to swing with his weight.

Soon he was swinging up and down, back and forth, giggling with each swing up and down. Hearing and seeing Ralph having the time of his life, the older boys ran to the other side of the water tank. Clambering, they got up on to the rod that connected the water tank to a jeep. (The College used the jeep to pull the tank to haul water for campus use.) With their hands, Andy and his friend lowered themselves and hanging on to the rod, began swinging, with Ralph at the other end. Soon tiring, the two boys let go of their hold. The weight shifted suddenly, crashing down on Ralph's head. Hearing a thud and a whimper, the older boys ran to the other side and found Ralph's head pinned down by the rod. Blood seeped from his ears and mouth.

"I couldn't get my brother out, so I ran to get my Mommy," Andy said.

The grief-stricken parents put up a brave front to prove their faith. They believed death to be but a sleep in God's sight, didn't they? The jolt of this sudden death and their wanting to live up to their faith served only as a mild tranquilizer to them. They must make immediate arrangements for their little boy in the morgue. Alfonso called the funeraria, and they decided on a simple coffin in which to lay their son's body.

Faculty and close friends suggested plans for the internment. The benumbed couple accepted their friends thoughtfulness, appreciating all their help at a time when grief shackled them.

Son, I'll not be getting you dressed this time as I dressed you for Sabbath a few days ago. How you loved to go to Sabbath School. Thoughts tumbled in her mind as she packed her little boy's clothes and shoes in a box to send to the funeraria. She would no longer hear her little boy say, "Mommy, I know my mem'ry verse."

Later, dean of men D. M. Hechanova, then pursuing his medical education, related what he considered providential timing: He was returning from MCU after his classes that afternoon when after entering PUC gate, he noted a crowd behind the boys' dorm. He quickened his steps to investigate, and saw what seemed the lifeless body of a little boy. He stooped down, and seeing blood oozing out of his ears and mouth, gently placed his hand over the boy's head. He felt the skull broken like a hard-boiled egg. With no other option, he pulled his clean handkerchief out of his pocket and wrapped the boy's head with it in hopes of keeping mangled ragged bone edges from causing more injury to his brain. Atty. Tabu, then a PUC student, cradled little Ralph in his arms, laid him on his lap, they drove back to MCU. Before they could take off, a caring neighbor and friend hopped in the jeep to lend a hand.

Uniformed students took turns 'round-the-clock-vigil on the lifeless body laid in a small yet impressive coffin. His own father took his turn. Loving hands buried two-year-old Ralph Reginald Roda on October 20,

1960, exactly on his parents' seventh wedding anniversary. Needless to say, this day forever changed their wedding anniversary celebration.

"Darling, we must pay attention to Andy, love him even more…." Lydia told her sorrowing husband. Seeing her son's grief deepened the pain in her heart. They took extra effort to comfort their remaining son, doing their best to be supportive of him in his own loss.

Why? Why must this tragedy happen? Ralph was such a well behaved little boy, Lydia kept turning question after question over and over in her mind. *Why didn't the angel of the Lord deliver my son from death as He promised to them that fear Him? His father loves Him, serving Him, giving his all…. There's no question that I, too, love the Lord, serving Him the best way I know how.* Nothing made sense to her now.

Alfonso tried to be strong for both of them. "Sweetheart, some day we'll understand," he said, trying to comfort his beloved. In dispensing comfort, he felt his own pain assuaging.

God created man in His own image, He surely must feel this grief, missing Ralph so, Lydia comforted herself. *Emotion surely is a part of God.*

Thought-Sharing. "I know how *Mamang* grieved over *Kuya* Arding's death, even at age 30, a responsible adult. Giving herself time to mourn and to shed tears doubtless brought about her healing. Look at her now, rejoicing to see all of her children and their spouses in His service," he said.

"She's a very strong woman, I admire her," said Lydia.

"My preoccupation with my work, and other responsibilities helps," he said. "Yet when I come home," his voice choked, "I miss the patter of my little boy's feet running to meet me. I miss him in my arms." Pausing to take a deep breath, he added, "Surprisingly, after verbalizing my feelings, as if the weight, the ache in here," he said pointing to his heart, "lifted."

***

I answered the knock at the door,
Someone asked to see Laughter.
Sorry, Laughter no longer lives here,
Someone had taken away Laughter
I know not when he'd again be here.

Chapter IX

<u>THOUGHTS</u> OF A FAMILY

Train up a child in the way he should go.... (Prov. 22:6)

Miguelito (Mike) Orlando (Orlie) and Edgardo (Pepe)—Lydia's younger brothers—had accepted the offer to live with them in their home as long as they were students. They had promised to be diligent in their studies, they would be helpful, and they would abide by their home regulations.

The adjustments to be made went well, and they became one big family. An occasion the entire household always looked forward to was their anniversary, the celebration with pizza and ice-cream, that is. It was a pleasant change from their school life routine, for this time, everyone at the APR home was a student with the exception of the head of the house.

In the past few years, Lydia has gained competence as a home manager, a topnotch in stretching the family budget and in delegating home chores to her brothers and to their student helpers. Her husband, the head of the house, wasn't beyond the division of labor. He volunteered to join the *Bayong* Club, often driving the bus the College supplied the faculty and staff to do their weekly grocery trip to Divisoria. And whenever the family needed more food, he rode his motor bike to Balintawak market to buy the items Lydia wrote on the grocery list.

Despite their busy life, Alfonso and Lydia took the time to connect. At one time, feeling the need to share thoughts on his mind, he began his theolo-gymnastics. "The depth of sorrow Adam and Eve must have suffered over the death of Abel from the hands of his older brother must have been intense. Did they see the tragedy as a swift retribution of their separation from God? Did they see the link between their choice to eat the fruit and Cain's act? It is apparent their boys were born after their Eden exile and it was in their youth when Cain killed Abel."

Lydia muttered something, but Alfonso continued. "Did Adam ever question God's forgiveness for their disobedience? Having walked with God in the Garden, he surely knew from communing with God that even if God forgave them, nature's laws, being as immutable as the moral law and the Author, the results were inevitable. I believe Adam discerned God had something good coming out of their disobedience: *The woman's seed bruising its* (Satan) *head* resulted from its bruising her heel. Their disobedience would uncover Satan's character for the whole universe to see. The important role Adam played in the Lord's plan of salvation is clear to me.

This thought to me is comforting despite the millenia since the bruising of her heel. My question is, how much longer must we, who believe in our Savior, should occupy 'till He comes?'"

Lydia forced a smile. "It had been difficult for my mind to follow your discourse," she said. "I admit I'm still recuperating from an emotional shock. Although Andy took the blame for the tragedy, Ralph's death was an accident, while Cain let Satan take control over his emotions. Yet, wasn't Satan behind both deaths? At work then, and with all the years of experience he has had, he's working harder yet." She let out a deep sigh. Her husband wrapped her in his arm. "We experienced a repeat of history. Did Adam and Eve suffer more than us, in witnessing, with their own eyes, the results of their disobedience?"

He began singing softly. "God understands your sorrow, He sees the falling tear. Then let Him bear your burdens, He understands and cares." Drawing a deep breath, he said, "Singing always lifts up my spirits. Praise the Lord for the therapy of song on my sagging heart. He's willing to give anyone desiring the ability to use the language of heaven, music, song."

"You had looked forward to singing with Ralph, I know."

He nodded, and switched to another song. "Someday, He'll make it plain to me. Someday, when I His face shall see. Some day from tears I shall be free, For some day I shall understand."

In her peripheral vision, Lydia saw her husband's Adam's apple bob. She saw him draw a deep breath.

"Songs bring tears as well as inspire," he said, blinking tears that threatened to spill. Lydia, too, was wiping her own.

"I'm glad Andy's grade school activities is filling his life. Each day he's getting more independent," she said. "The papers he brings home carry excellent marks. He takes pride in presenting them to me."

"I see the refrigerator turn to bulletin board for a display of his schoolwork," he chuckled. "I like your resourcefulness. I also like to see his eagerness to welcome the Sabbath for he knows we have more time for him. And he is raring to go for our family Sabbath afternoon nature stroll."

They were happy to see their son enjoy being read to and reading the books they had brought for him. "Is it too early to influence him into a career?" Lydia wondered. *Why not give it a try,* she thought.

When an opportune time came, she asked, "Andy, what would you like to be when you grow up?"

"I want to be like Daddy."

"Good, Andy. Would you like to hear a story?" His reply was a nod and he moved and sat close beside his mother.

"One day a rich family went to take a vacation in the country where their boys could enjoy nature. The boys were excited to see the small lake, and down they went to wade in the water. One of the boys stepped out too far into deep water. He didn't know how to swim and soon he was drowning. His brother screamed for help. When the son of their gardener friend heard the cries, he jumped into the water and rescued the little boy.

"Thank you for saving my son," the rich man said, then turned to his father. 'What reward would you like for your son?" He asked.

"He wants to go to college and want to be a doctor," replied the gardener, "but we can't send him. We don't have enough money."

"He shall go to school," the rich man said. "Were it not for him, my son would have drowned." And the rich family paid the son of the gardener to go to school. The young man studied hard and became a doctor-scientist. "Many years later during World War II, Prime minister Winston Churchill of England was very sick with pneumonia. And he was dying. The king called for the best doctor to attend to make the sick man well.

"They found the best doctor—Alexander Fleming—the scientist who discovered penicillin. He was the young man who saved the little boy from drowning. This time, he saved Churchill's life from pneumonia."

Again, Lydia asked what Andy would like to be when he grew up. "I want to be like my Daddy."

Lydia could only smile, and asked, "Do you want to be a teacher?"

"I want to be like my Daddy."

Too early to talk about careers, she concluded. It was enough that his father was Andy's role model. To Lydia, her husband was an easy going man with laughter in his eyes, and she often guessed his thoughts. He was serious in matters spiritual, in matters about God, and about the feelings of his fellow human beings. He had accompanied her on her grocery shopping trips for many years, because he wanted to help her. He also had kept some of his boyish ways, like sampling ice-cream flavor of the month, whenever they happened to go to town together for an errand. She said they were having a regression, but to him they were having marriage enrichment and progressive selfless intimacy.

Even if they had figuratively become one flesh, they maintained their own personal identities. Rough spots that rubbed against smooth sailing in their marriage, they worked to smoothen together bit by bit. Lydia always respected his seemingly unperturbed ways. She felt especially safe in the way he spoke, normally low that rarely generated excitement.

One day as Lydia and her student help were cleaning up after dinner, *Inday* started giggling. "What's funny?" Lydia asked. "Let me laugh, too." But *Inday* kept it up, giving Lydia no clue. She could no longer contain herself and started laughing, too—at her, at *Inday.* She managed to say, "If you don't tell me what's making you act like crazy, I'll suspect a screw in your head is getting loose."

Inday finished stacking the clean dishes neatly, wiped her hands, and said, "Ma'am, promise me not to take offense?"

Assured, *Inday* began. "I was walking out of my class today when I overheard a girl complaining to her friend about her inability to sleep. She said if she lacked sleep, she couldn't function that day. Her friend was silent for a while, then said, seriously. "I have a suggestion. Take Prof. Roda's history class at one o'clock."

The two burst out laughing. When they were spent laughing, *Inday* said, "Ma'am, may I ask something?" Consent given, *Inday* went on. "I like the way Prof. speaks—in an even, low tone—but I noticed a few times you suddenly appeared upset when he spoke a little louder than he normally does. Maybe I'm misjudging you, Ma'am."

"Yes, I do feel slighted when he answers me louder than he normally does. You probably saw him come to me, perhaps overheard him say, 'I'm sorry, please forgive me.' Often he'd add, 'When I raise my voice, it's for emphasis, nothing more.' Sometimes he'd remind me, 'See, I'm always the one asking forgiveness.' Of course, I'd tell him, 'Because you're at fault.'"

"I never saw him get angry," *Inday* said.

Just then they heard their topic of conversation singing. Worship.

"Let's go," Lydia said, and started out to join the evening worship.

After worship, Alfonso asked Andy to stay by while the others left. He thought it was time for a father-son talk, for when he asked if he could have a baby brother, Lydia told him to ask God about it. And since then, a baby brother for him had been in Andy's every prayer.

"Do you remember how Ralph came to us when he was a baby?" he began. "You were a little boy then when your mommy let you feel your little brother tucked away in her big tummy."

Andy's face showed little recall of the events as a three-year- old. *God fashioned the mind for questioning for growth,* Alfonso affirmed himself.

"Andy, what I'd like to tell you now is that God answers prayers in other ways than how we expect or want. Like when your brother Ralph was born. It was time for him to come out. We prayed for your baby brother to be healthy. You know we pray at worship every morning, asking God to take care of us all. We always prayed for angels to take care of you and Ralph. Why didn't God protect Ralph from the accident? We also prayed for his healing, for God to save his life. We don't know why He answered, 'No.' Can you tell how God may answer prayers at other times?"

After trying to understand the question, he said, "Wait." Then looking up at his father, he said, "Daddy, I don't want God to answer, 'No,' again."

"Remember your memory verses in Sabbath School, "If you have faith as a mustard seed ...' and another,'whatever ye ask in my name, I will give it to you....' Can you think of other similar verses?"

"I do," the little boy replied brightly. "Ask, and ye shall receive...."

"Good. Let's go to your room and ask God to fulfill His promises in His own good time. Let's wait for your mommy." They saw her coming.

"It did not take us long to wait for your Mommy."

"Yes, Daddy, but it is so hard to wait for God to say yes."

"It takes prayer to understand God's ways," he said. "One day is with the Lord a thousand years, and a thousand years as one day," (2 Peter 3:8).

Andy's face was a question mark, his dad noted his son's serious look. "Let's take these puzzling verses to God," Alfonso said.

They knelt down to pray their sentence-prayer. After his parents' prayer, Andy came in, "Dear Jesus, thank You for giving me parents who love me... and... for giving me a new baby brother soon, if it's Your will." Three voices blended in an amen. Andy's arms stretched out for the hugs.

Alfonso and Lydia had the living room to themselves, as the students had gone to their own rooms. They had their own reading to do, but first they would talk. "A beginning," he said. "Looking back to my own childhood, I don't recall having questioned much about the subject. I found good books to read to satisfy my thirst for knowledge. We were always busy, we had no spare time to think about ourselves. For Andy, he has both of us, his three uncles living with us, and the live-in student helpers."

"The Lord set up in His crowning work of creation brains and emotions to handle this part of growing up. Without conscious effort led by His wisdom, man repeats the cycle of 'replenishing the earth.' He chuckled. "The Roda brothers are doing their part well. Five in *Papang's* family—if he lived longer than 33...? Uncle Alvaro, ten, and uncle Tony, seven."

"Seven in my parents, too," she said, "but ours is planned parenthood."

"Now, what was the smile on your face when you came for worship?"

He only grinned when Lydia repeated *Inday'* s story about his class.

"You've never taken any of my classes," he said. "My history class always met after lunch. In tropical countries, it is the time when the body wants a siesta. I, too, sat in a history class at exactly the time I teach this class. I recall struggling to keep awake. But when one has to teach, it is something else, no matter that teachers repeat the same facts in their lectures year after year. I sympathize with my students trying to stay awake, particularly the working students. However, many students add life to the class. That alone gives me inspiration to keep going."

"Why not ask the Registrar to assign a different time for your history class in the future? I took history classes only because they were requirements. Past events and dates, who needs them?"

"That's what many generally think, but without history a gap remains, a disconnection to the present occurs. We don't see Bible classes as history, but they are. The birth of Christ, events surrounding His life, His ministry, His resurrection. Without the Old Testament, what would Christianity be?"

"The history of the nursing profession was interesting," she admitted.

"Right you are. Florence Nightingale 'hi'story in nursing…."

She nodded, and changed the topic. "Miss Manalaysay said Andy shows interest in his music lessons, and that piano is always a good start in music. She suggested to get him to learn to play other musical instruments."

"Andy can take lessons in any musical instrument he cares to learn," he said. "As a young boy, I wanted to take music lessons, but the opportunity never opened for me. We'll see that Andy develops whatever musical ability he inherited. Ahem," he chuckled. "I enjoy singing. Singing is a noble and uplifting form of self-expression."

"I enjoyed the vespers in PUC, especially when the faculty trio—Mr. Romeo Brion on the organ, Mrs. Paz Poblete on the piano, and Dr. Man, the violin. I thought we students were so lucky to listen to the gifted faculty play good music. I forgot I was sitting on a hard bench at the gymnasium, I got lost enjoying the music, imagining what heavenly music must be."

A few weeks later, again after evening worship, an occasion arose for Alfonso to re-word the question he asked his son earlier.

"Andy, tell me, do you think God always answers 'yes' to prayers?"

He thought a moment. "I think God sometimes tell us to 'wait,' he said.

'Right, Son," he said patting him on the shoulder. "In God, there's no such thing as time. It takes faith to understand that, Son."

Andy nodded. "Then I'll need to wait when God says it's time for my baby brother to come in His own time. I don't want God to say No," this time. He side-glanced his father and mumbled the question he'd always wanted to ask. "And how did Ralph get inside my Mommy… to grow?"

"That's a very good question, Son, and I'm glad you asked me that. Do you remember the short memory verse you learned as soon as you could talk? We also sing the verse in many songs. And we even sing it at worship time." He cleared his throat, and softly began singing. "Tis love that makes us happy, Tis love that smooths the way." He invited him to sing along, and father and son blended in, "God is love, We're His little children, God is love, We would be like Him…."

"God created us in His own image—like Him. He placed in us a part of Him—love. The word 'create' becomes 'procreate' in human beings, whom God created in His own image. When He made our first parents, Adam and Eve, He gave His love to them and what love can do—to procreate—so they could have their own children. Just like when your Mommy planted tomato seeds in her garden. Soon tomato seedlings came up and grew, and later bore flowers that became fruits that had seeds. That's how God's creation continue His work of love. Your Mommy and your Daddy love each other, it's an expression of their love to each other to plant their human seeds to grow. An ecstatic and wonderful experience for married couple to do with God's sanction. Son, as you grow older, you'll understand it better."

Andy listened, and since he had always trusted his parents, he took his daddy's explanation without question.

***

Chapter X

OF PEACE HIGHER EDUCATION

Show me Thy ways, Good and upright is the Lord ...
(Psalms 25:4, 8)

1962. Alfonso came bouncing home. "Sweetheart," he called, "here's fulfillment of your dream to be a foreign missionary." He handed her a letter. He watched for her reaction as she read ... dimples beneath the corners of her lips told of her delight. "Andrew's University scholarship from FED," she mumbled. "Are you taking it?"

"All of us will. The scholarship stipend is far from sufficient for the three of us, but we will go in faith. I don't want to leave you and Andy here. We'll entrust our lives in the care of the One Who *clothers the grass* (Matt. 6:25) and Who sees the sparrows fall.(Matt. 10:29). He had taken into consideration that less than two years ago they had buried their son. Much prayer and buoying of spirit from relatives and friends gave them reason to cling to Alfonso's initial decision to go in faith. Accordingly, they bent their efforts to prepare for adventure in Berrien Springs.

Three set to sail for N America. L-r: Lydia, Andy, Alfonso, in *barong tagalog*.

Thanks to Mrs. Paz Villanueva Peng for posting the following article in the Cyberlink by Dr. Flores about the *Barong Tagalog*:

During the Spanish regime in the Philippines (1561–1898) the Spanish government required the Filipinos to wear *barong tagalog* at all times to differentiate the rich from the poor. The poor serving the rich must always be in uniform, and must adhere to these particulars:

1. Shirttails must not be tucked in (the mark of inferior status).
2. Transparent material (to reveal any weapon).
3. No pockets (a precaution against thievery).

By the turn of the century, a new middle class emerged among the Filipinos, known as 'The Principalia.' They have mastered Spanish laws and were able to obtain title to lands, became successful in business and agriculture, their sons went abroad to be educated. Only The Principalia could be addressed by the title 'Don—and Dona—' and only they could vote. Years later, the first Filipino president Don Manuel L. Quezon, declared *barong tagalog* The National Attire for men.

***

Their transcontinental voyage was uneventul and they arrived on time to attend the General Conference session held in San Francisco in June, 1962. With Lydia's older brother Felicito Fernando and his family, they drove east, and in July they settled in a one bedroom apartment in Berrien Springs. Lydia had prepared her mind to manage, by God's grace, without an *Inday*'s help for the three of them.

And she went to apply for a job at the hospital within walking distance of their new home. To her dismay, she learned Michigan did not participate in the Nurses' Exchange Program. However, she was given assurance that she'd have no problem getting a job in domestics, in janitorial work, for example. That was beside the point. They'll have to manage with the General Conference $95.00 monthly stipend, and trust in the Lord to lead.

They enrolled Andy at AU Elementary School, where he readily adjusted to his new environment. He was soon enjoying his new friends. ("He's cute, smart and athletic and could run the fastest to catch the ball," they said of him.) Andy also met the challenges of school surprisingly well.

As for Lydia, she was becoming ill-at-ease over their financial affairs. Alfonso tried hard to influence her with his unfaltering faith in God.

One day while at the AU post office, Alfonso happened to meet Elder R. Figuhr and Elder Blake, then G. C. treasurer. They asked Alfonso how he was doing. *The Lord's leading*, he thought, and unburdened his heart to the two Church leaders. His monthly stipend increased to $165.00, for which Alfonso was grateful. However, Lydia could not stretch this amount to meet their needs. Her hopes to augment their stipend by working as an R.N. did not materialize, and it devastated her. Dr. Manalaysay's remark to her before they left PUC—*your financial status will depend much on your earnings*—kept going through her mind.

To begin with, she felt insecure over having to keep up with the profession after nine years as a stay-home wife and mother. Esther, her older sister, told her that Illinois had nurses reciprocity, and Hinsdale Sanitarium needed nurses. If she had to work, she would have to live apart from her husband, and she did not want this to happen. Fretting over these caused her insomnia that led to anorexia that made her restless and depressed. Even her prayers for God to rebuke Satan from pursuing after her proved futile, as was her own, "In Jesus' name, Satan, get out of my way!" She prayed for faith, but her prayers seemed to her so ineffectual. All these sank her deeper into depression.

"Whatever happened to my darling wife," Alfonso cried, wrapping her in his arms. "Lord, please heal her. Return her sweet, happy disposition."

Lydia, hearing and seeing her husband affected so, feeling guilty over her runaway mental state beyond her control, and her sense of inadequacy plunged her deeper into depression. Esther offered her home to Lydia and suggested for her to seek psychiatric help. Alfonso saw this to be the only way. He took Lydia to see Dr. Charles Anderson, an Adventist psychiatrist, and a member of the Medical Staff at Hinsdale Sanitarium & Hospital.

Dr. Anderson observed his patient as he listened to the answers to his questions, and after a thorough analysis and evaluation of her case history, advised electroshock therapy and hospitalization. Lydia declined both. He then prescribed antidepressants and gave her a follow-up appointment.

Alfonso and Lydia drove to Chicago—to Esther's place—in silence, deep in thought, barely communicating. They would take Esther's offer for Lydia and Andy to stay with them during the duration of the treatment.

Jun was on surgical residency in Chicago, and he and his family lived in a two bedroom apartment with a living room open to a dining room/kitchen in one, and a den. Jun's mother, Esther Vizcarra, Sr. (Sr. Esther) who came to live with them after her husband died, had the den. She'd share the den converted-to-a-bedroom and her double bed with Lydia. The boys, Edred and Rodney, would share their bedroom with Andy.

September. Esther helped Lydia enrol Andy at North Shore Drive Seventh-day Adventist Elementary School, where her own boys attended. It warmed Lydia to see her nephews' delight over having their cousin with them, and Andy's response to his cousins, but now she was having tremors.

On her follow-up, Dr. Anderson agreed with Lydia that her tremors were adverse effects of the antidepressants. Again, he suggested electroshock therapy and hospitalization. But again Lydia refused both. Dr. Anderson thought of the only alternative—referral to the Great Physician. The doctor and the nurse-turned-patient knelt for divine consultation.

While Esther drove home, Lydia shared with her the details of her visit with Dr. Anderson. Esther said Lydia made the right decision in declining electroshock therapy and hospitalization. "We are warring against powers and principalities," she said. "I'm a hundred percent for prayer therapy. 'Prayer is the key that unlocks heaven's storehouse,'" she quoted from the pen of inspiration. Esther reminded her younger sister of how the Lord had intervened in her behalf, in her healing especially, in the not too-long past. He will also carry you through this," she said.

"I'll grow up one of these days," Lydia said. "I appreciate you and all you have done for me; God loves me enough to put me through all these."

"This is another opportunity for us to grow closer together as sisters, and draw closer to God even more," Esther replied.

Alone in Berrien Springs, Alfonso had his own adjustments to make. He saw how his training as a growing boy in a fatherless home—helping his mother and siblings with daily chores—came handy. Going for grocery—his self-assigned duty up to the time before Berrien Springs—was no problem. Early in the week, he wrote Lydia making fun of his life as a bachelor: of making his bed, preparing his own meals and eating alone, housecleaning, doing dishes and laundry. He also wrote a short note to Andy, which he always ended with, "I'll see you this weekend," which he always fulfilled.

One weekend in late October, they piled in their second hand station wagon. "There's room for everybody," Andy said to his cousins, and away they went. Outside the city limits, they came upon a spectacular grove.

From the back seat,"Daddy, Mommy," Andy called, "see those trees? Why aren't the leaves green? They have the color of flowers!" he said, pointing at the maple trees in full autumn regalia. Then he noticed a tree devoid of leaves. "Is that tree dead, Daddy?"

The children, and even Lydia, listened as their driver described fall, winter, spring, and summer, comparing it with the Philippines' dry and rainy seasons. "About the leaves," he explained, "the colors like flowers are there all the time, but the green color outshines them all. When the days get colder and shorter in autumn, the chlorophyll that gives the green color in the leaves fade, giving a chance for the bright-like-flower colors to show. Fall is the other name for the season." Getting the attention of the boys, he asked, "Can you tell me why?" Just then a gust of wind hurled multicolored leaves from the trees in to space. Watching the leaves fly and playfully dance in the wind, the boys chorused, "Because the leaves fall down!"

Boys—Edred, Rodney," their uncle Alfonso called, "Do you like winter?"

"Yes!" the boys chorused.

"Why?" their uncle asked as he drove along.

"Because we can build a snowman!" Edred and Rodney replied. "Do you like the cold winter weather?"

"It's OK," said Edred. "We wear coats and galoshes to keep us warm."

"I also like springtime," said Alfonso. "It's the time when leafless trees bud and blossom. The bright flowers blooming on the ground and on shrubs and trees bring life to the earth. It's the time when the birds begin to sing and build their nests." Briefly turning to Lydia, he whispered, "Sweetheart, I'm sure you'll like spring, the time when crocuses, daffodils, flowering dogwoods, forsythias, redbuds, and the fruit trees blossom. Apples, plums with pinkish white flowers, apricots, cherries, peaches, in pink array, the pears carry white nosegays." Sideglancing her, he added, "Fleeting beauties of the earth, through them God talks to human hearts."

"I like fall already," she said. "I wish the multicolored leaves stayed longer on the trees, wish the wind would not blow them away so soon."

On their return drive, the boys started a game: counting bright-leaved trees and red cars. Tiring of that, they began to talk to themselves. Edred said, "We are leaving Chicago soon. Andy, come and attend school with us where we are going." Echoing his older brother, Rodney said, "Yes, Andy. Come with us to Urbana. Dad said it's not far from Chicago."

Silence.

Overhearing the boys' talk, Lydia sighed. "I wish this depression would lift. I feel like… imprisoned," she sighed. "Hinsdale San needs nurses, but I am unfit to work." Another sigh.

Alfonso reached for her hand and gave it a squeeze. "I think your outlook has improved since coming to Chicago. I praise the Lord for that. I can't thank Esther enough for accommodating you and Andy."

Driving closer to Esther's home, Alfonso said, "I wish I could stay with you longer, but I must get back to Berrien." He drew a deep breath.

"I know," said Lydia. "You have to study plus other work I should be doing. This depression has reduced me to being a burden to you."

He gave her hand another squeeze. "Sweetheart, for those the Lord loves, He allows adversities to happen to them for a good purpose."

"I think Dr. Anderson is hinting that I submit an application for work, in faith." And drawing a deep breath, she added, "By God's grace, I will."

"He is a praying doctor, we can trust a Christian like him. Take heart, Sweetheart, the God whom we serve will carry us through. He promised to. As for me, days are swiftly fleeting. Here today, gone tomorrow."

"Wish it were like that for me," she said. "Days go so slowly for me."

"I'm glad to see Andy having fun with his cousins," he said. "My next trip over will be on Thanksgiving weekend." He cast her a sideglance. "I have a paper to research on," he explained, as he slowed down to park. After letting the boys out, he went around to open the door for Lydia. He took her hand, and slowly they walked up the steps hand in hand.

"We'll try to be fine," she finally said. "We'll look for your letter."

Esther met them. "Wow," she said, "You look radiant!"

"Thank you," Alfonso.said, grinning. "Colorful autumn influences."

The Sr. Esther came out and greeted them with a tentative smile.

"You should have come along," Alfonso said to her, "for our chaperon."

"I'll be seeing a lot of autumn foliage in years to come," Sr. Esther said. She reached out to tuck a hair lock of Lydia's. "This is the first autumn for you, isn't it?" she queried with a bigger smile. "Do you like fall?"

Lydia returned her smile. "Yes, my first. It is glorious, I love it."

"I like to see your dimples flash when you smile," Sr. Esther said.

Alfonso put his arms around the two Esthers "Thank you so much for encircling us in your arms of love. I must be on my way," he said.

"Wait," Esther said. She ran to the kitchen and returning, "Take this with you," she said to her brother-in-law, handing him a small cooler. "It's Ma's idea," she gushed. "*Pancit* and *pinakbet* to save you some cooking."

"How thoughtful of you," Alfonso mumbled, his Adam's apple bobbing. "Now I see why you declined our invitation to join us for a drive," he said addressing the Sr. Esther. "I will have a feast on these for several meals."

Sr. Esther switched her eyes from Alfonso to Lydia, then to her daughter-in-law, and back to Alfonso. She laid both hands lightly on his shoulders. "May I call you my son, too?" she said, a hint of reticence in her tone. "You know I have only one child, don't you?"

Alfonso wrapped her in his arms. "Please do," he said. "Please do." He drew a deep breath. "My wife Lydia is your daughter, too," he added.

"Exactly," she said, her smile reached her eyes. "You knew it," she said. "You have good intuition."

The two sisters blinked misty eyes.

Lydia stepped out to call Andy. His cousins trailed along with him. Andy went to his dad and threw his arms around his trousered legs. Spontaneously, the boys put their arms around each other, and bowed their heads. Alfonso committed them all in the care of their heavenly Father. Andy jumped up to his dad's arms for a big, long hug.

***

AUTUMN MUSINGS

Why do trees turn colorful in autumn?

Some say, shortening of days,
*   decreasing supply of light*
change the cells in the leaves and
*   chlorophyll integrity.*

Some say, sudd'n weather changes
*   when long sultry summer days*
turn cold and cut off the flow
*   of the green hue in the leaves*

Letting warm colors to show
*   the emerald to subdue*
ever present through all clime
*   silently waiting for their time.*

Matters not to me why, how
*   leaves turn aflame on the bough:*
orange, magenta, maroon,
*   red, yellow, gold, brown, crimson.*

Autumn colors shout: lives end
*   gloriously as one opened*
his heart to the Lord's warm love
*   for renewal up above.*

As nature relies on God
*   to guide and direct its course*
throughout all the four seasons
*   pray, direct and guide me, Lord.*

Like leaves respond, change colors
*   in fall foliage, strewn rainbows,*
I think of one Who promised,
*   "For you, I'll return, Dearest."*

 ***

At Esther's initiation, she and her siblings reached a consensus. They would meet on Thanksgiving day for potluck at Mike's home in Hinsdale. Mike was beginning his year of internship at HSH. His wife Lucy, a lab tech worked at the laboratory department. The get-together would celebrate Mike's recent acceptance for residency at a teaching hospital in Chicago.

"A double occasion," said Esther, "call it a family reunion." For in a few months the Vizcarra family would be moving out of the windy city and Mike and Lucy would be moving in after Mike completed his internship.

It was understood that Alfonso would say grace. "Before we bow our heads," he said, "I would like to say that words are inadequate to express my deep gratitude to all of you—our kind kin—for opening your arms of love to my family." He put his left arm around Lydia. "We say a million heartfelt thank yous, especially to," gesturing with his palm-upturned right hand to the younger Esther and then to Sr. Esther. "You are Christian love personified," he said, voice choking. He drew a deep breath. "We can't thank you enough." Then he offered a prayer of thankfulness, 'for the blessings before us and for the hands that prepared the good food.'"

As dinner progressed, their talk led to the origin of Thanksgiving Day.

"Another mark of Philippine Americanization is the Thanksgiving Day celebration there." Jun said, his eyes disappearing with his 'heh-heh-heh.'

"Ehum," Mike nodded. "Credit the missionaries for that," he said.

'Yes, every moment of the day, we have many things to be thankful for," said Alfonso. "Think of it. We—boys—are all students." Looking around he added, "Two big boys pursuing medical specialization, one is upgrading in the educational field, and three little boys in church school."

"Hey! A discovery!" Jun practically shouted. "You are right," he said.

"And the girls stay home, except me," Lucy interjected. "To help the boys go to school, but soon, the table will turn, eh," she added chuckling.

"Lucy, must you say that!" Jun tried to scold and his eyes went to hide.

"Auntie," Edred turned to Lydia. "Can Andy come with us to Urbana?"

"We may be moving to Hinsdale," his aunt replied, shaking her head.

"Hey," Jun said. "We would not be too far away from each other."

"That means," Esther explained, "we could easily visit each other."

After the goodbyes, Alfonso left for Berrien. The Vizcarras with Lydia and Andy drove home to Chicago. When the boys tramped outdoors, Lydia told her sister she felt the need for solitude.

Perceptive Esther said the best place would be the room the boys shared. Lydia slipped in the room, shut the door behind her, and knelt beside the bed, propped her elbows on a pillow—palms cupped over her eyes—and in whispers began to pray.

"Lord, my Father in heaven Who sees the sparrows fall, also hear my prayer. I thank Thee for inviting me to come boldly to Thy throne of grace with my burdens. I'm so tired of being depressed, Lord, of being unable to function. Lord, lift up my emotions with Thy healing hands. I thank Thee for a loving older sister, but I cannot and I do not want to have to lean on her each time I need a round of chastening for refining this life of mine. I thank Thee for opening my eyes to see that as I can rely on my sister's willingness to help, I, too, could rely on Thee, for Thee to be ever present for me.

I'd been through so much already in the past, Lord. Thou must love me so. I thank Thee for pointing out the rough edges in me that need polishing, Lord. I thank Thee for making me realize that I'd been apt to snub those who could not help acting in ways that do not please me. I thank Thee for making me aware of my tendency to be quick to judge others, using my own standards I was brought up with. As Thou have been caring and sensitive to my needs, Lord, give me a more tolerant heart to my fellow beings' humanness. I want to be more loving and empathetic, more understanding to the circumstances influencing my fellow beings to act in the way they do, but I know not how. Lord, show me, teach me how.

I thank Thee for bringing me and my wonderful husband comfort in the loss of our precious Ralph." Drawing a deep breath, a sob escaped. She wiped the tears with her fingers, and dried her fingers on the bedsheet."Let me realize that the short life of my dear little Ralph was a blessing perhaps in disguise, that I should not forget. I still don't understand why his life was snuffed out so suddenly from us. Perhaps in the future we'll understand why, there must be a good reason for him to be taken away from us. I thank Thee for bringing the comfort we needed, and please erase the pain from this aching heart of mine. Lord, touch me, give me faith to keep trusting Thee, if thou are willing, lift this depression...." She sighed.

"I thank Thee for granting the desires of my heart, for opening a job for me at the San—Thy work. I thank Thee for a Christian psychiatrist whom Thou had stirred to seek divine consultation, and for impressing him to tell me of the hospital's need for Christian nurses." Suddenly, Lydia realized she had inadvertently asked for something she dreaded. "Lord, I don't want to live apart from my husband," she cried out in anguish.

My dear child, where's your faith? Put your complete trust in Me.

"Lord, I thank Thee for awakening me to the fact that 'without faith it is impossible to please Thee.' I ask Thee to give me faith to discern Thy power to rebuke Satan from piling this despair on me. Give me the courage to come to Thee and trust Thee to solve our financial problems. I hand this problem to Thee, Lord. I thank Thee for taking over my burdens."

Lydia reached for her Bible, "Lord, please speak to me through Thy Word," she pleaded. She let her fingers leaf through the New Testament, stopping in Philippians 4. Her eyes were drawn to verse 6. *Have no anxiety about anything but in everything let your requests be made known to God.* I thank Thee for showing me this verse, Lord. I claim Thy promise, 'Whatever you ask in My name, you will receive.' "I claim this promise now, Lord. Please enable me to sleep at night so I could function as a cheerful nurse, bringing comfort to the sick in body and spirit."

Now she thought of a place to live within walking distance of the hospital. "Lord, thou would know where we could stay, where Andy would be able to walk to school. If living in Hinsdale apart from my husband would be the best solution to our financial problems, Lord, give me fortitude to accept this temporary distance separation. I ask for a definite sign of Thy leading, Lord. If at my next medical follow-up, Dr. Anderson would suggest for me to apply for a job and he would have me fill an application form, and that the hospital would have housing available for me, I would take this to be Thy plus sign. I trust Thee, Lord. I thank Thee for answering my prayers. May I bring Thee glory. I pray in Jesus' name."

She looked at her watch. *I'd been on my knees for over two hours!* She got up, her heart felt light. No oppressive feelings of depression weighing her down. As she looked out the window, she saw the sunshine brightening every building, when in the past, they looked drab.

"I praise Thee for healing me, Lord, for delivering me from Satan's clutches. It feels so good to be free of the heaviness of depression. I give my whole life to Thee. Use me as Thou see fit to bring glory to Thy name."

As she got up, she became aware she was softly singing, "Jesus, Jesus, Jesus. Sweetest name I know. Fills my every longing, keeps me singing as I go." She was still softly singing when she walked to the kitchen.

Esther looked up from preparing supper to see Lydia. "Wow!" she said. "Singing and smiling! Did you have a good nap?"

"The Lord healed me, and I praise Him so. No, no nap. I was on my knees pleading for healing, and He healed me completely. My worries over having to work after years without practice are gone. I feel I'm ready for a full time job. I thought of Dr. Anderson's remark that Hinsdale San needs good nurses."

She gave Esther a tight hug. "I thank the Lord and I thank you very much, too. We'll meet my next doctor's follow-up appointment as scheduled. I know Dr. Anderson will give me a good recommendation, and somehow I feel he'll suggest for me to fill an application for a job."

"Good! I've heard they need good nurses there. You'll fit right in."

"Your mother-in-law comes handy, doesn't she. Lucky you. She'd been very good to share her bedroom and double bed with me. I also prayed the San would accommodate me with housing. I have faith they would. Now, I will have to pack our things for the move."

"No need to hurry now," said Esther. "Pack after supper. I need your help. Will you set the table? You know what to do but ask if you don't."

Supper had an extraordinarily festive mood for Lydia. Sitting across Sr. Esther, she thanked her for sharing her room and double bed with her. "I know a job and housing are waiting for me at the San," she said.

The hospital gave Lydia an apartment at the Ana Pederson Hall, and a complimentary cafeteria meal ticket for the weekend. Lydia set up housekeeping and prepared for the Sabbath. Alfonso, Lydia, and Andy walked hand in hand to the hospital cafeteria and found the line open. The serving team was cheerful, courteous and professional.

As they looked for a table, Lydia met familiar faces. She had heard a few Filipino nurses were working there and had anticipated bonhomie with them. Meeting former MSH employees was like homecoming to Lydia. The nurses lived at the hospital apartment complex. Soon, they were catching up with news about each other, their families, friends, and so forth.

Hearing and seeing all this social interaction assured Alfonso of his wife's welfare. He delighted to see her bubbling with joy over her new employer's hospitality. She'd not worry about food, they'd return to the cafeteria for their Sabbath and Sunday meals. His concern was over Andy, who had been unusually quiet during their meal. *Uprooted from his cousins' companionship, it would take some time for him to get acquainted with another way of life,* he reflected. Mentally preparing for his return to Berrien Springs, he anguished over having to bid his son goodbye.

"Son," he said on Sunday, "God willing, I'll be here next Friday."

Andy nodded his head slowly. After his father left, however, he turned to his mother and began an outburst of 'whys.' "Why do we have to live here, away from my daddy. Why can't he stay with us. Why can't we stay with him. Why are we not all going home. Why can't we stay with my cousins."

No matter how much Lydia explained in simple terms for him to understand the 'whys' to this arrangement, her son remained unhappy.

I need the solace, Lord, she prayed silently. The Lord granted her prayer in Andy's schoolteacher's report."

"Andy is adjusting very well. He's making friends easily, he's a fast learner and takes great pride in his work. He is a bright pupil." The papers Andy brought home proved the reports true. Yet the boy lived waiting for Friday, to his daddy's return for the weekend. The hour before bedtime remained his loneliest moment, for he sorely missed his daddy at worship. He missed his bedtime routine, his hug. Mealtime problems persisted. Picking at his food, he'd say between bites. "I want my Daddy here."

"Lord, make me accept this situation," Lydia prayed. "Grant me peace, Lord. I'm a mature person and I believe in Thy goodness. Let me be brave for Andy. Let Andy accept this temporary separation." Doing bedside care distracted her nagging loneliness, yet she began to dread getting back to their apartment. She, too, began to look forward to Friday afternoons.

When Mike and Lucy invited Lydia to double with them in their home at Hilgrove Road, Lydia promptly accepted the kind gesture. Alfonso felt great relief for God's leading. With a support system under the same roof, he could relax more over their temporary distance separation. Yet Andy's longing for him remained like a thorn in the flesh for both parents.

"We'll keep living one day at a time, Sweetheart," Alfonso whispered to Lydia when she told him she worried over Andy more than ever. "Young as he is, he can learn to accept this temporary arrangement. As long as you are living with Mike and Lucy, I trust Mike's presence would fill in Andy's man-figure needs. This is God's answer to our prayers."

That Friday afternoon, Andy came bounding home, and sidled against his dad. "I'm the luckiest boy now, Daddy," he said as he and his dad hugged. "But I wish you'd be with us all the time."

"How do you like school?"

"I have many friends now," he boasted. "At my school and in Sabbath School. And I joined the Pathfinders."

"What do you do at Pathfinders?"

"We memorize our pledge. We hear stories. We learn to tie knots. We study animals, birds, flowers, and insects, and other things. We have drills, and we will go climbing mountains, and we will go swimming, too."

"Then you are enjoying yourself very much, aren't you, Son?"

Andy nodded his head. "You should come to tell us stories too, Daddy, and join our fun. Other boys' fathers come some time."

Alfonso drew his son to his knee. He flipped through the calendar and said, "I have commitment on these dates. I'll have to stay in Berrien," he added. "Son, will you keep yourself and your Mommy from crying?"

"No!" Andy whined. "You promised to be with us every weekend." Tears filled his eyes, flowing down his face. "I want you with me, Daddy."

"Why don't we tell Jesus all about this now, Son." With his eyes he called Lydia to kneel down with them. Clasping hands, Alfonso prayed "Our most gracious Father in heaven, we thank Thee for Thy promise to hear us when we pray. We thank Thee for wanting us to talk to Thee about our problems. Look down from Thy throne of grace, dear Father. Hear our prayer. We want to be obedient to Thy will. We praise Thee for sending Jesus to earth to be with our forefathers long ago. Thou must have missed Him, too, when He lived on earth so far away from heaven. It must have really hurt Jesus, too, but He came to Thee in prayer. Let us realize that we can be near Thee when we pray, that in thy presence we are together as a family. Please help Andy realize that when Jesus was his age, He, too, lived far, far away from His Father. Jesus understands how Andy feels now with me away from him all week. In our minds let us perceive that distance shrinks in Thy presence. Let us be aware of unseen holy Angels keeping watch over us. Let us experience Thy presence in our lives moment by moment everyday. Please be very close to Andy and his Mommy when we are far apart. Lord, let us feel Thy loving arms around us. I thank Thee for listening to our prayer. We ask these in Jesus' name."

Alfonso gave Lydia's hand a squeeze for her to pray next, but she shook her head. She couldn't pray aloud. The lump in her throat had grown and tears streamed down her cheeks. She wiped them away, forcing herself to believe in her husband's prayer of faith. It lifted her spirits to see her son quietly accept his dad's prayer. Silently, she prayed for her son's faith to grow. She must not allow her grief for Ralph to return. *Lord, give me a childlike faith,* she pleaded. *Give me a sound mind and a sunny outlook. Rebuke Satan from inflicting me with loneliness.*

Before Alfonso left for Berrien Springs, he specified the hours of the day and the night when he would be on his knees. "Meet with me at the altar of prayer on those hours," he suggested. She promised she and Andy would. They let their hugs and kisses linger to make up for the weekends.

As the days dragged on, Lydia felt the heaviness weighing down her heart grow heavier. Having never relished letter writing, she bought a tape recorder. Listening to their voices on cassette tape would be less expensive than long distance phone calls. She sang into the tape recorder songs such as, "When My Heart is Filled with Sorrow," "No, Never alone."

She let Andy speak to his dad on tape. Alfonso returned the tapes filled with his spoken love for them. Their evening and morning tryst on their knees and hearing her husband's voice on tape brightened the weekends.

Like any innovations. the taped communication, too, lost its novelty, but Lydia determined that *when the Lord laid His hand to take my depression away, it was a permanent cure. It's up to me to do my part.* And she knew where to go. *I feel like I'm deep in a quagmire of sadness, Lord,* she complained. *I know Thou has not withdrawn Thy love from me.* Andy's courage had also dwindled. He resumed telling he wanted his Daddy and his Mommy together. His attitude worried her.

Lydia forced herself to focus on all the blessings the Lord had lavishly poured on her. She began praying in whispers, *Lord, I totally surrender my whole life to Thee. Free me from all the cobwebs of petty concerns and self-awareness entangling my peace of mind. I open my mind for Thy holy Spirit to fill with peace. I give my all to Thee, Who will lead ...Help me to accept things I cannot change, and to change what I can, by Thy grace.*

She listened to a quiet voice speaking, "Take Andy with you for a weekend at your sister's." Lydia thought of the many ways her older sister had been an ever-help for her. She dialed her phone number.

"Come on over," Esther's sweet voice came on the line. "Pack up and get ready. I'll pick you and Andy tomorrow." Andy perked up when his mother told him of their trip.

Lydia felt her heart lighten when Esther greeted her with a hug as she cried. "*Mang* Es, it's so good to see you in flesh and person again."

"The car is busting its seams," Jun declared after packing their things in. The sisters chatted all the way to Chicago. "Chattering like monkeys," he teased. Andy, however, remained quiet most of the time.

Upon arriving at her sister's apartment, the heaviness in her heart returned, but Lydia kept it to herself.

Esther's 'feel-at-home' was like a red carpet of welcome. "As in the past, the boys will camp in the boys' room. Get settled," she said. "The weekend accommodation will be a repeat of the past," she said. "It's Friday, we have Sabbath preparations to do. My mother-in-law helped clean the house but we need to prepare for supper." Lydia offered to help, and put her weekend luggage away.

As the sisters prepared supper, Lydia told Esther she had been chosen to represent the Philippines as Miss Hospital in the float for the upcoming hospital day. "I plan to wear my Filipina dress and a matching fine-weave bamboo hat," she said. Esther was visibly happy for Lydia and promised she would try her best to take her family along for the occasion. "It looks like your dream of being a foreign missionary is coming true," she added.

"Andy's daddy said that, too, I might as well enjoy it. I enjoy working. My worry over my inability to keep up to date with the current nursing trends, having had no professional bedside nursing since completing my clinical practicum, was energy wasted," she laughed. "How do you manage to live on Jun's salary as a surgical resident?" Lydia wanted to find out.

"Fine," Esther replied. "Ma has funds, and I know this mode of life is temporary. Jun's happy-go-lucky nature is definitely a plus. Hardly anything upsets him, not even Ma's throwing well-meaning motherly advices." She gave a belly laugh. "He said he was lonesome as a growing boy, being an only child, and now he would like to have as many children as we could produce," she chuckled. She looked around and seeing no one else, she asked, "Is Andy still begging for a baby brother?"

"Not since arriving in the States. Too many distractions. I count them as blessings in disguise," Lydia replied. "You don't seem to mind the limited varieties of fruits and vegetables in the grocery stores. Do you...."

"At first I missed our home grown native greens," Esther interrupted. "The *ampalaya, malunggay,* squash blooms, sweet potato tops, even the *kang kong!*" she laughed, "but not lately. The children took after their father. They eat what's on the table. I think they have American taste buds," she added. "I vary the preparation of whatever vegetables we get. I serve not too many kinds of food at one meal, a la Mrs. White's counsels."

Lydia regarded her older sister with admiration. "The Lord must not see any rough spots on you that need polishing. Or, you are just fortunate. Satan has not touched you one bit, as far as I recall."

Esther shook her head. "I took the death of our mother more seriously than any one of you, I think including *Papang,* at that, remember?"

After some silence, Lydia said, "I don't see how anyone could forget a spouse so soon, or at all. I, for one, would never think of remarrying… if…."

Two heads turned simultaneously toward the door and saw Sr. Esther smiling. "Neither would I," she said.

"You have good ears!" the siblings said in unison as if rehearsed.

"I am glad that you—my son and my daughter-in-law—had taken an older mother Esther to live with you. That's one disadvantage of having an only child," she added. "No where else to go."

The two sisters exchanged furtive glances. "I think *Mang* Es is so lucky to have you with them, a built-in baby sitter," Lydia. said softly.

"Ma comes in handy," Esther chimed in. "We enjoy her presence. Ma is very good with the children, and she helps in almost every house chore." Turning to her mother-in-law, she said, "I thank you for that, Ma."

"Thank you," the older Esther said, eyes glistening. "I try to do my best. As I grow older, I trust I will not become a burden to anyone."

At that Esther rang the dinner bell, and called out as the children started coming in, "Be sure to wash your hands thoroughly."

The children took their places. Esther looked at the clock. "Their father should be here any minute now, but he always tells me not to wait for him. Whose turn is it to ask for the blessing-before-meal this time?"

Edred, the oldest child, raised his hand, and everyone bowed their heads as he offered grace.

***

"As a renewed person, Mrs. Roda," Dr. Anderson said, "I expect you to be able to handle things now. I believe it constructive to review your recent past. You will realize there had been many changes within a short period in your life recently. You scored stress points beyond one normally could handle." Standing up, he extended his hand. "Congratulations for overcoming the setbacks. I believe you'll no longer need my professional help, but my door is always open for you," he added. "I'll be seeing you as a professional nurse helping care for some of my patients in the hospital. You'll find this experience as others say, 'having been in their shoes' invaluable. You'll be a more sympathetic professional care giver."

Lydia thanked Dr. Anderson for his encouragement and for his professional care. As she walked away from his office, she thought, *That's another chapter in my life. How fragile life is. As Dr. Anderson said, it helped me become a more perceptive health care giver.* She wondered of the change in climate. From a humid-sultry climate to wintry weather. *Did I suffer from what others call the winter blues?* Her depression began to lift in December. In spite of the frigid clime, she fell in love with the pure white fluffy snow flakes daintily falling, at times swirling in magical ways.

Even Andy, still very much missing his dad, showed signs of adjusting to their new life. Fitting himself to the school routine, making new friends, he no longer mentioned missing his cousins and friends back home.

As Dr. Anderson stated, Lydia now saw patients in a new light. *I had to experience their feelings to understand them better,* she admitted. More and more she proved this to be a reality. Work became a source of enjoyment—financially rewarding and emotionally fulfilling. *I can regard myself as a foreign missionary,* the thought gave her emotional fulfillment.

Until one day, when no sooner than his dad had left for Berrien Springs, Andy had turned quiet and rather morose.

"Andy, are you ready to hear a story?" she asked, tousling his hair. He kept a lugubrious mood, unresponsive to her offer, so unlike him. "Will he be away all the time" he asked. "I want my daddy," he sobbed.

"I miss him, too, Son." Lydia's mind flashed back to the time soon following Ralph's death. Alarms rang, realizing her feelings now reminded her of those days. *Lord, I cannot give in to this feeling after healing me of depression.* She would try the cathartic effects of reviewing the past.

Her mind went to the times when she had asked her husband not to raise his voice when replying to questions she may ask him. For she felt demeaned and felt he'd lost respect for her when he talked to her louder than he normally did. She recalled the time when she quietly slipped out and sat down on the protuberant root of the mango tree. Soon Andy's arms were around her neck. "Daddy said to forgive him. He loves you. I love you, too, Mommy. Daddy asked me to kiss you." And she felt the wet kiss on her cheek, and the pull of a tiny hand leading her home. She recalled her husband chuckling, "Is that all?" to her, "You shouted at me!" in reply to his "Darling, what upset you?"

The young Tabucol family with unidentified relatives. Front l-r: Felicito, Esther on mother Adelaida's lap.

The young C. C. Vizcarra, Jr. family, l-r: Luella (front) Edred, Richard on Mom Esther's lap, Dad Jun holding Susan, and Rodney, standing.

Chapter XI

AND NOT OF EVIL

1964 Andrews University GRADUATION.

Alfonso successfully completed the Bachelor of Divinity requirements in the first semester. Instead of staying for the commencement, he opted to return to PUC by way of Europe. Being chair of the Department of Religion, he felt it worthwhile to get a first hand experience walking in the land where Jesus lived when He was on earth.

Lydia supported his decision, for she, too, believed in the educational value of travel.

Only after much prayer and carefully weighing matters regarding their future did they decide for Lydia and Andy to remain in Hinsdale. As a first grader, Andy had survived attending three different schools and they felt it was their duty to give their son the benefits of continuity now that it was possible to do so.

This arrangement would also extend Lydia's work experience at the surgical unit while earning at the same time. "And," she said, "it would also boost my sense of independence and develop my self-reliance." She was happy to stay and work to fund his scholastic trip. And she'd try to save as much of her earnings as possible.

This time, Andy willingly acquiesced to the distance separation.

***

RESPONSE TO SPRING

What makes me sing
  makes me tingle
  makes me feel like dancing

When Lady Spring jiggles
  bright colors
  on crocuses and jonquils

On forsythia bowers
  lilacs and redbuds—
  armloads of purple flowers

On tulips and rosebuds
  promise of hues
  from awakening buds

Fragrance to diffuse
  and charming faces
  who could refuse?

Ah, Spring that blazes
  exquisite loveliness
  that makes me sing praises!

cj ***

MARCH

March is traipsing
Now and then pirouetting
*   with wintry beaus*
*   on March sequinned toes.*

Maybe some snow
Fickle March will know
*   of fog, or mist,*
*   a downpour harvest*

Of nimbus clouds
To wash off the shroud
*   that hides the fun,*
*   the warmth of the sun.*

Spring now whispers
To buds: shake off winter's
*   hypnotic spell*
*   wake up every cell.*

Lord, open my eyes
Let me see the prize
*   of a changed life*
*   devoid of strife*
And filled with Thy love.

cnj ***

The American Way—the theme of the Hospital Day float—that featured Lydia, representing the Philippines, and a twelve-year-old European girl, representing her country, won first prize. The float depicted how America is helping other countries.

Perhaps the proudest spectators were a father and son. Andy watched his mother alight from the float. As fast as his feet could go, he ran to meet his mother. "Mommy!" he cried, "you could win Miss Universe!" Alfonso was proud of his wife and the role she played, and prouder yet of his son's enthusiasm over the activities of the day. Lydia hoped the occasion opened her son's eyes to a future career in medicine.

Some of Lydia's friends remarked about her resemblance with Jackie Kennedy. "A Filipino version of Jackie Kennedy," they said.

Alfonso had his own opinion of the physical-feature-semblance of his only love with the first lady. He just had to tell them, "To me, Lydia is more beautiful."

It had been a long yet exciting day for everyone. Now Alfonso had his packing to do, and while so doing, he and Lydia began bantering back and forth, making things light, verbally teasing each other. He reminded her of the day—on one of his first visits—when she came out in her student nurse's blue uniform, underarm sleeves wet. And then, he said, "Not long after I die, many will be at your door wooing the beautiful, rich widow."

"Oh, that's what you think," she retorted. "Soon after my burial, you would have someone else to take my place. As for me, my wedding vow goes beyond the grave. No one could ever take your place in my life. I would not feel like a Christian with another man. I'd feel it a sin…." She was serious about all this, never mind that they were in a jocular mood.

***

SHOULD YOU GO FIRST

Should you go first and I remain
  To walk the road alone,
I'll live in memory's garden, Dear,
  With happy days we have known.
In Spring, I'll wait for the roses red,
  When fades the lilac blue;
In early fall, when brown leaves call,
  I'll catch a glimpse of you.

Should you go first and I remain
  To finish the scroll,
No lengthening shadows shall creep in,
  To make this life seem droll.
We've known so much happiness,
  We've known our cup of joy,
And memory is one gift of God
  That death cannot destroy.

Should you go first and I remain,
  For battles to be fought,
Each thing you have touched along the way
  Will be a hallowed spot.
I'll hear your voice, I'll see your smile,
  Though blindly I may grope,
The memory of your helping hand
  Will buoy me on with hope.

Should you go first and I remain,
  One thing I'd have you do:
Walk slowly down the path of death,
  For one day I'll follow you.
I'll want to know each step you take,
  That I may walk the same.
For some day down that lonely road,
  You'll hear me call your name.

—author unknown

from <u>The Ladies Home Journal</u>

***

Mother and son once again were by themselves, now without the weekend-with-Daddy to look forward to. By now, however, the temporary distance separation had become a way of life for them. Pre-occupied with their own lives, nonetheless, they looked forward to receiving his letters. And they were never disappointed. As they read Dad's letters, they enjoyed vicariously walking where Jesus walked. And now, they looked forward to viewing the pictures he took in the land where Jesus trod.

Upon arriving in PUC, Alfonso continued to write them, now about his life in PUC and how he was missing them. For busy people, days fly fast. Before long Lydia booked for two to leave for the Philippines on the first week of December. Andy's school friends gave him a farewell party as well as to wish him von voyage. Everyone at the elementary school signed a large beautiful card to remember them by.

Mother and son proved to be good sailors. In the long days at sea, they met new friends. Sailing was a relaxing time and a diversion. For Lydia, no reporting for duty. For Andy, no school. When the ship docked at ports, mother and son took the time to stretch their legs on tierra firma as time permitted. With their new friends, they visited places. Having bought *pasalubong* (gifts) in Chicago, Lydia spent her time sightseeing.

Their Christmas at sea would last them a lifetime, so would the twenty-one days they lived at sea. Alfonso was first to come up the dock to welcome his loved ones home.

1965. The months from January through April had been a period of adjustment to being back home for Lydia and Andy. Being the milder months of the year, it gave them time to gradually re-acclimate to the hot and humid weather in the islands.

"I really didn't care for the cold winter months," said Lydia, "but I miss watching the fluffy snow, the cascading and floating flakes of white."

And she rejoiced over the many varieties of fresh fruits and freshly picked vegetables all year round. She would also grow a garden to enjoy.

As for Andy, the weather mattered little. He was happy for again there were different kinds of bananas to eat that 'don't-taste-like-paste.'

May 9, 1965. In an all College ceremony, outgoing President Arthur Corder formally handed the symbolic Key of Presidential Responsibility to Professor Alfonso P. Roda. It was the fulfillment of a dream.

Dr. Reuben G. Manalaysay had been the first Filipino PUC president. Both are sons of two of the first three nationals ordained to the Seventh-day Adventist ministry: Emilio Manalaysay and Leon Z. Roda.

The months following were exceptionally busy and challenging days for the Alfonso P. Roda family. Each day, they packed their prayers full of petitions for divine guidance from the Source of all wisdom and strength.

Lydia handled tasks to relieve her husband from responsibilities that she felt belonged to her. Yet she remained open to share matters with her husband that would reflect on him. She made sure that their table provided for their individual physical nourishment for the day. From experience, she learned to be ready to welcome company for meals without notice. Her husband had a habit of bringing home company for Sabbath dinner. The family's spiritual nurturing were Alfonso's—he led in the morning and evening family worship and other church related activities.

Planting and tending a garden had always been one of Lydia's favorite pastimes, and she wished to share with her husband the joys of gardening. But lucky would be any day when he'd say a word or two of admiration over the colorful flowers and lush vegetables in her garden.

One of her student helpers accepted the assignment to prepare the garden, but had not found the time. Eager to start her garden, she took the shovel and started digging. When she saw her husband walking home, she also saw a chance to get his interest in gardening, his welfare in mind. She thought, *The exercise would be a good form of relaxation after a whole day of administrative duties.* As he greeted her, she asked him to help. It elated her when he said he would put on his work clothes. *Now, he'd get the third dimension of education—the physical.* Lydia inwardly reveled.

Back and properly attired, he took the shovel from her and began digging in earnest. Lydia got down to pull the weeds. She was mentally congratulating herself for her success, thinking, *another chance to be with each other and enjoy each others company,* when a few minutes later, he stopped digging. "Sweetheart," he said, "I do not really enjoy doing this." Lydia turned to face him hoping he will read her disappointment. She saw his face flushed, beads of perspiration trickling down. Their eyes met, "I only do this because I love you," he said.

Christmastime '65. Alfonso's theological horizon grounded him on the pagan origin of Christmas. Moreover, its commercialization added to it a worldly trim, yet he—nor the Adventist community—forbade not its celebration. The College has never prohibited re-enacting the tradition. Celebrating Christ's birthday on the 25th of December, paganese or worldly though it be, was opportunity to reflect on God's love for the human race.

The College Voice editor Eliseo Bautista walked to the elementary school to ask the children what they wanted for Christmas. Earlier, Eliseo and the teacher talked about this project. He instructed them to write their wish on a card. With the help of their teacher, each child made a Christmas card with their 'want' written on the card. It made the children proud to see their own work. They flaunted their hand-made Christmas cards, and eagerly waited to get the approval of their teacher and the visiting young man. Their work having been pronounced 'good', their teacher showed them how to tie a ribbon on the card with which to hang it on their Christmas tree at home, or wherever the family placed their cards or gifts.

That afternoon Andy walked home clutching his own Christmas card. He went straight to their Christmas tree, hang it but made no mention of it, yet he could hardly wait for his parents to see what he had written in it.

December 25. Finally their family morning worship ended, and they gathered around their Christmas tree. Andy watched as his mother lifted his Christmas card, watched her open it, watched her as she read it. **All I want for Christmas is a Baby Brother.**

Lydia's eyes met her son's and he dashed in her arms. His Dad, too, read the Christmas card. He wrapped them in his arms, a grin on his face. Lydia's heart melted. How could any mother deny her son's Christmas wish? *Only a very cold-hearted mother would,* she thought. In her mind she considered her varied roles in a more serious way. She enjoyed each of them: a wife, a mother, and most recently, as one of the nurses at the College Clinic, plus her part-time teaching. And now, a role closely linked to her most important first two. *I foresee no problems. I'm only 33,* she affirmed herself. So she began looking forward to be 'expecting.'

Months rolled along. Another month, then another, and still another. The thought came that perhaps bearing another child was not the Lord's will—the condition she gave and specified in her promise to Andy. Yet she felt disappointed, although initially she felt it unfair to bring another child to grow up in a cruel world.

And to make it worse, her husband began teasing her. "Mommy, you're probably too old to expect." When another cycle came around, he'd shake his head while muttering, "Mommy, *wala na, bogok na"* (it's hopeless, impaired, functionless).

The more he teased, however, the more Lydia set her mind to prove him wrong. *I've just turned 34,* she consoled herself. She had seen mothers much older than 35 deliver full term healthy babies at the San. Then a thought struck to divert her mind. *I'll pursue a master's degree.* Her husband gave her his blessings.

More months of disappointment. Lydia determined to steel herself against her husband's incessant taunting. She refrained from blurting out what was on her mind, *Could someone about nine years older be the guilty party?* She kept her emotions in check when she verbalized her thoughts.

"Darling, are you still grieving over Ralph?"

All of a sudden, Alfonso felt the deep hurt she harbored. He took her in his arms. "Sweetheart, please forgive me. I didn't realize my efforts to cheer you up, making light a weighty matter to you was thoughtless of me." The tender emotions that warmed his every fiber during their courtship days and after their wedding, came back to life. "My love, I value your perceptiveness. Yes, I could be on denial, still sorrowing. I could be at fault, come to think of it...." his grin was of embarrassment. "I'm going on forty-five." Shaking his head, "I can't believe it! Honest, I don't feel that old," he said, kissing her. "My young beautiful queen. My love, my Miss Universe with more staying power that surprises and pleases me. I praise the Lord for blessing me with a wife and a friend nonpareil in you."

"Thank you for letting me know," she said, wiping her tears. "Were it not for your strength and abiding faith in God, I wouldn't have been able to bear losing Ralph. I do miss him." Then in a brighter tone, said, "Andy stated his choice of gender in his Christmas wish."

"Neither did he say a brother to replace Ralph," he muttered.

Now Lydia broke in a smile. "It's irony, but with *Mang* Cheding's six girls to one boy, do you think there's a chance our next child would be a boy? I agree with you, it would be wonderful to have a girl."

"Stop teasing," Alfonso said, again taking her in his arms. "As you well know, I own the responsibility in more ways than one, Sweetheart. For didn't science find that man's Y chromosome is the determining factor for the gender of a new life?" He paused as if to gather his thoughts. "Along this line of thinking, I recall a verse in Isaiah 49 appealing. It's about God knowing one before his formation in the womb. You were wise in laying the responsibility in God's hands. Yet, even endowing man with the power to procreate, He absolved us not from cooperating with Him. I repeat—you bloomed in the months you carried Andy and Ralph under your heart. I'll say it again, your expecting state enhanced your beauty many times over."

"Thank you," she said. "Man carries the Y chromosome, I know that, but in consenting to carry another baby according to His will, beauty had not been in my agenda. Honest, I have never given that a thought."

***

A PRECIOUS TRUST

by Ellen G. White

Children are committed to their parents as a precious trust, which God will one day require at their hands. We should give to their training more time, more care, and more prayer....

The sympathy, forbearance, and love required in dealing with children would be a blessing in any household. They would soften and subdue set traits of character in those who need to be more cheerful and restful. The presence of a child in a home sweetens and refines. A child brought up in the fear of the Lord is a blessing.

Care and affection for dependent children removes the roughness from our natures, makes us tender and sympathetic, and has an influence to develop the nobler elements of our character.

Remember that your sons and daughters are younger members of God's family. He has committed them in your care to train and educate for heaven.

The Adventist Home, pages 160–161.

***

Chapter XII

<u>TO GIVE YOU</u> HAPPY CHALLENGING DAYS

Sing unto Him, sing psalms unto Him, talk ye of all His wondrous works. (I Chronicles 16:9).

September 25, 1967. "Andy," his dad called soon after their family morning worship. "Your mommy and I are going to the hospital and will come home with your baby brother." Andy gave a whoop, and ran to his room. His parents exchanged knowing glances. They must be on their way.

Recently, they had noticed their son evolving a quiet personality. He had been keeping his emotions to himself. "Hmmm, I suspect he went to his room to thank the Lord for giving him his Christmas wish for a baby brother," Alfonso said. "And perhaps to hide his excitement," Lydia added.

At 10:00 a.m., Dr. Elton Morel delivered a bouncing baby boy, and presented the long awaited one to his parents. Alfonso and Lydia had a name ready for their prayed-for baby, Reginald Todd. Reggie, for short.

Andy could hardly wait to see his belated Christmas gift. As soon as the baby came home, he had to hold him. "I love you, my little brother," he crooned. His parents shared the unquenchable joy.

One day, Lydia greeted her baby with, "Hi, Bong!" The nickname caught. *Of all my babies, Bong has the biggest cry, he's my crybaby,"* Lydia thought. *If what they say of a big cry is true, Bong will be a great singer. Good for his daddy.*

Growing fast, Bong was soon preferring his supplemental feeding. "Now, I ought to get on to my dream," Lydia told her husband, "before Bong gets to be a toddler." His reply, "Sweetheart, you have my blessings."

May, 1968. UP (University of the Philippines) processed Lydia's application, and she started working toward her Master's Degree in Nursing Education. Circumstances in her life a few years earlier determined Psychiatric Nursing as a major. The more or less 15-minute daily drive each way to and from UP were blissful minutes for her—she had her husband for chauffeur. On their drive they could talk on matters mundane.

Between 4 and 5 p.m. every school day, Alfonso arrived at the UP campus to fetch his special passenger. Both of them looked forward to the 15-minute precious sharing time, talking about how they missed each other, and going over the happenings while apart that day.

"It feels so much lighter lugging my books instead of a baby," ebullient Lydia said one day. Seeing the grin on her husband, she added, "My mind absorbs my class assignments, thanks to my past experience." She was reflecting on the long dreary days when Satan inflicted depression on her, now proving of value for self-understanding and insight on others lives.

One afternoon Lydia noticed something in her husband's demeanor, something amiss, which she could not pinpoint. *So unusual of him,* she thought, *to let me do most of the talking.* Casting him a side-glance, she confronted him with, "Darling, are you keeping something from me?"

He drew a letter from his shirt pocket and handed it to her.

"Far Eastern Division," she said, and began reading. Noting she had finished reading the letter, he mumbled, "My concern is over disrupting your studies. I hope we can go as a family for another upgrading for me."

"It should not," was her cheery reply. "I should finish my classes in a few weeks and I could request postponement of my comprehensive."

"That sounds promising," he said, a sense of relief in his tone. The remaining minutes' drive home flew as they discussed tentative plans. "I ought to be able to work while you and Andy go to school," she said with a laugh. "History repeating itself, this time minus reasons for depression."

"Those were the Dark Ages for me," he said. "I pray, no repeat of it."

"Those Dark Ages built me up, made me stronger," she said, "made it easier for me to understand my textbooks," she chuckled. "And someone at FED thought to give you a fair amount of stipend this time, but we need cookware, dishes, and other things. There are four of us, now. So I need to work to get these and other incidentals to make life more pleasant for us."

Alfonso drew a deep breath. "Bong is still a baby. He needs his mommy. I really hate to see you go to work. Andy and Ralph had you...."

Lydia practically interrupted him. "I'll have to make an appointment to see my adviser as soon as possible," she said. "I hope to finish all the requirements in all my subjects before your scheduled date of departure."

Finally, Lydia met with her adviser, and found out, to her dismay, that there was no way she could complete everything on time to leave for L.A. together as a family Yet she knew she had strength enough to handle the matter. *It is another chance to toughen me up,* she consoled herself.

After much prayer, they decided Andy would go with his dad. They would stay with Alfonso's niece, Tita and her husband Romie Torres, until they could find a place of their own after Lydia and Bong arrived.

Much earlier, the College Board voted for Dr. Ottis C. Edwards, PUC Dean of Faculties, to be interim president while he completes his upgrading.

Once again, Lydia would rely on her relatives. For a baby sitter, she thought of Sr. Esther, her older sister's mother-in-law. Only a few years back, Lydia experienced the bigheartedness of Sr. Esther during what she considered the darkest period of her life. Since she didn't have to work outside of her home, Esther had in mind to suggest this arrangement, anyway.

And while at the dinner table and on Esther's mention of Lydia's predicament, Sr. Esther actually offered to be amah for Lydia and Alfonso. "They are my children, too," she bragged, adding, "I need to feel needed." And in a jocular mood muttered, "I think we share a mutual feeling sometimes that two Esthers under the same roof makes a crowd."

Upon learning of this arrangement, Alfonso's mother said to Lydia, "When I get to join you in the States, I'd like to be a relief for Sr. Esther."

Finally, after a few months that seemed forever to Lydia, she and her baby boarded a plane for California. And before long, Bong began crying. The flight attendants did everything they could think of to help Lydia comfort her baby to no avail. Lydia knew Bong wanted his security blanket, which unfortunately, she had forgotten to take along. It made the flight seem oh so unending. At long last, the plane reached its destination. Distraught and worn out Lydia fell into her husband's arms. Immediately, Alfonso took charge of everything, including his crying baby.

Tita and her hubby Romie opened their hearts and home to Lydia as they had for their uncle Alfonso. Their home in Los Angeles was but a few minutes commute to UCLA, where Alfonso had chosen to earn his doctoral in Administration in Higher Education. Much, much earlier, FED directed Alfonso to take this field of learning in keeping with his duties as PUC president. Santa Fe Memorial Hospital hired Lydia as a staff nurse.

When Tita and Romie moved to Glendale, Lydia and Alfonso, too, found a three bedroom house with a spacious living room for rent. It was but a stone's throw behind Glendale Sanitarium & Hospital, where Lydia took the 3–11 work shift. She walked home for supper to be with her family and Sr. Esther, to enjoy the meal together.

This time, unlike the Berrien Springs days, Lydia's heart sang praises to God for His loving kindness. For her devoted husband, their boys, and for Sr. Esther, who dotted on them. When Alfonso's mother Maria arrived for a long visit with her grandchildren, Tita and Romie, she began coming to Alfonso and Lydia's home, relieving Sr. Esther of her amah duties, and to enjoy Alfonso and Lydia and their boys.

Lydia luxuriated on having two loving grandmas to her boys, who, she was sure Bong especially enjoyed as much as she appreciated them. They, too, were great cooks. One day, Bong snuggled against his mother. "Mommy," he said, "let my grandmas go to work, you stay home with me."

Andy, now a veteran in the temporariness of life, had adjusted well to his transfer from San Gabriel Academy to Glendale Academy. It was at Glendale Academy from where he later graduated with honors.

Lydia felt thoroughly equipped and happy working at Glendale San's Mental Department. Occasionally, in a teasing mood, she'd say she was proud of her two scholars working hard at their studies while she was enjoying her work, and would jokingly add, "to help keep you in school."

The two sisters—Esther and Lydia—kept in touch by phone-talk which frequently ended on their agreeing upon a convenient date for the Roda family to drive to Loma Linda to the Vizcarra's capacious home.

During one of their visits to Loma Linda, Esther said that when all her children were in school, she would join the work-force outside the home. And on second thought, since she has not worked outside the home through all the years while raising her five children, she thought it best to take her master's degree to get the 'warm-up' to qualify her for a good job. She had set her mind to major in Public Health. "Jun supports my decision," she said. "Edred had hinted on his desire to follow in his dad's footsteps in Medicine. To get our five children through school, we must be a two-income family."

"*Hoy*," said Lydia, "That would make all of you scholars, but Jun."

***

Lydia holds 3 month-old prayed-for baby Reginald (Bong).

Andy holds 3 month-old brother Bong, his Christmas-wish come-true.

1968. Andy was president of his elementary graduation class. Here he is flanked by his parents and Bong. Andy says, "Dad was always proud of my accomplishments. In leadership ability, I am only as good as his little toe."

1972 UCLA graduate Alfonso P. Roda, EdD (Administration in Higher Education)

Lydia's UP graduation, M.Sc. Nursing Education. 1974

A moment of pride in the family: APR's 1972 UCLA Ed.D. graduation. L-r: Esther Vizcarra, Sr. (Sr. Esther), Maria P. Roda, Lydia, Alfonso, Andy. In front is Reginald (Bong).

September, 1972, Homecoming. The whole PUC faculty/staff and students met their returning college president, Dr. Alfonso P. Roda, and his family with bright waving "Welcome Home" streamers at the College east gate. It was a never-to-be-forgotten gesture to the APR family, a memory they will long cherish. PUC family missed them and were celebrating their homecoming.

Interim President Dr. Ottis C. Edwards had updated Roda, in his absence, of the most important events at PUC. Changes worthy of mention include: FED began subsiding the PUC Graduate School in 1971 ($50,000 a year). The College Board's decision to purchase a property in Silang, Cavite, to be the future home of PUC, and the plan to place the Baesa property in the market. It was understood that the transfer of PUC to Silang property, and its building, would be the responsibility of the returning president.

The Sale of the Baesa PUC Property and EGMP (Eternal Gardens Memorial Park). We owe Dr. Don Van Ornam, then PUC Financial Adviser, the following facts. In his own words:

PUC received many offers for the Baesa PUC property. Some were preposterous, others interesting but high risk or not doable, still others wanted our title so they could go to the bank and get a loan to develop the property. We were confronted with the problem of needing sufficient money to move off the campus before we could relinquish the property. We could not build without money—most investors would not give money without us vacating the property. The only plan that made sense was to develop the new campus in stages whereby a portion of the PUC property would be relinquished for development while retaining the other portion for ongoing classes. This would generate funds initially that would enable PUC to begin construction and then the rest of the campus would move over a period of time. This plan allowed both parties to meet their needs. The proposal was developed by the Valencias, well-known realtors in Manila. It allowed for PUC to retain title on all campus portions of the property not turned over for development. Thus, PUC was assured of security of title for the area retained for teaching purposes, in case the project did not prosper initially.

At that time, with the peso still relatively strong against the dollar, we projected that we could purchase the land and build sufficient of the new campus—if built immediately—to move the existing student body for some twelve million pesos.(P12,000,000). We also recognized that inflation could impact us adversely, if the development of the Baesa PUC campus took too long. So we proposed a cash purchase of 12 million pesos and we should get off within a stipulated time, or we received 40% of gross sales (after the perpetual care portion was deducted from sales) with a guaranteed series of payments in the first several years to give us money to begin building of the Silang site. The agreed amount of the payments came from a blend of how many lots could likely be sold within the first three years while providing us sufficient funds to build so that we could vacate the Baesa property in a timely manner. The rationale for the 40% was that as sales prices increased with inflation/value of lots, our share would also increase to offset inflation. Sale of lot projections were for seven-year sell out at optimum, or ten years maximum. (These figures may be off slightly but the general picture is correct.)

To achieve the concepts embodied above of a guaranteed minimum sales price and a safeguard against inflation, our attorneys developed two linked contracts that allowed for a sale of 12 million pesos and the 40% share of gross sales. This gave us a guaranteed minimum amount of revenue with the assurance of a larger amount when all lots were sold. In the meantime, we had title to the portion of the campus we retained for our use. NPUM corporation executed a deed of sale only for the portion of unused land initially developed. The agreement also called for additional land to be deeded over as we vacated the campus and they sold the existing lots. It was only a joint venture in that we had the land and shared in a percentage of the revenues generated.

Because we were reasonably sure that an agreement to develop PUC property was imminent, we paid a small earnest money to hold the Silang property while we negotiated the sale of the Baesa PUC property. We did not want to risk losing the Silang site and have at that point to begin again looking for a new site. While negotiations were proceeding with the Valencias, our option time to purchase the land was near to running out. At a Board meeting in Manila, attended by the Division officers, we requested an advanced to make the first land payment, which would be repaid from the EGMP payments. Initially, they declined but then agreed (this is a story in itself). This allowed us to sign contracts to purchase the Silang site.

Problems of collection arose after a shake up in EGMP leadership, about three years into the project. EGMP replaced Valencia as president of the corporation, and that is when things began to change. As I remember, we had received the guaranteed payments by that time and were receiving our 40% share of gross revenues. At that time, there were still many lots to be developed and sold—maybe 50% of them. EGMP was just getting well into the marketing phase. Stalling tactics began. The contracts were challenged, but failed because the contracts were indeed binding. I think the challenge was their obligation was satisfied under the sale contract, therefore the 40% contract was not valid. Then things began to happen. Our title to the land—which we had for fifty years—was challenged. The former owner declared that he was still the rightful owner and therefore entitled to the money we were receiving. Certain records pertaining to PUC ownership could not be found in the city hall. Our attorney was able to offset this challenge eventually, but in the meantime payments were withheld until the 'rightful owner' could be determined. When that was settled in our favor, they came up with another reason not to pay. We appealed to the courts, which became a challenge in itself. It did drag on in the courts for a long time but not because our claim was invalid. In the end, the Supreme Court upheld our claim, including a sizable amount of interest for all the years in between, and ruled that EGMP must pay the full amount. EGMP claimed the money had been used and was no longer available. Nor would they allow the court to review their records.

A Larger Perspective. In reflection, perhaps the Lord used this project with EGMP to get us moved from Baesa but then He provided from other sources to complete the building of the campus. If we knew from the beginning what we learned later, we might still be in Baesa because the Division would likely not have given approval to move. Thus, we are continually reminded that this move was His blessing, not our wisdom. If PUC had received all the money due from EGMP, it would have been easy to think, 'We did it, and look at all the money we got.'

We have a lovely campus but none of us can take the glory. When we reflect on how the Lord provided just at the right time from a variety of sources over and over again, we can only praise Him. PUC is a faith campus, a monument to God's great benevolence.

In closing, let me make one more comment. I know of no one, overseas or national, who personally benefitted from any of the transactions in connection with the sale of the Baesa PUC property and the development of the new campus. I do know of so many who tirelessly and unselfishly gave of themselves to see the project to fruition, who moved forward as God opened the way. This is the story that should be shared.

At some point, we need to move on and watch the Lord continue to pour out His blessings in unexpected ways. This is His work and He will see it through. If we choose to continue to focus on a past that cannot be changed, we will waste much energy unnecessarily. If we use those same energies to move forward as His Providence opens the way, we will continue to see and experience new evidences of His leading.

We have nothing to fear for the future, except as we shall forget the way the Lord has led us, and His teaching in our past history.

Ellen G. White, <u>Life Sketches</u>, p. 196.

***

Chapter XIII

A FUTURE AND A HOPE

Sample letters. SWK, in large letters on the flap of each envelope.

Batu Fernygu 11-17-75 (Note: Lydia was in Glendale, CA.)

Dearest Sweetheart,
Today will be the last day of the session. There is a fever of restlessness among the delegates to be on their way home ....

We had a very good study this morning from Elder James Zackary of MVC. I can see why MVC has been so successful in its evangelism thrust... I can see in Zachary a really dedicated person who is close to God.

Yesterday, after the morning devotion by Ray James, the new MV Director, a recognition program was given in honor of Pastor M. M. Claveria and Elder & Mrs. Kong, the secretary of S.A. Mission (he's the father of Arthur Kong). Words of appreciation was given by Elder Bruce Turner, a FED, for the Kongs, and Pastor Diaz on behalf of Pastor Claveria. It was the same words of appreciation that is usually given to returning workers, but what a distinct honor Pastor Claveria had as a retiree.

Yesterday the business of the season was finally completed and the budget voted on and all the resolutions of thanks and gratitude, etc. and we adjourned. In the afternoon, we went out to the town and looked at some stores. I had not intended to buy, but when the others were buying and the prices were reasonable—even cheaper than in Manila—I succumbed to the temptation and, of course, I wanted to buy you something nice so when you come back I have some little token to give to you. Batik cloth is much nicer here than in Indonesia. The cloth they use is much finer. Maybe when you come we can have some matching clothes—your dress and my shirt. I also bought Bong a watch. I hope he'll like it. I also got him a suit. I hope it fits him. I got Andy some colored T-shirts—the printed over—those which are so much in style. I also got a few for myself.

In the evening, the chaplain of the hospital invited us to eat in a Buddhist restaurant, and then we were taken to the revolving restaurant on the 14th floor of a hotel to see the whole city. What a sight. Penang is not too large a city, but nice and clean and the people—Chinese and Indians, a few Malays—are all quite friendly.

I have to go now and will be writing you next from Manila after arriving from Bangkok. In the meantime, may the good Lord bless and keep you, my Sweet. Love and kisses to you....

(signed) *Pons*

February 8, 1976 (Note: Lydia still in Glendale)

Dearest Sweetheart Mine,

It's the time of the year there when sweethearts express words of love and devotion and appreciation to their sweethearts. And even though I've been saying it all along and every time these many, many years, now is as special, emphasis on our being so far from each other. Darling, I love you more than ever before and miss you so much. You're the sweetest girl in all the world to me....

"I never knew that life could hold A happiness as true As the happiness I find, Sweetheart, In sharing life with you ... So I chose this Valentine as the one way to let you see That the home we share and the love we share Mean everything to me."

The weather has been ideally cool the last few weeks—the mornings have always been in the low 60s and for me here, that's cold. As the song goes, "When day is done, I think of all the joys we knew, the yearning returning is always in my heart won't go. Love, I know love without you, life has lost its dreams.... And though I miss your tender kisses the whole day through, I miss you most of all when day is done." (Parang naring na ng aking kumanta sa iyo. (Make believe it's me who sang it to you.)

.... I had just written you ... telling you to please write, and early Monday morning, I received the letter .... it had been taken to the post office but not delivered to the office.... I got your very thick envelope! I was thrilled. You 'pala' (after all) *had been writing all the while, for over a week, 16 pages! My, that was a real document. Thanks so much, Darling. I needed that....*

Sweetheart, please don't start thinking of extending your stay there. After my work of campaigning (S.O.S.—Save Our Silang) *we'll go home together. I do not think continual separation after June will be looked at with favor. In fact, I think now the Board is just winking their eyes because they know I'm going there soon for this S.O.S. You'll have to sacrifice your 'hanap buhay'* (livelihood).... *I'll make a campaign letter and send also to all the alumni as you suggested.*

Friday vespers I gave the sermon on Sabbath Keeping—its deeper meaning, acceptance of the salvation provided by Jesus at the cross.

Well, Darling, I'll sign off now. May your day be filled with joy and happiness and don't forget there's someone here who is deeply in love with you.

as ever, yours,
(signed) *Pons.*

***

THE SOS LETTER (reprinted from **SPOTLIGHT PUC**
1st quarter, 1976):

Dear Friends,

Costs of running schools have risen tremendously. As consumers of goods and services in an inflation-ridden society, we cannot escape its dire effects. Everyone groans under the burden of escalating costs and high prices. Salaries of all employees as mandated by Presidential decree have risen 8½ percent over last year and will do so again this year.... Taxes on schools, no longer guaranteed tax exemption status by the 1973 Constitution.... (President Marcos has given another year's grace....)

Where can we turn? Tuition and fee increases? How much higher can we go before pricing ourselves out of our market—the SDA Church membership? Many feel we have already reached this point. If we are to run a viable program of quality worthy of our name, help has to come from somewhere.... It seems to me that the only solution is YOU, our alumni and friends. You have benefitted from this school. You who have been nurtured and fed by your Alma Mater, we need your help. PUC graduates number- ing thousands have gone forth from its portals into a world of service. Hundreds have given honor and glory to God and PUC. A growing number are a affluent in this world's goods. To you I direct this pointed question. What have you done for your Alma Mater lately? At this time when we are beset by financial problems as we faced the gigantic task of transferring a campus to a new site and when we are faced with financial problems operating our present campus, we need your financial help. Any amount you give will be gratefully acknowledged, but I would like to challenge you all—loyal sons and daughters of PUC—who remember with poignant memories the years of your stay here. Give something that will make a difference. Give sacrificially by denying yourself some luxurious item.... Please give. If we ever needed your help, it is now....

....Your gift may mean the difference between our continued service to our youth and to the Church or otherwise.

Sincerely yours,
(signed) *Alfonso P. Roda* President

April, 1976, SOS (Save Our Silang) **Crusade**. Early in the month, Dr. Alfonso P. Roda (APR) arrived in Glendale, California, to join Lydia and their seven-year-old son Bong to launch the SOS Crusade.

To the alumni group that met while at the home of Dr. Celedonio & Mrs.(Adela Pumarada) Fernando, APR said, "I believe it was for a time as this that many PUC alumni are in the States."

Alumnae Mrs. Priscilla Atiga Catalon and Mrs. Adela P. Fernando volunteered to join the SOS group as solicitors. Dr. Fernando (Lydia's *Tiong Dons*) offered the use of his station wagon for APR to drive around to the many alumnae listed in their itinerary. With a list of PUC alumni and their addresses, and prayer in their hearts, APR, Bong and Lydia with the other two alumnae solicitors left Glendale on April 11 for Tuczon, Arizona.

Their first stop was in Tuczon, at the home of Mr. Solomon & Mrs. (Esperanza Aquino) Mopera, who welcomed them with open arms and treated them royally. They gave a liberal donation—to launch the SOS —with a promise to follow the crusaders with their prayers as they travel to visit the PUC alumni all over the States and Canada.

April 13–16, Texas. In Baird, they stopped at the home of Dr. & Mrs. Laurence Gayao, and in Santa Ana, at the home of Dr. Filemon & Mrs. (Lily Alvarez) Cabansag. They also looked for other PUC alumni in Keene city.

17th in Tennessee: Collegedale, from there they drove to Limestone to Dr. Felicito and Mrs. (Fely Garcia) Fernando.

18th in Kentucky, Manchester, Mr. Norval A. & Mrs. (Consuelo Roda) Jackson; in Danville, Dr. Florentino Martin; in Prospect, Dr. Ildefonso & Mrs. (Melu Jean Timple) Campomanes.

19th in Indiana. Indianapolis: Dr. Samson and Mrs. (Lorenza Salomon) Cadiente, Dr. & Mrs. (Noli Calderon) Primero, Mr. & Mrs. Calderon, and Dr. Peter & Mrs. (Esther Dalisay) Pacamalan.

Same day, to Ohio. In Dayton, Dr. Arturo & Mrs. (Tomasita Pilar) Roda, Mr. Nehemias & Mrs. (Adela Soberano) Velasco, and former MSH missionaries Dr. & Mrs. Elvin C. Hedrick.

20th, still in Ohio. In Worthington: Drs. Irineo & Linda Bautista Pantangco. In Marion, Dr. Ben Arthur & Mrs. (Esther Hernando) Sanidad, and Dr. & Mrs. Samuel Lardizabal.

21st, still in Ohio: Dr. Imelda Lanzanas Yu. From there they drove to W. Virginia to see Dr. Ephraim & Mrs. (Anita Acopio) Imperio

22nd, Maryland. Takoma: Mr. Ben & Mrs. (Teodola Ocampo) Martin, and Drs. Chakarat and Kanchana.

23rd, still in Maryland. In Laurel: Dr. Rosella Decena and her husband Israel Castro.

24th: still in Maryland. In Takoma Park: Dr. & Mrs. Gideon Mercurio, Mr. Emil and Mrs. (Presentacion Dalusong) Balay, and in Tappahannock, Virginia: Drs. Prospero and Elma Lou Roda. In Riverdale: Mr. Alvaro & Mrs. (Nellie Hilado) Roda, Jr. In Silver Springs: Dr. & Mrs. Joshua Dee, Dr. & Mrs. Joseph Hwang. In Beltsville, S.E.Washington D.C.: Dr. Elias Umali.

25th Pennsylvania. In Morrisville: Dr. & Mrs. Jaime Arcilla.

26th, New York. In Elmhurst: Thelma Fernandez and Pastor & Mrs. Primitivo Reyes. In Newburgh, Dr. & Mrs. (Perla) Tojino.

New Jersey, in Teaneck, Mr. Miguel & Mrs. (Pilar Roque) Balisnomo, Dr. Oseas & Mrs. (Miriam) Sulatan, Lydia Barberan Gellioe, Purita Argosino Baylon, Patrick & Miriam (Tupas) Stablein.

26th at midnight, the SOS group left for Canada (they slept in the car!)

27th—time for relaxation, they saw Niagara Falls (U.S. side)

28th, at Branson Hospital: Dr. & Mrs. Fiel Poblete, Dr. & Mrs. Eliseo Arevalo, Jr. In Willowdale, Toronto: Priscila Pedro, Anna Salting and her niece nee Daphne Manalaysay, Dr. Sam & Mrs. (Virgie) Primero, Rey and Rodel Sinco, nee Charity Roda and Lim. Atty Jose & Mrs. (Lydia Garcia) Desamito, and other loyal PUC alumni in North Toronto Church.

From there, they drove back to the States.

29th, Michigan. Detroit: Dr. Napoleon & Mrs. (Nita) Imperio.

30th, at South Gate: Dr. Ruth Lamadrid and husband Felix Drapiza, and Dr. David & Mrs. (Ruth Balinao) Pulido. Drove to Berrien Springs,

May 1. Berrien Springs: Dr. D. M. & Mrs. (Fidela Senson) Hechanova, Jr. Dr. Rudy & Mrs. (Annie Sarno) Quion, Dr. Marcelino & Mrs. (Virginia Cabansag) Medina.

May 2: Dr. Ernesto & Mrs. (Loida Sarno) Medina, C. Cabardo-Munar and daughter Eve.

May 3, Illinois: in Skokie: The Vigilia and the Valenzuela families. Chicago: Rey and Esther (nee Lapena) Foliente. (They took Adela Fernando to O'Hare Airport for her to return home, to Glendale, California. We owe her this itinerary list.) In Hinsdale: Dr. Pedro & Mrs. (Evelyn Ritumalta) Roda, Norma Sumicad Mondejar, Edwin and Naomi (Tagle) Cabansag, Bernardo and Judy Begmin.

May 4: Marven and Divina Tingzon, Sofronio and Dolores (nee Uzzaraga) Mitra, and Segundito and Carol (nee Bautista) Tortal.

APR noted the road becoming icy. Suddenly, the vehicle went on a skid and hit the ramp. "Lord, save us!" they cried. Right away, the angel of the Lord helped APR stabilize the car. A big dent on the back of the station wagon proved that the Lord delivered them from danger and injury.

The Lord blessed this SOS Crusade with some $30,000 plus pledges.

It was the first time, since EGMP stopped their payments, the College was able to make their timely payment for the Silang property. The AWESNA alumni pledged to raise $50,000 annually for their Alma Mater.

This, being the first and the last presidential SOS Crusade, it was the beginning of active participation of loyal PUC alumni to the support of their Alma Mater. Alumni in western United States organized into what is now AWESNA, and in the east, into EASNAC. Each association consists of sub-chapters, meeting regularly between the annual conventions the two organizations hold separately.

In the 2002 EASNAC Alumni Convention held in Arkansas, under the leadership of Dr. & Mrs. Andy Roda, Dr. Conrado Miranda IV presented the One Million Dollar Endowment Fund, instituted in 2000 when he assumed his term as EASNAC president. The project will continue for the next two years (2002–2004) with Dr. Prospero Roda as president.

The Endowment Fund will be administered from the U.S.A. by the Foundation. The principal will remain untouched: only the interest will be appropriated for projects. None of the funds will be used for infrastructure projects, such as buildings, road improvements, or other capital projects by their nature are responsibilities of the university and its sponsoring organizations, such as the Union Conference…. from The PUCian

***

GROWTH, CONSOLIDATION and RECOGNITION

*Dr. Alfonso P. Roda's quadrennium Presidential report,
excerpt-summary.

"… praise the Lord for His bountiful blessings on PUC and His continual guidance and direction in carrying out of our work.…"

Highlights of the report include the following :

*The completion of the transfer of PUC from Baesa to Silang in 1981.

*A list of PUC graduates topnotching Nutrition and Nurses Board.

*The students' many missionary outreach programs bringing souls to God.

*Continued progress of building projects, including landscaping. Tribute given to Mr. Sam Robinson for procuring needed materials.

*Dr. Howard Detwiler's pledge of a million dollars for the proposed medical school, but because of disapproval of this project, the amount was directed to build the library (still to be in honor of his third son, Dr. John Lawrence Detwiler) its inauguration to coincide with the 70th anniversary of the founding of (the mother institution Pasay Academy in 1917) PUC.

*PUC Alumni Association (AWESNA) pledged to build an Alumni Center, completion also targeted for the 1987 inauguration.

*Purchase of rice land. Mr. & Mrs. John Grillmeir of Australia, who had been sponsoring students in PUC, donated P449,000+ with which a 7.4 hectares of irrigated rice land was purchased.

*Operational gains despite escalating costs and spiraling prices… total assets grew from P18M to P39M. Net work doubled from P15M to P35M.

*On Problems: The separation of the Seminary from the College as a separate institution: "It is with the hope and prayer that these two institutions on this new campus work together in unity and love, so that there would be harmony and understanding prevailing among the administrators and staff so as both programs may be carried on in strength and unity rather than in weakness and disunity."

*On the FED annual committee's decision in November to move the Seminary off campus. "It is with a sad heart that I accept this decision as the solution adopted, especially as the commission that has been appointed to study this matter, which included Dr. George Akers and Dr. George Babcock, from the Education Department of the General Conference, had recommended a reunification of the Seminary with the College.…"

*On EGMP nonpayment to PUC. "We are hoping that a decision might be made on the writ of execution on the decision of the regional Trial Court regarding EGMP payments to PUC."

*Dr. Roda presented this report on November 2, 1985. Summarized from <u>The Spotlight PUC</u>. Dr. Alfonso P. Roda died on March 5, 1987.

(As this book goes to press: In an out of court settlement, negotiated by Ambassador Bien Tejano, who represented NPUM, EGMP paid P100,000,000 (amount given to SSD, 40% of which will go to AUP) resolving the 27-year Eternal Gardens impasse. Ban B. Alsaybar's <u>Dingball</u>, Jan. 2003

***

PUC's president for nearly 22 years, Dr. Alfonso P. Roda

Dr. Alfonso P. Roda and the first lady pose in front of the Finster Chapel.

Dr. Roda officiated in many, many weddings. One of the last weddings he performed was his own son's—Andy—to Loree Villanueva on June 15, 1986. The newlywed's most cherished advice that day was, "Andy, Loree, ...make God first in your lives." Bong served as his older brother's best man.

Alfonso and Lydia with family members pose on the steps of their home, the PUC Silang presidential home.

In their home, the APR family always had student help, students working their way through school. Here, the College president and the first lady pose with the Guarin twins—Nelson and Wilson—(standing) on their graduation flanked by their (the twins') parents.

Alfonso and Lydia (4th and 5th from left) enjoy entertaining visitors in their home. "Almost every Sabbath, we had company for lunch," Andy recalls.

The last family photo, taken 6–86.
L-r: Bong, Alfonso, Lydia, and Andy.

The APR family members pose behind Dr. Alfonso Roda's flower-strewn casket before entombment. Andy stands above his father's photo. To his left, his mother Lydia, Bong, Dr. C. E. Fernando, Cheding, Ely, and uncle Tony.

Lydia and her grandchildren her husband did not live to see.
L-r: Alfonso Leon, Andrea Lauren, and Ellysa Raquel.

ALFONSO P. RODA

SECTION 2

<u>A COMPILATION</u>

REFLECTIONS

RELEVANT QUOTES

COMMUNIQUE DECRYPTIONS

THE AIIAS/PUC CONTROVERSY

DIALOGUE—POINTS OF VIEW

DOCUMENTS

A DEVOTIONAL

REFLECTIONS on the LIFE of
Dr. ALFONSO P. RODA

I have always considered Dr. Roda as an outstanding individual and as a very personal friend. When we were both teachers at PUC—not involved in administration—we made a visit together to Legaspi and Mount Mayon region. We had a delightful time, one which I shall always treasure in my memory bank. We have always enjoyed being together. I have always regarded him very highly and know that he accomplished a great deal to make PUC/AUP an institution that has made a tremendous impact on the lives of thousands of students. I look forward to meeting him at the resurrection, and being able to share with him throughout eternity....

Dr. Ottis C. Edwards,
1969–72 Interim PUC President, letter, 3–2001.

. . .

Three of us overseas families moved to Silang in early December. There was no electricity or running water. We bathed in the river, gathered drinking water from a spring, and ate by candlelight at night. It was Christmas eve, a Sabbath evening at sunset. We had completed sundown worship at the one building which would serve as the first church, classroom, and library, and were sitting on the porch watching the deepening twilight when we heard a car approaching. This was unusual as people felt it was risky to drive out there at night. The car came up to the porch and to our surprise, Dr. & Mrs. Alfonso Roda (President and his wife) got out. They said, "We were sitting at home thinking about the blessings of family and Christmas. Then we thought of you folks out here by yourselves, so far from your families and homes, and we just wanted to come out to be with you."

Sacrificing their own comfort and quiet family evening, they chose to be with us so that we might feel 'community.' At that moment, we were no longer overseas missionaries and nationals. We were brothers and sisters sharing a common bond.

One reason I enjoyed working with Dr. Roda was that, we might not always agree on everything, but we could share disagreeable things with each other and still be friends and compadres. He was as loyal to the Church and PUC as he could be.

Dr. Donald Van Ornam,
former PUC Financial Consultant,
from The Link, part of his address
given at AWESNA Convention,
Ca., 6-19-94.

. . .

309

I have a great deal of cherished memories of my professional and personal relationship with the Roda family. As an expatriate, Dr. and Mrs. Roda treated me with profound fairness and friendship. Through them and a few others, I came to better appreciate something others ... seemed not to have grasped... that the Christian message of brotherhood and integrity transcends nationality, ethnic affiliation, language, position, hemisphere, and the like.

Dr. Hedrick Edwards,
former PUC Dean,
International Institute of Public Health,
from his email, 8–2001.
...

I first saw Ponsing in Baesa when I came to PUC in 1937. He was a fourth year academy student, I was freshman. He also worked as a student like me, he was often with Gershon Brion playing basketball. I enjoyed his singing in a quartet with Gershon, Dionisio and Catalino Bautista. He sang, "So Send I You," when Victor Cabansag and I were ordained in NLA (Northern Luzon Academy) on March 31, 1961.

When he and Lydia were in honeymoon on the campus, he sent a card of thanks to the faculty with personal words, "... we are very, very happy."

I found out Ponsing had a higher MQ (mechanical quotient) than I when we took auto mechanics under Dr. Arthur Corder. Fair enough, for he was to own a car ahead of me when he became PUC president.

In April 1965, I received a letter from him. (I had just given a sermon in PUC and somehow I felt unfulfilled.) He thanked me for my sermon and wanted me to know how someone else appreciated my sermon. "Nehemias Barnedo said he was going to stop being average in his Christian life...."

As a classroom teacher, Ponsing was not exciting, neither was he an impelling speaker, but his messages were well-prepared and packed with good things. I never expected him to become college president, but when God chose him, he really surprised me. Speaking of presidency, isn't it significant that two children of pioneers became PUC president? In this, I see God's message, "Him that honor me, I will honor." Placing Reuben G. Manalaysay and Alfonso P. Roda in the top post was not merely a human decision. God had an active hand in it.

Pastor Bangele B. Alsaybar
...

I came to PUC in Baesa with my parents for the first time in 1976. I was a little girl, an elementary pupil. Dr. Roda was the president of PUC, and we were next-door neighbors in campus. When I passed by their yard, and he happened to be there, he would always smile and wave at me. I remember when he came over and patted me on the head and said, *"How are you feeling, little girl? Do you enjoy staying at your new house? Do you like studying at PUC?"* I was thrilled—the president of the college spoke to me! In 1978 when he and his family were still at Baesa campus, he came all the way to Balibago ... to spend the Sabbath with us.

On a Friday, in December, 1986, PUC Silang: I was on my way to the main gate when Dr. Roda, in his Hi-Ace, slowed down, and asked where I was going. "To Manila," I replied. "Hop in," he said. When we reached the gate, he offered a ride to two students, whom he had not met until then. They were going to Binan .... Upon arriving in Binan, he advised the girls what jeepney to take, and as they alighted, he said, *"magingat kayo, huh"* (do be careful). The girls thanked him, went on their way, but Dr. Roda did not start the car. Wondering why, I glanced at him and saw him watching the girls, concern on his face. Only after he saw them get their ride did he start the car....

My Indonesian friends told me how Dr. Roda would always greet them when they happened to meet, even without knowing their names. Or, if riding his car, he'd slow down, smile and wave his hand for a greeting.

I remember the day when our family and all the graduate students moved to the new PUC campus. We were all tired and exhausted when we arrived at the campus. It was already dark when we moved in to our apartment, which was half-finished and without water supply. I opened the door to a knock, and saw Dr. Roda standing there, forehead full of sweat and thick dust on his T-shirt. "Do you need anything?" he asked.

Oh, that Dr. Roda could hear me now.... Nevertheless, I must say it, *"Dr. Roda, I returned to finish my studies in PUC because of your influence. You were a great leader. I shall never forget you."* * Caroline Katemba, Indonesian Graduate Student

Etched in my memory forty years ago, in my three and a-half years' stay with the Roda family—I found them to be deeply religious, naturally quiet, serene, reserved, refined and cultured in their manners. I was closer to his mother and to his two sisters than to Dr. Roda and their youngest brother, a medical doctor. My first impression of Dr. Roda was that he was aloof, for he seldom talked—a man of few words who spoke only when necessary and always spoke in low tones—but how wrong was I.

When Ralph, his second son, met a tragic accident that caused his life, Dr. Roda's calm and peaceful spirit showed in his countenance. A man of prayer, he was spiritually strong.... His consistent close relationship with his Maker was no secret. The evening and morning worship were important to the family ... By his hearty and sweet singing voice, I could tell he enjoyed every bit of their family worship... he attended all religious meetings that were held. ... I saw him to be constant in prayer and in *earnest in the study of God's word. He undertook nothing without earnest prayer.*

Many of us ... are witnesses to Dr. Roda calling the faculty and staff for seasons of prayer when the security of PUC was at stake. An example of his intelligence and vision was the moving of PUC from Baesa to Silang campus. The great undertaking proved the mettle of the man he was for indeed he was the target of destructive criticism and malicious suspicions. Yet he bore it all in quietness and deliberate calm.... His constant abiding with his Lord gave him the patience—never retaliating in kind—he brought us all to inherit Silang campus.... For his calm and serenity in solving personal, academic and institutional problems, we respect Dr. Roda as a person and as a true servant of God....

.... During one of the faculty meetings, some faculty members became careless and unkind to point accusing fingers at him, insulting and offending him.... Worth emulating was his generous forgiveness to the insults and injuries thrown at him.... He fished out his handkerchief, wiped his face, but I sensed deep down in his heart, he was bleeding and crying... he did not deserve the unkind accusations of his subordinates.

Dr. Roda ... knew how to solve problems great and small. I remember the time when their youngest son wanted to go to Manila with his parents, who said, "No." They did not want him to miss his classes. Wish thwarted, he struck the window glass of the former library with such force that broke the glass and severely wounding his hand. When Dr. Roda saw his son's bleeding hand, he did not scold him, but calmly took him to the medical clinic and then to MSH. On their way out, he never raised his voice. I recall another more recent incident. When he was in critical condition, he refused to let anyone tell Mrs. Roda of his condition—to save her from worrying. He tackled problems carefully with due consideration to other existing difficulties. As much as possible, he'd spare others if he knew there were ways to solve the problem. He tried to minimize involving others in solving problems in an effort to keep peace at any given moment. He appeared to be a very secretive man.

His readiness to stoop down when necessary proved him to be ... a real gentleman. His faith, his hope, his courage to face the most trying hours, his self control, his tact and patience... made him a great leader—a stable man in all his twenty-two years as president of PUC.... I consider Dr. Roda a great man. —a man of intelligence and vision....

Mrs. Maria F. Roman, an excerpt.

...

On March 5, 1987, Dr. Alfonso P. Roda, then PUC president, died of a broken heart. He was entombed on the 8th.

The fact that FED advised the PUC Board to pressure Dr. Roda to sign the retraction letter to the Ministry of Education, Culture, and Sports against his will, really broke his heart.

Earlier, after coming back from a yearly meeting in Singapore, Dr. Roda (Ponsing) told me that FED offered to create a position for him—that of director of education in Bangladesh. These Division officers advised him to consult with me on the matter. Before leaving Singapore, however, he wrote FED declining the offer. I think he mentioned in his letter that he was very much aware of the usual procedure of easing out a worker....

Nestor Arit showed to Ponsing a letter from Michael I. Ryan, associate director of education of Far Eastern Division, dated January 26, 1987. The message was, "Exercise the option of retirement for Dr. Roda." Ponsing's term was to end on December, 1989.

In his 6th term as PUC President, Dr. Roda was largely responsible for developing the School of Theology, which later was appropriated by FED, developing it as Far Eastern Division Theological Seminary.

I wish Dr. Roda were alive to witness the loyalty of PUC/AUP Alumni, especially those in the U.S., financially and morally helping to keep not only the Graduate School going but also to AUP in general.

Ponsing has always been a Christian gentleman and very professional in his dealings with other people and in the manner he carried out the affairs of the College. He didn't easily share his concerns with people, except his confidants. But a week before his death, while having his July physical checkup at Manila Sanitarium & Hospital, he confided his feelings to a young nurse preparing him for the tests, and to a clinical instructor, who told me recently that Ponsing, completely stressed and feeling guilty, kept repeating, "Why did I ever sign that document? I should not have signed it."

Seeing him suffering from so much stress, I told him to 'let go' and take a vacation with me where my siblings were living. He took a deep breath, shook his head slowly and replied, "You are my best counselor and that is the worst advice you had given me...."

Lydia T. Roda,
reprinted with permission,
from the International Filipino Network **(IFN)** Aug. 1994.

My father... Alfonso Roda, never gave up on me. He was always there for me. I am lucky to have had him for my father.

One incident will always stay in my memory. It happened the year before he died. I don't know what came over me that day, but I left home without telling anybody. It was senseless, of course, I wandered in the streets of Manila for two days. When I came back to the campus (Silang, PUC) I felt like the prodigal son—embarrassed and afraid that he would not welcome me back. I sat down under the mango tree thinking of what to do next. I did not know that my father was looking for me. It must have been close to midnight. When he saw me, he came up to me and said, "Hi, Son. I love you. You are always welcome home." Then he embraced me. That moment changed my life.

My understanding of the heavenly Father became clearer, His love more vivid, because my father's love illuminated my mind and heart....

Reginald (Bong) T. Roda, reprinted with permission, from **IFN** Dec. 1994, an issue dedicated to celebrate the life of Dr. Alfonso Roda on what would have been his 73rd birthday.

The first recollections I had of Dad were happy ones. It was a family outing, my first airplane ride.... I remember Daddy, Mommy, and me between them, their about three-year-old boy.... This was the start of many such outings. Dad put a priority on his family. I remember trips to Mountain View College, Baguio, Banawe, Kaliraya, and in the States, to Yosemite, Washington, D.C., Sequioa, and Florida. Many happy family outings I could look back on with fondness.

Another event that stands out vividly in my mind was when Mom and Dad had a quarrel. (I was about three years old.) I don't know what they had quarreled about, but it affected me so. It was near sunset. Mom went out to the front yard and sat on the swing trying to hide her tears. My dad knew that if he approached her alone, he would get a snob, so he sent me to her. When Mom saw me, her heart must have melted. Dad saw it, he soon joined us, and without a word, they hugged. I knew all was fine. My Dad was like that, always tactful. He knew and understood human nature. In my grown-up years, sometimes we had disagreements, and even when we both knew I was wrong, he didn't wait for me to say, "I'm sorry." He initiated the healing process, it made me respect and admire my Dad.

One of the most significant events in my life was when he baptized me. I remember that Sabbath afternoon well, at the Tagalog Church where baptisms were held then. I was one of the last in a long line of 4th graders.... As my father clasped my hand in his and raised his other hand to pray for me, I felt a bond and a closeness only a son-and-father could feel. My father was deeply concerned over my spiritual life, but he never forced religion on me nor on any one else. We had morning and evening family worship every-day. The ring of a bell called everyone for worship. and often we had lively discussions about the Sabbath School lesson. Whenever we got into a diffi-cult snag, we always turned to Dad to clarify the passage. Many times before the sun was up, I'd see light in the living room, or at times in my parents' bedroom. I knew he was reading his Bible. Often he and Mom studied the Bible together. I believe this was the source of peace and strength in his life. His relationship with God gave him strength and wisdom to face the problems of the day. I saw no inconsistencies in his life. Times came when it was his turn to give the message of the hour, and as I sat in church listening to his sermon, I was never disappointed for he practiced what he preached.

On June 15, 1986, Dad was the officiating minister at my own wedding. I shall always treasure the wedding sermon he delivered that day, for he poured out his heart to me and to my bride. "Andy and Loree," he said, "remember God is the answer to your love life. Always have Him in your hearts." These words were immortalized in my mind....

On February 26, 1987 early in the morning, I received a telephone call from my sister-in-law, and a second later, from my mother. Dad was seriously ill. I laid in bed numb, shocked. My father had never been seriously ill.... Tears started down my cheeks as I realized the gravity of it all. My wife Loree and I started reminiscing all the good times we had together with Dad. We took the earliest flight possible to Manila.

When I arrived in the ICU of Manila Sanitarium & Hospital, the father I knew—strong and vigorous—lay still and helpless. A respirator was breathing for him. In my deep anguish, I embraced my dad—his thin and emaciated body. "Daddy, I love you!" I cried, but there was no response.

There is a passage in the Bible that characterized my father. I'll now read it from 1 Corinthians 13: 'Love is very patient and kind, never jealous or envious, never boastful or proud, never haughty or selfish, or rude. Love does not demand its own way. It is not irritable or touchy. It does not hold grudges and will hardly even notice when others do wrong. It is never glad about injustice but rejoices whenever truth wins out. If you love someone, you will be loyal to him no matter what the cost. You will always believe in him, always expect the best of him, and always stand your ground in defending him."

*given by Andy (Ferdinand Roda, M.D.)
...

My reflection of Uncle Ponsing was his cheerfulness. When I was in the grades and I stayed with Lola (grandma) Uncle Ponsing (then single and living with Lola) had a cheery good morning greeting for us all every morning....

A trait I admired in him was his thoughtfulness of his mother, my Lola, (Maria Roda)and even to me. The first Bible I owned was a gift from him.

He was not a fiery speaker, in fact, I heard that some students became sleepy in his history class, but when he spoke, those who listened profited.

Corazon Arevalo Coo
for many years, a PUC Music Professor.
...

Some moments of recollection to ponder on a man of humility and what he had extended to us. We have been mutually attached to each other for years, being both neighboring institutions for the character building of youth....

The name of Dr. Alfonso P. Roda became our common words whenever we had significant occasions or important affairs. Never did he fail us—he always attended our invitations, neither did he refuse to assist us in our needs. He was ever ready and willing to share the gospel with our children and men. Let me ... enumerate the marvelous things Dr. Roda did for us.

Being the president... he made available the sports facilities of PUC accommodating our officers and men to the extent of athletic competition. The vast land area of the command (Philippine Constabulary) always requires proper landscaping in preparation for every military celebration, which Dr. Roda unhesitatingly provided us—the use of lawn mowers and tractors. Also, he arranged conduction of instructor's course, a live-in training programmed for our instructors. This initiative of his brought beneficial results to our commands' corps of instructors, student officers and men alike. He also served as technical consultant on KKK projects—the production of fruits variety in our plantation bloomed from 1964 to 1985.

Aware of difficulties due to hospitals being far away, Dr. Roda offered the PUC medical clinic for the medical needs of our dependents, and even programming herbal medicine seminars. He offered religious services every summer, sending his staff to conduct Bible study for both adult land children dependents of our command. In mid-1986, he programmed a seminar on effective communication wherein our organic and student officers and men including our civilian employees participated with immense enthusiasm. We never thought this would be his last endeavor for our benefit. Truly, his untimely death shocked us all.

Dr. Alfonso P. Roda, we will miss your greatness, humility, and magnanimous spirit. We came to know you are an achiever as a doctor, civic leader, and president of this institution. Your achievements will remain a shining monument of your deep and abiding concern for mankind. We all will never forget what you have done for us. You have accomplished your mission here on earth. You are worthy of heavenly glorification, and we unite in praying for your eternal repose.

Paulino B. Silau, PC (GSE) Assistant Supt., Philippine Constabulary (where police officers are trained) an excerpt. *given at Dr. Roda's funeral service, March 8, 1987, PUC Silang Campus.

As an administrator, Dr. Roda possessed courage and integrity of character. He stood for the right even when he was alone. He was open-minded, cool-headed, humble, and a model in life-style: simple living and a faithful regular participant in religious activities. He was sensitive to the needs of the faculty, staff, and students. Often from his personal funds, he distributed rice, clothing, soap, and other toiletries to the needy ones. He provided scholarships for some children of the faculty and staff and working students. He provided some small children whose parents were abroad, especially during Christmas, free rides to the city to enjoy Christmas sights, decorations, etc. He always had 'pasalubong' for his staff when he came from official visits to places such as Singapore or the U.S.

He was connected to prestigious organizations dealing with the improvement of the quality of education, like the Coordinating Council for Private Education, Executive Board of the ACSC, Federation of Accrediting Agencies of the Philippines, and the SDA Board of Higher Education. Through his leadership and determination, PUC was accredited for Academic Excellence by several accrediting agencies, among them ACSC, PAASCU, GC Board of Regents.

Dr. Roda was a recipient of awards, citations, plaques of recognition from several organizations. In June, 1986, he was honored as one of two outstanding FED educators receiving the Medallion of Merit award from the General Conference (of Seventh-day Adventists).

Less than a month before his death, at a faculty meeting he presided on, Dr. Roda said, "I am not asking anyone of you to sign this letter I've written to define the stand of PUC to the MECS. I've signed it alone and I'm ready for the consequences. This may be the last fight I shall have. I am putting my head on the line, and when it rolls, you can catch it."

Dr. Maria Tumangday,
Coordinator, PUC Graduate School.

···

Although born in the same year (1921) as my father, I have always thought him younger, because his oldest son, Andy, is several years younger than I, Ban's panganay (oldest). *Those of my generation knew very little about Dr. Roda's multifaceted personality and career. To most of us, he was the learned, soft-spoken comely tennis-playing prof., and later college president, with a beautiful wife and handsome little boys, whose departure for upgrading at UCLA denied us the chance to get to know him better.*

Who among us knew, that in his younger years, Dr. Roda sang and even directed a church choir? That aside from tennis, he excelled in swimming and also played basketball? That at one time he was the fastest typist under Quintina Geslani Tamayo, and that around the time (perhaps even on the day) the Philippines was granted independence, Dr. Roda was working at gas stations and picking fruit to support himself at Emmanuel Missionary College (now Andrew's University)?

317

Perhaps unknown even to those of his generation is that Dr. Roda was a regular concert goer and longtime season supporter of the National Philharmonic Society. During the years before his upgrading at UCLA, Dr. Roda would pick me up... and together we would attend concerts of the National Philharmonic Orchestra conducted by Redentor Romero.

At that time I was a budding violinist in my high school years, and it was thrilling and inspiring to see live performances of such legendary artists like violinist Ruggiero Ricel, cellist Janos Starker, and pianist Ruth Slenecynsks, accompanied by a symphony orchestra in which I would later become a member. I remember those evenings when Prof. Roda would invite me to his home to listen to recordings of those great performers we had met backstage after those concerts at the Philamlife auditorium.

By the time Dr. Roda came back from his doctoral studies, I had graduated from PUC and moved on to University of the Philippines (Diliman) where I started anthropology and eventually got recruited to teach and do research at the Asian Center. While our paths never crossed again, destiny led me to Dr. Roda's alma mater at Westwood, and the resurrection of the AIIAS controversy led me to analyze his pivotal role in sparking anti-colonial sentiment in the Filipino Adventist community.

During my first year as a graduate student at UCLA, I went to Moore Hall (house of the School of Education) to take a look at Dr. Roda's professional/academic background (which included upgrading at University of the Philippines, that met the tough admissions standards of UCLA. It also revealed that Far Eastern Division ... had granted him full support for the three years he spent in UCLA.

(Historical note: The late '60s was a turbulent period of rising ethnic pride and activism in America with UCLA being one of the centers of unrest at the time Dr. Roda was there.... Incidentally, Dr. Ottis C. Edwards, president of FED at the time Dr. Roda was institutionally roughed up, obtained his doctorate from the economically elitist University of Southern California (USC a.k.a. 'University of Spoiled Children'), UCLA's crosstown rival. Although farfetched, it seems uncanny how the fabled 'Bruin-Trojan' rivalry was sort of played out in the AIIAS-PUC conflict....)

Dr. Roda has been widely praised for his strength of character: his humility, generosity, courageous leadership, and faith in God. He was a loving husband and father. Lydia cannot be faulted for not remarrying, ... for she considers him irreplaceable, rightly so. The last of the Filipino presidents of PUC who had the intellectual flair, finesse, and stature to lead an institution of higher learning, he had many achievements as church worker and administrator—the most laudable, according to many observers, being the transfer of PUC from Baesa to Silang.

In my opinion, Dr. Roda has secured a place in history, not merely for presiding over the transfer, but more significantly, for being the transitional figure bridging the colonial and post-colonial Philippine

Seventh-day Adventist Church. Although nurtured and supported by the colonial Establishment which he served loyally and with distinction, he decided, in the end, to do the right thing: to fight and die for his own indigenous community's interests. In the future, no one, historian or layman alike, can properly examine the pre- and post- AIIAS eras without considering Dr. Roda's central rule in opening the doors to revitalization and change.

Alfonso P. Roda was the kind of person who reminds me of that old but timeless saying, 'still waters run deep.' He was not a firebrand or orator like his father, Leon Z. Roda, or his uncles, Alvaro and Antonino Roda. Neither was he the kind of lecturer who could keep students awake during an after-lunch lecture. In the lingo of second generation Filipino American youngsters, he might be aptly described as 'laid back.' Yet, rather enigmatically, the defining image and legacy he left behind is that of the fighter who stood up to the colonial Adventist Establishment.

Bangele D. Alsaybar
reprinted with permission, from <u>IFN</u>, Dec. 1994.

HE WORKED FOR A DREAM

I've seen men striving solely for the best
  Like huge trees tow'ring high above the rest,
Whose lifes like music have inspired my heart,
  I know such one so selfless from the start
Whose faith in God was like a solid rock
  Resisting firmly each incoming shock.
In God, not man, he set his hope and trust
  To stand for truth—that was for him—a must.

A teacher principled, yet e're so kind
  He knew the strength or weakness of each mind.
A leader, loving both by word and deed
  He muffled every voice of pride and greed.
His brother's keeper, he did prove to be,
  For in each soul, great value he could see.
All teachers, students—hostile, or a friend—
  Admired his guts, which lasted to the end.

He dreamed that some day PUC would be,
  By merit, a full-fledged university.
He scoured the world in search for every tool
  To help build here the finest medical school.
In committees he gladly helped us frame
  The guidelines to ensure such school's good name.
Aye, no one traveled, worked as hard as he
  That some day, this dream achieved would be.

For honesty and unity, he sought
  On moves to weaken PUC, he fought.
Oh, nothing grieved him more than see us split—
  With hearts an arrogant for heav'n unfit!
Silang implies (the school's new location)
  God's radiance will illumine each situation.
Some glad day, we shall know the real story,
  When no more we'll toil save for His glory.

*Ulysses M. Carbajal, M.D.
***

RELEVANT QUOTES

On History and the Future: *The past is a source of knowledge, and the future is a source of hope. Love of the past implies faith and hope.*
Stephen Ambrose, from The Fast Company.

...

On Past Mistakes: *Those who bury their past mistakes are likely to repeat the same mistakes.*

selected

...

On Talking Matters Over: *I believe we build credibility when we are candid about the problems the church faces ....questioning may ... be an essential step ... in the process of identifying what continues to contribute to the completion of the mission the Lord assigned the Church.*
Robert s. Folkenberg, from Ministry, June, 1989.

...

On Forgiving: *Forgiving does not erase the bitter past. A healed memory is not a deleted memory. We change the memory of our past into a hope for our future.*

Lewis P. Smedes

...

The real miracle of forgiveness is to remember and still forgive.
Len D. McMillan, in his book Person to Person.

...

On Human Nature: *As long as there has been organized religion, there have always been people who tried to use it to control others. Why do humans have the need of control? .... Perhaps it is just a part of the sinful condition that humans suffer from ... Control has never been a part of the Most High plans.*
Mark, in The War of the Invisibles, by Sally Dillon

...

On Romans 13:1, 7: *All of us should understand that regardless of what country we live in, our duty as Christians is not to resist the existing government, but to bear a positive witness to Christ in the midst of adverse circumstances.*

Theodore Carchich

...

On Presidential Decree No. 2021: *Atty. D... can reveal you where a big amount was given and accepted by Dr. R.... in exchange of permits granted to certain schools.... The only instance I know for which she played a significant role, was the preparation of the implementing guidelines/rules and regulations ... establishing the AIIAS whose governing Board comprised of foreigners, not Filipino citizens as provided under Section 4 (2) Article XIV.... This she did in total obedience to the orders of her*

321

immediate superior, Dr. R... despite her personal conviction ... that such is contradictory to the written provisions of the basic law of the land ... which specifically provides that "the control and administration of educational institutions shall be vested on citizens of the Philippines.... For the role she played in preparing the documents, she was transferred to another section of the city of Manila. Can you imagine ... the investigations that went on...

Excerpt of letter, copy received by Dr. D. B. Salmin.

...

Dr. Roda was a respected person in the academe. They could not understand why that happened to him.

dbs

...

On Wastefulness: *We ... are a prodigally, even a wickedly wasteful people: wasteful of our natural resources, ... of food, ... of time and money. Few of us waste the good experiences of life, many of us probably wasted most of the harder experiences of life, those that we labeled evil when we were passing through them....Our instinct is to forget all such events, seal them up in the tomb of lost memories....That attempt is psychologically impossible and probably psychologically dangerous.*

Leslie Stephen ... on his critical essay on Wordsworth's ethics, wrote: "All moral teaching,... might be summed up in the one formula, "Waste not." Sorrow is deteriorating so far as it is selfish. But it may, if rightly used, serve only to detach us from the lower motives and give sanctity to the higher.

Willard L. Sperry, from his, <u>Sermons Preached at Harvard</u>.

...

On AIIAS: *I have my own reservations on the establishment of AIIAS, which in the least is and will remain a controversial issue. However, I do not have the temerity to express my views and reservations for the simple reason that I do not have the full knowledge of the circumstances that led to its establishment. I can express just one thought that would have changed the unfortunate picture which has caused much distress and stress among those at PUC—stress especially on the administration of the College.*

I feel that the Theology Department of the College should have remained as part and parcel of PUC, and when eventually upgraded to a Seminary, the more should it remain under PUC. Then there would not have been two administrators in the same campus sharing the facilities of the institution—two heads and one body—two principal pilots of the same airplane. Can one imagine the Theological Seminary of Andrews University to be a separate entity from the University? If separating the Theological Seminary from PUC is the best model, they should do the same with Andrews University, Loma Linda University, etc.

Now that plans are to divide the former FED into two divisions AIIAS should belong to the division that includes the Philippines. As of now it is a division institution belonging to the former FED. ... Better yet, if and when the FED is divided, AIIAS should revert back to the now Adventist University of the Philippines....

Dr. Reuben G. Manalaysay, his letter Oct. 12, 1996.

(Dr. Manalaysay was the first Filipino appointed PUC President). AIIAS became a General Conference institution, <u>R&H</u> article. Nov. 1997.

***

COMMUNIQUE DECRYPTIONS

FROM: The Ruler of Planet Earth

TO: Videl, Luzon, Philippines

MESSAGES:

1. *Learn from the past. Your territory is current on technology. Microbes scored us victory on two of their Big Three, and on a promising young son of Leon Roda—cut down by tb—but failed on the young woman whom the second son of this Leon Roda, later married.*
Discouragement tool worked on Bib Panis. Your man now is this Panis'nephew—summon genes. Sharpen the tool, add teeth—stress. Find ways to put him under this sharpened tool. Persistence pays. Divide and conquer.

2. *80s. Sow seeds of greed in the minds of the corporate-purchaser. Then instigate EGMP breakup, capitalize on those Christian leaders' naivete using their faith in their fellow human beings. Get EGMP to hold and stop payments to PUC. Try harder yet to stop the flow of Christian love among those Adventists. Sow seeds of discord and distrust. Divide and conquer.*

3. *The islands had for years been colonized. Now sow hybrid seeds of colonialism, and score another victory.*

4. *Make leaders ignore the laws of the islands. Get them to pay the price. To your advantage: The country's current president's grandmother, whom he adored, was an Adventist—the fruit from this Leon Roda and brothers'influence. Divide and conquer. Score us victory.*

5. *Jan-Feb. 87. Blind visions. Capitalize on their church organization's passion for progress to keep up with the times and their world mission. Cripple communications. Minimize respect for cultural differences. Supplant loyalties. Muddle financial accountability. Divide and conquer.*

6. *Blow up their church's reputation for good works. Keep the rippling effect ever widening. Sow seeds of dissension and distrust in their midst. You succeeded in dividing the tribes of His chosen people. Discord, distrust, dissension never get outdated on humans. Human heart is fertile ground for these seeds. Divide and conquer—still among our most effective tools.*

7. March, '87. *Now sound the death toll. Annihilate the island leaders—repeat on their Big Three wipe-out. Fever the emotions of the students who love their school and their president. Make them vent their feelings of anger sans inhibitions. Cancel their once-upon-a-time respect for missionaries. Mobilize the media. Turn this into a feast for the radio. See how we score another grand victory in devastating the good our Enemy nurtured in the hearts of the community.*
Never mind that our Enemy manages to work together for good to those who love Him. Secure victory by any means. Slow the progress of their church's Cause. Time is running short. Divide and conquer.
Congratulations, Videl. But don't rest on your laurels. There's still work to do. Stay at your post. You have the tools to use.

***

The AIIAS/PUC CONTROVERSY

A DIALOG, POINTS OF VIEW

PUC and the AIIAS, excerpted (italicized), from The Link, March 15, 1990:

In 1957 during Dr. Reuben Manalaysay's presidency, the PUC Graduate School opened as a locally-supported (by NPUM) department of PUC.

In 1971, the FED started subsidizing the PUC Graduate School....
During the same year, the FED took over the PUC Seminary and continued to operate it within the same campus, but the full control given to the expatriates, directly under the FED, based on the premise that whoever gives the financial support should be given the control.

In 1984, (a Mr. Ryan wrote) *a letter addressed directly to Elder W. T. Clark, then FED president (bypassing PUC channels) and written in his capacity as research consultant, proposed the creation of the position of Coordinator of Graduate Programs, in order "to bring a greater degree of efficiency and quality to those programs: because the Graduate School "seems to lack an international outlook and is inward focused." He wanted this coordinator to be attached to the Education Department of the*

FED and to be the secretary of the Graduate Coordinating Council, which was already in existence, "to resolve the differences among graduate programs."

...this proposal was partly acted upon later on by the PUC Board by appointing Dr. Maria Tumangday as the coordinator.... he voiced his sentiment in Bangkok, in one of the FED meetings, that the PUC Graduate School should be taken out of the control of PUC in the same way as they did in the Seminary. The dean of the Graduate School at that time was Dr. Delfe Alsaybar, who obtained his doctorate in education from the United States. All graduate school professors, be they local or expatriates, were supposed to be under his supervision.

Then PUC Financial Adviser Don Van Ornam addressed this issue in a letter dated February 24, 1985, sent to the FED Officers and the Educational Department Personnel, the NPUM Officers, the Educational Secretary, the PUC Administrators and Deans, to Dr. Charles Taylor and to Dr. George Babcock of the General Conference. This letter, addressed—Brethren—is reprinted below with the permission of Dr. Van Ornam:

For several weeks thoughts have flowed through my mind. Last week these were jotted on scratch paper but left there. Again I feel compelled to write.

The Seventh-day Adventist Church has been given special commission to carry the gospel to all the world in the spirit and example of Christ. Implied in this commission is the idea that we should be as effective as we can to maximize the effects of our ministry and outreach. It also implies that each of us individually and institutionally needs to be continually open to better ways and approaches as well as opportunities to serve in greater ways. There are times when it seems various factors converge to a focal point creating an opportunity to make a greater impact. If as leaders we grasp the opportunity, the Church can hopefully accomplish even more. If the opportunity is allowed to slip away, we continue as we were, maybe thinking all is well, when in fact we failed to come up to a higher level of service. Often, once the opportunity slips away, it is lost forever. As leaders, the Lord measures us not only by what we have done, but by what we could have done. This does not imply a hasty jumping into anything new, but rather a well reasoned, prayed-through advance as the Lord opens the way. He opens the way but He will not push us through. We must follow of our own volition. Force is out of context with His character.

Some honestly believe we have come to an opportunity whereby the Seventh-day Adventist Church has a unique chance to meet the higher educational needs of our young people more effectively and on a broader scale, both in terms of academics and accessibility. Perhaps this opportunity has been approached in a wrong way. In thinking back, perhaps the root considerations were overshadowed by more immediate considerations. It would perhaps have been better to recognize the situation by saying—we need a different approach, a different structure to handle the growing needs of the graduate education in the FED—rather than focusing on problems which were perhaps symptomatic of these needs. This in turn has put some of us on the defensive, leading us to bypass the real issue. It is a fact that we are outgrowing the reality of a union institution providing international graduate education even with Division help. A new approach is called for. We see it now but it wasn't as clear before. As a result, many hours were spent discussing things which some felt didn't exist, but which others felt did. This has had negative effects for some. But this should not blind us to the basic possibilities confronting us at this time—the opportunity to obtain authorization to operate an international institute which can possibly enable us to serve our Church in the whole of the Asia Pacific region in a far greater way. Whenever new possibilities arise, there can be fears, doubts, suspicion of motives, or opposition to change because of the possible effects. Yet, if we are to be effective leaders at all levels, we must do our best to evaluate new possibilities on their merits—on how they benefit the whole Church—and not merely along personal or nationalistic lines. At the same time, genuine national interests must be considered and preserved, if this is in the best interest of the work—including the local work. Our focus needs to be continually on the good of the work and its impact on people.

At the same time, the Lord also stresses unity among the brethren. It is the devils's delight to create distrust, division, and ill will among God's people. The gospel is to unify and bring together. Sometimes we may not be ready to handle opportunities that come. Certainly, the history of Israel is full of examples. Even though they were called God's people, they left much to be desired. God met them where they were and led them to the extent they could willingly follow. Unfortunately, they missed many opportunities in the process.

The opportunity before us has tremendous potential. Some may not see it that way, or maybe better said, they see certain advantages but fear possible results in certain areas. Because of this, it seems to be shaping into a nationalistic issue. This does not best serve the needs of the Church at large, and is in fact creating a deep division on the campus both emotionally and along national lines. In the end, this will only bring bitterness and confusion. Those who may be opposed should be heard. If the opposition is founded on a legitimate basis, it should be given all the serious consideration it deserves. And if the Filipino constituency as a whole feels this is not best for God's work in their country, certainly it is not wise to move ahead here. If, on the other hand, the constituency feels, upon mature reflection, that this can be a real benefit and they want it to happen, then those opposed should accept and pull together. As leaders we set the tone of those working with us. If we determine to make it succeed, then the atmosphere will be more conducive to bringing it about. What troubles some of us is that among the local constituency, some may see the value but do not feel free to differ with some in authority who are opposed, if indeed they should want to. From soundings, it seems that outside of the PUC campus, most either don't know, don't care, or like the idea so long as they are assured of good education for their children. But on the campus, it seems the issues are being presented only in nationalistic terms, for whatever reasons. This does not best serve the Church, and if it continues to be fostered will only result in negative attitudes regardless of the decision made by the Union and/or FED, because of the deep feelings generated. It also prevents an objective evaluation of the basic issues.

We need to keep in mind that history will judge us not by the political considerations of the present moment, but rather by whether we, as leaders, foresaw and met the future needs of the Church in this part of the world by our present decision. I know that when La Sierra College was combined into Loma Linda University, there was much anguish. If the college faculty and staff had been polled, the college would not have agreed to merge. Even today a few still have feelings against it. ... But in spite of it, the Church moved ahead because the leaders, after considering all aspects, felt it was good overall for the Church. It did not mean the undergraduate colleges had failed in their role but that the needs of the Church had changed and there was a need to restructure. The same is true here. It is not an indication of failure on the part of PUC, but rather of growth and success of our work here and elsewhere which has impelled us to a new point of meeting the growing needs of the international church. The future, then, depends on the ability of our leaders to see and accept this newly emerging reality.

In view of the foregoing, would it be wise to consider the following?

1. Does the Filipino constituency want/welcome an International Institute (with its implications of an international staff—not all foreign but not all Filipino either) which can serve not only the needs of the Filipinos but other countries effectively as well?

2. If the constituency does want it but certain of the college personnel do not, how can this difference be resolved amicably? It should probably be resolved by the national leadership if they desire the institution to be here. It is not for us as missionaries to impose, but rather to respect the informed, objective, mature decision of the people—all the people—among whom we work. Our role is to uphold a certain vision, certain potentials as best we can see them, and then place the matter in the hands of God and our national brothers and sisters, under His guidance.

3. If it is felt that such an institution can serve the Church well from this place—whether jointly or as two sister campuses side by side—then everyone must somehow be willing to actively work in a spirit of unity and harmony, to heal wounds, not accentuate differences. In an international community, there are sufficient national differences which can cause friction, even when everyone is actively seeking to pull together. Responsible leadership, on all sides, implies sincerely working to overcome, not exacerbate such tensions, in accord with the well-considered, prayerful decisions of the Church's appropriate governing bodies.

4. Unless such a spirit of unity and brotherhood can exist, it may be better to scrap the idea until such time as it may be more acceptable (if indeed such an opportunity could ever be resurrected) or, even relocate to an area that would welcome such an institution. There are invitations already. A number have expressed concern that it stay within the Philippines. It is unwise to push ahead in the present environment on this campus, creating more tension and division among the brethren. If those opposed do not speak for their people, then they must be addressed first. If indeed they do, then, of course, we must not proceed with the idea of establishing an international institute here at this time. Other alternatives would need to be considered.

Some may view this as an attempted international takeover. That is not the intent or purpose. Neither must our purpose be a nationalistic defense. The work cannot best prosper under either. It is simply an effort to address the broader needs of the Church in training leaders and workers throughout the Far East and beyond. The international institute can provide training in the art of training leaders. The Church and all groups need experience and exposure to this. If the Church is truly international in its focus and mission, then those who train the future leaders must themselves have an international vision that transcends any one culture. ...If such an institute is to be truly responsive to the broad needs of the Church, and if the Church is to be successful in training all groups of people for leadership, then an organization must exist that is designed to provide the framework and an environment in which this can happen. It would seem that the most efficient and practical way to achieve this is to make provision for all constituent people of the FED to be trained and to have a direct and active part in the training of tomorrow's leaders. This can be achieved through a truly international institute of higher learning under international governance —if indeed the time has come.

Please, let us consider the opportunity on its own merits, its strengths and advantages and then decide from that objective point of view whether it can best serve the needs of the Church—including the local Philippine church. Otherwise, let us drop the idea. Those who can fit into such programs as PUC may offer will stay and others may need to be relocated.

We can only maximize this opportunity if we can go forward in a spirit of working together as God opens the way. In closing, let me share a thought which again emphasizes the international concept. "There is no person, no nation, that is perfect in every habit and thought. One must learn of another. Therefore, God wants the different nationalities to mingle together, to be one in judgment, one in purpose. Then the union that there is in Christ will be exemplified." Testimonies, vol. 9, pp. 180–181.

This concept can apply here: to choose the best among the various nationalities both for instruction and leadership, regardless of who they are, because we need one another in training international workers. Let us pause and re-evaluate and then unitedly move ahead for the good of God's church as His providence indicates.   DVO

Opposition of Western USA Alumni Association (PUC-AIIAS Story)

On September 11, 1985, the alumni association voiced its opposition to the take-over of the graduate school and submitted a position paper to the Far Eastern Division stating, among other things:

"We are concerned with PUC's welfare and nothing more. If, after we have expressed our opposition and opinions regarding this matter, the FED leadership still decides to go ahead with this proposal with the consent and approval of NPUM constituency and the College Board, then we cannot do anything but weep over the matter and continue to pray for our dear PUC, and leave everything in God's hands.

"... Without the Graduate School, the status of PUC will be downgraded as an institution of learning.... Taking over the Graduate School would mean decapitating the head from its body. PUC would lose its high academic status in the educational field in the Philippines. It would become a second-rate educational institution. Without a graduate school, no school can be elevated to university status, the ultimate level in the development of educational institutions. Removing the Graduate School would mean the capital punishment of a dynamic institution. Dismembering it would mean reversal of the progressive trend of Seventh-day Adventist education in the Philippines. The position paper submitted the following recommendations to the Far Eastern D:ivision:

1. Transfer the Theological Seminary and create an entirely new International Graduate Institute elsewhere, or

2. Entrust the Theological Seminary back to PUC with continued FED support and to increase its support to the PUC School of Graduate Studies. Teachers who do not agree to this set-up should be recalled permanently and only those who are of humble minds in trusting local leadership should be sent there, or

3. *Upgrade the whole Philippine Union College (with the Seminary as a part) as a regional or Far Eastern Division university (with Philippine government approval) in Silang, Cavite, Philippines campus and operate under the existing laws or decrees in the country without resorting to politics in order to circumvent law or decree.*

It is our prayer that the Lord grant our leadership wisdom from above in reaching a decision that is in accordance with His will.

Presidential Decree 2021. *During the later part of 1986, to the surprise of the PUC leadership, they were informed by the Ministry of Education and Culture* (MEC) *that representations have been made by some expatriates through a well known lawyer in Manila who urged them to enforce a Presidential Decree of President Marcos, PD No. 2021, signed Jan. 31, 1986, a few days before he was removed from power. The decree "recognized the AIIAS as an educational institution of an international character and granted it certain prerogatives conducive to its growth as such, and for other purposes."*

To this Dr. Alfonso P Roda, then president of PUC, responded to the MEC in a letter dated January 6, 1987, opposing the enforcement of said decree on the ground that the decree was issued just a few days before Marcos was toppled from power and that PUC and the highest leaders of the NPUM opposed its enforcement because:

1. *PUC was never consulted, although the address of AIIAS was Puting Kahoy, Silang, Cavite.*

2. *The objectives and goals of AIIAS were identical with those of PUC.*

3. *Its establishment therefore was just a duplication of PUC graduate programs.*

4. *The decree (PD 2021) was not in compliance with "the letter and spirit of our constitution because it provides for international management, composition and content which the government cannot allow under the present laws.*

5. *Circumstances and conditions in the obtaining of the decree were highly irregular.*

6. *The process of securing said decree was opposed by the leadership of NPUM and PUC.*

The letter appealed to the government ministry not to allow the AIIAS to operate at or near PUC campus, and not to allow them to offer courses offered at PUC.

However, on January 21, 1987, the PUC Board acted to write a letter to the government ministry stating:

1. *That PUC welcomes the establishment of AIIAS through PD 2021,*

2. *To request the MEC to recognize PUC, AIIAS and the FED Theological Seminary as candidate for university status.*

3. *Request the General Conference to set an Ad Hoc commission from the FED ... which would recommend campus allocation for AIIAS at minimum expense utilizing as many of the facilities used by the Seminary and Graduate programs.*

The deadline set by the Board was April 7, 1987. The death knell of the graduate school was sounded....

However, it became clear to the FED that PUC was not a willing participant to its disadvantage. The death of Dr. Roda on March 5, 1987 unified the PUC faculty and students in opposing the take-over of the graduate school by the establishment of the AIIAS within PUC campus and admonished the leadership to put it outside the Philippines. Later on, Dr. Esmeraldo de Leon, the interim president of PUC, in June, 1987, acted not to allow the absorption of the graduate school by AIIAS, and the PUC Board resolution, signed by the new NPUM president Pastor E. Macalintal, allowed the PUC graduate school to continue its operations and reversed the action of Jan. 27, 1987, by deciding not to turn the graduate school over to the AIIAS.

After it was demonstrated by PUC and the leadership in the Philippines that they are determined to keep the graduate school ... the FED decided to stop the annual subsidy of $50,000 to the PUC graduate programs and instead to give it to the AIIAS, which was to be built separately a few miles away from PUC campus still in Silang, Cavite, along the national highway....

THE FED SIDE OF THE STORY. *Don Van Ornam, former financial consultant of PUC, who was in the thickness of the question regarding AIIAS back in the Philippines, appeared to be the spokesman for the FED. He attended two meetings :—in La Sierra on Feb. 24, 1990, and on March 10, 1990, in San Diego. He said:*

The FED has the responsibility of supporting graduate education in the region and therefore has all the right to establish the AIIAS in the same way the Unions have the responsibility over undergraduate levels of graduate schools in the region such as in PUC, Korea, and Hong Kong, which latter constituents were complaining why PUC was being supported by FED while their graduate programs were not.

This was one of the reasons for establishing the AIIAS—the need for an international graduate studies program that will be sensitive to the needs and input of all the constituents of the FED and not only for the Philippines. It was therefore envisioned having Indonesian, Japanese, Korean, etc. professors, not only American expatriates and Filipino professors.

Don Van Ornam cited some feed back which came from foreign gradu-ate students who said they were not coming back because of the unwhole-some situation existing in PUC (what with the conflicts most of the time arising from the existence of the FED Seminary within PUC campus).

...the basic issue is that if the FED is funding a graduate program, then the FED should be given the control to run it, he said.

... He also said that the FED decided to put the AIIAS elsewhere but they could not find any place better than the Philippines because the people are very hospitable, standard of living is not so high and therefore easier to live in the Philippines. ... Also, the present administration of PUC told the AIIAS not to leave PUC campus, but this time the AIIAS became firm on establishing it elsewhere. in Silang... not far from PUC ... to preserve the synergy existing between the two institutions.

He further said, ..."now that the Ministry of Education has authorized the establishment of AIIAS outside a perimeter of 20 kilometers from PUC, there should not be so much apprehension because there will not be much threat to the enrollment in the PUC graduate school due to the high tuition being charged by the AIIAS. The main thing is to look for other alternatives in funding the PUC graduate programs....

Dr. Van Ornam was invited to dialogue on the "PUC/AIIAS, A 'story'," published in The Link, Feb., 1990 (the story excerpted above in italics. His response—by email March 2002—follows, in his own words.

Basically, the article is factual. Information and truth can free us from misconceptions and misunderstandings that bind us into groups.

There are several points that are different to what I remember. What does impress me is that after all these years, we still seem unable to put the past behind and move forward. The truth is that no one intentionally meant to hurt anyone else. On one side, our action was 'protective' as we saw it. The other side was a felt need that we must serve all of our constituency, and if one way wasn't providing it satisfactorily, then we must be open to other ways.

One point that I must take issue with is the idea that the expatriates were devious ("scheme and behind the scenes method...without regard to the effect on PUC") and should have talked with the locals first.

We did talk about the problems and possible solutions on numerous occasions. I talked to Dr. Roda several times about the criticism that we were receiving, but he did not want to accept it. Nor did the national faculty. So there was no discussion regarding foreign students' perceptions and concerns. Thus, feelings built up over time until at one Division meeting, various national leaders from other FED countries told the committee that the problem (as they perceived it) was not being addressed by PUC and they were no longer willing to send students or funding from the Division. At that point, basically we had passed the opportunity for PUC to fix the problem.

Probably few, even today, will agree with my assessment. That is OK. Leadership is not always easy, especially in such circumstances where there is not a mutual recognition or acceptance of problems to be resolved. Sometimes, one must choose what seems to be the best in spite of some of the outcomes. The Filipinos would have been delighted if PUC had retained the graduate programs, but others would not. So in such circumstances, the outcome risks engendering emotional outcries. (… many still seem to harbor strong feelings of injustice by Church leaders but still ignore other causative factors that led to the decision that could have been avoided.)

… PUC had a golden opportunity to rise to an even higher level as a player in the international education of Adventist students. But we didn't step up to the plate. Perhaps we at PUC should have asked a different question. "Were we at PUC adequately and properly serving the needs of the whole Division? And was it perceived as such by various constituents?"

I think that Dr. Roda sincerely believed that his position was correct. However, the day the Union Committee voted against his stand may have been the day when his stress took on a new dimension. After that he talked about standing for what he viewed as right regardless of the outcome. And he did…. I do know that he was not the only one under heavy stress. That was not the kind of experience to add years to the life of anyone deeply involved in the situation.

Even with the decision to separate the programs—two campuses side by side collaborating—could have been a powerful force. But it was not to be. As I remember, it was only after this became obvious and some plan had to be developed to fit the Division needs did we consider other alternatives. My push was always that we find a way to work together even with the differences that arose. But one cannot push water uphill. Yes, the effect on PUC was a consideration. PUC also needed to consider the effect on others if nothing was done to address the situation. It had to be a two-way street, and that was where the separation grew from.

If the past is any indication, most minds will remain unchanged. I had put this to rest but you have stirred my halls of memory to recall some of our most treasured experiences. Our Philippine journey was one of our best because we so often saw the hand of God leading through both the sweet and the not-so-sweet. And we were enriched as a family with Filipino friends and culture. It changed our lives for the better.

(Dr. Van Ornam indicated his appreciation for P. J. Barayuga's work as AUP president, and wished others to pull along with him for success. Dr.

THE GIFT OF CHOICE

Van Ornam. former PUC Financial Adviser, at the time of this dialogue was with Southern Adventist University, Tennessee, in a similar capacity. In the summer of 2002, he traveled to Bolivia, yet he managed to email the information about the EGMP—in Book 2, Chapter XIII.)

Dr. Ottis C. Edwards, 1969–1972 interim PUC President, and later FED President, now a retiree, keeps very busy with Church involvement in his home in Vancouver, Washington, where he and his wife reside. He kindly obliged to dialog on the issue. His response follows, in his own words:

Let me say that my stay in the Philippines for some thirteen years has made that country and its people very dear to my heart. I have many very close friends who are now living there or are here in the U.S.A. One former student of PUC is so close to us that he and his wife call my wife and me, "Mom and Dad." His children refer to us as *Lolo* and *Lola.*

Having been a teacher and administrator at Philippine Union College for eleven of those thirteen years made that school also dear to my heart. It was while I was president there that PUC purchased the present property. For these reasons I have a great deal of love for PUC/AUP. And that admiration will not change with the passing of years.

As I have read many of the things that have been said about FED, AIIAS, myself, and other personnel involved in the happenings that have brought stress between the institutions, PUC/AUP and AIIAS, it has brought a great deal of sorrow to my heart. I believe that Dr. Roda and his administrative staff were sincere Christians. I believe that the leadership of the FED and AIIAS also were sincere Christians. Both sides were trying to do what they saw as right. Both desired to have the Lord lead and work out what would be best for His work and the good of students that would be affected by the future educational programs established.

Just as Paul and Barnabas were sincerely following the Lord but came to such stress between them that they had to part ways, yet both of them were still used by the Lord. All of us are human and sometimes that humanity gets in the way of what God wants to happen. That does not mean that we are not still trying to follow where He leads us. Both Paul and Barnabas went on to do great things for God, even though not working together as before.

When I arrived in PUC in October of 1960, Dr. Manalaysay had already established a graduate program in education. Shortly after my arrival, PUC, with the financial help of the Far Eastern Division, began a graduate program in various aspects of Theology. The Division was interested in this because it would provide additional training for its ministry. Some of us felt that teaching was just as important and we requested the same financial assistance for PUC's graduate program in education. Shortly thereafter, that happened. Some time later, the Division established a bursary program which enabled many teachers of PUC to pursue doctoral studies. This was a great blessing and greatly strengthened the academic qualifications of the teachers.

In laying the background for the separation that eventually came between FED and PUC in financing graduate courses, one must realize that the Division recommended that the Seminary program become a separate institution under the Division a few years prior to the time that the separation came for the other graduate programs which PUC was offering.

There came the time of stress between the Division and PUC, which was underwriting the financial expenses for operating the graduate programs at PUC. The Division was concerned about several aspects of the way these courses of study were being operated.

More than ten years have passed since these problems were experienced. That amount of time erases some of the awareness of all that happened. Three of the issues that were present during the time of the problem were:

1. The Division felt that, since sizable amounts of funds were going into the program, that there should be representation from the Division and the other Unions of the Far East in the decisions that were made regarding the graduate programs.

2. The Division was concerned for the quality of the programs offered.

3. Another issue had to do with the Dean of the School of Education being given only a half load so there would be time enough to do the administration and supervision necessary for the graduate programs to be carried on at the desired level of quality.

Basically, these were the main issues. Regarding the representation, (No. 1) we were given to understand that it was not possible for the FED to have representation on the PUC board.

Regarding the quality of programs offered (No.2) the Division felt that teachers who taught in the graduate programs should not be overloaded. This became quite an issue and the graduate load of these teachers was reduced to what should be appropriate, however, the undergraduate load of these same teachers was not reduced so that the teachers were overloaded from that perspective. The Division felt that it was difficult for these teachers to carry those extra load and give attention to the high quality needed.

After much dialogue, satisfactory solutions were not found to resolve the problems and bring agreement between the FED and PUC. At one time, the Division paid for the transportation of the two chief administrators—the president and the business manager—to travel to Singapore to discuss the issues and find solutions. An agreement was reached that, we believed, could have solved the issues and could have kept Division funds flowing into PUC for the graduate programs. We were extremely happy regarding this. However, we were informed later by PUC that the agreement could not be materialized. This was very disappointing.

Eventually, the Division made the decision to separate from PUC. Therefore, it found property several kilometers from PUC where it located the Seminary program, which it was already administering and developed a graduate study programs in other academic areas in an institution called AIIAS. This decision was very painful to PUC as all of us can understand. It brought a great deal of stress for many individuals, strains that have lasted through the ensuing years. Funding for PUC's graduate offerings was gradually diminished over a period of time.

As we look back upon that decision we could wish that we had put forth greater efforts on both sides to find a more compatible solution, but as with Paul and Barnabas, once the break was made, once the decision to separate had been finalized, even though like these men of New Testament Times, they were Christians, and Paul, himself, was an apostle, still it was not possible to reverse the situation. Both men went their separate ways, both still working for the Lord, still reaching people with the gospel of Christ, winning them to His Church, accomplishing a great mission for God. And so the two institutions continued to serve the needs of the field as separate entities, striving to fulfill God's purposes.

Today, we are a decade beyond the decision for PUC and the AIIAS to separate, let us find ways to make the most of a situation that may not be to our liking. Let us forgive and move on to greater service for both institutions. For my part, even though many unkind things have been reported about me and about the decision the FED reached under my leadership, I harbor no hard feelings toward those who have made them. I have forgiven and am anxious to seek unity. I would hope that all who have felt badly regarding the decision that was made may also be willing to forgive me and others responsible for the hurts and injuries they received because of the action.

Our Sabbath School lesson this week (*3-20-01*) was about Christ's prayer in John 17. One of the great burdens of that prayer was for unity among His followers. Can we somehow find a way to bring about that unity and have the love for one another that Christ has prayed for, that we might be one as He and the Father are one? That thus we might cooperate together for the good of God's work, even though the past is not all that we might like it to be.

I was delighted when PUC became AUP, the Adventist University of the Philippines. My love for this institution will not fade. Whenever I meet people here in the U.S. who are from the Philippines, I am proud to tell them about my years at that institution. I am glad that I had the opportunity to have a part in its development during the time I was a teacher and administrator. I continue to pray for God to lead in its future. I continue to watch its progress with a great deal of interest and am praying for *Dr. Barayuga and his staff as they face the issues before them today.

Very sincerely yours,
(signed) Ottis C. Edwards, Retiree
(undated letter was received 3-24-01)
*Dr. P. J. Barayuga, the newly appointed AUP president at that time.

Note to Readers, interested to know the background of The AIIAS/PUC Matter from PUC Point of View. The following documents are included in the book only to set the background of the AIIAS/PUC Matter, as perceived by PUC. (see also Foreword and Relevant Quotes.)

DOCUMENTS, PUC GENERATED

GRADUATE SCHOOL STATEMENT
OF BELIEFS, DISAGREEMENTS

and

RECOMMENDATIONS, submitted to the FED.

BELIEFS

We believe in quality education.

The recognition for the programs we now operate and the autonomy in the conduct of the oral defense granted by the MECS, and the kind of alumni and leaders from PUC attest to this belief. We believe in internationalization—in character and dimension, in faculty and studentry. The PUC graduate school has always been international since the beginning. We believe in the speedy finishing of God's work. We believe in openness and participatory democracy which democracy-loving missionaries in the past have taught us. We believe in the philosophy of mission as enunciated by the General Conference Institute of Mission—that we have now entered the phase of consultancy. We believe in the indigenization of leadership, program, management, and personnel consistent with and in keeping with current mission trend and practices. Southeast Asia Association of Theological Schools goes by this philosophy and practice. Missionaries only play a supportive role through funding and personnel assistance. We believe that, in the final analysis, the interest of God's work in any country can best be served and its burden borne by the indigenous faithful. We believe in unity, in giving and taking, in the mutual operation of the Biblical golden rule. We believe in receiving some measure of input from leaders in the FED who are supportive of our program within the context of Philippine laws. We believe that the Philippines deserves to be heard concerning this graduate school issue because the human resources and environmental factors conducive to operating this academic establishment, perhaps unvalued in terms of dollars, are provided by this country. We believe that the continuous and onward development of PUC is a legitimate and proper concern. We believe in putting up a sort of mechanism by which we can receive input from the participating unions.

<u>DISAGREEMENTS</u>

We disagree with the dismemberment of the College program. A take-over of the graduate school will mean a decapitation of PUC, a loss of the program recognized by the government for which PUC has struggled to gain over the years. We disagree with the idea of a divided campus. The confusion and division, even now evident, are not exhibits of Christian witness. We disagree with the proposal of take-over or transfer of the graduate school. It is demoralizing to faculty morale. We disagree with the proposed institute duplicating the programs now being offered and will be offered by PUC. We disagree with the proposal to divide the present campus on points of unity and aesthetics. We disagree with the notion repeatedly expressed—that the control of the graduate school should be in the hands of the FED, since they provide the finances. The Philippines, comprising almost sixty percent of the Division is a contributor to the world fund. We disagree with the idea that the demand for control originated in the different unions of the Division. Indonesia, our biggest student source outside the Philippines, wholeheartedly supports the present program. We disagree with the survey instrument used. It was slanted towards the desired goal of the questionnaire makers and shrouded the implications of the proposed institution for PUC. We deplore and strongly oppose the method utilized in the whole transaction. We disagree, and are saddened by what we observe and hear—that in discussing the issues relevant to this campus problem, threats and innuendoes on certain personalities, coercion, and deceit have been employed.

RECOMMENDATIONS

Based on the forgoing statements of Beliefs and Disagreements, we are recommending the following options:

1. That the AIIAS work with the PUC administration, as recommended by Dr. Akers of the General Conference and MECS, so there will be no duplication of courses with PUC, nor confusion.

2. That, if the forgoing option is not acceptable, AIIAS build on a separate campus, no less than three kilometers away, according to the MECS requirement.

3. That, in the event that the FED decides to withdraw financial support of the PUC graduate program, we make known to the Board our willingness to seek ways and means to be self-reliant in order to carry on the graduate school program. Since more than half of the Division membership comes from the Philippines, and its three unions contribute to the Division fund, we appeal to your sense of fairness and justice to give consideration to these stated beliefs, disagreements, and recommendations.

The PUC GRADUATE FACULTY
February 7, 1987

***

THE ISSUES AND QUESTIONS IN THE PLAN
TO ESTABLISH The AIIAS on the Campus of PUC

I. The Presidential Decree Method (Means) was opposed by the highest leadership of the North Philippines and the College.

A. Basis for strong opposition.

1. Amendment No. 6 which enabled the President to issue decrees states that it is only when "there exists a grave emergency, or a threat or imminence thereof, or whenever the interim *Batasang Pambansa* or the regular National Assembly fails or is unable to act adequately on any matter for any reason that in his judgment requires immediate action, he may, in order to meet the exigency, issue the necessary decrees, orders or letters of instructions, which shall form part of the laws of the land.

QUESTIONS:

Was there a grave emergency, threat, to the country?

Was the National Assembly not meeting?

Statement: The Presidential Decree method should not have been used since it was clear there was no emergency and the National Assembly was doing its work of legislation in the normal proper way.

II. The decision to follow the counsel of the Quasha Law Firm to pursue this course when such method was opposed by the leadership of God's people in the North Philippines is, to my thinking, going to the 'gods of Ekron' (2 Kings 1:3, 6, 16 and chapter 2).

QUESTIONS:

Why did FED leadership go to the Quasha law office and followed its advice when the leaders of the local union said they were opposed to this method?

Shall this word of the lawyers prevail over and above that of God's leadership in the Union?

Statement: There is, I believe, a place for lawyers/legal counsel in the church, but when the Division leadership sets aside counsel from the leadership of the local/national church, then, I believe we have gone to the gods of Ekron and put to nought the counsel from God's people.

III. After the decree was approved, our Division-appointed personnel went about working for its implementation in a quiet, covert, secretive way which makes us think they were afraid we would find out and thwart their efforts. They were working in the dark—in a covert way—which makes me wonder if even they were uncertain whether they were doing the right thing. E. G. White says, "Everything that Christians do should be as transparent as the sunlight. Truth is of God; deception in everyone of its myriad forms is of Satan; and whoever in any way departs from the straight line of truth is betraying himself into the power of the wicked one." Mount of Blessing, p. 68.

Statement: In our recent FED and NPUM meetings, we approved guidelines on how we should deal with government. We should be open, truthful, honest, with no intention to hide facts or to deceive.

IV. This establishment of the AIIAS contradicts our General Conference policy of missions—in giving greater and more responsibility to nationals and less and less to missionaries and/or non-residents of the country. Dr. Gottfried Oosterwal, in an article in the Review, says that there are four stages in mission strategy:

1. Pioneering
2. Managerial
3. Specialists, and
4. Consultancy.

Our present status now, I believe, is No. 3—Era of Specialists. This AIIAS would bring us back to stage No. 2.

The work in any national geographic area should be carried out under the laws and provisions of the country in which we are working. The work will be brought to completion through the Holy Spirit using all means, but in the final analysis, it would be the nationals who would carry on the work after the expatriates are gone. Let us not repeat the tragedy of China, Vietnam, Cambodia. Let's trust the nationals and give them the responsibility and make them loyal to God and His church and His work—not distrust them, nor cut them from growing.

V. Christian leadership focuses on procedure/method. Mr. Bruce Powers, in his book Christian Leadership, made research on "How to be an Effective Leader." He says that any effective Christian leader is not so much concerned in knowing a formula or acting a particular way, as he is in adopting a lifestyle based on certain principles. These principles are process-oriented. Effective Christian leadership is not so much a goal to be achieved as it is a means or a lifestyle that must be developed.

QUESTION:

Were the FED-appointed personnel so engrossed with their goal, their desire to enforce a policy (FED takes care of graduate level education and therefore should exercise control, administration) and regardless of what MEANS or PROCESS they adopted, whether this goes against the will and the sensitivities of the people whom they are supposed to serve, they would go ahead and do it anyway?

Statement: Life-giving leadership is dependent on close personal relationship with God and with fellow believers. Life-giving leaders cannot function effectively in isolation. These leaders also must be part of a loving, caring, supportive body of believers in which they may develop.

VI. The pursuit of this objective—establishment of the AIIAS—was accompanied by a subtle kind of "force." 2 Cor. 3:17, RSV: "Where the Spirit of the Lord is, there is freedom." Dick Winn, in his book, His Healing Love (Morning Watch Devotional for 1987—Jan. 1, 1987, states: "But if there is in one's religious experience such a feeling of oppression, of heavy demands for submission to power, then we can be sure that the Spirit of the Lord is not there. He is not involved in such religion. For the Spirit of the Lord does not work by force."

We must recall that there is more than one kind of force. Far more subtle (and therefore more effective) than physical force is emotional force. And that comes in myriad forms: the threat of withholding appropriations...

...God doesn't need to use force to support His truths for they are well able to stand on their own merits.

In human structures, whenever leaders become deficient in truth, they must immediately compensate with a display of power. Such leaders either do not have truth behind their schemes or they do not trust the ability of their subjects to grasp what truth they may have.

But God has neither problem. Not only is His government rooted in sensible, coherent truth, He also has great confidence in the capacities of His creatures to perceive that Truth! To use force is to deny both these principles.

QUESTION:
Could we not have sat down together and arrive at a consensus? Involving those most directly connected with the graduate programs and not using high-handed methods, and threatening with loss of appropriation, or even the threat of moving the "problem" out?

VII. The National Leadership in PUC has had the experience—30 years of operating the graduate school—from 1957 to 1987. We have had hundreds of graduates. We are now international in student body. We are now international in faculty/staff. We are continually concerned with quality. We are continually concerned with being relevant. We are continually concerned to do things within a context of Christian scholarship. But we must do these under the context of the country's laws and regulations.

We will need more missionaries, not less, but we will do our witnessing in the open, not following an exception to the rule, but within the context of the country's laws and regulations.

Success is something we do not wish to parade around, and yet, we are not embarrassed to admit the quality of our graduates, here in the Philippines, as well as those who have gone back to their homelands. All throughout the world, our graduates are serving with dedication, efficiency and loving care.

Any talk of quality must be brought about and carried on within the context of the present administrative set-up. We will not only be law abiding, cooperating with the MECS, which has suggested this option, but we will also bring into a cooperative venture our present faculty/staff who are hard-working, efficient and dedicated to the work of highest quality.

VIII. Money is a very important commodity. It makes things go—it builds schools and makes possible continued operation of established institutions. It pays salaries, it makes possible research and the advance of knowledge.

But why should MONEY—**monies contributed by the world church from all believers**—be the overruling force or factor—the deciding element on this very sensitive and important matter?

Why is money more important than people?

Is money more important than honesty and integrity?

Is money more important than a witness of the true character of God whom we worship?

Is money more important than being a caring and loving person?

STATEMENT: Money is important, but true witness—loving, caring, and the like, are vastly more important. To make money ALL important, the deciding factor on this matter is decidedly WRONG and will be a negative factor in the witness of this Church.

IX. At a time of our Adventist history when we all, regardless of our color or station of life, should be striving for UNITY, we are being divided between missionaries and local workers. It is taking on a color of nationalism. Although I maintain the issue is not nationalism, the effect and perception is that the missionaries want to continue lording things OVER THE NATIONALS. This is unfortunate. It is not good for the Church. Jesus prayed for unity. John 17: 21, "That they may be one in us." Gal. 3: 28. NIV, "There is neither Jew nor Greek, slave or free, male or female, for YOU ARE ONE IN CHRIST JESUS." Acts 10: 34, 35 NIV. "God does not show favoritism, but accepts men from every nation who fear Him and DO WHAT IS RIGHT.

Unity is a worthy goal, but it should be genuine unity, not a plastic one—not a veneer to be 'displayed' to others.

Unity must be the inevitable result of love and treating each other as equals, treating with dignity and respect.

Unity is the outcome or fruitage of justice and fairness in dealing with each other.

Unity cannot be attained where there is continuing injustice and unfair dealing, and discrimination in any form.

The time for unity was yesterday. But it is not too late. The necessary changes must be accomplished NOW.

X. The principle of freedom of speech, the freedom to vary in thinking, even from those above you, if warranted, is a freedom we value highly and which should be guaranteed by our leaders.

This Church should not be threatened with genuine opposition to ideas, plans, and projects, specially when the issues involved are basic to our existence, the very essence of what we should stand for, i.e. our witness of what kind of God we worship and the resulting response in acts of love and caring—and all the components of the fruit of the Holy Spirit.

Any attempt to muzzle this genuine airing of variant alternatives cannot but be foreign to the Spirit of Christ.

The greatest American president ever was not Richard Nixon of the infamous Watergate 'cover up' even which eventually led to his resignation from the presidency, not Ronald Reagan of the recent and ongoing Iron Gate 'cover up', but Abraham Lincoln, the great emancipator of the American Negro slaves. He was the one who said:

> *"I am not bound to win but I am bound to be true. I am not bound to succeed but I am bound to live up to what light I have. I must stand with anybody that stands right. Stand with him while he is right, and part with him when he goes wrong."*

PRAYER: May God give us the wisdom to do what is right even at this stage of the problem that has been brought about by the establishment of the AIIAS. Amen.

Dr. Alfonso P. Roda, January, 19, 1987.

***

*LEST WE FORGET

by Dr. Miriam Sarno Tumangday
excerpted from <u>IFN</u>, October, 1994, reprinted by permission.

A Sense of History. We Seventh-day Adventists treasure our history. Surely, we do not want to turn our backs on the events which shaped us as a denomination: the struggles of our pioneers, the issues that rocked our fledgling church then (especially the 1888 confrontation that continued until now) and the leaders who stood up for the then unpopular cause all of which contributed to what we are now.

I believe we should nurture a sanctified sense of history and be willing to face the past and learn from our mistakes, and see God's hand leading His people in the midst of conflict. History can be written accurately only as we review objectively and with the illumination of the Holy Spirit what has happened and how it affects the present.

That painful phase in PUC's development—the issues with AIIAS—was a crucial point in her history. And that important turn at the fork of the road has to be recorded for everybody's information and edification.

Scripture brings before us vivid details of Israel's story, their sojourn in Egypt, the burdens they bore, the humiliation they suffered, the representations made in their behalf, the stubbornness of the Egyptian leader, and finally their deliverance from bondage. This part of their history was to be reiterated, according to divine instruction, to their children and future generations, so God's intervention would not be forgotten.

.... *Some time in 1984*, we professors of PUC Graduate School received communication that FED wanted to claim the graduate school in order to "internationalize" its academic standards. Led by Dr. Alfonso P. Roda, then college president, we asked to dialog with the Division officers. Several reasons for the takeover were advanced: academic quality, a bigger umbrella for the expanding programs, among others. All these were quickly invalidated by documented evidences presented by Dr. Roda and the PUC group.

We at PUC maintained that for the sake of the educational work in the Philippines, the graduate school should be retained. As you may know, the Philippine government requires academy and college teachers to be holders of masteral degrees, which ... could be acquired only in a graduate school.

The proposed Division graduate school could admit an enrolment of only one-third Filipinos as mandated by presidential decree. And the tuition would be six or seven times higher than what it was at PUC. Add to this the fact that a mission or institution could sponsor only one upgradee; and you'll realize why we resisted the idea of a takeover. This would mean that PUC would lose its graduate school and the majority of our graduate students, largely self-supporting, would filter out to secular schools.

Dr. Delfe Alsaybar, Dean of Graduate School, and President Roda's Untimely Deaths

What would the face of Philippine Adventism look like ten years hence if our institutions' leaders were trained in non-SDA centers of higher learning? The future loomed darkly before us. But we were determined to stand for the cause of principled SDA leadership preparation for the Lord's work in the Philippines.

It was for this cause, as I saw it, that Dr. Roda, wearied and stressed by the constant buffetings on his psycho-physical resources and conscience, valiantly stood for—until he died on March 5, 1987. Dr. Delfe Alsaybar preceded him in death by a few days.

Dr. Roda's untimely passing stilled the dialog somewhat, but not the stand of the graduate school professors: that the cause for which Dr. Roda died should be pursued with determination.

Shortly after this presidential loss, it became my privilege, as the new dean of the graduate school, to take up the challenge. Fortunately, the College Board … decided to keep our graduate school. Yet an enormous problem lay before us. Since the Division's annual appropriation of one million pesos was to be diverted to its own AIIAS…, we were left to solve this financial deficiency. Otherwise, we wouldn't be authorized to operate our graduate school, we were told by the powers-that-be.

Forward in Faith. I presented this matter to my fellow professors and the graduate students, and the faith wheel in the graduate school began to turn. Sessions of prayer several times day and night targeted the problem: Where will that immense amount of money come from? At graduation time that year, Dr. Celedonio A. Fernando, then president of WUSAC (now WESNAC) came to be our commencement speaker. I laid bare our need for money to keep the graduate school going. He suggested that I go to the United States and present this need to the alumni at reunion time.

Atty. John G. Tulio Establishes AMSA…. Dr. Fernando gave me prime time Sabbath morning, and Saturday evening at the Alumni banquet to appeal in behalf of our need…. Atty. John G. Tlio, stood up and came forward. Urging the alumni to get involved and respond to the call of their alma mater, he proposed that the Adventist Mission Society of America (AMSA) foundation be established for the purpose of raising funds for PUC.

....He led out in making AMSA a reality. Rising to their feet as one, the alumni pledged $50,000 each year for three years to help the graduate school survive. Romulo Valdez, M.D., the incoming president at that time, indicated his willingness to carry out and implement the commitment....

With assurance we can look forward to the kind of leadership in our Philippine institutions that is distinctively SDA, and truly Christian. It must be remembered that each graduate student represents not just one individual, but an academy, a union, a mission or hospital.

Today we live with the consequences and implications of that stage of PUC's growth—through the overwhelming providence of God—born in that historic PUC-AIIAS controversy. Then why should that dramatically significant account of PUC's courageous few and its impact on her progress and commitment be consigned to oblivion?

*Given at WESNAC's 17th annual retreat held in Aug. 1989. As a result of this, the Western Chapter organized the Adventist Mission Society of America (AMSA) a foundation to raise funds for PUC's Graduate School.

STATEMENT OF CONCERN

by John G. Tulio, Attorney At-Law

Atty. Tulio personally handed this document to then GC president Robert Folkenberg, in August, 1992, when he was the guest speaker at the PUC Alumni Western Chapter annual retreat, with a request to enter into a dialog on the issues. It was learned much later that the document was transmitted to the FED for consideration. To date, no dialog had ensued.

Introduction. This statement was prepared in order to provide a unique perspective for the president of the General Conference ... regarding very important developments in the Adventist higher educational system in the Philippines. Because of the major impact of some of these developments on the future of both Church and our nation, it is necessary that these views be presented to the leader of the world church in this fashion.

(Omitted information on membership growth in the Philippines, the establishment of the graduate school and the work it had accomplished, the separation of the Seminary from PUC and placing it under expatriates' leadership, FED funding and de-funding of the graduate school arising from the establishment of AIIAS, and the results of the stress produced.)

The Role of Christian Education in the Philippines. Education plays a major role in Philippine society. When this factor is combined with the Adventist Church's commitment to its education system, one gets an idea of the importance of our schools to Filipino Seventh-day Adventists.

Our schools train and prepare church workers and help members (converts mostly from the lower class) to move upward economically and socially. Reflecting the country's population, the majority of church members today in the Philippines are below age 40. About 67 percent of the church's school-age youth attend our schools....

PUC has played a major role in preparing and training educators who now staff three senior colleges, scores of academies and elementary schools throughout the country. Its Graduate School provides advanced degrees in education, administration, nursing, and in public health to educators, administrators, health care and public health professions. Skills and expertise in these fields are sorely needed in the Philippines today.

...The Adventist Church in the Philippines has worked fervently to improve society through evangelism, health and welfare programs and

Christian education for almost a century now. The gospel is needed to instil a new morality and code of ethics based on heart religion.

The medical and welfare programs are necessary to improve the health and physical condition of the citizenry. Schools are indispensable if the youth are going to be educated not only for a useful vocation but for service to God and country.

To Promote Survival and Advancement of PUC. Perhaps no other country today feels the impact of Christian education more than the Philippines. The Adventist education system in the Philippines does make a difference! This is the reason why Adventists operate one of the largest sectarian education systems in the Philippines, second only to Roman Catholics in number but first per capita.

This is also the reason why its alumni and supporters are extraordinarily passionate in advocating and promoting the survival and advancement of Philippine Union College.

Colonialism, Nationalism, and Missionaries. Through the centuries people of the dominant nations have advanced the idea, by direct assertion and implication, and more recently by insinuation, that colonized peoples are unable to govern themselves. As a result, a 'colonial mentality' both on the part of the colonizer and the colonized began to develop, which espoused the ideology that the supremacy and dominance of the white race and the inferiority and subservience of the darker races was a most 'natural' order of events.

Colonization produced certain characteristics among the colonized—such as inferiority, laziness, lack of initiative, lack of creativity, as well as lack of self-confidence—disabling factors which prevent them from developing leadership qualities.

Filipino Psyche Affected by Foreign Domination. The experience of the Filipinos under the Spaniards, then the Americans, and the Japanese, deeply affected their psyche. To this day, Filipinos have yet to free themselves from the shackles of colonial mentality, which is so apparent in the way they deal with other nations, with foreigners, and with themselves.

Centuries of authoritarian rule under the Spaniards and decades of manipulation by the U.S. have created a confused style of leadership among Filipinos.

Stanley Karnow, in his Pulitzer Prize-winning book, <u>In Our Image</u>, describes the authoritarian system of the Spaniards.

"Under three centuries of Spanish rule, the Philippines suffered as much from neglect as from tyranny. Its officials, soldiers and priests brought to the archipelago the archaic, parochial dogmas of their sectarian society—demanding total obedience to their absolute authority as they sought to reap profits and save souls.

"By the early 17th century, five religious orders had each carved out its distinct sphere of influence.... In theory, the natives were to rule themselves under Spain's guidance.... In fact, the friars ran the show....

"The friar exercised power through a staggering panoply of functions. He audited the parish budget, conducted the census, registered the residents, directed the tax board, managed health and public work projects, screened recruits for military service, presided over the police and reviewed conditions at the local jail.... Most of all, he oversaw education and religion." (In Our Image, pages 48–52.)

Americans Were No Different. While the Americans were more altruistic in their approach, their attitude towards the natives was no different from the Spaniards. Karnow describes this attitude:

"Taft went to Manila with the preconceived notion that the Filipinos were unsuited to govern themselves, and his first impressions only confirmed his prejudice. The great mass of the people are 'ignorant and superstitious,' he observed, while the few men 'who have any education that deserves the name' were mostly intriguing politicians, without the slightest moral stamina, and nothing but personal interest to gratify.' They were oriental in their duplicity, and, he estimated, it might take a century of training before they shall ever realize what anglo-Saxon liberty is. However, he declared, the United States had a sacred duty to Americanize them. With that, he launched his program to instill in them the values that had made America the greatest society on earth: integrity, civic responsibility and respect for impersonal institutions. No matter that the United States at the time was itself riddled with corruption, racism, and appalling economic disparities. America's mission was to export its virtues, not its sins." (In Our Image, p. 19.)

Leaders and educators of the colonized society need to re-study and understand the reasons, causes, and results of colonial mentality. Once these things are understood, the 'ghosts of the past' can be exorcized and a new and healthy relationship can be re-established between the colonizers and the colonized. Since these attitudes are passed on from one generation to the next, educators should go beyond simply dispensing facts in teaching history to the next generation, but they should also deal with the sociological and psychological impact of colonialism.

Colonial Adventism. This issue should also be addressed within the context of the Adventist subculture. Many have observed that the Adventist missionary program grew and profited from the colonial situation in the mission fields. Both the missionary and the mission community have acquired, whether consciously or not, the mentality of the colonizer and the colonized and these attitudes have continued to this day.

Adventists do not seem to be immune to the tendency of citizens of superpower nations to treat citizens of less powerful nations with an air of superiority. The servile attitude of church members in the mission fields has helped reinforce a situation which creates a fertile breeding ground for arrogance. Missionaries from America, for example, view the people of the Third World countries as recipients of their 'expertise.' Church members in the mission fields, on the other hand, see the missionaries as givers of help. In spite of the fact that many expatriate workers take up their assignment as novices, they are looked upon as superior in ability and wisdom. In this kind of situation, all of the elements of an unhealthy dependent relationship continue to exist.

Thus, the thought that the American way is superior to all others was likewise reflected in the mission work of the Adventist Church. Barry Oliver, in his doctoral dissertation, Seventh-day Adventist Church Organizational Structure, Past, Present, and Future (Andrews University, 1989) describes the Adventist mission approach:

"Throughout the 19th century, a sense of manifest destiny had permeated American religion and society. But by the end of the century that sense of destiny had become strongly ethnocentric in orientation … white, Anglo-Saxon, Protestant social and cultural values where regarded as the norm for everyone. Even the pattern of government which had been established in the United States was considered by many to be the ideal pattern for all peoples in all places.

"Seventh-day Adventist missions were not particularly adept at promoting autonomy. Even in the early stages of the 20th century, their missionary methodology was based on the institutional or mission situation approach. Insufficient attention was given to the selfhood of the younger churches and the development of the indigenous leadership."

No Training in Goal Setting, Negotiation, or Institutional Design. "It appears that in the history of Adventist work in the Philippines, the Filipino national workers were not given or "allowed to learn such essential skills … as goal setting, negotiation, or institutional design. These had all been done for them by their colonial masters."

(Robert Greenleaf, Servant Leadership, p. 308).

***

In his doctoral dissertation Breaking Through (Fuller Seminary, 1981) Herman L. Reyes chronicles the development of national leadership:

"The Japanese Imperial Army of occupation decreed that all leadership positions of churches occupied by foreigners be given to

Filipinos. Thus on September 2, 1942, the executive committee of Philippine Union Mission (the majority of its members being missionaries) elected nationals into office.... It is interesting to note that the Filipinos elected to become presidents of the six missions were called 'associate presidents', although the minutes showed no other persons elected president.

"Immediately after the missionaries were liberated from the concentration camp, on February 23, 1945, the leadership positions of Philippine Union Mission were taken back by the overseas missionaries who had elected to remain until their replacements arrived (including the presidency of PUC which has been given to Reuben Manalaysay in 1943).

"Had the Filipinization of church leadership in the Adventist Church in the Philippines been too slow? Compared with the Methodist Church, it was rather slow. It appears that all Methodist district conference superintendents (corresponding to presidents of local missions) were already in Filipino hands before the outbreak of World War II. Its Council Of District Superintendents appointed an acting head of the Church in 1942 and then in 1944, its first Filipino bishop (corresponds to union mission president) .... Methodist world policy was ahead of Seventh-day Adventist world policy in this regard.

"The story of the Seventh-day Adventist Church during these two decades (1920 to 1940) reveals that the majority of the missionaries were not yet psychologically ready to allow Filipinos to lead."

Dr. Reyes goes on to propose that indigenous leadership helps to avoid having a 'foreign' church.

"A myriad of factors affect the growth of the Church, the... above seem to indicate that indigenizing leadership is a factor that contributes to church growth. Using Pentecostal missionaries in South America as a frame of reference, Peter C. Wagner explains why this happens:

"Many non-Pentecostal missionaries have been much slower in turning over new churches to national leaders. This lingering paternalism almost invariably produces two results which retard church growth. The first is foreignness about the church so that it appears to be something both exotic and irrelevant to outsiders. The second is a development of a strong anti-missionary sentiment, particularly in the second-generation believers."

Adventist Leadership in the Philippines Colonialistic. There appears to be explanation for the slower nationalization of Adventist leadership in the Philippines other than what appears to be the colonialistic tendencies of the missionaries in charge. The alternative explanation is not any better—that Adventist missionaries have been outperformed by the Methodists and Pentecostals in training indigenous members for church leadership.

The nationalization of church leadership in the mission fields will not completely solve the problem of colonialism in such a way as to open the way for servant leadership. Without an understanding of the deeper issues involved in the colonial mentality of both the colonizer and the colonized, colonialism may still be perpetuated by national leaders. It has been observed that when colonized nationals take on leadership positions, their style is that of their former masters whom they have been imitating: authoritarian, paternal, and autocratic.

Damaging Result of Financial Support From North America. One damaging result of the colonial mentality in former mission fields is over-dependence on financial support from North America. In the past, very little organized effort was made to build economic self-sufficiency among church members and institutions. The progress of the Work was always made possible with funds from North America.

Unfortunately, very little of these funds went into making the mission fields self-supporting. Rather, these offerings funded expansion of institutions which could not be maintained without the continuing support of North American money, thus perpetuating a cycle of economic dependency.

This situation is not only damaging to those in the mission fields, it affects the mentality of the North American church members. They have become the providers of funds to the point that they believe that nothing can be accomplished in the mission fields without their help.

A corollary to this thinking is the belief that they are also responsible for controlling the use of these funds in the mission fields because 'people who cannot support themselves cannot be trusted to make wise financial decisions.' And so, the Church must keep sending missionaries from North America to build administrative positions to places where the national workers should have been prepared and trained to function, if they could be trusted. Often, this had cost the Church many times more than if the national worker had done the job.

This kind of colonial mentality, which continues to linger in the minds of both the 'colonized' and the 'colonizer,' has prevented the Church from not only utilizing its funds and personnel effectively, it has also prevented personal growth in the area of human relationships. In many Third World countries today, there is a continuing and silent struggle for control between national and expatriate church workers.

THE GRADUATE SCHOOL ISSUE:
OUR PERSPECTIVE

Based on the discussion above and our analysis, we believe that the following factors contributed to the conflict involving the Graduate School of PUC:

1. Lack of spirit of cooperation.

There has been a perception on the part of many Filipinos that organizational and organizations and institutions administered by expatriates do not work in cooperation with national leaders unless the expatriates are in charge. They see a lack of confidence in their leadership on the part of expatriate workers. As a result, some national workers have become defensive in their attitude toward missionaries, often expressed in indifference to the ideas and concerns of expatriates.

During the period when the FED-sponsored Seminary operated in the PUC campus, a cooperative relationship would have been quite beneficial to PUC and the Seminary. Instead, each unit went about their activities independently, failing to combine their efforts in point projects unless it was absolutely necessary. The Seminary operated its own 'church' apart from the mission-recognized congregation, the Philippine International Church, named as such in order to accommodate overseas students and expatriate faculty—certainly an act of Christian love.

Thus, when the issue of administration of the PUC Graduate School was brought up by the expatriates, it was not perceived by the Filipinos as a cooperative gesture but, rather, as a direct challenge to the administrative capabilities of the Filipino leadership of PUC.

Without an underlying spirit of cooperation, the FED leadership should have known that any discussion of reorganization of the Graduate School would be seen by PUC administration as a step backward in the development of Filipino leadership and as a sellout to the expatriates, who were now viewed as competitors, not helpers. From that point, all attempts to convince PUC leaders that giving up the Graduate School to direct FED jurisdiction would be beneficial to the Filipinos, as well as the rest of the Division, were futile.

2. Colonial Mentality on the Part of Both National and Expatriate leaders.

There continues to exist in the minds of the national workers and expatriates that the nationals just are not good enough to be trusted to lead without the help of the expatriates. Filipinos have been brainwashed to think that anything Filipino is inferior to anything 'stateside.' This has resulted in a love-hate relationship where Filipinos seek the help and approval of American missionaries (believing that they cannot succeed without them) and hating themselves (and the expatriates) for being so dependent on the Americans.

This kind of mentality has never been acknowledged by all parties. And so it continues to undermine any serious attempt to promote true cooperation—one based on equal partnership and mutual dignity. With this brainwashed subconscious mentality, expatriates are seen by Filipinos as being arrogant and controlling. They often are indeed, in spite of the biblical injunction to be humble and loving. National leaders are perceived by expatriates as being defensive and provincial, and therefore not capable of leadership beyond their national boundaries.

In this atmosphere, the issue of who controls the Graduate School becomes a power play, rather than a cooperative venture for the good of the wider work of the Church in the Division. The heavy handed tactic of FED in withdrawing financial support to coerce PUC to accede to what was perceived as the expatriates' demands only validated the suspicions of the Filipinos that this plan was anti-Filipino.

To complicate the situation, the expatriates never really understood the Filipinos' view of the Filipino-American relationship. It is a view that defies logic but nevertheless reasonable, in the light of the colonialistic history of the development of the Philippine Adventist Church.

It is a dependent relationship where Americans are viewed as providers (even if they are controlling) and protectors of the Filipino inter-est whenever other nationalities are involved. In this relationship, it is acceptable for Americans to dominate the Filipinos and for the Filipinos to complain about the Americans. But when other nationalities are involved, Americans are expected to fight for the interests of the Filipinos. Colonial-ism has bred strange relationships, indeed. But after all, we fought and died for American interests in Bataan.

This is why, when the issue of the Graduate School was addressed by FED committee, the Filipino leaders were not as vocal as they should have been. They expected the Americans to speak for their—the Filipi-nos'—interests. When this did not happen, the Filipinos felt betrayed, not realizing that their understanding of the relationships and events were different from that of their American colleagues.

3. **Lack of Sensitivity to National Aspirations.** Expatriates are generally not sensitive to the feelings and hopes of Filipinos. Both the Filipino and expatriate workers think that 'preaching the gospel' is the only concern of the Church. It is quite reasonable for individuals on mission assignment not to be concerned about local problems, especially long-term issues. They are there to do a job within a limited time, then they return home.

National workers, on the other hand, must not be narrow in their approach to the work of the Church. They must not forget that they are Filipinos, and as such, they must also be involved in nation-building, they must also prepare the next generation of believers to be moral leaders in their communities and in their country.

In this regard, PUC is seen by the Filipinos not merely as a church institution for the work of the Church, but also as an important educational center for future leaders and productive citizens of a country badly in need of Christian leadership and influence. That is why throughout the existence of PUC, it has endeavored to maintain a reputation for moral leadership and scholastic excellence among the Protestant colleges and universities in the Philippines. Since its establishment, the Graduate School has been the cornerstone of this grand strategy.

For the FED to suggest that this important segment of PUC's identity be surrendered for the 'good of the rest of the Division' exhibits a lack of sensitivity to the national aspirations of church members in an underdeveloped country. Why couldn't the wealthier parts of FED and the expatriates 'sacrifice' their egos in favor of a less developed country which **has more than 60 percent of FED membership?**

4. **Inefficient Management of Limited Resources.** Both the national and expatriate workers have become financially over-dependent on North American resources that they do not really try to accomplish their mission with local resources. There is a lack of creativity in financial planning on the part of the leaders because of the attitude that funds from North America will be available to bail them out. (No longer true.)

In the Graduate School situation, we are not satisfied that all parties tried their best to find a solution to the problem. Indeed, ignoring the reality of the limited resources of the Church, FED somehow found the money to build another facility. Rather than learning to understand the national aspirations of the Filipinos and humbly, in the accommodating spirit of Christ, accepting the leadership of PUC administration (however imperfect these people were) it was thought wiser to indulge in pride of control by building a separate facility at great expense... of Church money.

The FED-sponsored graduate school must now charge a higher tuition as its operating budget is increased....

In a country where more than half of the population live in extreme poverty, it is the height of arrogance for our Church to use its limited resources on more buildings, especially when compassion and humility would have been not only proper but cost effective. The Church cannot afford to continue to squander its limited resources.

5. **Failure of Church Leadership.** The leadership failed to see the moral issues involved here. Equality, justice and compassion for each other

are not peripheral organizational matters which are effectively addressed by re-organization and separation. These issues need to be faced openly and honestly by Church leaders. The process may be painful and would appear divisive, but our people cannot grow in this important area of human relations without going through it.

Filipinos continue to see AIIAS as a symbol of the inequality among expatriate and national workers, the ineffectiveness of their national leaders in providing courageous leadership, and the poverty of the Philippine Church.

The Church could no longer safely ignore these issues because it will continue to fall behind the other institutions and sectors of society in this area. We cannot pretend that our people are unaware of what is happening in the Church institutions. Our leaders must deal with these issues if the gospel is to have any meaning at all in the minds of our people and the world.

Because of the 'mission' status of the Adventist Church in the Philippines, the voice of its members have been mostly through 'representatives' (and these representatives are still to be approved by the next higher body). The officers of the local missions and union missions do not get their administrative authority from the constituency that they serve, but from the next higher organization. In this system, many leaders feel a higher sense of responsibility to the people who placed them in their positions.

Officers who get their administrative authority from the constituency tend to be more creative in their leadership than those who get it from the higher organization. When the laity is not really involved in selecting their leaders, the leaders do not feel that they are accountable to them. In many cases, decisions are made by leaders without taking the best interest of the membership into consideration.

In the matter of the PUC Graduate School, others have pointed out that the North Philippine Union Mission leadership voted to go along with the FED plan of separating the graduate program from PUC even though it was aware of the opposition of the PUC staff and students. Most observers of the Philippine scene (former national workers and administrators) believe that if these officers were elected by the constituency that they are supposed to serve, they would have seen the issues from a different perspective.

A situation like this could not have occurred in other parts of the world where the church organization has a 'conference' status. The leadership in such a setting would be more in tune with the desires of their constituency and would do their best to further the best interests of the people they represent and serve.

OUR RECOMMENDATIONS

In order to improve the work in the Philippines, as it relates to the issues we have raised in this document, we urge the Seventh-day Adventist General Conference leadership to give serious consideration to the following recommendations:

1. Re-examine the goals of the FED-sponsored graduate school.

2. Eliminate competition and the adversarial relationship between PUC and AIIAS and promote cooperation between the two institutions.

3. Recommend university status for PUC.... (PUC achieved a university status in August 1996 and accordingly was renamed Adventist University of the Philippines).

4. Develop a church structure which allows the laity to choose these leaders and to participate in decision making.

5. Recognize the importance of national aspirations in structuring church institutions.

6. Provide assistance in upgrading national workers for leadership.

7. Develop a new 'missionary system:

    a. Work to eliminate colonial mentality or colonial Adventism.

    b. Develop self-sufficiency in the 'mission fields.'

    c. Design mission assignment to be mutually beneficial.

An Adjustment to the Mission Service. Russel Staples proposed an 'adjustment' to the mission service:

"It is more or less axiomatic that the ecclesiological concept of true mutuality and equal partnership in mission will lead to altered patterns of missionary service in many parts of the earth. Pioneering missionaries go forth to found and organize where it has not yet been planted, but many missionaries go to assist an already established church. There can be little doubt that, increasingly, missionaries will offer their services as 'servants' of the church rather than pioneers.

"The real question is not whether there should be missionaries, but what kind of missionaries are needed, and what roles they should perform. As already noted, it is possible to have too many of a certain kind of missionary in one place. This is particularly so if they stifle local initiative by performing functions that the local church should undertake for itself.

"We have already urged the case for the partnership of the world and the local churches in mission and suggested that under such arrangements, the 'servant' missionary will go out to help the church in some other area in the fulfillment of its responsibilities. A high level of mutual confidence and maturity will be required of both the servant and the served to make this pattern of missionary service a success." <u>Seventh-day Adventist Mission in the '80s, Servant of Christ</u>, 1980.

Certainly, major adjustments need to be made in Seventh-day Adventist missions. But more important than these is that both sending and receiving parts of the church should make the needed effort to rid themselves of the colonial mentality which continues to breed arrogance and servitude, instead of servanthood, after the example of Jesus Christ… who came to serve.

***

A DEVOTIONAL
by Lydia T. Roda

Let me share with you a topic closest to my heart. It is very simple and yet it touches each of us because we all go through this process at different times and in different degrees of intensity.

Of all the gifts that heaven can bestow upon men, fellowship with Christ's suffering is the most weighty trust and the highest honor. <u>Ministry of Healing</u>, p. 478

We know that people suffer due to cause and effect, or the effects of sin on the human race, or because God permits suffering among His people as proof to the world that it is possible to love God and to be faithful to Him despite sufferings.

The bitter experiences I went through after the demise of my husband have provided me with a glimpse of what God's people will go through at the time of trouble. Christ Himself has promised that He will never forsake us, that He will ever be our source of comfort, security and love.

God provided me with all the possible human support a grieving person could ask for. I thank God for an uncle *Tiong Dons* (Dr. Celedonio A. Fernando) who accompanied me on the lonely and scary trip home to the Philippines to be with my husband, Dr. Alfonso P. Roda (Ponsing), who was in the hospital and was not doing well. (I was in the U.S. seeing to my son Bong Reggie's health when my husband was taken to the hospital.) *Tiong Dons* left his practice for a couple of weeks, canceling all his appointments and surgeries. He brought his instruments with him should they be needed to save Ponsing's life. Relatives and friends in the U.S. followed me to the Philippines a day after we left to join us in our grief, to hover around me during those most difficult days. My younger brother Mike and his wife Lucy, auntie Dels (wife of *Tiong Dons*) and Precy Pilar, my younger sister, flew to the Philippines to be with me. Dr. Gideon Pilar, Precy's husband, wrote telling her to stay with me as long as I needed her (she had never left on any trip without her husband). *Manang* Ely (Elizabeth Roda-Roeder) *Manang* Cheding and her husband *Manong* Eling Arevalo were there to give me emotional, spiritual and mental support. Dr. Reuben Jabola and his wife Naomi Jaurigue flew to the Philippines to share my grief and greatest loss.

So Touching and Comforting. The sea of faces of mourners and comforters—friends, college faculty and staff crowding the hallways of Manila Sanitarium & Hospital that midnight Tiong *Dons*, Bong and I arrived touched our hearts and embraced us with comfort.

The telephone rang constantly and needed my attention. Cablegrams, enormous sympathy cards, letters of condolences poured in the mail for me from former missionaries, former students, co-workers, friends and loved ones from around the globe.

Church members supplied abundant food. MSH assigned us two suites to use for rest and sleep overnight. The Seminary offered the guest houses for my relatives and guests.

The spacious pulpit of Philippine International Church (PUC Church) was transformed into a beautiful garden overflowing with bouquets of flowers—fresh and gorgeous orchids, roses, lilies, mums, antoriums, and more—from Adventist institutions, local universities, colleges, schools all over the country, from embassies (all friends of Ponsing) from the National Police training Centers of the Philippines with one common message: they, too, were hurting and that I was not alone in my grief.

To my surprise, the campus practically convulsed with students refusing to attend their classes. The intense emotions could not be quelled. Placards on sidewalks from the main gate into the campus were put up by students. Big streamers hung over the main gate. Posters mushroomed all over the place—the classrooms, offices, walls, doors—with one common sentiment: I was not alone in my great loss.

Finally, a long caravan of mourners in their own private cars, pickup trucks, buses, motorcycles and jeepneys from the surrounding barrios joined the long funeral train. It was nearly noon when we left PUC campus for Loyola Memorial Park to entomb Ponsing's mortal remains in his temporary resting place.

I thank God for the human support the Lord gave me. It greatly assuaged my grief, but I'd like to share this with you. At midnight when all human support was cut off and I was utterly alone, I had to fight the dark panic of loneliness, the drowning feeling of emptiness, the desperation of groping in the pitch darkness of abandonment.

How to Survive Spiritually and Emotionally. One must be prepared long before the coming of any crisis. It is a daily preparation. My

Bible has marks all over and the pages are dog-eared, as does Ponsing's. He and I made it a habit to read the Bible at break of day. I thank God for the promises ... which are indelibly etched in my memory, and which I have always claimed. Here are some familiar statements I would like to mention:

All things work together for good to them that love God.

Death is only sleep.

Suffering is God's way to purify His children.

God does not allow trials beyond what we can bear.

The Lord is my Shepherd, I shall not want.

Nothing can separate us from the love of God, nothing whatsoever.

We must be thankful for all things, pleasant or not.

A merry heart doeth good like medicine, but a broken spirit drieth the bones.

Reciting John 3:16 and John 14:1–3 gave me peace and lulled me to sleep in my days of deepest grief and loneliness. Dwelling on God's promises surely strengthened my faith and confidence in God.

Forgiveness Does Not Pretend That Evil Has not Happened.

Another factor that kept me alive spiritually and emotionally during those desolate days was forgiveness. I had to learn to forgive those who hurt me—those who perhaps inadvertently caused the stress that led to Ponsing's demise. I chose to initiate the healing process, too. I talked to certain individuals to clear the air in a Christian and mature manner.

I agree with Elder Paul C. Hewback that "*True forgiveness does not retreat from suffering. It does not pretend that evil has not happened. Nor does it resign itself to the idea that things can't be changed. A forgiving Christian responds by reaching out to those who caused his suffering. This response makes suffering an occasion for pursuing something good. A forgiving person refuses to be a mere victim of others mistreatment. Instead, they become masters of the situation. Far from a display of weakness, forgiveness is a sign of enormous strength.*"
Excerpt from Elder Hewback's article on "God and Suffering."

Faith in God's Saving Power. My passion for the presence of God provided the key to my survival during those very bleak moments. The feeling of void and emptiness was so acute and intense that I felt raw, bleeding and hurting emotionally. The loss of my loyal, loving, devoted companion was so excruciating—it seemed humanly impossible to bear.

I cried to my God day and night to relieve me of my suffering. I cried for faith that could move mountains that I might peek through the clouds of loneliness and depression, and see Jesus, my Lord and Redeemer.

God Saves My Sanity. Casting myself completely in the mercy of God, I felt His awesome power and had a foretaste of Jacob's encounter with the Angel. I pleaded with God not to leave me unless He relieved me of my distress. Like Job, I said, "Though You slay me, yet will I trust in You." One thing I asked of God was that He save my sanity. I was close to losing it, but I held on tenaciously to God's everlasting and powerful love.

Someday you, too, perchance will undergo being lost in an unfamiliar place, frightening surroundings, abandonment, isolation, dejection, rejection, and the feeling of being cut off from all you love and cherish.

We soon will face the greatest 'crisis as has never been since there was a nation,' a crisis far from what we could imagine. Something should take place in our lives while everything goes well so we could be ready for any eventuality. "Where everything goes well, our faith and feeling may be in harmony, but when we face abandonment and persecution, our faith and feeling parts company," says an Adventist preacher.

This is the issue we face at each crisis in our lives. This will be the issue we would face in the time of trouble. Could God expect a people whose faith is unshakable despite the feeling of being lost and forsaken of God? When this happens, you and I can reach up and take hold of the reassurance that we are not alone. God is always there. He will save us.

God will reproduce the victory of faith that Jesus had claimed for each of us at the cross. Jesus felt abandoned of His Father. "My God, my God, why has Thou forsaken Me?" He cried.

By faith He felt victorious, thus He announced to the whole universe, "It is finished."

To close, I would like to read Romans 8:18: "For I reckon that the sufferings of the present time are not worthy *to be compared* with the glory which shall be revealed to us."

Given at the AWESNA Board Meeting, October, 1993, and published in the IFN December, 1994 issue, reprinted with permission.

***

We'd love to send you a free catalog of titles we publish
or even hear your thoughts, reactions, criticism,
about things you did or didn't like about this
or any other book we publish.

Just write or call us at:

TEACH Services, Inc.
Brushton, New York 12916
1-800/367-1844

www.tsibooks.com